# THE
# CATHOLIC
# MARTYRS
## OF THE
# TWENTIETH
# CENTURY

# THE
# CATHOLIC
# MARTYRS
## OF THE
# TWENTIETH
# CENTURY

### A COMPREHENSIVE
### WORLD HISTORY

# ROBERT ROYAL

*A Crossroad Book*
The Crossroad Publishing Company
New York

The Crossroad Publishing Company
370 Lexington Avenue, New York, NY 10017

Printed in the United States of America

Library of Congress Card Number: 00-102839
ISBN 0-8245-1846-2

1  2  3  4  5  6  7  8  9  10      06  05  04  03  02  01  00

*For My Mother and Father,*
*who made everything possible*

THE EARLY TIMES OF PURITY AND TRUTH have not passed away! They are present still! We are not solitary though we seem so. Few now alive understand or sanction us; but those multitudes in primitive time, who believed, and taught, and worshiped as we do, still live unto God, and, in their past deeds and their present voices, cry from the Altar. They animate us by their example; they cheer us by their company; they are on our right hand and our left. Martyrs, Confessors, and the like, high and low, who used the same Creeds, and celebrated the same Mysteries, and preached the same Gospel as we do. And to them were joined, as ages went on, even in fallen times, nay, even now in times of division, fresh and fresh witnesses from the Church below. In the world of spirits there is no difference of parties.

— JOHN HENRY NEWMAN, *Sermons*

*Under the Wormwood Star bitter rivers flowed.*
*Man in the fields gathered bitter bread.*
*No sign of the divine care shone in the heavens.*
*The century wanted homage from the dead.*

*They traced their origin to the dinosaur*
*And took their deftness from the lemur's paw.*
*Above the cities of their thinking lichen,*
*Flights of pterodactyls proclaimed the law.*

*They tied the hands of man with barbed wire.*
*And dug shallow graves at the edge of the wood.*
*There would be no truth in his last testament.*
*They wanted him anonymous for good.*

*The planetary empire was at hand.*
*They said what was speech and what was listening.*
*The ash had hardly cooled after the great fire*
*When Diocletian's Rome again stood glistening.*

— CZESLAW MILOSZ, "The Wormwood Star"

# CONTENTS

# ACKNOWLEDGMENTS

T HE BIRTH OF A BOOK is at least as complicated as the birth of a human being. Before a single word has been put on paper or the vaguest outline been sketched, a number of lucky coincidences or providential interventions have to take place. The present volume is living proof of that truth. I have written several books, but none of them has made me more aware of the debt I owe to my mother and father for a whole range of human and divine possibilities. They showed me my first examples of quiet fidelity and courage in everyday life. In my mind, they occupy a natural place in the larger vistas of Christian virtue alongside some of the figures described in these pages.

The immediate genesis of this book reflects the powerful and unpredictable action of martyrs in the world. When John Paul II issued his encyclical *Tertio Millennio Adveniente* ("On the Third Millennium") in preparation for the Jubilee Year 2000, he mentioned, almost as an aside, that the twentieth century was a century of martyrs whose *witness should not be forgotten*. A group of lay people reading the encyclical at Saint Aloysius Parish in New Canaan, Connecticut, were somehow galvanized by those brief words. They began collecting files on twentieth-century martyrs. Word of their activities spread spontaneously, and people from every continent sent books, pamphlets, martyrologies of religious orders, private correspondence — a blizzard of material on martyrs, previously scattered over the face of the earth, became one of the most extensive archives about the subject in North America. Carole Pinard bravely kept track of this increasingly complicated material. Monsignor J. Peter Cullen, pastor of Saint Aloysius, generously supported the project at every stage. My brother, Father Kevin Royal, rector of Saint John Fisher Seminary, encouraged the burgeoning excitement about the martyrs' stories and provided hospitality during consultation of the Saint Aloysius files. At a certain point, the lay people and clergy involved in this miraculous growth realized that order should be drawn out of these disparate materials. I hope the present book fulfills everything they hoped for.

For help with research into some difficult and obscure material, I would first like to thank Greek Catholic bishop Michael Hrynchyshyn, president of the Commission for New Martyrs, and Professor Marco Bartoli of the same commission for his hospitality while I worked in their picturesque offices on the Isola Tiberina in Rome. The following chapters make extensive use of the work that Didier Rance and the Aide à l'Eglise en Détresse in Paris have produced about the persecuted churches over the past two decades: several of his volumes should be translated into English some day. Also, though I only discovered his work well into this project, Father Vincent Lapomarda, S.J.'s bibliographies on twentieth-century martyrs around the world are a veritable gold mine deserving of further attention. Thanks also to the Ukrainian Study Center and the Most Reverend Basil H. Losten, bishop of the Ukrainian Catholic Diocese in Stamford, Connecticut.

For various kindnesses, recommendations, encouragement, and services rendered let me recognize: The Most Reverend Edward M. Egan, Ralph McInerney, Michael Novak, Virgil Nemoianu, Seamus Hasson, Lee Edwards, Margaret Heckler, Richard Higgins, Edward Feulner, Brad Miner, Annette Kirk, Jeff Nelson, Deal Hudson, Bartholomew De la Torre, O.P., Dennis Bartlett, and Paul Goble.

My wife, Veronica, improved my understanding of various figures in this book in a myriad of ways. Elizabeth Royal helped retype the manuscript. Jason Boffetti, as ever, guarded against the ever present danger that the electronic version of the text might slip into an ignoble eternity in cyber-limbo.

An extensive research project like this one can take place only with substantial financial help. I would like to thank James Piereson of the John M. Olin Foundation for early and quick support that got the ball rolling. Michael Joyce and Daniel Schmidt at the Lynde and Harry Bradley Foundation came to the rescue more than once as the well was running dry. Bob Lockwood and the Our Sunday Visitor Foundation went out of their way to help. The Strake Foundation in Texas kept body and soul together at a crucial juncture. Mrs. Anne Seggerman, occupied with many causes and commitments, still managed to be personally generous to this endeavor, as was Foster Friess. And Mary Schwarz and Monsignor Eugene Clark of the Homeland Foundation made the final months less precarious. To all these benefactors, heartfelt thanks and hopes that the product repays the investment.

Finally, Gwendolin Herder was once again a perfect publishing partner and among the first enthusiasts about the idea for this book. John Tintera of the Crossroad Publishing Company also helped greatly, not only by seeing to it that the book got into print on time, but that the world would know that it was about to be born.

# INTRODUCTION

S ACRED SCRIPTURE TELLS US that God does not try any of us beyond our strength. If so, the Lord seems to have had a high opinion of believers of every kind in the twentieth century. He allowed hundreds of thousands — perhaps millions — to be tried, even to the point of martyrdom, all over the world. In absolute numbers, the century's martyrs far surpass those of any previous century. Among them, Catholics form a great, perhaps the greatest, part. To a certain extent, those figures have something to do with the sheer size of Christianity in general and the Catholic Church in particular at the dawn of the new millennium. There are over a billion Catholics, making it the single largest denomination in the world. It was only to be expected that, in a century of widespread religious persecution, many Catholics would become martyrs.

But there have been other factors, primarily the appearance of virulent anti-Christian ideologies and brutally repressive regimes seeking to impose them, which led directly to the widespread suffering and slaughter of religious believers. In a century that rightly prided itself on its scientific and technological advances on the one hand and its commitment to human rights on the other, refined methods of torture and control, physical and mental, also emerged with a vengeance all around the globe. As one of the deepest sources of opposition to oppressive trends, religion was a logical target for tyrants. The twentieth century, by any measure, presents a brutal spectacle that may be remembered historically as one of the darkest periods of martyrdom.

Relatively few studies have appeared, however, documenting this indisputable part of modern history. Accounts of the twentieth century are generally written from an almost purely political perspective that admits the presence of martyrs, if at all, only tangentially. The terrible Turkish attempt at genocide against the Armenians in the early part of this century, for example, is duly recorded in most history texts. It is rarely noticed, however, that many Christians, Armenian Catholics and Orthodox, died during the same massacre precisely because they were Christians. The Armenian Catholic Church counts 7 bishops, 126 priests, 47 nuns, and around 30,000 lay people among those who lost their lives for their faith under the modern Turks.[1] About the same level of courage

1

occurred in 1900 in only a few months during the Boxer Rebellion in China. As chilling as these numbers are, they represent a rather midrange body count of religious believers under persecution in many countries around the world in the twentieth century.

This is also a century in which one pope, Pius XII, was almost kidnapped by the Nazis near the end of World War II in order to hold him hostage in Germany. And another pope, John Paul II, was shot and nearly killed in an assassination attempt by a Turk, Mehmet Ali Agca, operating under Bulgarian handlers, who were following the orders of the Soviet KGB. Unlike Hitler, the Soviets did not long hesitate about the decision: according to Czechoslovak and East German intelligence files that have been opened up since the 1989 fall of Communism, the prospect of an anti-Communist Pole leading the Catholic Church convinced KGB officers within hours of his election to give the death order, if needed. Two covert operations — Pagoda and Infection — were organized by the Warsaw Pact countries to infiltrate the Church and spread "disinformation and provocations that do not exclude [the pope's] physical elimination."[2]

Despite these and similar facts, it is not easy to write about martyrdom in the contemporary world. Martyrdom is not one of the common categories of modern thought. In addition, a great deal of the material produced by religious sources only complicates the problem. Anyone who begins looking at that literature will soon grow tired of pious accounts about people who "nobly went to their deaths" or "ardently desired martyrdom." Martyrdom is a gruesome affair, and few of the true martyrs of the twentieth century, who saw it close up, looked upon it in a conventionally pious or romantic light. Still, these expressions are true enough, in their way. If we already know how to understand them, they reveal a little recognized source of heroism and an exalted state of the human spirit.

In recent years, a great deal of ingenuity and energy have been devoted to trying to show that our genetic code hardwires us either for ruthless self-preservation (the "Selfish Gene") or, through a complex mechanism of game theory and natural selection, for selfless care for others (the "Altruistic Gene"). Each of these hypotheses tries to explain by naturalistic premises the mixture of good and evil which we see in human societies all around us. But the martyrs introduce an unanticipated wrinkle into this neat scheme. They clearly are not driven by a selfish gene; and any mechanism we can think of — desire to propagate offspring or preserve the species — seems inadequate to explain the nature of martyrdom. There seems to be little biological advantage to individuals or the race in the kinds of sacrifices willingly embraced by the martyrs included in the present volume, too little, certainly, to overcome the immediate fear of death. The only way to understand the martyrs is from the standpoint of the particularly human thrust toward truth and goodness, the realm of the spirit.

It is worth noting that martyrs are real human beings, human beings like ourselves who were fearful when they were placed in extraordinary circumstances and yet managed to act in extraordinary ways. In the abstract, there is not a great deal of simple consolation in religion for those of us who begin to think about such persons. As John Henry Newman pointed out, the central Christian story itself is a tantalizing mystery that *"increases our difficulties."*[3] Why it was necessary for the Incarnate God to die for the salvation of the human race is beyond us. Why it continues to be necessary for human beings to die after that redemption is another mystery. Why some of those who die have to do so in such horrifying conditions at the hands of wicked men is a stumbling block for our imaginations and intelligence. But since there is a God, these facts must mean something. In the long run, they mean the salvation of the world. But in the short run, they leave us struggling to understand.

From the outside, martyrs present difficulties. From the inside, they manifest luminous conviction. One element that returns again and again in the following chapters is how people undergoing unjust suffering and degradation frequently found their faith and their very lives becoming purer, more meaningful, more ardent. Their accounts of this experience and the stories told about them by survivors who knew them offer an unusual testament to the nature of Christian faith. There is even a kind of dark humor that hovers around the lives of martyrs and confessors. Willingness to die liberates. For example, Václav Benda, one of the heroic Czech Catholic dissidents, observed serenely about the regime's retaliation against him: "If a man is so eccentric as to allow himself to be thrown to the lions, it would be very silly of him to complain that their teeth were not clean enough."[4] After the reality of trial by fire, the modern intellectual objections to religion seem bloodless abstractions. Martyrs do more than entertain various possibilities; they put their lives behind the truth.

Most of us need to approach the exemplary lives of modern martyrs by way of the often brutal details of their deaths. When we understand concretely the enormous price they were willing to pay for no earthly reason, we might just catch a glimpse of what they achieved and why. The brutal details themselves are often numbing. Realistic accounts of the martyrs, as spectacular as they are, soon become all too familiar. There is a relatively small number of ways human beings can be killed: "tortured and then executed," "killed with a bullet to the back of the head at point-blank range," "throat slit," "drowned," "hung" — from trees, lampposts, telephone poles, statues, balconies, anything that will bear the weight of a human body — in public squares, desolate outposts, churches, palaces, police stations, military barracks, parks, cemeteries, the bodies often left to rot in public as a warning to anyone who would even think about similar witness. It is just as difficult to retain a lively sense of the realities behind these repetitive litanies of horror as it is to see real human beings behind pious descriptions.

Thinking about martyrdom at the beginning of the new millennium, then, requires a kind of spiritual discipline and intellectual adventurousness. It takes focused attention and unrelenting sympathy to keep the sheer numbers and predictable deeds of evil from turning into a commonplace. Like any extensive evil, it would be easier to explain it away as a historical aberration or lessen its human poignancy somehow so that we can go about our daily business without having to recognize that such evils exist in the world. But they have and do exist, even in our own time. There is an almost otherworldly logic that requires not only unbelievers but, at times, misguided believers to hate, persecute, and kill authentic followers of Christ.

Jesus himself warns the disciples that "the hour is coming when everyone who kills you will think he is offering worship to God" (John 16:2). That, he predicted, would be the reaction among pious Jews. "You will be hated by all nations because of my name," is the Lord's warning about the larger perspective. If the twentieth century proves anything it is that, far from being pious generalities, these words are as literally applicable today as then. Most of us, most of the time, are less certain about Jesus' promised compensation: "Happy are those who are persecuted for righteousness' sake, the Kingdom of Heaven is theirs" (Matt. 5:10). But the martyrs' stories confirm that much happiness indeed can accompany persecution and death.

Why should such persecutions exist? The early Church seems not to have been much in doubt about this question. Its members knew that the Savior they followed was a Sign of Contradiction who would bring them into conflict with the world: "See how the kings of the earth stand in array, how its rulers make common cause, against the Lord and his Christ" (Acts 4:26). All of the Apostles, with the possible exception of John the Evangelist, died violent deaths. Saint Paul, tradition has it, was beheaded in Rome near the church now known as Saint Paul Outside the Walls. Saint Peter, the leader of the Church after Christ's crucifixion, was probably crucified himself, upside down, and set on fire at the present site of Saint Peter's Basilica. In the first Epistle of Saint Peter, the Apostle counsels the Christian community: "Beloved, do not be startled at the trial by fire now taking place among you to prove you, as if something strange were happening to you; but rejoice, in so far as you are partakers of the sufferings of Christ" (1 Pet. 4:12).

Saint Paul makes the same argument. When he reflects on the Old Testament stories, he notes: "As then, he that was born after the flesh persecuted him that was born of the Spirit, even so it is now" (Gal. 4:29). Paul is thinking of the special reaction in the Roman world to the new revelation: "All that will live godly in Christ Jesus shall suffer persecution" (2 Tim. 3:12). Some will hate the Word because they envy its goodness; others will hate it because it is a reproach to the evil within them. In either case, they will seek to eliminate it. As strange as it seems to modern sensibilities, both Peter and Paul took it as a foregone conclusion that persecution of Christians was not an odd occurrence, but the normal course of affairs in a world where good and evil are in competition with each other for our ultimate allegiance.

The modern world has a distorted perspective on this truth because many core Christian values have become so natural to our way of thinking that they seem like the tritest truisms. But in many parts of the world where the Christian message has not yet reached or is just arriving, the faith appears quite different. Bishop James Edward Walsh, one of the first Maryknoll missionaries in China, saw things differently after his many years' experience, even before spending nearly two decades in captivity: "Christianity is not a private way of salvation and a guide to a pious life; it is a way of world salvation and a philosophy of total life. This makes it a sort of dynamite. So when you send missioners out to preach it, it is well to get ready for some explosions."[5] The same, it might be said, is true when Christianity bumps up against anti-Christian currents even in formerly Christian societies. That clash repeated itself in Mexico, Spain, Germany, Russia, and a host of other countries in the twentieth century.

Christianity made its first appearance in an empire that in many ways resembled the regimes with which Catholics have contended in modern times. The first persecutions, and the first large crop of martyrs, occurred as the Roman empire was beginning its decline. When Nero blamed the Christians for the massive fire that gutted Rome in July 64 A.D., he could count on the fact that the new religious movement, expanding remarkably all throughout the Roman world only a few decades after the Crucifixion, could be attacked without negative repercussions. The early Church had shown itself absolutely unyielding in religious purity. It would burn no incense to the emperor-god, however meaningless the gesture was thought to be, even by the Romans. There was good reason for this resistance. Just as the Jewish people on their first coming into the Holy Land had been warned by the Almighty not to adopt any of the ways of the Canaanite peoples, the early Christians had to resist — and ultimately reform — a good bit of the evil in the classical world. In short order, unfounded rumors spread about cannibalism and ritual orgies among the new Jewish sect. The Roman historian Tacitus, who harshly judged Nero and the other corrupt emperors, nonetheless accepted the popular slander of Christians as "men who were abhorred for their villainous practices, and convicted of nourishing a hatred toward the whole human race."[6]

Christians immediately became victims of the cruelest punishments available in the Roman world, confirming Christ's warning to them: "I am sending you out like sheep among wolves" (Matt. 10:16). As is still the case, in worldly terms, the martyrdoms were absurdly out of all proportion to any conceivable offense, suggesting something unusual lay behind them. Not only were believers summarily executed for the mere fact of being Christian by the Roman justice system, which was otherwise admirable in many ways. Early believers were made to put on animal skins and were then pursued by mock hunting parties with fierce mastiffs in the imperial parks. In the Colosseum, they might simply form a part of brutal spectacles in which they were hacked to death by gladiators or torn to pieces by wild animals. Some were forced to reenact the bloody or lubricious stories of classical mythology in front of jeering crowds.[7] There were few apostasies among the Christians even in the face of such horrors and many noble deaths that began, ever so slowly, to turn the whole classical world away from the evils that, unfortunately, had lodged themselves among the many real achievements of Greco-Roman civilization.

The hatred of Christianity was not based solely on its refusal to participate in pagan emperor worship. The Jews of ancient Rome had worked out a compromise with Roman authorities by which they, ever the people of a jealous God, prayed for the emperor to their own Deity. But Christianity was about to introduce a new ethos into the world which would upset no small number of existing practices. Ancient slavery, sexual immorality, injustice, and state-sponsored brutality would change and, in large degree, simply disappear under that influence. By the second century, the Christian apologist Tertullian could use the Romans' own sense of what was right against them: "What can you think, then, of laws which have only been executed against us by impious, unjust, infamous, cruel, extravagant and insane princes, which were partially ignored by [the "good emperor"] Trajan, and which Vespasian, the slaughterer of the Jews, and Hadrian, Antoninus Pius and Verus never applied at all?"[8]

Tertullian was wrong in detail. Though the better emperors did not go out of their way to enquire into who was a Christian, belonging to the Church was a punishable offense during their rule all the same. Saint Ignatius, the second bishop of Antioch, for instance, was torn apart by wild beasts in Rome during Trajan's rule.[9] And after his day, under the emperor Diocletian in the third century, persecutions were resumed that, in sheer numbers, surpassed those of the earlier centuries. The anti-Christian furor knew no limits. Old men, women, and children made up a large percentage of those killed. Tertullian knew that there was some fanatical spirit behind these acts: "If the Tiber floods, or if the Nile fails to flood, if the skies darken, if the earth trembles, if famine, war or plague occurs, then immediately one shout goes up: 'The Christians to the lions! Death to the Christians!' "[10]

As this description suggests, it was not just the Roman mob that perpetrated these outrages. All over the empire — in Egypt, Asia Minor, Gaul, and Greece — as well as Rome, recognition that Christianity represented a new order infuriated people and leaders alike. The aged bishop of Lyons, Pothinus, was martyred as was the eighty-six-year old bishop of Smyrna, Saint Polycarp. In North Africa, near Carthage, twelve Scillians were put to death for refusing to worship the emperor.[11] In another notorious incident at Lyons, a slave girl named Blandina was terribly tormented by torturers taking shifts in order to make her confess that Christians practiced abominations. She refused and said only instead: "I am a Christian, and not one of us has done anything wrong." Heroic scenes like this were repeated all around the Mediterranean. Innocent people were ripped to pieces while displaying great calm and dignity. The Church remembered them as witnesses, *martyroi* as they were known in Greek. The nineteenth-century French writer Ernest Renan summed up the cumulative effect: "Blandina the slave girl showed that a revolution had taken place. The true emancipation of the slave, the emancipation through heroism, was, to a large extent her work."[12] It was her work and the work of countless and nameless others who followed the Master in witnessing to the truth and bearing the consequences courageously.

The ancient world had admired similar heroism in the figure of Socrates as the great philosopher Plato had depicted him, who refused to escape from prison and calmly accepted his own execution out of love for the truth. But the Socratic/Platonic way was for a special few. Christianity inspired multitudes. One of the elite, Saint Justin, later himself a Christian martyr, observed: "When I was one of Plato's disciples, I listened to the accusations being brought against the Christians. They faced death so intrepidly, they were so fearless regarding the things that all mortals dread, that I told myself that it was impossible to believe that they really lived evil lives, spent in immoral pleasures."[13] Justin was highly literate and left a record of his change of heart. He also bore witness through his death; he refused to betray fellow Christians and suffered decapitation along with six other believers in Rome as a consequence.[14] Thousands, then millions, of more humble, illiterate people, reacting to what they saw and discussing it among themselves afterward, found a new dignity.

Except for a tiny number of fanatics, who were discouraged by Christian leaders, none of the martyrs sought death. They simply bore with it like people more than human when it was forced upon them. Any hint of an unhealthy desire to commit suicide would have stopped the spread of the Church dead in its tracks. Instead, legends grew up around the martyrs to such an extent that modern scholars are still trying to sort out fact from fiction. The Church itself, recognizing the human means by which it spread, venerated these early saints/heroes. Masses usually were and are said on altars containing relics of the martyrs. The practice is ancient. The Book of Revelation records a deep sense of the connection of martyrs to all of salvation history:

> And when he opened the fifth seal, I saw *under the altar* the souls of those who had been slain for the word of God, and for the witness that they bore. And they cried with a loud voice saying, "How long, O Lord (holy and true), dost thou refrain from judging and from avenging our blood on those who dwell on the earth?" And there was given to each of them a white robe; and they were told to rest a while longer, until the number of their fellow-servants and their brethren who are to be slain, even as they had been, should be complete. (Rev. 6:9–11, emphasis added)

This passage is read to this day at the consecration of new churches. Behind this honoring of the martyrs is a recognition that, just as it took God Himself to suffer and die to redeem the human race, it took, in human terms, the Christian martyrs to spread the belief in that redemption by their own participation in the very suffering and death of their Lord. The very survival of the Church depended on there being people willing to value its truth above life itself.

All of this is a very old story, though little known or appreciated by contemporary Christians. The Christian revolution succeeded in time, the Church grew, and, at least in some Christian countries, the dignity of all human beings as children of God slowly came to be taken as a given. For roughly the last thousand years, being a Christian, except in mission territories, has meant to be part of an established way of looking at things. Martyrdoms were few. Christians might occasionally persecute one another in inquisitions, denominational disputes, witch-hunts, or religious wars. In a rare case, someone like Thomas Becket could die in a conflict with his own Catholic king or a Joan of Arc might even be martyred by clergy of her own faith. But being a Christian per se did not typically demand the heroic witness of the early martyrs — until modern political upheavals began.

When they did, it is no exaggeration to say that, in quite a few countries, Christianity was saved again by martyrs. As the following chapters indicate, the price for this witness was often as high or higher than it was in the ancient world. Christians were once again deliberately ripped to pieces by wild animals, probably for the first time since the fall of Rome. Under Nazism and Communism, Christians were sometimes crucified during blasphemous parodies of the first Crucifixion. As the century drew to a close, reports of similar crucifixions were heard from the Sudan in Africa. In addition, Christians in the twentieth century were subjected to scientifically engineered persecutions whereby sophisticated brainwashing techniques were used that, in many cases, resulted in people going mad or committing suicide. The world needs a full assessment of what these facts mean about modern secular movements.

In his encyclical *Tertio Millennio Adveniente,* Pope John Paul II made a point to remind the world of the old truth, *the blood of the martyrs is the seed of Christians:* "At the end of the second millennium, the church has once again become a church of martyrs. The persecutions of believers — priests, religious, and laity — has caused a great sowing of martyrdom in different parts of the world.... *This witness must not be forgotten.* The church of the first centuries, although facing considerable organizational difficulties, took care to write down in special martyrologies the witness of the martyrs." Observing that these lists were constantly added to, the Polish pope, who had witnessed persecution from several quarters in his own country, recommended a twentieth-century updating to accord simple justice to the many who have perished of all religious faiths. The task is not an easy one: "In our own time the martyrs have returned, many of them nameless, 'unknown soldiers' as it were of God's great cause."

The present book is intended to be a comprehensive survey of the twentieth-century martyrs. But in the nature of the case, it can only partly complete that task. As the Holy Father has noted, most of the hundreds of thousands of people killed for their faith in the modern world are not known by name. Even where the local churches have tried to keep track of who disappeared, many people simply vanished into the maw of various killing machines. In Latin America, for example, "to disappear" became a verb used in a new way, e.g., "three religious were *disappeared*." People were classified as *desaparecidos* ("disappeareds"). The neologisms tell us that something new about the modern world was perceived by those who experienced its injustices. Systematic and secret elimination of groups of people became common toward the end of the second Christian millennium. Most of their names and fates are unknown, and may always remain so. A significant group may have had their final days recorded in official documents, but the regimes that slaughtered them will not open up those archives for some time to come. So at best, any attempt to do justice to the martyrs at this point in history must begin by acknowledging inescapable limitations. It will be decades before a really comprehensive study of twentieth-century martyrdom can be fully done.

In addition, martyrdom comes in many forms, some that make it difficult to judge whether they are even martyrdoms at all. A few cases are quite simple. The Church quickly declared Maria Goretti, a young Italian woman who died resisting a rape because of her faith, as a modern martyr. Other cases are complicated. For instance, in the 1990s, three of Mother Teresa's Missionaries of Charity were murdered in Yemen by a so-called Muslim "madman," who believed they were preaching the Gospel and seeking to convert Muslims. In fact, the nuns were doing what they do everywhere — caring for the sick, poor, and forgotten — without any verbal proselytizing at all. So the questions become less than entirely straightforward. Were they, nonetheless, proselytizing by example, as their killer believed? Was he a "madman" who was mentally unstable, a fanatic, or merely a careful observer of Islamic law, which forbids Muslims to allow their fellow believers to be converted to other religions? There are no easy answers to any of these questions.

But it seems fair to say that the nuns were martyrs in a general sense, even if the Church never decides that they fit into the necessarily careful definitions of martyrs used for official beatification processes.

Complex modern political events also make it difficult to judge whether a particular death constitutes martyrdom. By far the largest number of recent martyrs died because some government or political faction believed Christianity was "reactionary" and had to be eliminated to usher in some better society of the future. It is not uncommon to find in recent political ideologies language that resembles Tacitus's charge that Christians manifested "hatred toward the whole human race." The pope, bishops, and even ordinary Christians have been branded as opponents of social progress and apologists for various forms of exploitation. The charge has a kernel of truth in that the Church's basic role is not to rush to embrace every new social trend, but to remind individuals and whole societies of eternal principles. When Socialism began to succeed in Europe, for example, it appeared that the Church was opposed to the aspirations of workers. Many simple workers consequently stopped practicing their religion. But in retrospect, the Church was right, perhaps righter than any individual knew. The first great modern social encyclical, Leo XIII's 1891 *Rerum Novarum,* observed in passing that if Socialism were implemented, the workers themselves would be the first to suffer. Socialism is a complex movement, but it would be fair to say that the Polish dockworkers who in the 1980s opened the first crack in the Communist system under the leadership of Lech Walesa, a pious Catholic, knew in their bones what Leo meant. Because several political systems in the twentieth century had mistaken notions about human nature, they felt justified in committing terrible crimes — allegedly out of a desire for human happiness.

As a result, the present volume may appear to suffer from certain prejudices. Many of the examples included here resulted from Communist persecutions in various countries. This reflects the fact that the largest numbers of innocent dead in the twentieth century are the direct victims of several bloody forms of Communism. The best estimate is that at least a hundred million people have died from Communism in this century, fifty million in China and twenty-five million in the Soviet Union alone.[15] (The Soviet dissident Vladimir Bukovsky has reminded us that Communism typically killed as many people in a day as the much-criticized Inquisition killed in all the centuries of its existence.) Nazism killed about another twenty million people. The "dirty" anti-Communist campaigns in Latin America or the Philippines and the large massacres in sub-Saharan Africa, terrible as they were, pale by comparison. So it is only fair to the reality that the Communist victims occupy the largest amount of space.

A large portion of the people described here died in Europe. Again, this was not because of any intentional prejudice. Paradoxically, some of the most literate and advanced civilizations in the world witnessed the worst atrocities in the twentieth century. As a result, we have better documentation and written records for these outrages than is the case for Africa and much of Asia. For example, Spain's Civil War lasted only three years (1936–39); at its end, memories were still fresh and over seven thousand names of martyrs could be submitted to the Holy See. Places where wholesale murder and repression lasted for decades and, in no small number of cases, still continue — Sudan, China, Cuba, Vietnam, North Korea, and a host of others — have not yet been carefully enough studied to allow us to piece together the full accounts of martyrdom. In the new millennium, one of the unfinished tasks of simple justice will be to recover, as much as possible, the names of all those whose faith brought death.

There are many types of martyrs examined here, again, not all of them easily classified as such. In the fall of 1999, for example, when Indonesia and pro-Indonesian militants went on a murderous rampage in East Timor, dozens of Catholic priests and nuns were murdered. Thousands of lay people and secular leaders were massacred as well in an attempt to prevent the former Portuguese colony from becoming independent. But it would be wrong to exclude religious motivations of several kinds from consideration of their deaths. First, Catholic clergy, though politically neutral in principle, were among the popular leaders of the East Timorese. Their care for the people, even when they might have fled to safety, at least raises the possibility that they should be thought of as martyrs to Christian duty. Also, as the world's largest Muslim country, Indonesia did not seem particularly concerned to stop the violence against non-Muslims. The large number of Catholics left in East Timor by the 1975 withdrawal of Portugal from its former colony bore the brunt of that failure.

Another delicate question — one that returns regularly in the following pages — is whether the attempts by clergy to protect basic human rights for Catholics and others, an activity that is arguably part of the Church's social witness, also provide grounds for declaring their deaths martyrdom. As chapter 13 of the present volume argues, this is clearly true in cases such as that of Archbishop Romero in El Salvador, where his preaching of the dignity of all God's children led to his dramatic death. But many other situations are not so clear-cut. For example, Father Pino Puglisi was a priest in a Palermo, Sicily, neighborhood, who was killed by the Mafia on September 15, 1993, for trying to defend the lives and property of his people out of his sense of his obligations as a Catholic priest. He knew the risks he was running. But was he a martyr or just another mob hit? The Congregation for the Causes of Saints approved the opening of his cause for beatification in the fall of 1999, specifically noting that the case could be examined to see if it was martyrdom. There is no assurance that the Congregation will eventually find him to be an official martyr. But cases like his indicate the subtle interplay between worldly circumstances and religious commitment always found around the figures of martyrs.

A final word about the methodology of the present volume. The Catholic Church conducts a meticulous process before it officially declares any person, however celebrated, a martyr. There are two general categories for such people: first, those who died for refusing to give up their faith, both those who were pressured to make a formal denial and those who would not perform some act inconsistent with faith or morals; and second, those who died *in odium fidei,* that is, at the hands of persons who had a hatred for the faith. Both of these categories, of course, allow for wide ranges in interpretation. Do the large groups of people murdered because some political leader or local brigand found the Catholic Church an obstacle to his designs — as often happened in the twentieth century — come under the heading of those who died *in odium fidei?* Or do Catholics engaged in promoting justice in a given society, a direct expression of one dimension of their faith as they see it, qualify as martyrs by that fact? Ultimately, the Church, as the keeper of the Keys of the Kingdom, must make the determination.

This book takes a different approach. The author has no authority to decide any of the issues outlined above. He can only try to present as full a record as possible of those who died as martyrs or lived as what have traditionally been called "confessors" of the faith. The latter term denotes people who suffered heroically and survived as living witnesses to the truth. The appropriate authorities will perform their work at times and in ways that they think proper. A martyr, like a saint, is inextricably bound to the Church founded by Christ.

Unfortunately, even within Christian churches, there is some resistance at this moment in history to the very notion of martyrs. For many modern Christians, the idea is somewhat quaint, a holdover from another age, and does not seem to connect with their own daily sense of a religious life. The stories collected in the following pages should dispel that impression. The Second Vatican Council restated what is and always must be a basic truth of Christianity:

> Since Jesus, the Son of God, has manifested his love through the surrender of his life, no one has greater love than the man who surrenders his life for Jesus and his brothers (cf. 1 John 3:16; John 15:13). To give this highest witness of love for all, particularly for one's persecutors, has been the calling of some Christians from the earliest times and will always be. The Church considers martyrdom, which makes the disciple similar to the master in the free acceptance of death for the salvation of the world and which makes them equal in the shedding of blood, as a splendid gift and as the highest proof of love. Even if there will only be a few, all must be ready to acknowledge Christ before all and to follow him in the persecutions that the Church will always encounter on the way of the cross.[16]

In the twentieth century, the numbers who were called on to bear witness were not few, but their value, for all of us, is great.

# -ONE-

# MIGUEL PRO AND
# THE MEXICAN TRAGEDY

**M**EXICO IS, and has always been since its creation in the sixteenth century by Spanish explorers, one of the most Catholic nations on earth. Because of its long connection with the Spanish Crown, however, it experienced great difficulties in the transition to an independent and partly democratic country. As occurred during the French Revolution a century earlier, Mexican leaders who tried to create a modern system mistakenly believed that they had to "jumpstart history," in part by destroying the Church to achieve their goals. Even leaving aside the obvious violations of conscience this entailed, it was highly quixotic to expect such a deeply Catholic people to forgo their beliefs for brutal and corrupt secular politics. In addition, Mexico's political traditions tended toward highly centralized, bordering on dictatorial, rule. Charges were often raised at the time that the Church was a reactionary force fomenting revolution against the Mexican government. But, if anything, high-handed Mexican governments set out in the twentieth century on an unprecedented, revolutionary war against not only Catholic resistance to its policies, but against Catholicism per se.

Since 1857, the time of the first constitution of independent Mexico and the dictatorship of Benito Juárez, the Church had already been stripped of much of its power and property. It represented little threat to anyone or anything as long as its basic rights and functions were respected and its adherents were not outraged. During the long, essentially quiet dictatorship of Porfirio Díaz (1876–1910), Church and state in Mexico had found a way to coexist, even if uneasily. But the 1917 Mexican Revolution resulted in a new, socialist constitution — the first in the history of the world, even predating the Soviet constitution. It contained radical political elements, including several articles meant to all but stamp out Catholicism. Article 3, for example, mandated that "the education imparted by the State [which was to have a monopoly over

15

instruction of the young] shall be a socialistic one and, in addition to excluding all religious doctrine, shall combat fanaticism and prejudices by organizing its instruction and activities in a way that shall permit the creation in youth of an exact and rational conception of the Universe and of social life." Like many such appeals to rationality in the twentieth century, this provision would lead to bloody fanaticism and prejudices of its own.

The visitor to Mexico today sees many churches and a believing population. Visitors usually know little about Mexican history. So it may be hard to understand that for almost a century outrages were committed against the civil and religious rights of Mexican believers. Churches were destroyed, desecrated, confiscated, and turned into army barracks; religious items were profaned by soldiers drinking from chalices, chopping up statues for firewood, and using religious art for target practice; orders of priests and nuns were outlawed, and teaching about religion prohibited; religious buildings or private homes where religious activities occurred might be subject to forfeit. Religious activities were limited to churches and, when those were closed by the government, were not permitted even there. Priests had to seek government licenses, a procedure used to all but eliminate their work in each state (the number allowed might be one or two for anywhere from ten thousand to a hundred thousand Catholics, effectively denying Catholics the sacraments). In the state of Tabasco, the governor, Tomás Garrido Canabal, who, to express political and religious radicalism, had named his children Lenin, Lucifer, and Satan, expelled any priest who would not marry.[1] Few did. The vast majority refused and were driven off, meaning that the state, except for a few priests working in secret, was essentially without clergy. The same governor tried to destroy all existing churches. Harsh, if slightly less radical, measures were taken in other states. Even the first church erected in the Americas by Cortés in Veracruz — a historical and cultural treasure by any standards — was closed and partly burned by the radicals.[2]

Out of sheer desperation, some Catholics took up arms — after over a decade of sporadic then more and more systematic persecution — against the government forces that were slaughtering lay people and priests and closing and destroying Catholic churches, schools, colleges, and hospitals. They are sometimes referred to as Cristeros and their uprising as the Cristiada. But contrary to the government's claims that the Church was promoting revolution, these efforts, which might have succeeded among the vast Catholic population against a small group of radicals, were never endorsed by the Catholic hierarchy in Mexico or by Rome. In fact, constant episcopal teaching, following established Catholic social thought on the evils of armed disorder within societies, was that Catholics should obey legitimate authority and try to convince public officials who were violating basic rights against individuals, families, and religious institutions to act on principles of fairness that the officials themselves often acknowledged — at least in theory.

This restraint is all the more remarkable because popular sentiment in Mexico would have made the call for a Catholic uprising quite easy. An American bishop visiting with the Mexican bishop of Querétaro in the 1920s observed that the Indians, let alone the Mexicans of Spanish descent, in that region, who were frequently portrayed by government ideology as needing to be liberated from Catholic control, would instantly rise in rebellion if the local bishop gave permission. To which the Mexican replied:

> Were I only to lift my finger I could have twenty-five thousand of [the Indians] sweep into this city and, even with their bare hands, kill every persecutor in it. And I am but one of the bishops who not only could do that but knows that he could do it. Our enemies are living by the unfailing toleration of Christ. They know as well as we that the finger will not be lifted, no matter how they make us suffer.

And when the American noted that Mexican Catholics had a legitimate right to self-defense, the bishop concluded with a scriptural and theological argument the Church has made in every age: "Christ said, 'Put up thy sword into its place for he who takes the sword shall perish by the sword.' But let that pass as something hard for the world to understand. We cannot be responsible before God and man for bloodshed. It is better that we should die and that out of the blood of martyrs should come a new growth — as it is sure to come."[3] The deaths came in abundance. New growth was less apparent, though at the very least Mexico did not become the secular, socialist society the government was trying to create. Mexico remains an overwhelmingly Christian nation in no small measure thanks to its martyrs.

Of the martyrs of those days, no one caught the attention of the public in Mexico and the rest of the world as much as the Jesuit Miguel Agustín Pro. Pro was killed by a firing squad in front of news cameras that the government had brought in to record what it hoped would be the embarrassing spectacle of a priest pleading for mercy. It was one of the first modern attempts to use media images to manipulate public opinion for antireligious purposes. But instead of wavering, Pro displayed great dignity. He walked out to the execution bravely, asking only to be allowed to pray before dying. After a few minutes, he stood up, extended his arms in the form of a cross, a traditional Mexican posture in prayer, and with a steady voice, neither defiant nor desperate, movingly intoned words that have since become famous: "Viva Cristo Rey," "Long Live Christ the King."

Far from being a propaganda triumph for the government, the photographs of Pro's execution became objects of Catholic devotion in Mexico and of government embarrassment throughout the world. Officials tried to suppress their circulation, declaring the mere possession of the photos a treasonous act, but without success. Pro's story, though remarkable enough in its way, was only one of many similar acts of bravery and fidelity during the persecutions of the time. But it bears looking into more carefully because, like many of his contemporaries, Pro was quite ordinary in his early life; he would probably have been considered a very unlikely candidate for the high calling of martyr. In the course of events, he clearly turned into someone quite remarkable.

Despite the best efforts of his sometimes pious biographers, there was little conventionally pious in the young Pro. His family, especially his mother, Josefa, was deeply Catholic and practiced the usual devotions — frequent confession and Communion, regular Mass attendance, family recitation of the rosary. But there is no evidence that Miguel Pro was unusually attached to religion in his early years. According to one anecdote, at around six he carried a long candle in the Corpus Christi procession, when the family was living briefly in Monterrey. The experience so moved him that he told his mother, "I want to go to a procession that never ends!" Yet for some unknown reason, he adamantly refused when the local pastor asked him a little later to become an altar boy.[4]

It is indicative of the all-embracing nature of anti-Catholic persecution in Mexico, however, that Pro's first contacts with the faith were linked with a later martyr. Father Mateo Correa Magallanes, the humble local priest who gave First Communion to Miguel and baptized his brother Humberto, was to be martyred himself a few months before the two Pro brothers in February 1927. Arrested on charges that he was in league with the Cristero rebels, an obvious falsehood, Father Correa was ordered to hear the confessions of militants about to be executed.

After the confessions, General Eulogio Ortiz, the officer in charge, demanded that Correa break the seal of the confessional and reveal what the condemned men had said. When the good priest refused, he was executed himself.[5]

But despite the gathering storm clouds in Mexico, Pro lived a happy home life, made even more pleasant by his naturally cheery disposition. He was born into a comfortable, but modest, middle-class family on January 13, 1891, in the village of Guadalupe near Zacatecas, in central Mexico about three hundred miles north of Mexico City. His father, Miguel Sr., worked as a mining engineer, a job that would take the Pro family to the capital as well as several other parts of the country. Not only did the younger Miguel enjoy fun and games and show an early talent for acting; he was something of a wag, playing practical jokes on family and friends which might have been annoying in less sympathetic a person. The practical joking and acting never stopped: when, years later, he was a hunted priest, he posed in civilian disguise, cigar in hand, for a photograph in front of the residence of the rabidly anti-Catholic president Plutarco Elías Calles, the "Mexican Nero" — one of the few surviving photographs in which a smile is on Pro's face.[6] Stories abound about the many times he improvised disguises and identities on the spot to escape capture during the height of the persecution.

The Pros were a large family; ten children were born and seven lived into adulthood. They apparently had substantial musical talents, since several of the children learned instruments and formed an ensemble that played frequently at public events under the baton of Miguel, an accomplished guitarist, mandolin player, and arranger. Along with his jokes, music would be a central part of his whole life. Pro experienced several early health crises that would dog him until his last years. Otherwise, there is not much of note in his early childhood. He was always an indifferent student, though not unintelligent. Indeed, his raw memory for songs, poems, business details, and other matters was quite evident to all who knew him. The family had a hard time finding the right schools for him. Once when they had moved to a new mining town, Concepción del Oro, they even mistakenly sent him to the Protestant Colegio Acuña in nearby Saltillo until a serious illness required the presence of his father, who then discovered his error. What formal schooling Miguel Pro received came from home tutoring by Miguel Sr. Even that ended by about age fifteen.

After that, Pro worked in his father's mining office, where his prodigious memory for the exact contents of files of business contracts and

law suits made him a valuable clerk. The powers of memory were a natural gift, because Miguel took little interest in the business per se. He
had far greater concern for the mines and miners. Even as a child, he
had carried water and candies to the miners waiting in pay lines and
gone down with them at times into the ground. He identified with their
problems. (One of the code names he would use for himself when he was
a hunted priest was *barreterillo,* "the little miner"). Though as a mining engineer Señor Pro was a quasi government official, the whole family
sympathized with the unbreakable cycle from which the miners suffered:
low pay, the need for credit from the company stores, and unescapable
debt. Josefa founded and operated a hospital for the miners (a radical
mayor in 1905 forced her to open it to all classes, not just miners, and
took the ominous step of forbidding patients to receive Last Rites there).
And Miguel's concerns for workers would later lead him to study *Rerum
Novarum,* Pope Leo XIII's encyclical on modern social problems along
with other Catholic analyses of social questions. His sense of humor
and concrete experience with working men seems to have given him a
rare ability to talk about religion with them. When he studied in Europe, he gravitated toward workers. And when he returned to Mexico
he labored on their behalf.

But the three years Pro spent in the mining office until he was eighteen
left him feeling his life was going nowhere. He began to be uncharac-
teristically moody and quiet. For a time, it seems, he was wrestling with
his faith. He stopped going to Mass and Communion. When his oldest
and favorite sister, María de la Luz, took the nun's habit at a convent
in Aguascalientes in 1911, Pro was the only member of the family not
to receive Communion. What was happening inside of him at the time
has never been entirely clear. It may have been only the usual adolescent
turmoil, or a profound spiritual passage from a child's faith to a mature
commitment. There are hints of girlfriends, one a Protestant. Some biographers have recorded that not only did Miguel resent losing María,
with whom he was very close, to the religious life; he feared the impulse
he felt within himself toward a similar step. In its quiet piety, the Pro
family seems to have been fertile soil for vocations. Miguel's second sister, Concepción, decided at María's reception into the convent to remain
there herself. For Miguel, the loss of a second sister brought him to tears
and made him remark that "the heavens had fallen on his head."[7]

Within a short while, however, this formerly cheerful young man resolved the various tensions he felt and arranged to join the Jesuits. The
Jesuits, of course, already had a long and distinguished history, not least

in the Spanish-speaking countries of the New World, particularly Mexico. Contrary to a general prejudice against the old Jesuits, they were neither reactionary nor obscurantist, and their history in Mexico proved it. Prior to their expulsion in 1767, around the time that the Society was suppressed, they had founded twenty-five colleges, eleven seminaries, and many other educational institutions in Mexico. In the eighteenth century, they had promoted a form of Mexican humanism, bringing the work of modern philosophers like Descartes and Leibniz to a country that had not been very intellectually adventurous. Jesuits became prominent in opposing slavery, advocating popular government, and helping to create a sense of Mexican national identity that had not earlier existed during "New Spain's" close identification with the mother country.

Around the time of Pro's decision to enter the order, two Jesuit friends asked him to go with them on a mission. He seems to have arrived at some sort of peace, confessing and taking Communion. Returning home with the old cheerfulness, he is said to have explained: "Do you know what I'd like best? To be one of those saints who eat and sleep, enjoy their little frolics — and then work so many miracles!"[8] The Jesuits in the area were not above their own little jokes. When Pro first approached them, he was told that he had to talk about his potential vocation with Father Gabriel Morfín, rector of the Colegio of Saint John Nepomucene, a noted Jesuit establishment near the Pro household. When Miguel arrived for the interview, he found the good *padre* reading the newspaper and unwilling to be disturbed: "It is best that you come back tomorrow, my son, since, as you see, I'm rather occupied today." For a high-spirited and eager candidate like Pro, this cavalier treatment drove him crazy. The next day, things were no better. Morfín was not reading, but writing something this time. Leaving in a huff, Pro ran into some other Jesuits loudly complaining about religious life. When he thought about it, he realized that this Zen-Buddhist-like treatment had a purpose: testing whether he had the seriousness and patience for entering the Society.[9]

He decided he had what it would take and joined the Jesuit *hacienda* El Llano outside of Zamora on August 10, 1911, but soon found himself wondering whether he had been right to do so. Unlike the imaginative ways in which he had been tested before entry, day-to-day life in the Society was glum. The other novices and the novice master were not joyful about their work, but serious and stressed. Pro is reported to have told the novice master: "Before I came here, I liked the Jesuits very much, but now they all repel me — beginning with you."[10] The master laughed and encouraged Pro, with his natural cheerfulness, to help out the other novices, who were younger and less mature than he was. This gave Pro a chance to organize outings and sports, play the guitar and sing, and invite the novices to do dances from their native regions.

Yet underneath all this surface cheer, something was moving deeply, as no small number of Pro's colleagues recognized. Just as the decision to enter the Jesuits had been made quietly, in some inner chamber of his spirit, so his development of an active spiritual life was carefully concealed beneath an energetic heartiness. He was fortunate that his novice master, Father Santiago, was the kind of man who was wise enough to allow for the workings of the spirit in this unusual seminarian. It says something about Pro that, though everyone who knew him has remarked on his unusual degree of high spirits, not one of his superiors ever gave the slightest hint that Pro was anything other than a serious and promising Jesuit scholastic.

Meanwhile, the Mexico outside the Jesuit oasis was in complete turmoil. Marauding bands claiming various political goals, but often really little more than bandits, were destroying and looting large sectors of the nation — churches, government buildings, and businesses. Religious communities were sometimes held hostage, nuns raped, men dispersed or sent into exile. Father David Galván Bermúdez, a priest of the Guadalajara archdiocese, became a martyr in 1915 because he disobeyed a military order and had ministered to the dying on both sides after a clash between the bandits led by Pancho Villa and the troops — little better than bandits themselves — under the direction of General Venustiano Carranza. To a colleague who had refused to carry out this mission on the grounds that it was not his responsibility, Father Galván had replied that he should join him: "Not out of obligation, but out of charity." His heroic charity earned him a place in front of one of Carranza's firing squads.[11]

In the general chaos, Pro's own father lost his job when the mining office where he worked was burnt to the ground. He took the youngest daughter of the family, Ana María, with him to Mexico City in search of work. The train on which they traveled revealed a country where railroad stations had been destroyed, social order overturned, and the victims of various factions left hanging publicly from telegraph posts. This grisly situation, never before seen in Mexico even in the worst earlier uprisings, bode ill for the Pro family, not least the members in religious houses.

The novitiate at El Llano had a close brush with another band of

Venustiano Carranza's followers. (Carranza would later continue his antireligious campaign as president of Mexico.) The Jesuits knew that they had to disperse before their library, religious articles, and furniture were destroyed. These were hidden or shipped away. Priests and novices disguised themselves in secular clothing to pass more securely on the outside. Disguised as a rancher, Pro made his way to Zamora. Though the city was safe for a brief time, it quickly turned dangerous when the general commanding local forces ordered all priests to be rounded up. The Jesuit novices began a harrowing journey that forced them to evade soldiers, to sleep hiding in fields of tall corn, and to make their way carefully to the large city of Guadalajara. There they found that General Alvaro Obregón, another brutal military leader who would also become president, had taken control of the city, expelled all foreigners, and — once again — ordered priests to be rounded up. The cathedral was turned into an army barracks, and religious objects and art were desecrated, as might be expected, by the lawless soldiers.

Happily for Miguel, his father and the rest of the family had moved to Guadalajara, where, Señor Pro had been told, work might be available. They were able to visit with one another before Miguel went into exile. The Mexican Jesuits knew the situation made study impossible for the novices. So they ordered the students to take the train to Laredo, Texas, where they would receive instructions about what to do next. Pro said goodbye to his mother, whom he would never see again. It was the beginning of a long pilgrimage that would take Pro across the United States to California, through the Panama Canal and over the Atlantic to Europe, and then back to Mexico for his crowning achievement. He was still in his early twenties, but circumstances in his native land would cause him to grow up quickly.

His story was the culmination of several currents in Mexican history. For much of the nineteenth century, Mexico was torn by efforts to establish a nation independent of Spain and prepared to meet the modern world. For those who are only familiar with the poverty and authoritarianism of Mexico in the twentieth century, it will come as a surprise to learn that at the beginning of the nineteenth century Mexico was one of the more remarkable success stories in the New World, not least because of the exertions of the Mexican Church. The University of Mexico was founded in 1553, a little over thirty years after Cortés's conquest and

a century before the foundation of Harvard. But this was only the tip
of a massive educational and scientific system that the Church had created for both Spaniards and Indians alike. The educational efforts led
to economic and scientific advances. Mexican land was under intelligent
cultivation and social institutions were strong. When the great scientist
Alexander von Humboldt visited Mexico in 1803 he remarked: "No
city of the new continent, without even excepting those of the United
States, can display such great and solid scientific establishments as the
capital of Mexico."[12] Humboldt thought the public monuments in Mexico would have excited admiration even had they been built in Paris,
Berlin, or Saint Petersburg. Scientific institutes had discovered many new
plants and done original work in mineralogy, while other educational
establishments were introducing the population to the humanities.

The difference between Mexico and the United States at the time was
that America had already had its war of independence from the mother
country and made a moderate revolution that respected the habits of the
people. The same was not to occur in Mexico. The separation from Spain
occurred amid the confusion of Napoleonic Europe. Napoleon put his
own brother on the Spanish throne, complicating the position of those
in Mexico who wanted to remain loyal to Spain and those who wanted
to revolt. Problems and disorders at home made the population restless.
Ironically, the figure usually credited with inaugurating the Mexican War
for Independence (1810–11) was a priest, Father Miguel Hidalgo. One
of Hidalgo's seminary students, José María Morelos, continued the revolution when Hidalgo was arrested and executed. Four hundred armed
priests joined Morelos until he, too, was captured and executed. Though
the motives and methods of these figures have been both praised and
criticized, Catholic clerics, contrary to the portrayal of the Church as
monolithically reactionary, are universally recognized as founders of the
Mexican Republic. Despite decades of rabid anticlericalism and bans on
public religiosity, Hidalgo and Morelos remained honored figures: they
have given their names to two states near Mexico City.

The Mexican revolutionary path, however, was a rocky one. Like
other nineteenth-century revolutions that were influenced by French
ideas, they went through various periods of upheaval and reaction,
as France itself did until well into the twentieth century. The Church
was often denounced as exploitative or antidemocratic by revolutionary
movements. But the Mexican people were deeply Catholic, and measures
against the Church could be justified only by claiming — quite undemo-
cratically — that the people did not know what was for their own good.

Furthermore, the revolutionaries of various governments grew quite rich themselves by expropriating church lands. By most measures, the Church, even in the colonial period, had been far more deferential to the people and certainly nowhere near as greedily corrupt as the new "popular" governments.

Early restrictions on the Church and confiscations of its property and income occurred in the mid-nineteenth century under Benito Juárez. But Juárez's legislation was conveniently ignored by the man who, from 1876 to 1911 (with only one brief interruption of power) kept a reasonable and peaceful compromise in Mexico: Porfirio Díaz. Díaz believed the antireligious legislation of Juárez both ill-advised and utopian, but for political reasons (he wanted to retain anticlerical support), he did not repeal it. Instead, he mitigated its effects by quietly ignoring its provisions and drawing all sides in Mexican society into a workable compromise. Díaz's methods could be harsh, but there is no question about the results he achieved. Mexico enjoyed a long period of peace, security, order, and prosperity extending for thirty-five years. That Mexico was the nation Miguel Pro and most people alive in the 1920s at the height of the persecution could remember in contrast with the Mexico of more recent decades. When Díaz was finally driven out in 1911, the Mexican government fell prey to a succession of variously oriented but consistently anti-Catholic bigots: Carranza, Obregón, and — for a long period both before, during, and after his presidency — the man who pushed for Pro's execution, the archpersecutor Plutarco Elías Calles.

Calles was a strange figure, at times inclining toward Socialism, at the end of his life an admiring reader of Hitler's *Mein Kampf*.[13] It has been argued that there is no way to explain his boundless hatred for the Church except as a desire to concentrate all power in his own hands. That seems to put the matter in understandable terms; the reality may be something far more sinister. But besides his personal animus, Calles also put his stamp, political as well as antireligious, on subsequent Mexican history by founding the National Revolutionary Party (PNR), which monopolized all political power in the country despite elections held for show. The PNR became the PRI (Institutional Revolutionary Party), which still has a stranglehold on the Mexican presidency and has set a record by being the only party to hold the highest office in a nation for the whole of its existence, which almost coincides with the whole of the twentieth century.

It was into Calles's Mexico that Pro was to return. But before that he had a relatively tranquil period of several years' formation and teaching to prepare him for his final work. From his first place of refuge in Texas he and the other Jesuit brother were ordered by their superiors to go to Los Gatos, California. In that city, they continued their novitiate at an American Jesuit center. But the lack of teaching materials in Spanish and the makeshift conditions were not conducive to the serious formation program the Jesuit system demanded. Pro's outgoing personality made him a favorite of the Americans, even though he knew little English. According to one report, Pro communicated his good-humored spirit through "a charmingly confused mixture of English, Latin, and Spanish."[14] An American student at Los Gatos at the time remembered the impression Pro made: "Due to the general ideas in those days of what a saint should be, if we Americans were asked to vote on which of the Mexican brothers would someday be considered for beatification, I believe Brother Pro's name would be way down on the list. Yet even then, he showed many of the characteristics that made him loved by the Mexican people and hated by the police."[15]

These confirmations of Pro's character from people of a very different cultural background were repeated during several years he spent studying in Europe. The Jesuits, seeing the impossibility of working at Los Gatos, asked the Mexicans to transfer to Granada in Spain. In that city of romantic Spanish tradition, Pro flourished as much as a man, separated from a family enduring difficult circumstances, could be expected to. He worked hard, both to make up for his earlier lack of formal education and to develop along the lines laid out by the Jesuit system. Languages, literature, and moral theology came naturally to him. Philosophy — a central part of the academic program — did not, and he had to review the course carefully after failing his second year in that subject.

But in Granada there also emerged another natural dimension of his personality. Pro began working among the small villages surrounding Granada, drawing both children and their humble and largely uninstructed parents to his catechetical activities. He also began to study social questions, particularly the circumstances that had set workingmen in Europe at a distance from the Church. His natural aptitude for these subjects seems to have been an outgrowth of his interest in the people they were intended to help. Also, unmistakably, something else was going on. His pranks continued nonstop in the seminary and outside it. But at a deeper level he was quietly bringing his life into line with the rigorous practice of patience and the other virtues. As his end would show, he was quite successful in that effort, so much so that his room in Granada would later be converted into a chapel, until the Spanish Communists destroyed it in 1937 during the Spanish Civil War.

One of the ways in which the Jesuit program of formation develops virtues is to prescribe a period of teaching during the novitiate. Pro could not return to Mexico, so he was assigned a post as prefect and teacher at a school that the exiled Mexican Jesuits had opened in another Granada, in Nicaragua. For a man who had health problems all his life, assignment to the tropical climate of Central America was not conducive to well-being. But Pro threw himself into helping to organize the newly formed school with a great deal of enthusiasm. As usual, he made sure there was a lot of physical exercise and outdoor activity in addition to study, even going so far as to organize baseball games in the hot tropical sun. Guitar music and popular Mexican songs also played a major role in his teaching program.

In 1922, after two years along Lake Nicaragua, Pro was assigned to the College of Saint Ignatius in Sarria, outside of Barcelona in Spain. It was his third trip across the Atlantic, but it brought some unexpected opportunities. Since his ship, the *Pero,* landed in Le Havre, he took a train to Paris and visited the sights, including the place where Ignatius of Loyola and his six companions first took their vows. As happens to many Americans who have studied in Europe, direct contact with the sites of Catholic history moved his soul. During his two years at Sarria, Pro made one of his annual retreats at Manresa, where Ignatius wrote the *Spiritual Exercises.* Pro seemed to draw from these places, as he would from others during his last years in Europe, a strength of conviction and purpose that even his joking exterior could not hide.

The enthusiasm spilled over into his studies. Theology and canon law opened themselves up to him. The Jesuit instructors seem to have intuited where his gifts were taking him. They assigned him in 1924 to the School of Theology at Enghien in Belgium, a lovely and tranquil place to study. But Pro knew that at that very moment back in Mexico, Plutarco Calles, the most rabidly antireligious president in Mexican history, had been elected and was beginning to go on a virtual rampage against the Church. This must have driven Pro to read even more deeply into Catholic social thought, especially on workers' issues. And his interest was not merely speculative. He asked and received permission to go into the coal mines of Charleroi in Belgium. There he not only came into contact with workers like those he had known growing up in Mexico, but he also encountered the Catholic Worker Youth Movement, or JOC, as it was known in French. For Pro, a similar movement at home might have spared Mexico many troubles by putting the Church at the center of a movement toward justice. The JOC made an impression on him, and he made an impression on its members. They remembered him years after he had become a martyr.[16] The priest who founded the Jesuit school in Nicaragua and had seen what Pro was capable of doing in that small country described him as "born to be dedicated to the worker,"[17] and suggested to the Jesuit superior general that the Mexican should be sent to Orizaba when he returned to his home country, a city famous as a center of hardline Communists.

Remarkably, Pro was even-tempered enough to see within Socialism and Communism an admirable zeal, despite the errors of their systems. Just before his return to Mexico, he wrote: "The Socialists are more interested in the fate of the workers than we are. The popular masses know this; they can see it and from this consequences can be drawn. We ought to talk, to shout against injustices. We should have confidence and should not be afraid. We should proclaim the principles of the Church, the kingdom of charity, without forgetting that of justice, as sometimes happens." Even the Communist, he observed, "has a brutal sincerity. He is moved by a savage hate and he is ready to spill blood on the altars of triumph."[18] Given this passion on the part of those who had a mistaken view of human beings and society, mere critiques of their errors would not suffice. Something more positive had to be both presented and heroically labored for. Pro studied and made plans to go deeper into various works on the question of labor and social justice and to implement the results in action.

It is one mark of his spiritual growth that he did not restrict his social concerns to the merely intellectual realm. His burgeoning interests and warm personality won him acceptance by a wide variety of people, even in Belgium where language difficulties and cultural differences hampered his work. But he took no personal credit for his successes: "The facility with which I pass from one social class to another is not, as I used to think in my joyous youth, owing to my physical advantages nor to my sound and sweet piety. . . . It is all due to the fact that, poor rascal that I am, I belong to the Society of Jesus. The name Jesuit is enough to open up the doors of all types to me."[19] Pro's own witness on this point must, of course, be given weight. But it is difficult for an outside observer not to believe that being a Jesuit would have normally closed as many doors, with some people, as it opened with others. It was the kind of Jesuit Pro was that made the difference.

Pro was doing all this work and study simultaneously with preparing for ordination. When the day finally came on August 31, 1925, he was ready to carry out the work for which his whole previous life had readied him. His family was not at his ordination, though he thought of them. Despite his usual cheeriness, worries about them seem to have been taking their toll. In his first months as a priest, his stomach, never in very good shape, gave him increasing trouble, which at first he concealed. When he could do so no longer, he went through three operations for "ulcers," one of which involved cutting away large parts of the stomach without any anesthesia. Pro prayed his way through the pain. Given the state of medicine at the time, it is no surprise that his digestive system did not heal well. To add to his misery, news arrived from Mexico that his mother had died. In his prayers and masses afterward, he was gripped by the conviction that she was already in heaven and would do great good with her intercessions for those she had left behind. For another person, this might have been a pious illusion. In Pro's case, there is something strangely confident and perhaps prophetic in his words.

The Jesuits at Belgium decided that there was no hope for Pro to recover without drastic steps. More out of desperation than anything else, they came to the conclusion that he should go back to Mexico, where the more familiar food and surroundings might help with his recovery. How to do this presented several problems, since in 1926 priests were banned by the Calles government in Mexico, and Pro certainly would not be admitted by customs officials. It did not help matters that his passport quite openly declared him to be a "religious." Perhaps because of the general ignorance about conditions in Mexico, Pro's Jesuit superiors and the European officials he consulted thought this would create no problem. In any event, it appears there was no way to change the passport and Pro would have to take his chances.

The only thing he asked to do before embarking was to be make a short pilgrimage to Lourdes. Like his visits to other significant Catholic sites in Europe, this one moved him deeply. He spent only one day in Lourdes, mostly in a state of emotional exhilaration at the sight of the simple pilgrims and the various religious activities. He wrote that it "produced and released in my soul things I have never felt before," and he even remarked that the experience was a kind of Nunc Dimittis, a crowning event that put an end to the European period and made him ready to be sent to Mexico.[20] He felt the Virgin had promised him an easy voyage.

On board the *Cuba,* the ship taking him home, there were almost five hundred Mexican Catholics. Pro did not hide the fact that he was a priest and was frankly welcomed as such. Many of the passengers took Communion from him and came for confession and advice. It was an anticipation of the same spiritual hunger he would find when he landed. The sea experience was so satisfying that he claimed he had forgotten he had ever been ill. And he remarked that God, who seemed to be calling him back to Mexico, had given him special faculties to carry out his work.

But he still had to enter the country. Since so many passengers knew his true identity, he had already run the risk that someone would betray him to the authorities. He had things in his bags that customs might find suspect. There was the matter of his passport. A reasonable person might have expected that he would be turned away. He and his superiors had taken no steps to mislead the port authorities. For some unknown reason, the Veracruz customs officials miraculously passed him through without opening his bags and did not notice the markings on his passport. Pro got on a train that evening and arrived at Lerdo, the Jesuit provincial headquarters in Mexico; the next morning, he spoke briefly with his superior and by 11:00 a.m. was working at the Jesuit Church of Our Lady of Guadalupe, Calle Enrico Martínez, Mexico City.

The Mexico of that time was far worse for Catholics than the one Pro had left. His arrival in July 1926 nearly coincided with the Mexican bishops' decision to suspend all public worship in view of the harsh laws imposed by the Calles government. When the bishops sought redress through official channels, they were put off by the president and his ministers with the lame excuse that the Mexican constitution forbade the executive branch from interfering in religious affairs. The prelates were told they had to petition the Congress. The bishops protested that the Congress was in the hands of men who would not pay any attention to their complaints. But since there was no other recourse, they decided to try anyway.

By September 1926, they had collected two million signatures on a petition requesting the same kind of church/state separation that existed in the United States and European countries. In truly democratic nations, that many signatures would have made election-conscious politicians worried. In Mexico, where elections were a sham, they had no effect. In fact, the bishops were stripped of their Mexican citizenship on the absurd charge that article 37 of the Mexican constitution prescribed such a penalty for clerics who publicly opposed constitutional provisions. So not only would any desiring constitutional change, even according to constitutional forms, be denied it by the constitution itself; they would, also on allegedly constitutional grounds, no longer have a right to call themselves Mexicans.

This and many other provocations seem to have been part of a deliberate attempt by the government to goad Catholics into taking violent action, which could then be ruthlessly suppressed as allegedly necessary for public order. The event that most directly caused an armed Catholic uprising was the execution of Father Luis Batiz Sáinz and three laymen (David Roldán, Salvador Lara, and Manuel Morales) on August 15, 1926, at Chalchihuites in the state of Zacatecas. All four were involved in setting up the National League for the Defense of Religious Liberty. Morales, the League's president, had made a point of stating an important principle at the public organizational meeting: "The League will be peaceful, without mixing itself in political affairs." Nonetheless, they were accused by the government of trying to stir up sedition and were arrested.

When the local townspeople protested the arrest of the League's leadership, they were told that the four would be taken to the capital of the state to give legal depositions. But no legal proceedings ever took place. Instead, the four were shoved into cars, driven into the mountains, and offered a choice. If they accepted the Calles legislation against the Church, they could go free. If not.... None of them accepted the offer. Father Batiz tried to save Morales, who had children. But Morales said: "I am dying for God, and He will take care of my children." All four were shot and killed near Puerto Santa Teresa.[21]

Despite their peaceful intentions and heroic deaths, the incident sparked an uprising, the famous Cristeros Rebellion, particularly in the states of Jalisco, Michoacán, and Guanajuato, some of the most Catholic areas in Mexico. At the time of the uprising, the National League for the Defense of Religious Liberty had three hundred thousand members in Mexico City alone.[22] So the government had reason to worry despite the League's pacifism. The official Church position was ambivalent. The bishops and the pope seemed to counsel peaceful persuasion and patience, as did many of the martyrs themselves. But the Catholic lay people had had enough. In fact, according to several analysts, if the United States had not backed the Calles regime and that of his equally persecuting successor Portes Gil with arms, money, and moral support, while prohibiting private arms shipments to the Cristeros, there was a

good chance that the rebellion would have succeeded. It was an unfortunate choice by the United States, a country that had no love of religious
repression, but sought stability and financial predictability for American
citizens on its southern border.

When the Mexican bishops were expelled in July of 1927 for supposedly inciting the rebellion (more than seventy years after the fact,
when tempers have cooled, there is no evidence of any such incitement),
the Cristeros went into even higher gear. Enrique Gorostieta Jr. became
their commander-in-chief. Several federal generals joined the Cristeros.
The rebels were so successful that Calles, no longer president, but as
*Jefe máximo,* the power behind the president, persuaded his friend, U.S.
Ambassador Dwight Morrow, to bring two exiled bishops back from the
United States to negotiate. But by this point, the lay people had taken
charge of what they believed to be a properly lay initiative. In May of
1929, Gorostieta publicly declared that the bishops' negotiations with
the government were not relevant to the Cristero cause. For him, the
problem was not essentially a religious one:

> Liberty has been proscribed, and the National Guard [i.e., the Cris-
> teros] has been constituted to defend all liberties. Its vitality must
> be ascribed to the fact that it represents the people in a genuine
> manner. . . . The foregoing and other considerations that we will
> not enumerate authorize us to demand, not to petition, that the
> solution of the problem be left to us, that the Mexican people who
> wish and are determined to be Catholic, who have demonstrated to
> the entire world that in defense of their religion they are generous
> with their blood, their money, and their dearest interests, in spite of
> the selfish apathy of the wealthy aristocracy and the intellectuals,
> be left unhampered to struggle for the recovery of their freedom.
>
> Let the bishops have patience; let them not despair that the day
> will arrive when we summon them in company with our priests to
> return and carry on their sacred mission in a nation of free men.
> The voice of our martyred dead commands us to carry on![23]

This was not the typical tone that Catholics adopted toward bishops in
the Mexico of the 1920s. If there was any genuine question in the Mexican government whether the bishops were in charge of the rebellion,
words like these would have put an end to such speculations. But the
charge was never meant as a statement of truth, merely an instrument
of destruction. Tragically, Gorostieta died in an ambush shortly after, a
dramatic end to a dramatic life.

Miguel Agustín Pro Juárez, S.J.'s last days, however, were even more dramatic and memorable. But his and Gorostieta's cases were far from unusual. In 1928, President Calles himself admitted to a British journalist that he had executed fifty priests up to that time. Official records indicate that the true figure was twice that number.[24] These included other well-known figures such as the Augustinian Elías Nieves, who was pastor of a poor parish in Michoacán. In March of 1927, Father Nieves was captured by government forces in a village near his parish after the captain in charge threatened to torture the villagers if they did not reveal the priest's whereabouts. Nonetheless, two humble *peones* caught with Nieves refused to abandon him. A wealthy Catholic offered a large bribe for their release (the chance to make a tidy sum through extortion was one of the reasons why troops were often eager to pursue priests). But the captain refused the offer.

What then ensued has an almost Gospel-like quality. Nieves heard the two peasants' confessions and absolved them. They were executed. Before he followed them, Nieves gestured to the soldiers: "Kneel down. I will give you the blessing of a priest — and along with it my pardon for what you are about to do." The soldiers all knelt and made the sign of the cross. To the captain Nieves remarked: "Even for you there is a blessing and my pardon," which so infuriated the officer that he drew his pistol and killed Nieves on the spot.[25]

Countless other priests met terrible ends: shot in their vestments during Mass, thrown from trains, executed and dragged behind vehicles, tortured for information, "disappeared" — a term that would be commonly used decades later for similar cases all over Latin America. Where the locations of death are known, they have often been turned into shrines and places of pilgrimage.

But it was not only clerics who suffered these outrages. One of the distinguished American experts on Latin America at the time, Carleton Beals, was shocked when he went to Guadalajara and was proudly informed by government officials that forty old men and women had been caught at Mass and shot. (Beals noted that the wives of the same military men heard Mass themselves, at home and in full security.) Martyrdom, however, also came to more prominent lay people. In another notorious case in Guadalajara, a lawyer named Anacleto González Flores paid the price for being a Catholic. Though he was president of the Catholic Youth Organization, involved in Catholic Action, and a founder of the Unión Popular, none of these activities were the reason for his murder.

Instead, he and two cousins were arrested and interrogated by the police, who were looking for the archbishop of Guadalajara, Don Francisco Orozco y Jiménez, who had gone into the mountains to evade an outrageous law ordering all priests to report to Mexico City — clearly for arrest or worse. The archbishop was so law-abiding that he wrote a letter to the president, explaining why he could not comply with an illegitimate request and was going into hiding. There is no reason why González Flores and the other laymen should have had any information on the archbishop's whereabouts. Torture resulted in nothing. Yet with no formal charges, no trial, no official reason for the action, they were put before a firing squad. It was April 1, 1927, a time of many heroic deaths. González Flores added to the legends. His last words, glinting like gold and representing many in similar straits whose last words were never recorded, were: "I die, but God does not die!"

To their shame, journalists rarely reported these events, even in foreign countries. Mexican officials had shrewdly paid off journalists, especially in the United States, to help give favorable interpretations of events. The result was that one of the most serious and systematic violations of basic human rights in the century did not enter world consciousness at the time and continues to be largely overlooked — or at most given a few passing words — in histories of the twentieth century. The great modern Catholic novelist Graham Greene wrote a stunning record of the atmosphere in Mexico as late as the 1930s in his travel book *The Lawless Roads.* Greene then turned some of the material he had gathered into one of the most moving novels of the century, *The Power and the Glory.* Another distinguished British literary figure, Evelyn Waugh, visited Mexico and produced an incisive, if little remembered, study: *Mexico: An Object Lesson.* Because of the general lack of world interest in the plight of Mexican Catholics, even these remarkable literary efforts produced little response, being dismissed either as the work of Catholic partisans or as anecdotal rather than scholarly treatments. But the atrocities and persecutions Greene and Waugh documented were neither figments of overheated Catholic imaginations nor mere isolated incidents. They were real, all too real for the Mexicans who suffered them.

This was the world into which the returning Father Miguel Pro stepped on July 8, 1926. Many, clerics and lay people, had already made sacrifices as heroic as his. But no one's story from this sad chapter in Mexican history was to become more famous. At his parish, Pro would begin hearing confessions at 5:30 in the morning with few breaks. In a typical day, he might spend fourteen hours in the box. Twice he fainted and had to be carried out. Yet this man, whose health was not good, drew energy from the people who came to him. And he needed to: just a few weeks after his return, the Calles government issued an order suppressing all public worship and making all priests subject to arrest. The date deliberately chosen to announce the law was July 31, the feast of Ignatius of Loyola, the founder of the Jesuits.

But at least one Mexican Jesuit (and probably many more and members of other religious orders as well as diocesan priests) was undeterred. He set up various "Communion stations" around the city. Despite threats to those who even took Communion, the numbers swelled: 650, the first First Friday Pro distributed the host, 800 the following week, then 910. Police surveillance made this work difficult and dangerous, especially given the numbers and the fatigue involved. A good deal of bravado and no small amount of Father Pro's acting talent were needed to keep him out of trouble. Police might show up unexpectedly at the door. He would lead them boldly through the rooms explaining that nothing illegal was going on. Once he arrived at a designated site to find police detectives outside. Wishing neither to show fear by withdrawing nor to get anyone into unnecessary trouble, he pretended to flash a badge and said, "There's a cat [i.e., a priest in hiding] inside there!" Thinking he was an undercover agent, the detectives let him pass. He performed his duties and exited the house to the respectful salutes of the hoodwinked policemen.

Photographs from the period show him in various disguises. He gave retreats to all kinds of groups. When it was a women's association, he was dressed in a stylish suit and straw boater. For the workingmen, he put on overalls and a worker's cap; he looked like a fellow driver for a meeting of chauffeurs, a mechanic among mechanics. By various subterfuges he was able to hear confessions even in jails. He advised people who were preparing to be public speakers on behalf of the Church how to go about shaping public opinion.

After an event that particularly angered President Calles — the League for the Defense of Religion released balloons in the capital that showered down leaflets on the population — Pro, along with a group of others, was briefly arrested. He kept up their spirits by leading prayers and songs and attending to everyone. At the end, he made a bold, but perhaps foolishly impulsive statement to the jailers. They asked whether he would be willing to pay a small fine for his complicity in pro-Catholic actions.

He replied: "No, sir, and for two reasons; first because I haven't a cent; and secondly, even if I had, I would not want to feel remorse for the rest of my life for having contributed even a penny from my own pocket to the support of the present Government."[26] It was a minor miracle that this outburst did not end his life sooner.

In another notorious escapade, he managed to avoid policemen waiting for him only by jumping into a cab and ordering the cabdriver to speed off. Providentially, the driver was a Catholic who followed Pro's instructions. When they turned a corner, he bailed out, deliberately trying to attract the pursuing car's attention. He rolled to a stop and quickly composed himself, sitting up against a tree. The car passed by quite close, but for some reason Pro's pursuers thought the figure they saw was someone else. All these close escapes led him to reflect that the very precariousness of life under persecution was a blessing: "I feel the truth of that sublime answer, 'My grace is sufficient for thee: for virtue is made strong in weakness.'" By contrast, he reflected that the very strength of the oppressors would lead to their eventual demise.

One of the prerequisites for that demise would be Pro's own life. In a complicated series of events, he moved inexorably toward paying the highest price for being a believer. Following the first arrest, the police watched him even more closely. His Jesuit superiors ordered him to remain hidden though Pro wanted desperately to continue his work. In April of 1927, he got permission to be active again. He was not only tending to spiritual needs; he also managed to get food and shelter for several dozen families whose lives had been disrupted by the Calles legislation. His letters in these months show a growing awareness of dependence on Providence for everything, even though Pro was a genius at finding human agents to help support the poor. His words have the feel of deeply lived experience. He observes at one point, "The perils in which we live are terrible if seen with the eyes of the body and not with those of the spirit." And in the next few lines he reflects that if he had attempted to deal with these trials on his own, he would have failed miserably. Then the Gospel verse comes spontaneously to his mind, "For you did not choose me, I chose you," and he thinks, "God knows what a piece of work I was...."

Conditions had become so bad for everyone that instead of saying *adiós* people would make an Act of Contrition when leaving one another. Work was so burdensome that at times Pro fantasized that being in jail would at least be a rest. When he had a bad toothache, he confessed that he wanted to whack his penitents with the confession grille — but didn't.

The summer wore on and, almost absurdly, in September 1927 Pro was asked to take his final exam in theology to qualify him as a full member of the Jesuits. The opinion of his examiners — *Attigit mediocritatem* ("he has achieved mediocrity") — is comic in several senses, not least that, whatever his academic attainments in theology during his sixteen years studying to be a Jesuit, within two months Father Pro would show that he was at the top of the class in a far more demanding spiritual school.

In the meantime, he was now in the business of finding food for ninety-six families as well as performing his priestly duties "though we have no definite income upon which to depend." And strangely, this helplessness made him all the more light-hearted since he had already realized, not notionally but in concrete reality, that he and all his charges were at the Divine Mercy, a far more reliable source than anything anyone could arrange. However mad it may appear to people who live in orderly societies where the necessities of life are easily available, the system not only made profound spiritual sense, but it actually worked.

But he would not be in that business long. In the first week of October 1927, there were an estimated three hundred political assassinations, eliminations of mere worldly enemies having little to do with President Calles's furious assault on religious. Two presidential candidates were murdered. The whole society was becoming brutal. Fire hoses — and sometimes guns — were turned on little old ladies praying in priestless churches. The flimsiest pretexts were used to confiscate property, imprison "lawbreakers," extract bribes to stay out of jail for offenses that would never come before an honest judge or, often enough, any judge at all. Printing a prayer or teaching religion was regarded as sedition. The League for the Defense of Religion tried to use every means to stop the repression and terror. Some elements of the League, contrary to advice from Rome and the Mexican bishops themselves, resorted to armed resistance. Most members, however, merely sought redress of a terrible situation through persuasion.

In the midst of this titanic emotional situation, a bomb went off. General Alvaro Obregón, a past Mexican president, had conspired with current President Calles to be reelected, a direct violation of the constitutional prohibition against anyone serving twice in that office. After Díaz's long dictatorship, the writers of the new constitution prohibited reelection as a way to prevent recurrences of monopoly on political power. But Calles and Obregón were in cahoots and were planning to pass the office back and forth to each other. During the period between his fraudulent re-election by the party and his actual assumption of office, Obregón was leisurely driving one Sunday afternoon in November 1927 down the Paseo de la Reforma, as was the custom among the upper classes. A passing car tossed a bomb at the president-elect's car. Gunshots were exchanged. Obregón was slightly injured. His bodyguards chased the assailants' car. It appears to have held four people. They apprehended two: Antonino Tirado and Nahum Lamberto Ruiz. A third suspect, Luis Segura Vilchis, later made a full confession of having planned the attack without the knowledge of anyone else. This left one assailant unaccounted for.

The car used by the would-be assassins was traced. It belonged to Segura Vilchis, who had bought it from another man, who had bought it from Humberto Pro, Miguel's brother. By pursuing other leads, the police found bomb-making materials in a side room at a house where the Pros sometimes stayed. Even the owner had no idea that the materials were there. For the police, though, all these items pointed to the Pros as accomplices in the assassination attempt. It was an absurd pretext. On principle, the Pros had always stayed away from the ample opportunities that existed at the time to engage in armed struggle.

Be that as it may, the police were not interested in legal niceties such as evidence and guilt. They arrested three Pro brothers — Miguel, Humberto, and Roberto — along with other people without bother-ing to examine who, if anyone, among this group was actually guilty. Humberto had an alibi. Miguel was never even questioned about his in-volvement. Nonetheless, they all went to prison, where Miguel played his usual role of keeping up everyone's spirits. Another inmate, Antonio Mutiozábal, later recounted the agreeable and happy way that Pro faced the unknown dangers ahead. The last night of his life, Pro slept on the ground while Mutiozábal slept on Pro's mattress.

During their imprisonment, protests mounted. Confirmations of their alibis sent. No evidence had been offered of any wrongdoing. Public opinion — no small number of people in Mexico City owed something to Padre Pro — was running high in favor of the brothers, and the otherwise government-controlled press seemed to take their sides as well. General Roberto Cruz, however, received an order from President Calles on No-vember 21 to shoot the prisoners. Cruz was not a fool. He knew that martyring the Pros and others would not end well. He called his lawyer and asked what he could do, since none of the legal procedures had been followed. The next day, perhaps as a way of getting himself out from between Calles and public opinion, he allowed the newspaper *Excelsior* to interview Father Pro. According to what may be cleaned-up transcripts, Pro said he had no formal statement to make, but at least one passage sounds like it may actually contain some of his words: "I am grateful for the courtesy extended to me by those persons by whom I was apprehended. I am absolutely outside of this affair since I am a person of order. I am completely tranquil and await the enlightenment of justice. I deny positively having taken any part in the plot."[27] In other versions of the interview, Miguel and Humberto vehemently denied any involvement, and the interview was quickly closed by Cruz.

The same afternoon, Calles demanded that Cruz make an example of the Pros. In a battle of wits worthy of Pontius Pilate and the Sanhedrin, Cruz tried to talk Calles into allowing some legal cover. But Calles told him "to hell with" legalities and reminded him he had his orders and only had to obey. Cruz appeared before reporters and explained that evidence had been accumulated showing all the parties guilty in the attempted assassination. Apparently, Calles had also ordered that these executions were to have a high profile. So journalists and photographers from all over Mexico and the whole world were invited.

Even so the game was not entirely over. The morning of the executions, an enterprising lawyer, Luis MacGregor, had convinced a quite brave judge, Julio López Masse, to sign an *amparo,* a stay of execution. It is doubtful that Cruz and Calles would have paid any attention to this paper obstacle. But they did not even have to. MacGregor was locked outside of the proceedings at the police station, and the executions — quite odd for such widely advertised events — were carried out a half-hour earlier than scheduled. A last-minute request from the Argentine delegation to Mexico earned Roberto, the youngest of the brothers, a reprieve.

When Miguel's body and the body of his brother Humberto arrived at the family house, old Miguel Sr., ordered no one to mourn, for there was nothing sorrowful in such heroic deaths. Don Miguel opened the door later that night and found a half-dozen government agents outside. They came in, knelt, and prayed. A steady stream of workers, women, and professional people arrived. The Rosary was recited; other prayers were said. When the bodies were ready for transport to the Dolores Cemetery, there was an enormous crowd in the streets, even though President Calles had forbidden public demonstrations in support of the martyred brothers. But the crowd was much larger than the police could do anything about, somewhere between ten thousand and thirty thousand, according to some accounts larger than any ever seen in Mexico at a funeral. Around five hundred cars took part in the funeral cortege. As the caskets came out, someone shouted, "Make way for the martyrs!" The crowd fell silent. But as the coffins went through the streets "Viva Cristo Rey" was shouted everywhere.

The day after Pro's execution, the American ambassador Dwight Morrow (Charles Lindbergh's future father-in-law) and the humorist Will Rogers, who had become famous as a common-sense mocker of U.S. government foolishness, took a trip with President Calles through Mexico on the presidential train. Calles had deliberately set up the trip as propaganda intended to convince Mexican Catholics that the United States would not help them. Morrow is reported to have known this, but believed he could use the influence thus gained over Calles to turn his government in a different direction. In the next few years, the government killed 250,000 to 300,000 people, many Catholic, even after a compromise had been worked out.[28]

One of Calles's successors as president, Lázaro Cárdenas, announced in a speech in Oaxaca during the 1930s a more subtle form of persecution: "I am tired of closing churches and finding them full. Now I am going to open the churches and educate the people and in ten years I shall find them empty."[29] But Cárdenas also tolerated more direct assaults by his collaborators. He appointed Tomás Garrido Canabal, the brutal former governor of Tabasco, as his minister of agriculture. In December of 1934, Garrido Canabal sent several dozen of his thugs to Coyacán, a suburb of Mexico City, to confront a group of twenty or thirty lay people who had been alerted that the government might try to burn down the Church of the Immaculate Conception there. A young member of Catholic Action, María de la Luz Camacho, was gunned down along with four of the men. The incident was so outrageous that the murderers had to be punished. They were put in prison, but Garrido Canabal sent them a case of champagne. Shortly after, they were released.

One scholar of Mexican history sums up the result of the period of persecution in these unequivocal terms:

> By 1940, the Church legally had no corporate existence, no real estate, no schools, no monasteries or convents, no foreign priests,

no right to defend itself publicly or in the courts, and no hope that its legal and actual situations would improve. Its clergy were forbidden to wear clerical garb, to vote, to celebrate public religious ceremonies, and to engage in politics. Although in practice many of these prohibitions were ignored by both church and state, their existence was a constant threat.[30]

That uncertain existence, with few changes, continued in Mexico until the 1990s.

Yet the anti-Catholic bigots, for all their bloodthirstiness, did not prevail. Pro was right that their very appearance of strength was an illusion. Pro won the immediate public relations contest. The church/state question took longer to resolve. But he may have been instrumental even there. At one point, late in his life, he joked with friends that, if he were fortunate enough to be asked to give his life for the Church in Mexico, they should have their petitions ready because "he would deal out favors as if they were a deck of cards."[31] Mexico's fidelity to the faith and the eventual change in its laws on religion owe something, at least in human if not celestial terms, to Pro and his fellow martyrs.

Priests and believers were subject to harassment and occasionally murdered in the meanwhile, usually on trumped-up charges that they were involved in politics or drug smuggling. As late as the early 1990s, Cardinal Juan Ocampo Posadas of Guadalajara, the site of so much suffering during the height of the Calles persecution, was mysteriously gunned down at the airport for reasons that are unclear. Yet through negotiations with the Vatican carried out by the papal nuncio Girolamo Prigione, Mexican president Carlos Salinas de Gortari announced on November 1, 1991, that articles 3, 5, 24, 27, and 130 of the Mexican constitution would be changed to make the Church's position more secure.

Salinas's explanation for the move is interesting, because of his obvious attempt both to placate the hardliners in the central ruling party and to recognize the reality of international human rights standards at the end of the twentieth century:

Based on experience, the Mexican people do not want the clergy taking part in politics or amassing material wealth. The people, however, do not want to live a pretense or misguided complicity. The idea is not to return to existence of privilege, but to reconcile the definite secularization of our society with effective freedom of beliefs, something that constitutes one of the most important human rights.[32]

Even from a secular standpoint, this concedes the point to Father Pro and the many thousands of men and women like him who believed that the faith and modern Catholic social teaching placed no necessary conflict between the Church and the democratic state. Though some worrisome clauses exist even in the revised constitutional articles, it will be difficult for any Mexican government legally to oppress the Church again. The public witness of the martyrs and the private fidelity of many millions under harsh conditions assured that the cause finally triumphed. If the past century in Mexico ever receives a fair appraisal, it will be clear that, even in secular terms such as democracy and human rights, figures like Carranza, Obregón, Calles, Portes Gil, and Cárdenas were deplorable men. And their victims — Pro, Nieves, Batiz, Roldán, Lara, Morales, González Flores, Gorostieta, and countless, nameless others — in those same secular terms, but far higher ones also, deserve to be celebrated. They are a great rarity in any age: actors in a tragedy with a happy ending.

# -TWO-

# IN SOVIET RUSSIA
# AND ITS TERRITORIES

O N JULY 2, 1937, Joseph Stalin issued an order through the Soviet
Politburo to all levels of the Communist Party that all former detainees — especially kulaks, political prisoners, and religious ministers —
should be arrested or rearrested "in order to execute immediately the
most harmful elements through administrative steps taken at sessions
of the [Soviet] troikas."[1] Stalin was about to enter his most murderous
period, believing — or at least saying — that the real Communist Era
was about to begin, and that all enemies, therefore, had to be hit hard.
Nikolai Yezhov, Stalin's People's Commissar for Internal Affairs, duly
carried out the order, specifying that, among its other targets, it should
aim at "Church men currently to be found in prisons, camps, at forced
labor, and in [labor] colonies," as well as religious formerly convicted
of crimes and then in the countryside, in cities, or in factories. Such
sweeping measures could not help but produce a large bumper crop of
martyrs.

For as the categories included in the decrees show, there had already
been a sizeable number of religious people apprehended for various reasons. Furthermore, Stalin was not, as later apologists for the Soviet
Union have claimed, an aberration, but a culmination of a process begun from the very first with Lenin. In a famous passage, Lenin defined
a basic truth of the Communist regime:

> Religion is the opiate of the people. This dictum of Marx is the
> cornerstone of the entire Marxist world outlook concerning the
> problem of religion. All contemporary religions, churches, and all
> types of religious organizations, Marxism forever looks upon as
> organs of bourgeois reaction serving to defend the exploitation
> and the stultifying of the working class. . . . One must know how to
> battle against religion. . . . That battle has to be understood in con-

nection with the concrete practice of the class movement directed toward the elimination of the social roots of religion.[2]

This view did not remain in the realm of mere theory. Lenin invented the kinds of concentration camps and religious persecution characteristic of officially atheist regimes in the twentieth century. Though he began to put pressure on the Orthodox and other clergy at the outset of the Bolshevik regime, it was in 1921–22, during a terrible famine in Russia and Ukraine, that he sensed the time was ripe for a decisive strike. In a letter to Molotov that he ordered not to be copied, Lenin noted:

> It is now and only now, when in the starving regions people are eating human flesh, and hundreds if not thousands of corpses are littering the roads, that we can (and therefore must) carry out the confiscation of church valuables with the most savage and merciless energy, not stopping [short of] crushing any resistance. It is precisely now and only now that the enormous majority of the peasant mass will be for us or at any rate will not be in a condition to support [the religious resisters].

Further on, he argues: "The greater number of representatives of the reactionary clergy and reactionary bourgeoisie we succeed in executing for [resisting confiscation of church properties] the better."[3] Dmitri Voklogonov, a historian who had looked into the Lenin Archives, claimed to have seen another document in which the Soviet leader requested daily reports on the number of priests executed.[4]

In line with Lenin's views, even before Stalin's Great Terror, the Soviets had gone after all kinds of religious practice — Christian, Jewish, and Muslim — within the territories they controlled. But they hit Catholicism especially hard. According to Father Leopold Braun, an American priest who ran the Saint Louis Church in Moscow, by 1934, the 3,300 Catholic churches and 2,000 chapels on Russian soil had been reduced to two active churches, primarily meant to serve foreigners and serve as a public demonstration that Catholicism existed in Soviet Russia despite claims of persecution.[5] In addition to the destruction of places of worship, the Soviets rounded up numbers of clergy as well as active lay persons. And a French priest in Moscow during the 1950s reported that, even given the Soviets' desire to appear tolerant after the death of Stalin, two cooks, a driver, and other members of his staff disappeared without a trace.[6]

If the Mexican Revolution brought the first major persecutions and martyrdoms of Catholics in the twentieth century, the Russian Revolution invented the tools by which not only religious persecution but widespread oppression of large populations became common. Soviet Russia created an extensive network of prison camps, the *Gulag*, as Alexander Solzhenitsyn taught the West to call it. Much has been written about those camps, but not nearly enough that recognizes how — along with widespread torture, terror, executions, and surveillance for political purposes — they sought to wipe out religion. The most comprehensive and detailed account of these subjects, *The Black Book of Communism*, which admirably documents the sad history of that movement in the course of the century, devotes only one paragraph to the religious figures who disappeared, were killed, or merely imprisoned for decades during the Great Terror.[7] But mere justice requires that the memory of these martyrs not be forgotten or underemphasized.

Though Russia is often regarded as a primarily Orthodox country, it has long had large Catholic populations. When Poland was first partitioned in 1772, almost a million Catholics, in addition to those already under Russian jurisdiction, became part of the Russian nation. By that time, Catherine II had already reorganized the Germans, French, Italians and Poles, who largely made up Catholic congregations, especially in Saint Petersburg and Moscow, in order to make peace among them. Parts of Lithuania, Galicia, and other territories containing significant numbers of Catholics were joined to Russia in subsequent redrawings of borders. During all that time, Russia naturally sought to pressure Catholics into becoming Orthodox or otherwise subservient to Russian rule. When the czarist government finally issued an edict of toleration in 1905, at least a quarter million Catholics (perhaps many more) openly left Orthodoxy for Rome. It appeared that in the new century the Catholic Church might finally gain equality on Russian soil with other denominations. But that hopeful opening soon closed when the Bolsheviks came to power in 1917.

Catholics had welcomed the Provisional Government, believing it would lead to fairer treatment in an open democracy. The formation of a commission, headed by Catholic bishop Edward Ropp (later metropolitan of the Catholic Church in Russia) to deal with remaining Polish affairs seemed to promise serious improvements, and the Church was allowed greater freedom than at any time in recent Russian history. A Catholic-inspired Christian democratic program was inaugurated. Dioceses and bishops abolished by the czars were restored. Some churches, forcibly converted to Orthodox use in the previous century, were returned to Catholic hands. Schools, seminaries, and monasteries were opened or reopened. Freedom of conscience, with effective legislation to make sure choice could be translated into practice, seemed to be guaranteed. Church officials planned a newsletter and a catechism. The Church in Russia appeared on its way to a normal relationship in a pluralistic democracy such as it had in other democracies.

So when the Bolsheviks succeeded the Provisional Government, the Church in Russia — in its several forms and rites — was better organized that it had been for some time previously.[8] But it was not strong enough to withstand the tidal wave of antireligious action after the Bolshevik Revolution of November 1917. Two months later, to the great relief of many religious denominations, the Bolsheviks proclaimed separation of church and state. But as early as January 31, 1918, *Pravda* announced what that would entail: all church and monastic funds had to go to local soviets; commissars would run religious libraries and presses; "enemies of the people" had to be registered; that done the State could leave religion alone as a private affair.[9] Such decrees were not unprecedented in czarist times. They were serious, but more serious were the quick nationalizations of schools and seminaries, and then the ban on churches owning property. Taken together, these measures effectively stripped the Church of its independence.

In Saint Petersburg alone, this meant that twenty thousand children being educated in the eleven elementary schools run by the Saint Catherine Church no longer received a Catholic education. The vocational school and male and female *gymnasia* Saint Catherine's ran for another fifteen hundred students also closed. Atheistic ideology was one reason for closing the schools. Another was that the Soviets defined priests and other religious as members of the "exploiting classes." Not only were they restricted in their educational and catechetical missions, but they also were not accorded rights under the Soviet constitution, which reserved various freedoms only for workers.[10]

Under the circumstances, the Catholic authorities, meeting to decide how to handle government demands, were understandably divided about whether to sign agreements that potentially conflicted with canon law and unfairly curtailed religious action. They set up Catholic committees, consisting of two representatives from each parish, to organize action. Archbishop Ropp, of the Latin Catholic Mogilev archdiocese, the virtual primate of Roman Catholics on Russian soil, believed the Soviet regime would not last long in the fluid revolutionary atmosphere. With that in mind, he decided to sign several agreements that, at least temporarily, granted the Soviets certain powers over the Church.

But even that was not enough for the radical atheistic aims of the Soviets. In April of 1919, Archbishop Ropp was arrested. When the Vatican protested to Lenin, the Soviet leader lied and said that Ropp's nephew, not Ropp himself, had been arrested — for illegal economic speculation. But Archbishop Ropp had been arrested and would have been shot if some Soviet leaders had not convinced their more hard-line colleagues that he might be useful in an exchange for a jailed Communist prisoner, Karl Radek, instead.[11] According to reports, thirteen thousand Catholics paraded down to the headquarters of the Cheka (one of the precursors of the KGB) in Saint Petersburg after a Sunday Mass in protest. That night, the government tried to round up several priests; many of them, however, managed to escape into hiding. Four did not: Ladislas Issajewicz, John Wasilewski, Anthony Racewicz, and Aleksei Zerchaninov. Wasilewski and Zerchaninov were to die under arrest after a decade in prison camps.

Archbishop Ropp was moved to the notorious Lubianka Prison in Moscow and then to the Butyrka Prison for security reasons. A short time later he was allowed to live at Moscow's Immaculate Conception parish so long as he stayed out of church/state affairs and refrained from priestly duties. The Vatican intervened. An exchange of prisoners was arranged and Ropp was spared rearrest or worse by being deported to Warsaw. Karl Radek was sent to Moscow. Bloodshed had been avoided, but the steely determination of the Soviet government toward the Catholic Church had become clear.

Archbishop Ropp's successor, John Cieplak, would feel that steel more directly. In one of the most lurid trials of the early Soviet years, Archbishop Cieplak and his assistant, Monsignor Constantine Budkiewicz, would be condemned to death for anti-Soviet activity. As their names and those of many of the other Catholics arrested in the early days of Soviet rule indicate, a substantial part of the Church in Russia was Polish. Lenin's government was wickedly ingenious in finding ways to make it appear that these Catholics were in the pay of Poland, or Polish spies engaged in promoting the interests of a foreign or international organization (i.e., the Vatican), even when, as in this case, the Catholics were only defending the sacred core of the Church. The deception was only successful among those who were already believers in Soviet dogma. Undocumented rumors from other parts of Russia suggested that many priests elsewhere were being arrested or executed, church property was being seized, and church buildings confiscated. Sacrilege of sacred objects was common: during an "inspection" of a church at Gatchina, the Holy Eucharist was taken from the tabernacle and thrown on the floor. The relics of Blessed Andrew Bobola were desecrated. Catholics began fleeing the country.[12]

Ironically, though Budkiewicz would suffer the most from the Soviets, he had been the leader of a faction in the Catholic hierarchy that believed that the Church could find a *modus vivendi* with the new regime by hard negotiations. In his view, the Soviets would be careful not to arouse protests from Europe and could be talked into respecting basic religious rights. For instance, both Catholic and Orthodox leaders balked at the Soviet demand that they turn over sacred vessels to the state. Such an act would not only be unjust — the objects did not, as the Soviets claimed, belong to "the people." It would be a sacrilege. That was just what occurred: in Ukraine, fifty-two out of sixty-eight churches had sacred objects stolen.[13] Churches in Moscow, Novgorod, Rostov, and Minsk, among others, were forced to hand over valuables. As a noted scholar of the period has observed: "The strategy of Monsignor Budkiewicz avoided disaster as little as did the strategy of Archbishop Ropp, because no strategy could avoid it."[14]

Indeed, shortly after the Soviets came to power, Leonid Fyodorov, who would later be named exarch of the Russian Catholic Oriental rite by the pope, wrote to Andrei Sheptytski, the Ukrainian Greek Catholic archbishop of Lvov:

> The times of Diocletian [a Roman emperor noted for his persecution of Christians] begin for the Church. It is not a hyperbole, but a given fact.... Thanks be to God for all things! It is the just punishment of the clergy for their laziness, egoism, and little love for the flock entrusted to them. Our sheep look indifferently on God's abandoned and devastated churches. I live trusting in God and your prayers.... I would never have thought that we would be asked to carry such a cross."[15]

Fyodorov himself would die at only fifty-six after several stints in concentration and forced labor camps.

Around the country, confirmation of the Soviet policy began to appear. At the Polish border, where the Russians were involved in trying to absorb the newly independent Polish nation, there were massacres of Catholic Ruthenians and Poles. The brutality went so far as to lead to burying opponents alive, a rare form of terror even among the ferocious antireligious campaigns of the twentieth century. Along the Black Sea, which before the revolution had a Catholic population of about two hundred thousand, largely of German and other ethnic backgrounds, Bishop Aloysius Kessler survived by going into hiding: however three priests in his diocese were murdered. In Minsk and the huge Mogilev archdiocese, similar atrocities occurred.

At the same time, the Soviet government started a massive campaign of atheist propaganda. In 1921, it began censoring sermons, a step unprecedented even in the darkest czarist times. The Atheist Publishing House began churning out enormous numbers of textbooks and materialist tracts. That it did so, at enormous cost, when the country was in the midst of an economic crisis indicates how seriously the Soviet leadership took the propaganda struggle against religion. The campaign included all religious groups, from Jews to Old Believers. The crude blasphemies and jokes against religious belief convinced few church members. But the vilification had two main effects. In some places, it provoked a strong reaction in favor of religion. In others, it inhibited open practice. In Smolensk, for example, the Immaculate Conception Catholic Church had over 6,700 parishioners in 1904; by the early twenties the number had shrunk to 100.[16] In Petrograd, all Catholic churches were simply surrounded by troops and closed at the end of 1922. All thirteen Petrograd priests, along with Archbishop Cieplak, were ordered to Moscow the following year. Grigori Zinoviev, later an ally of Stalin's, was the prime mover behind this early effort at religious cleansing.

Along with its disruption of religious life, the Soviet government ruined Russia's economic activity. Industrial output plummeted. Even worse, the agricultural sector failed and famine ensued. In spite of the brutal religious persecution, the government felt no shame in turning to Orthodox Archbishop Tikhon, who had barely survived an assassination attempt, for help in petitioning the Western nations and the Vatican for relief. The archbishop refused to approach governments, but agreed to speak with Christian leaders — if the Church were allowed to distribute the aid. After an initial refusal, the government relented. But, at the same time, it continued to pillage churches of all denominations and synagogues (under the pretext that it needed the wealth for famine relief) and to pour out atheist propaganda.

Remarkably, the Western nations still responded to the Russians' plight. Popes Benedict XV and Pius XI not only sent Vatican aid but petitioned the League of Nations and other sources on Russia's behalf.

Pius tried to get religious freedom on the agenda at the Conference of Genoa, but most Western nations weakly excused themselves from doing anything on the grounds that they could not interfere in internal Soviet affairs. Pius did succeed in helping get large amounts of aid from the United States and other nations for starving Russia, and made a large contribution himself. To run this relief effort, Pius appointed the Jesuit Edmund Walsh, who was instructed to distribute help without regard to religion. Walsh's missions daily fed an estimated 160,000 people.[17] The Soviet government formally thanked Pius for his work in a March 1923 telegram. He was careful not to provoke antireligious backlash by his statements. But the Soviets were not nearly so delicate: they continued persecutions without letup.

March 1923 was the date when Archbishop Cieplak, Monsignor Budkiewicz, Exarch Leonid Fyodorov, the leader of the Catholic Byzantine rite, and thirteen priests along with a layman, James Sharnas, who had protested the closing of the Petrograd churches, were put on trial. Trial is too dignified a term for what actually occurred. The charges distorted all religious activity or resistance to Soviet persecution into political and counterrevolutionary crimes. The judges were virtual prosecutors. One of the prosecutors told Father Michael Rutkowski, who had knelt and started praying when he could not keep the militia from seizing objects in the Petrograd Church of the Assumption, "That was a counterrevolutionary act."[18] The same judge told the archbishop that teaching children religion was terrorism. Refusal to turn over church vessels to the government was lawless sedition; contact with Vatican representatives in Poland became a Polish conspiracy to damage Soviet interests. The Church had organized a counterrevolutionary movement. And so on. The prosecutor called for the death penalty for the archbishop and Budkiewicz, as well as for two priests, Stanislas Ejsmont and a Father Chwieko. The trial ended on Palm Sunday 1923: Cieplak and Budkiewicz received death sentences, the others prison terms of from three to ten years.

The Vatican, the United States, Belgium, Great Britain, and other countries along with religious leaders around the world petitioned Russia. Eventually, the All-Russia Central Executive Committee commuted the archbishop's sentence, saying he had been imprisoned under the czars and that it did not wish his execution to be interpreted as anti-Catholicism. Budkiewicz, though, had no excuses for his "criminality." More likely than not, the committee thought this a reasonable compromise. The monsignor was therefore shot — early on the morning of April 1, 1923, Easter morning, making Budkiewicz the first documented Latin Catholic martyr under the Soviet regime. And with his death, the fresh blooms of the Catholic Church in Russia were essentially extinguished.

By 1925, the number of Catholic priests in Russia had fallen from 245 to 70. According to good estimates, 200,000 Catholics disappeared and are unaccounted for in the eight years between the Bolshevik Revolution and 1925.[19] Some may merely have fled; but since so many of the victims of the Soviet persecution cannot be documented, a sizeable portion of those Catholics unaccounted for may have fallen to nefarious acts. In Moscow and Petrograd, various priests, nuns, and lay people were arrested, including a whole community of Dominican nuns along with their mother superior, Anna Abrikosova, a convert.[20] Where they were taken and their ultimate ends are largely unknown. Some were ransomed and expelled to Poland. Archbishop Cieplak spent about a year in several Soviet prisons before he was expelled to Latvia. He made his way to Poland, where he received a hero's welcome, then to the Vatican, where he was embraced by Pius XI in a very emotional private audience. The archbishop later traveled to the United States; he died in Passaic, New Jersey, in 1926.[21] By 1924, there was not a single Catholic bishop left free within the whole expanse of the Soviet Union.[22]

With the disappearance of the regular hierarchy and most of the clergy, such Catholic life as remained in the Soviet Union centered primarily around small groups that were outside Communist jurisdiction because they were run and staffed for the most part by foreigners. Since the fall of Communism, the KGB archives have been made partly available to scholars, so we have some indication of how the higher echelons of the party thought about and acted toward these groups.[23] In the heyday of the Cold War, it was a commonplace for Western intellectuals and politicians to denounce fervent anti-Communists for their "paranoia" toward the Soviet Union. But compared with the most ardent anti-Communism in the West — which at least had the basis in fact that atrocities and oppression were occurring in the Soviet bloc — the NKVD (a precursor of the KGB) manifested a truly murderous paranoia toward the small Catholic communities.

After Archbishop Cieplak was arrested, tried, and expelled in 1924, and
the rest of the Catholic hierarchy dispersed, the Kremlin refused to allow
the Vatican to appoint any more bishops unless the Holy See officially
recognized the Soviet government. Not wishing to leave Russian Catholics without ecclesial support while this diplomatic blackmail played
itself out, Pope Pius XI decided on the secret consecration of a remarkable French Assumptionist, who had been living in Russia for twenty
years, Father Eugène Neveu. The pope sent Father Michel d'Herbigny,
a French Jesuit himself consecrated as a bishop, to consecrate in turn
not only Neveu but three apostolic administrators for the churches in
Leningrad, Minsk, and Odessa. The French embassy knew of the move,
and Neveu was quietly made a bishop in the French church of Saint
Louis in Moscow on March 21, 1926.[24]

Neveu bravely and forcefully confronted the Communist persecution,
but he also believed that it might be possible to find a way to live with the
regime. His first homily at the French church ended with the observation:

> Since we live at the heart of the great Russian people, who give us
> hospitality, we must in turn recognize them and wish them peace,
> prosperity, and glory. We regard Russians as true brothers who are
> united to us through the bonds of the Catholic faith. To render
> unto Caesar the things that are Caesar's and to God the things that
> are God's, to love our enemies, to do good to those who hate us,
> to pray for those who persecute and offend us, if we happen to
> suffer such things, this is our only political position, because it is
> the position of the Gospel.[25]

Despite such sentiments, the secret police immediately started surveillance of Neveu and those with whom he came into contact.

As chaplain to the French embassy, Neveu could not easily be expelled
from the Soviet Union. So the KGB had to make a case against Neveu
that would expose him as "an agent of the Vatican." A normal person
would regard any priest as representing Vatican views. For the security
services, which read all activity as a mirror of its own entirely politicized
and brutally conspiratorial vision of the world, everything Neveu and
those around him did looked like a foreign plot. They placed spies among
his domestic help, the waiters at the French embassy, and even the Saint
Louis parishioners. Neveu was receiving reports about the Church from
all over Russia as well as the lists of clergy who were alive and dead in
the prison camps,[26] and he passed information on for publication in the
West. But there is a vast difference between conveying the truth about

a situation and the "counterrevolutionary" activities with which he and other Catholics were often charged.

A special charge against Neveu was that he received money from abroad and was, in effect, a subsidizer of "Catholic activists." Naturally, Neveu was helping religious orders as well as priests, orphans, and families who were starving either because the breadwinner was in prison or because of persecution and infringement on their rights. But far from being an international network of anti-Soviet subversion, it was — as any sane person might have seen — merely a philanthropic enterprise, and a small one at that. The NKVD was paying informants alone three times as much as Neveu was distributing in aid.[27] It justified these expenditures by inventing or exaggerating Neveu's network. An NKVD file on religious activities in Ukraine made public in the late 1990s characterizes Neveu's work thus: "We have had available for some time indisputable data according to which the Vatican has considerably strengthened its work of spreading union with Rome in the USSR, focusing as its ultimate aim on uniting the Orthodox Church and the Catholic Church in order to create a single counterrevolutionary church." According to the same document, Neveu was distributing "colossal sums,"[28] which of course demanded an equally large response from the secret police. But Neveu's only real "crimes" were that he was helping Catholics literally to stay alive and telling the truth about their plight and that of the Orthodox Church.

Among those he helped survive were some remarkable figures, both in their lives as Catholics and in the price they paid under Soviet persecution. The most prominent of these and the leader of a group in his own right was Sergei Mikhailovich Soloviev, a convert and priest, who was the nephew of the great modern Russian philosopher Vladimir Soloviev, himself a convert to Catholicism. The older Soloviev had prepared the way philosophically for a reunion between Russian Orthodoxy and Roman Catholicism, which might have begun to take place on a large scale had Russia become a democratic state after the fall of the czars. Several Orthodox leaders including Patriarch Tikhon were so inclined; that may have been one of the reasons the Soviets tried to assassinate him. Soviet fears of this potential moral revolution also probably lay behind the ferocity with which they rooted out the younger Soloviev and various other groups in contact with Neveu in Moscow.

Soloviev's conduct during his arrest was a disappointment. Not only did he come from a distinguished family and enjoy wide cultural contacts (his wife was related to Turgenev), he was himself an intellectual who had published some noteworthy poetry as a young man and had given signs of being capable of serious contributions to Russian cultural life. He was first arrested in 1931 when he was only forty-six, but from the first it was clear that he was not made of the stuff to resist the power of the NKVD. Anyone who meditates carefully on the kind of torture and terror Catholics and other believers faced at the time will find reason not to judge Soloviev harshly. But as much is expected from those to whom much has been given, we might have hoped that Soloviev would have finished differently.

He had about thirty followers in Moscow and was one of the Catholic leaders in the explorations of a possible union of the Orthodox Church with Rome. When Bishop Fyodorov was arrested, Soloviev was named vice exarch of Russian Catholics. But when Soloviev himself was arrested in 1931 with eight members of his community, he simply cracked. In part, Soloviev was terrified that the Soviets would arrest and murder his daughters; but he also seems to have suffered a complete psychological breakdown at the prospect of his own execution. Physical courage was a virtue that he had not developed in his mostly intellectual and cultural pursuits.

Among his signed statements are declarations abjuring his faith, accusing himself of converting Jews and receiving Orthodox priests into the Catholic Church, and passages such as this:

> I no longer wish to have any contact with Polish priests and Catholics, because their activity is directed, under the cover of religion, against the USSR.... Furthermore, I do not wish to have contacts with Bishop Neveu, a foreign citizen, because Bishop Neveu, whom I have always honored and considered a person of elevated spiritual life, plays a role precisely as a representative of bourgeois France.[29]

The very wording of the statement suggests that at least some of it was dictated by the NKVD. It is an open question whether Soloviev was even capable of writing such a statement after the NKVD got through with him. The friends who met him after he was released from the Lubianka Prison say he was incoherent and as distracted as a child. Even back in his own apartment, he startled at the sound of noise in the halls, fearing that they were coming for him or his daughters again. In this condition, Soloviev told people, "I have betrayed everyone and everything." Whether this is true or not only the interrogators know; the archives on his interrogation are not available. We do know, however, that Soloviev did not wish to see anyone, not because, as in his statement, he thought they were anti-Soviets agents, but because he could not face them. He was rearrested and ordered to set out for a work camp, but soon even the NKVD recognized that he was unfit for anything. Soloviev was sent instead to a psychiatric hospital — a real medical institution rather than the notorious so-called hospitals that the NKVD used to intimidate prisoners. He died in internal exile ten years later, having never recovered.

Soloviev was not an isolated case. The Soviets were successful in breaking down other priests as well. By contrast, the Catholic women in Moscow remained firm, but paid the price for their fidelity. For example, the Dominican nuns assembled around Anna Abrikosova, a convert, showed remarkable fortitude. The NKVD looked at these religious orders and saw its own face reflected in them, as we can now deduce from the reports available from the archives. One report informs Moscow: "At meetings, they spoke about the creation of cells of three to five believers, that would constitute the base for an organization to struggle against socialist ideas."[30] There may have been talk among the Dominicans about how to survive Socialism, but it is highly doubtful that they were in any way conspiratorial — especially in the cloak-and-dagger political mode the Soviet secret agents seemed to find in every group they examined.

The NKVD also twisted religious practices so that they appeared to be radical politics. Another file represents a woman as confessing that a Catholic friend had told her:

> ...that I was the only one to have been selected for a great task. I had to prepare myself for two or three months under the guidance of a priest, who then would tell me what to do. He told me that I had to concentrate every day on my examination of conscience and on contrition, to prepare myself for death. He cultivated in me the sense of sacrifice and readiness to die in the name of a great cause. All this made me into a person fanatically ready to carry out whatever deed to which they destined me.[31]

The misunderstanding of religious terms here is so large as to be laughable, if it had not led to such murderous results.

The nuns were quite direct about their religious beliefs. One remarked in front of her tormentors at a trial in Voronezh: "I am a Catholic and I boast of it, a Dominican and proud. You have no right to condemn me for this, because God is not head of a political party and because the teachings of Jesus Christ are not a political program, but a program of love and mercy." Neveu thought these nuns "heroic Russian women" who had added "a glorious page to the history of Holy Mother Church."[32] For the most part, their fearlessness brought them three- to five-year sentences in prison camps, which for some inmates turned into even worse outcomes. The NKVD was not squeamish about going after women. Camilla Krushelnickaya and Anna Brilliantova, two young women involved in the Catholic youth group in Moscow, were arrested and tortured into grotesque "confessions" that were used to portray the Church as a fanatical group of terrorists, plotting the assassination of Stalin, the return of capitalism, and other obviously trumped-up schemes. Both were sentenced to the camps. But going to the camps did not mean matters were at an end; surveillance continued and new sentences might be given for various reasons. In 1937, when the Special Troika of the NKVD, which Stalin and Yezhov had decreed to look into executing religious, revisited their cases along with those of several other Catholics, both of them, along with Father Epifany Akulov, were executed.

Some did not survive imprisonment long enough to fall to the terror of the mid-1930s. Victoria Lvovnova, for example, was a Jewish convert with intellectual gifts and a religious passion that might have made her into a figure comparable to Edith Stein. She was arrested with the rest of the Moscow Catholic group in 1931, but even her fellow prisoners never learned what happened to her. All we know, even with the opening of the KGB files, is that she died less than fifty days after her arrest; her case was closed by the NKVD because of "the decease of the accused."[33] Others did not go so quickly: Ekaterina Gotocheva took the usual route to the prison camps, but died just as the Terror was being unleashed under the rigors of solitary confinement.[34] Still others, like Father Potapyev Emilianov, endured their prison sentences and were released, but in such weakened condition that they died shortly after. In Emilianov's case, he never got beyond the railroad station that was to take him from the prison camp to exile. A large number of the twenty or so Dominican nuns died in ways that cannot be traced. Some were eventually released, but only three years after Stalin died, during a brief thaw in the 1950s ordered by Khrushchev.

The religious prisoners were only part of a much larger group of Soviet victims, and they are sometimes submerged into political or economic categories. Ukrainian and Polish Catholics, for example, are sometimes

classified among those the Soviets tried to wipe out for reasons of political unity. But even if that was one dimension of the story, another is that
Catholics and other religious were baited as such by interrogators and
guards who were militant atheists. Perhaps the worst taunt, because it
made all the sufferings seem useless, was that God did not exist. Father
Pietro Leoni, an Italian Jesuit trained to be a missionary at the Russicum,
or Oriental College, in Rome, reports in his autobiography a rather typical incident (he was in the camps from 1945 to 1955). A camp official,
hearing him mention God, launched into a heated exchange with the
priest:

> "God! But if God existed, he would not allow you to be here."
> "Why wouldn't He allow it? Look: I feel honored to suffer for
> His sake, and I am certain that He will give me an eternal reward,
> if I persevere to the end."
> "Vain hopes, because there is no God."
> "God exists, has always existed, and will always exist. While
> Soviet power...."[35]

Leoni was a particularly tough person who got the better of the camp
official. But many more prisoners were probably led to the brink of
despair by the thought that perhaps they had been mistaken all along or
that God had abandoned them.

The sheer number of people imprisoned in the Soviet Union is stag-
gering. Estimates of the number of prisoners overall in the Soviet Union
begin at nineteen million, of which seven million were shot or otherwise
killed or died from the overwork, poor food, disease, and the discour-
agement of the camps. Boleslas Sloskans, who became the apostolic
administrator of Minsk and Mogilev after the bishops were arrested or
driven out, kept a diary of his experiences in the camps on the Solovetski Islands in the White Sea. He estimated that seven hundred out of a
thousand detainees died there in 1928 alone.[36] His account of the rigors of the Solovetski complex of camps in the 1920s is also important
because, when the large roundups and rearrests of Catholics took place
in the 1930s, it was the Solovetski Islands to which many of them were
deliberately sent.

Many, as a result, died there. One of the earliest, Father Felix Lubycsynsky, was first arrested in Ukraine for "illegal instruction in the
catechism" — no attempt at hiding the reality behind a political rationalization in his case. Later the prosecutors would add the usual
pro-Polish, pro-international bourgeoisie, anti-Soviet charges. At his

Ukrainian Cheka interrogation, the priest revealed the lessons that he had learned during his recent experience: "Losing the Faith, man loses himself and morality at the same time and transforms himself into a beast. All the violent, without exception, no matter how they classify themselves, have the same philosophy: 'If God does not exist, everything is permitted.' "[37] That was in 1923. By 1931, Father Felix was dead from camp life. And he had only experienced the Solovetskis before the intensified persecution, inside and outside the camps, in the 1930s. In 1929, the Soviets unleashed a massive roundup of Catholic priests in the Ukraine when it seemed clear that the Vatican could no longer be of any use to the regime internationally.

Ironically, the Solovetski Islands had long been a spiritual center, where various churches and monasteries, surrounded by rich fields and abundant wildlife, had provided a pleasant place for the religious life. In the mid-1920s, the Soviets ransacked the buildings and drove out or arrested the remaining sixty-one Orthodox monks. The buildings, sturdy and situated on islands near the shore, were turned into prisons camps that became the model for the other camps that were established all over the Soviet Union. The prisoners in the camps used to have a saying: "The Solovetskis are the Soviet Union in miniature, and the Soviet Union is an immense prison camp of the Solovetskis."[38]

For some reason it was the place the Soviets often chose to send religious prisoners, both Catholic and Orthodox. There was no little tension between the two groups after the Bolshevik Revolution in spite of some recognition that union and a common front would be an of advantage to both. Orthodox leaders were particularly suspicious of the Russian Catholics who followed the Byzantine rite, and therefore could appeal to Russians without requiring them to change their mode of worship. The presence of Leonid Fyodorov, the Russian Catholic exarch, in the camp did not help matters. And long smoldering resentments between the dominant and officially supported Orthodox under the czars and the discriminated against, mostly Polish, Catholics provided additional fuel. But by all reports, Catholics and Orthodox reconciled with one another in the Solovetski camps and simply regarded one another as brothers in Christ. It was a hard school in which to have to learn charity toward one another.

In the early years, the Catholics were allowed to use the church of Saint German for Mass. As we know from accounts of prisoners in other camps throughout the Soviet Union over the whole period, there were camps where officials basically ignored religious activity as long as it did not threaten trouble for the officials themselves. In other camps and at certain times, including the Solovetskis, as we shall see, all religious activity was classified as illegal and might bring the harshest penalties. But at the outset, before harsh policies were implemented, religious services occurred regularly. It is difficult to judge whether this was the result of prisoner resistance or camp leniency. At least one of the people sent to the Solovetski Islands, Anatolia Ivanovna Novitskaya, told Neveu after her release that the camps had tried to set up a schedule that made Sunday Mass attendance impossible. The prisoners told the camp officials: "Shoot us immediately, but we will not violate God's commandments." When the officials tried to ban clerical garb, the people were equally adamant: "At work, we will be dressed like other prisoners, but in our cells, we will keep our habits."[39]

One prisoner, Sergei Karpinski, who had almost finished his seminary training when he was arrested, was even ordained a priest by another prisoner, the Russian Catholic exarch Leonid Fyodorov. In retrospect, for all the suffering, it was a relatively peaceful period. (Karpinski would later disappear into the maw of the Solovetski prisons in 1937, and Fyodorov died at a young age after his release into internal exile.) A letter from another young priest, Boleslas Sloskans, to his parents was published in the 1990s and shows a remarkable spirit in him and the other Solovetski prisoners:

Dear Mother and Father: Maybe you have already learned of my arrest from the newspapers. Only now, after six months, have they finally given me permission to write to you. Remember the words of Our Lord: "Do not fear those who kill the body, but have no power to kill the soul. Are not two sparrows sold for a penny? And yet not even one of them falls to the ground without your Father. As to you, even the hairs on your head are all counted; therefore, do not fear. . . . " It is exactly this that I am experiencing: everything that God disposes of or permits, happens only for our good. In the last fifteen years I have never experienced so many graces as in these five months of imprisonment. Prison has been the greatest and most extraordinary event in my interior life, if you exclude the sorrow of not being able to celebrate the Mass. Dear parents, pray for me, but without fear or sadness in your hearts. Open your hearts to this great Love. I am so happy, that now I am ready to love every human being without exception, even those who do not deserve to be loved: they are the most unhappy ones.

I ask you both from the bottom of my heart: do not let vengeance or exasperation make a crack in your hearts. If we allow that, we would not be true Christians any more, only fanatics. . . . I ask you one more time: pray. . . .[40]

It is worth remembering that these are not the words of a man in some play about prison camps, who can go home after the performance. These are the words and feelings of a man in the midst of a fierce Soviet camp where he witnessed large percentages of prisoners die each year. The Soviets wanted the prisoners to help construct a canal between the White Sea and the Baltic. The labor often consisted of backbreaking details ordered to transport blocks of ice or snow and to cut wood. The food was hardly adequate for such heavy labor in cold temperatures. And the barracks where they slept were so overcrowded that it was hard to breathe. It was a system intended to slowly break down all but the hardiest prisoners while extracting the maximum amount of manual labor from them sixteen hours a day, seven days a week. In short, it was simply slavery.

In 1929, the Catholics were forbidden to use the chapel of Saint German. In January 1930, a large group of Ukrainian lay people along with thirty five priests were arrested and sent to the Solovetskis. Others arrived from all over the country. The regime was cracking down. When Felix Lubycsynsky died, the camp officials forbade a religious service and were ready simply to throw him into an unmarked grave. Because of the repeated requests by several of the other priest-prisoners, he was allowed a decent burial, with some prayers at the grave side. But the antireligious storms were gathering. When those storms hit, many of the martyrs we have already mentioned were to be found in the Solovetski camps. The decrees of Stalin and Yezhov fell hard upon them in those once sacred islands. In the fall of 1937, at the height of the bloodshed, thirty-two priests along with many religious women were "retried" by the Soviet Troikas and shot.

In addition to the deaths, interrogations conducted under death threats led to the arrest of other active clergy and lay Catholics. Though anyone might see through the confessions the interrogations produced, they also sometimes succeeded in confirming others' involvement in Catholic activities — a betrayal that could cost them their liberty and even their lives.

Many who were arrested did not withstand the tortures and betrayed still other co-religionists. Sometimes this led the NKVD to bigger fish. For example, Bartholomew Remov, a Russian Orthodox archbishop, became a Catholic in 1932 after discussions with Monsignor Neveu at the Saint Louis Church in Moscow. The Vatican then made him the apostolic administrator of Moscow. Remov had already been arrested twice, in 1920 and 1928, simply because he was a prominent Orthodox leader, and then released, both times because of poor health. Through informers, the NKVD learned — or manufactured evidence — that Remov was giving Neveu information about the closing of Orthodox churches and religious persecution. He was arrested again in 1935 with twenty-one members of Catholic monastic orders. But his case was treated separately. Because of his eminence and importance, he was sentenced in a closed court session to "capital punishment by firing squad, with confiscation of goods. This sentence is definitive and does not admit of recourse to a court of appeals."[41] The sentence was carried out in the Moscow Butyrka Prison.

Remov's death was only the tip of a large iceberg. Antoine Wenger, an expert on religious repression in Soviet Russia who has studied both Monsignor Neveu's papers and the KGB archives, has noted that "Neveu's correspondence contains about fifteen hundred names of people, bishops, priests, religious, lay people, men and women, Catholics, Orthodox, less frequently Lutherans, whose Calvary we can follow from the moment of arrest until death."[42] Neveu's own assessment of these people, however, is worth reproducing:

> Despite the persecution, despite the traps insidiously laid for them, these generous people converted to the faith a good number of Russians and Jews, who became in turn fervent Christians. I am proud to give homage to the virtue of these saints. What would they not be able to do, in their ardor, if in Russia Catholics had a little liberty! In prisons, in concentration camps, in forced labor, in places of deportation: everywhere the nuns remained faithful to their own vocation and to their own holy vows; they have spread the fragrance of Christ and the light of our holy faith.[43]

With so many of his acquaintances falling prey to the NKVD, it was only a matter of time before the secret police found a way to get Neveu, despite his diplomatic protection. When, very much against his will, he had to go to Paris for surgery, the Soviets simply refused to give him a return visa. Without Neveu, the situation turned even more bleak. His replacement, the American-born Father Leopold Braun, wrote to Neveu in 1938:

> The persecution occurs with an ever increasing ferocity and an even greater hypocrisy. . . . It is fearfully sad for me to have to tell you that in the whole country, there is not a single priest at his post, except for Father [Michael] Florent [a French priest working in Leningrad] and your humble servant. . . . The miracle lies in the fact that in such conditions there still are, even among the Russians, believers who go to church.[44]

The Soviets were careful to keep open these two French churches in Russia's two most important cities during the whole length of their misrule. Tourists and other visitors could thus see for themselves that religious liberty, including freedom for Catholics, existed in the Soviet Union. But these Potemkin-village churches themselves continued to be harassed. Father Florent was expelled with no explanation in 1941, Father Braun for "anti-Soviet acts" during the war in 1945. Action against Braun was made easier by the fact that the United States and France believed Stalin's stance against religion was softening, partly because Stalin had chosen to open the churches to help him in his "great patriotic war" against the Nazis. Braun lost the support of both countries' embassies when he vehemently insisted that persecution continued without letup.

He was right. After Stalin died in 1953, Khrushchev denounced his errors, as did other subsequent Soviet leaders. But religious prisoners were not released in any large numbers, the churches were not allowed to reopen, and probably a majority of Russian religious perished in the camps. Since most of the people who were old enough to be arrested in the 1920s and 1930s would have been close to sixty by 1953, the persecution effectively wiped out one religious generation and prevented the appearance of two or three more. In fact, Khrushchev repudiated two parts of the Stalin legacy. He lamented the paranoid purges Stalin had carried out against political enemies. But he also seems to have thought Stalin's brief letup on the churches had outlived its usefulness. From 1959 to 1964 Khrushchev unleashed his own vicious antireligious campaign, reclosing churches that had been opened. In 1965 the Orthodox found themselves with about one-third the number open that had been open in 1955. Needless to say, Catholics were given no quarter.

The regime also stepped up antireligious propaganda again. Nikolai Ilyachev, Khrushchev's chief ideologist for this campaign, openly stated that the next phase in stamping out religion had to hit at the family:

> The facts show that it is the family which is the main center of sustaining the religious spirit. . . . We cannot and we shall not remain indifferent to the fate of children on whom their parents — fanatical believers — in reality commit an act of spiritual violence. We are not indifferent to the fact that, in Soviet society, a family is a cell of Communist education or a refuge of backward conceptions.[45]

This special targeting of families testifies to the seriousness of Soviet antireligious aims, even after Stalin. Essentially, up until Mikhail Gorbachev's assumption of power and even during his reign, religious repression continued from inertia if not great love for the struggle toward the end. But the campaign against families also suggests that, despite all public pressures, families had managed to continue to keep religion alive, enough so to call for a propaganda campaign fifty years after the Bolshevik Revolution.

Since the breakup of the Soviet Union, the Catholic Church has slowly tried to rebuild itself from its virtual liquidation. Even under the new constitution, however, it is classified as one of the "nontraditional" religions that is not granted full rights. Orthodoxy, Islam, and Buddhism are the only fully recognized faiths. Though as the century came to a close there were signs that Russia might rethink this classification system, the martyred Catholic Church operates well below its pre-Soviet level. Numbers are difficult to come by and generally unreliable. Crude estimates have been made on the basis of traditionally Catholic ethnic minorities that still exist in various parts of the former Soviet Union. But these are obviously flawed for several reasons. Many of the people who used to make up these minority communities — Poles, Germans, Lithuanians, and others — have chosen to emigrate to their home countries, usually because of the hard economic conditions in the new Russia. Actual Mass attendance gives a better count, but shows a tremendous drop-off from pre-Soviet levels. Church sources in Russia estimate that on a given Sunday there are about three thousand to four thousand people at Mass in Moscow, two thousand in Saint Petersburg, perhaps as many in the Kaliningrad region, six hundred to eight hundred in the Volga and Ural regions, even fewer in the North Caucacus and in Central and Northern Russia.

Clearly, the Church has far to go to restore its former presence. One of the factors in its favor is that it was not compromised in the slightest during the Communist era, a fact that counts for a great deal with the people and has led to some conversions. Furthermore, by an odd twist, the Gulag system distributed Catholics to places in which they had never before been seen. Siberia, for example, now has a sprinkling of viable new communities. But the project to heal the thousand-year-old rift between Catholics and Orthodox begun by the Solovievs has been put on indefinite hold in post-Soviet turmoil. Seventy years of repression weigh heavily on the Russian Catholic Church. It remains to be seen where and when the spirit of its many martyrs will blossom again.

# -THREE-

# THE TERROR IN UKRAINE

I N AN OBSCURE CORNER of Eastern Europe that is a crazy quilt of
several ethnic and religious groups, Soviet agents perpetrated one of
their most brutal and nefarious acts against the Church. On October 27,
1947, Bishop Teodor Romzha, head of the Mukachiv-Uzhgorod diocese
of Transcarpathian Ukraine (or Ruthenia as it is sometimes called), was
returning from the reconsecration of a restored church in the small village of Lavky to the city of Uzhgorod, the diocesan seat. Two priests and
two seminarians from the village accompanied him in his horse-drawn
cart — the Soviets would not allow him to use a car. At a relatively deserted point between two small towns, the cart had an "accident" with a
Soviet armored vehicle. Everyone in the cart survived the crash, however,
and soldiers jumped out of the vehicle to finish the job with rifle butts.
But the clergymen were tough: peasants took them to a nearby hospital
where they were treated and began to recover.

Bishop Romzha had his jaw broken in two places, almost all his teeth
knocked out, and severe bruises all over his body. He had to be fed
through a tube and regretted that his injuries prevented him from receiving Communion. After about a week of normal convalescence, he died
suddenly in the early morning hours between October 31 and November 1, 1947. A nun who worked in the hospital later recounted what
happened. The Communist hospital director, Dr. Abraham I. Bergmann,
ordered everyone out of the ward where the bishop was being treated.
A special nurse was brought in to take care of the bishop. Her treatment consisted in administering a dose of poison that brought about the
bishop's departure from this world.[1]

The Soviets had their reasons to fear Bishop Romzha. A young, energetic, and absolutely unyielding leader, Romzha had denounced the
pressures being put on his people by the combined efforts of the Soviet
authorities and the Russian Orthodox Church. The Orthodox themselves had suffered terrible persecution at Soviet hands and, no doubt,
quite a few of them deplored the persecution of their Greek Catholic

brothers and sisters. But the Moscow Orthodox leadership had been used by Stalin beginning in 1943 to help rouse the people for the "great patriotic war" against the Nazis. After the Germans were repelled, Stalin decided to continue manipulating the population by bringing as many believers as possible under the sway of the coopted Moscow Patriarch Sergei. In much of Ukraine, this led to violent acts against Catholics who refused reunion with the Orthodox and the state-imposed substitution of Orthodox leaders in Catholic dioceses and parishes. On Good Friday of 1947, in the Uzhgorod Cathedral, Romzha had publicly denounced these measures as "the lawlessness of the dark forces of hell."[2]

Romzha did not merely criticize. He strengthened his flock by telling them: "Divine Providence is watching over us at all times. So, let us rejoice that we have to suffer for our faith, because in doing so we are preparing for martyrdom!" He personally resisted all Soviets attempts to curtail his activity. And Romzha told his clergy: "Do not give in for anything in the world!"[3] His people listened: both clergy and lay people vigorously resisted Soviet pressures to convert and flocked behind Romzha. In 1945, fifty thousand faithful made the traditional pilgrimage to Černeča Hora on the Feast of the Assumption to hear him preach. In 1947, when the Soviets tried to coopt the populace by taking possession of Černeča Hora and installing subservient Orthodox clergy there, only three thousand made the pilgrimage. Instead, eighty thousand showed up at Romzha's celebration near Mukachiv. After that, the authorities kept him under close surveillance and would not allow him to leave his residence. His death came when, a few months later, he chose to go to Lavky anyway, despite all warnings.

To an outside observer, it might seem strange that the Soviet Union would fear a bishop who was merely going about his duties in an out-of-the-way corner of a territory that had only recently become part of the Russian empire. But the attention they paid Romzha is indicative of the strategy the Soviets adopted toward stamping out all potential centers of resistance to their totalitarian dominance of the peoples under the regime. Pavel Sudoplatov, who directed the operation against Romzha, has since revealed that then-Ukrainian Communist leader Nikita Khrushchev and Stalin himself knew of the plot, which was intended to clean out the "terrorist nest of the Vatican in Uzhgorod." Also, the "nurse" who administered the poison to Romzha was an MGB (secret police) agent.[4] In the various parts of Western Ukraine, the Soviet strategy aimed at liquidating the Greek Catholic Church, the traditional religion of many of the people and, in certain areas, a faith that claimed almost the entire population. The deputy director of the Council for the Affairs of the Russian Orthodox Church in Ukraine had visited Romzha and told him bluntly that the "Greek Catholic Church cannot exist in the Soviet Union." Romzha replied in a way that expressed the view of his people: "I would sooner face torture and death than betray the true Church of Christ!"[5] That heroic stance would bring torture and death to him and many people throughout Western Ukraine.

The portion of Eastern Europe commonly called Ukraine has a complex political and religious history. Its original title, Kievan Rus, or simply Rus, changed into the vaguer and larger term "Russia" of more recent times, and the reality to which it referred preceded the three large nationalities that stem from it today: Ukraine, Belarus, and Russia. Catholic Christianity has a long and distinguished history there. As early as 988, its leader, Wolodymyr the Great, grand prince of Kiev, converted with his whole people to Catholicism; Wolodymyr was later declared a saint for his personal piety. He was responsible for introducing the Old Church Slavonic liturgies of the Apostles to the Slavs, Saints Cyril and Methodius, into Ukraine. Catholicism, thus, was from an early date one of the elements that went into making the distinct Ukrainian nationality, even though Ukraine was only briefly an independent political entity at any time over the long course of its existence.

Catholicism in Ukraine has several distinctive features. Clergy are allowed to marry before they are ordained, though bishops traditionally must be celibate or widowers. The Ukrainian Church venerates icons, and individual church buildings usually have an icon screen in front of the altar. Ukrainian choral music is rich and moving, and liturgies are usually long and elaborate. At Easter, instead of palms, pussy willows are usually distributed, perhaps because palm branches were not readily available in the cold Slavic north. Though the Church in Ukraine remained in communion with Rome for over a thousand years, it thus had developed its own particular traditions of discipline, spirituality, theology, and liturgy.[6]

By the time the Soviets took over Western Ukraine from the retreating Nazis during the Second World War, there were over four million Catholics in Ukraine. In Galicia, the central region (not including Transcarpathian Ukraine, or Ruthenia), the population was close to 100 percent Catholic. Because of the various national influences on Ukraine over the centuries, Catholics there included Latin-rite believers of mostly Polish origin, somewhat smaller numbers of Hungarian and Slovak Latin-rite Catholics left over from the Austro-Hungarian empire, as well as other groups. Even in the 1990s, after a half-century of harsh Soviet persecution, about a half a million Latin-rite Catholics still existed in Ukraine. But the largest segment of the Catholic population belonged to the Byzantine-rite Ukrainian Catholic Church, which set its stamp on national life and culture.

The Byzantine-rite Church is referred to by several other names: Greek-Catholic, Oriental-rite Catholic, and sometimes even "Uniate," meaning a portion of the Church reunited to Rome at the Treaty of Brest in 1596. Since there is both confusion and an acrimonious battle between Ukrainian Catholics and Orthodox about how much the "reuni-fication" was a recognition of an existing pro-Roman Church and how much it was a forced political unification, the term "Uniate" sometimes has derogatory connotations and will not be used here. The best recent historical scholarship seems to indicate that the reunification was largely a sincere return to a faith disrupted by earlier Orthodox imposition by Russia.[7] But this is a technical dispute. Suffice to say that a significant portion of the Ukrainian population always felt an inclination toward Rome whatever political current was in the ascendancy. As we saw in the earlier chapter on Russia, when Czar Nicholas II proclaimed reli-gious toleration in 1905, two hundred thousand Ukrainians who had been "reunited" at that period with the Orthodox Church immediately proclaimed that they were Catholics.[8]

Given the combined religious and political currents that washed over Ukraine, it is not surprising that in the twentieth century Ukraine was one of the most harshly persecuted areas in the Soviet empire. Some of the persecution was intended to reduce the influence of "foreign" po-litical forces such as Poland and the Vatican. Some was meant to bring the Ukrainian Catholics under Orthodox control. But despite the argu-ments of certain scholars who interpret Soviet moves in purely political terms, it is clear that the ultimate goal of the Soviet machinations was not simply to establish political unity, but to eliminate Ukrainian and other forms of Byzantine-rite Catholicism — together with all religious belief — from the Soviet bloc. As John Paul II wrote to the European bishops on May 11, 1991, after the fall of Communism, *"Persecution reached its greatest intensity* in the cases where, as in Ukraine, Romania and Czechoslovakia, the local Catholic Churches of the Byzantine tradition were declared dissolved and nonexistent by the use of authoritarian and devious methods."[9]

In spite of the severe and almost singular nature of the Soviet religious repression in Ukraine, very little is known in the Free World and the newly freed countries of the former Warsaw Pact about the persecution, liquidation, and outright martyrdom of many believers there. The raw figures alone are startling. From 1946 to 1949, the Ukrainian Catholic Church, which started with 4 dioceses, 8 bishops, 2,772 parishes, 4,119 churches and chapels, 142 monasteries and convents, 2,628 diocesan priests, 164 monks, 773 nuns, 229 seminarians, and over 4,000,000 lay people was simply abolished, if sometimes to an underground existence waiting for better times. Many of the religious institutions were dispersed or "liquidated." Bishops, priests, and lay people ended up in prison camps, dead from overwork, or exiled. Not all of them were, of course, martyrs. But it is chilling to see official numbers indicating a flourishing religious community all simply reduced to zero.[10] The Ukrainian Catholic Church under the Soviets was the largest suppressed group of believers in the world.

Two great names appear among the leadership of the Ukrainian Catholic Church during its time of trial: the metropolitan Andrew Graf Sheptytskyi and his successor Joseph Slipyi. Both were highly talented and courageous men: the Ukrainian Church would have been in even worse shape without their heroic labors. Sheptytskyi was born into a Latin-rite Ruthenian family that had moved to Poland and embraced Polish customs. His mother was of the old Polish nobility. But in spite of family opposition, he decided it was his vocation to help restore the older familial tradition of Byzantine-rite Ukrainian Catholicism with the ultimate, and ambitious, goal of reuniting the Eastern and Western Churches, separated since the Great Schism in the eleventh century. After his ordination as a priest by the Basilian order, he rose quickly within the Church. In 1900, Pope Leo XIII named him metropolitan of Lviv and Halych, and thus head of the Byzantine-rite Catholic Church. Sheptytskyi was only thirty-five. The pope's confidence in the young priest was not misplaced. Sheptytskyi founded a theological academy in Lviv, believing that high-level religious education would make the Church a potent force for unity between West and East. He rebuilt the Studite order and imported the Redemptorists from Belgium and the Sisters of Charity of Saint Vincent de Paul from France. To reinforce and protect Church identity, he reformed the Byzantine liturgy and carefully avoided identifying the Church with any of the competing ethnic or political factions. He even took steps for the pastoral care of the large number of Ukrainian Catholics who had emigrated looking for work to Europe and North and South America.[11] Always inclined to the monastic temper, Sheptytskyi gave away a great deal of the fortune he had inherited to help support the arts and scholarship, as well as the Church's usual corporal works of mercy.[12]

The czarist Russians arrested him in 1914 and put him through a period of exile. But Sheptytskyi found his way back to Galicia where, after the Soviet Revolution, he was to become the figurehead of Ukrainian Catholic resistance to Moscow's designs. In the meantime, however, Galicia was in Polish hands, and Sheptytskyi distinguished himself not only for his leadership of Greek Catholics in overwhelmingly Roman Catholic Poland but for his defense of the rights of the Orthodox Christians to their own free exercise against the desire of then-independent Poland's authorities to Catholicize those Orthodox.[13] Respect for the consciences of all believers was a constant principle for Sheptytskyi amid a political situation in perpetual flux. When the Nazis invaded in the 1940s, Sheptytskyi showed that he believed in a Church independent of any worldly power, especially the anti-Christian dictatorships of both East and West. He personally protested to Hitler about the Gestapo and distinguished himself for his protection of persecuted Jews. Kurt I. Lewin, a Pole of Jewish background who was rescued by the metropolitan, testified at his beatification process in Rome. Asked why, as a Jew, he was interested in the beatification, he said that "the sanctity of the man was recognized by Christians and Jews during his lifetime. The Jews demonstrated their respect for him by greeting him carrying the Scrolls during his frequent visits to towns and villages where Jews were living next to Ukrainians."[14]

This is all the more remarkable because such an attitude toward Jews was not universally shared in Poland and Ukraine at the time, where policy toward Jews was shaped not only by Nazi and Soviet influences, but by age-old popular prejudices. Long before the ecumenical outreach of the last quarter of the twentieth century, Sheptytskyi had recognized the need for mutual respect among believers of various faiths even as he pursued the rejuvenation of the Byzantine-rite Church. Lewin remarks:

> The ideas of Andrew Graf Sheptytskyi, metropolitan of Halicz [i.e., Galicia] and Archbishop of Lwów [i.e., Lviv], are as valid today as they were in his lifetime. They are universal and point the direction

for pursuing the spiritual renewal essential to the survival of the civilization of Western man. A bridge between the Christianities of the West and the East, which the metropolitan foresaw as a mission of his church, but which remained only a dream during his lifetime, became a possibility with the collapse of the Marxist-Leninist ideology in the Soviet Union.[15]

If anything, this puts the Sheptytskyi achievement mildly. By the time he died in 1944, much of what the metropolitan had worked for had been destroyed, at least in human terms, by the back-and-forth decimations of Nazis and Soviets. And the main Way of the Cross for the Ukrainian Church, which basically took place between then and the early 1950s, was only beginning. Yet the foundation he had laid would not be entirely obliterated. When the Soviet nightmare dissipated, the Ukrainian Catholic Church resurrected itself in vigorous life, as it had several times in its troubled history. At Sheptytskyi's death, a family member of the chief rabbi in Lviv paid him the highest of compliments imaginable: "We do not believe in saints, but if there is such a thing, the first is metropolitan Andrew."[16]

The metropolitan's successor — the man who directly faced the severe persecutions described by Pope John Paul II — was an equally great figure. Joseph Slipyi became metropolitan immediately after Andrew Sheptytskyi's death. Within months the Soviets put him through a grand tour of the Soviet Gulag that took him to prison camps and places of exile in Kiev, Maryinsk, Kirov, Petchora, Kosiu, Inta, Boimy, Potma, Maklakovo, Novossibirsk, Sverdlosk, Vorkuta, Vychorevka, Novocunka, Ozerlag, Tajscet, and Mordovia.[17] This list is a good indication of the lengths to which the Soviets were willing to go to keep Slipyi from exerting his influence, which by all accounts (even those of non-Christians and atheists in the camps) was quite powerful. He ordained priests secretly, even there, and exercised a powerful spiritual ministry.

After his unbending behavior in so many camps, it was almost laughable that the Soviets thought they could tempt him in 1959 with an offer to make him Orthodox patriarch of Moscow — if he agreed to break with Rome.[18] He preferred, instead, to continue his life in the Gulag and exile, thirty-nine years in all. When he was free, he made his way to Rome, where for decades he organized efforts to support the Church in the mother country. Despite the many years of hard camp life, he lived to be ninety-two. At his death in 1984, John Paul II compared Slipyi to a very high predecessor: "He passed through the tortures and sufferings

of the Cross, similar to those of Christ at Golgotha.... May his memory
last forever!"[19]

The troubles for Ukraine began early in the century. Shortly after the
1914 assassination of Archduke Ferdinand at Sarajevo, which touched
off World War I, Russian troops moved into Western Ukraine, formerly
a part of the Austro-Hungarian empire. The capital of the region, Lviv,
changed names as various powers took control — Lemberg (Austria),
Lvov (Russia), Lwów (Poland) — but the effects of the various invaders
went deeper than mere name changes. First, Metropolitan Andrew Sheptytskyi was arrested by the czarist Russians and sent to Kiev and other
places of exile in Russia. The Russians, always eager to subordinate
the Catholic Church to the Moscow Orthodox patriarchate, tried to replace the Byzantine-rite priests. Few parishes willingly went along: of
the 1873 parishes, a hundred succumbed to the Russian pressure and
perhaps thirty priests. The vast majority of congregations remained firm
along with their leaders.

When the Soviets overthrew the czar in 1917, however, chaos ensued,
and the Austrians returned to Galicia. In October of the following year,
Ukraine proclaimed its independence and was recognized by the Aus-
trian emperor. But less than a month later, independent Poland invaded.
Russians, Poles, and Ukrainians battled over Ukraine and other interests.
The result was that in 1923 Poland was officially given Galicia. If the
Russians tried to Russify Ukraine, the Poles tried to Polonize it, going so
far even as to try to make the Byzantine-rite churches, with their strong
Ukrainian nationalist sentiments, into good Polish Latin Catholics. The
yoke was, perhaps, a little lighter, but the goal the same: moving the
people away from their age-old national identity and traditional form
of worship.

But these traditional struggles on the border between Eastern and
Western Christianity were virtually nothing compared to what was to
follow. In 1939, the Soviets invaded Ukraine, after signing the Molotov-
Ribbentrop Pact. This agreement formally put Hitler and Stalin on
record that neither would attack the other. By a secret protocol, they
also agreed to divide up Poland, meaning that Galicia, the main Catholic
region of Ukraine, passed into Soviet hands. Despite the clear interest the Byzantine-rite Church had in keeping a distance from Latin-rite
Poland, the Soviet propaganda organs immediately began to categorize

the Ukrainian Church as a Polish agent and an enemy of the regime. The Communist daily in Kiev made it clear that the Ukrainian Church was involved with "class enemies":

> The Uniate clergy headed by Metropolitan Sheptytskyi conscientiously served in the past the Polish large landowners and bourgeoisie. Uniate priests as a rule acted as agents of the Polish [counterintelligence] in the villages of Western Ukraine.... From church pulpits, rabid priests constantly called for action against the USSR. The priests acted as the most determined, most dedicated agents of counterrevolution in Western Ukraine.[20]

Given that during the Great Forced Famine Stalin had been willing to starve to death millions of Ukrainians in his war against the so-called "bourgeois peasants," or *kulaks,* such words had ominous implications.[21]

Yet the Soviets were careful at this early phase not to attack the Church too overtly or to apply Soviet laws that might have nationalized churches and forced registration of clergy. In part, this was because they recognized the wide popularity and prestige of Sheptytskyi; confronting him directly might have caused a popular uprising. Yet they began to take schools away from religious orders and to strip them of the traditional religious symbols. The teaching of religion was gradually banned. The NKVD sporadically arrested priests it thought a threat.[22] The regime struck harder, though, at crucial Church activities. All religious periodicals were taken over and publication suspended. Books were removed from stores and libraries, and destroyed. The seminaries were closed.[23] The metropolitan's resources were seized, as were those of the monasteries and convents, along with buildings and libraries. Religious congregations were dispersed. Because the Church was regarded as "socially unproductive," it had to pay exorbitant taxes. After one protest to Nikita Khrushchev, then first secretary of the Ukrainian Communist Party, some of the burden was lightened.[24] But given that even the less than entirely friendly Polish government had subsidized religion without regard to denomination (including Jews and Moslems), the financial disruption this caused is easy to imagine.[25] In Lviv, peasants and other believers had to provide financial support for Sheptytskyi and the Basilian order. Elsewhere, peasants refused, at substantial personal cost, to accept confiscated church lands from Soviets interested in redistributing the wealth the Church had "stolen" from the people. Soon, however, the puppet People's Assembly voted to join the Ukrainian SSR and began nationalizing any lands or property that might be used to support social resistance.

Metropolitan Sheptytskyi wrote a pastoral letter instructing Catholics to obey the law, so long as it did not contradict divine law, and announced that the Church would refrain from politics while continuing its ministries to the people. Foreseeing the religious vacuum that might arise among the people in the absence of Church schools or religious instruction, he counseled pastors to explain the catechism from the pulpit and to appoint trusted lay people who could perform baptisms and teach young people if priests became unavailable. To remedy the immediate situation, he released monks from their vows to work in parishes left without pastoral guidance. Another public statement to the head of the local Department of Education protested the violation of conscience and of rights guaranteed in the Soviet constitution under freedom of religion. The regime characterized Church activities as anti-Soviet agitation. In a private letter, Sheptytskyi informed the pope about impending threats and asked for Slipyi's appointment as his coadjutor so that if Sheptytskyi were exiled, as he had been in 1914, the Church would not be left without a leader. Slipyi was secretly consecrated with the pope's approval, though the Soviets appear to have learned about it almost immediately through agents within the Church.

It is a testament to Sheptytskyi's visionary leadership and near tireless hope that he did not content himself with these merely defensive measures. He thought of the situation — difficult as it was in every respect — as offering the Church an opportunity to evangelize the Soviets and reunite Catholics and Orthodox to the benefit of both the Universal Church and Ukrainian nationality. Consequently, he prepared himself and those over whom he was pastor for missionary activities. He created new exarchates inside and outside Ukraine and appointed bishops to govern them. He held priest conferences every Thursday at his residence to discuss how to implement his vision and even held two synods until the Nazi invasion interrupted his work. Two priests involved in the synods were martyred as a result of their participation. But all his labors were limited by the ruthlessness and single-mindedness of Soviet antireligious attitudes. As the most balanced scholar of the Ukrainian history has stated, "There was *nothing* the Greek Church could have done to avert the suppression by the Kremlin."[26] The brutality stemmed completely from Soviet aims, not Church policy.

When the Nazis broke their promise to Stalin in 1941 and invaded Ukraine, the retreating Soviets showed their hand more openly. They massacred hundreds of lay people and about a dozen priests.[27] At one point, they lined up Slipyi, several bishops, and other Greek Catholics in Sheptytskyi's retinue against a wall, but ultimately decided not to execute them. Metropolitan Sheptytskyi wrote to the papal nuncio, Angelo Ratta: "It is quite certain that under the Bolsheviks all of us were as sentenced to death; they did not conceal their desire to ruin and suppress Christianity, [to erase] its last traces."[28]

The incoming Nazis were, thus, initially welcomed as liberators, though Sheptytskyi had few doubts about their own brutality. From 1941 until the return of the Soviets in 1944, the Church walked a fine line between trying to find a *modus vivendi* with the Nazi reality on the one hand, and outrage over the Gestapo's treatment of Jews and other racial groups who did not find acceptance in Nazi ideology on the other hand. Slavs were certainly thought of by the Nazis as an inferior race good only for labor; in the first year of the Nazi occupation alone, a quarter million Ukrainian Catholics were sent to Germany to work in labor camps.[29] Calling the Nazis "diabolical" and describing their behavior as "if a pack of rabid wolves had fallen upon a poor people," the metropolitan did whatever he could to protect all Ukrainians. As a scholar, he admired high German culture; but as a pastor he could not help but see Nazi barbarism.

Kurt Lewin, son of the chief rabbi of Lviv, has noted that Sheptytskyi gave orders to various church organizations to protect the Jews of Ukraine:

> This labor of saving Jews was possible only because of the cooperation of a small army of monks and nuns together with some priests. They gathered the Jews into their monasteries and convents, orphanages and hospitals, shared their bread with the fugitives, and acted as escorts with total disregard of the danger. . . . For two long years no outsider knew about the Jews who were hidden in each and every cloister, and even in the Metropolitan's private residence.[30]

Despite overt and covert resistance to Nazism, Sheptytskyi was accused by the Soviets when they returned of having been a Nazi collaborator. In particular, they charged that he had given his blessing to the "Galician" SS Division, which had been formed by a faction of Ukrainian nationalists who hated the USSR. Though the Germans wanted the blessing, Sheptytskyi never gave it, merely allowing two priests to serve as chaplains.[31]

Sheptytskyi and his advisers believed the USSR would not survive the war. But by 1944, the situation in Ukraine was so anarchic under the crumbling German administration that Sheptytskyi speculated that the return of the Bolsheviks might at least restore minimum order.[32] The Soviets themselves took a somewhat conciliatory stand when they first returned to Western Ukraine. Soviet military officers openly attended church, and Moscow may have calculated that, under the circumstances, it would be a good idea to gain popular support among Catholics, as it had already gained Orthodox cooperation — at least until the struggle with the Nazis was settled.[33]

Remarkably, it seemed that the Soviets might even be ready to normalize relations with the Greek Catholic Church and the Vatican. Sheptytskyi proposed sending a delegation of Church leaders to meet with the Soviet officials. And in light of the new *modus vivendi* with the returning Red Army, he asked the faithful to collect money to be sent to the Red Cross to aid Soviet wounded. But before any of this could take place, Sheptytskyi died on November 1, 1944. An enormous funeral was held at the Church of Saint George in Lviv. The new metropolitan Slipyi officiated, priests carried the coffin, and a funeral procession of five thousand people stretching for over a half a mile paid homage to the Ukrainian leader.

In spite of, or perhaps because of, this indication of popular piety, the Soviets moved quickly against the Church after his passing. Georgii Karpov, head of the Council for the Affairs of the Russian Orthodox Church (CAROC), prepared Instruction No. 58 and submitted it to Stalin, Molotov, and Lavrentii Beria on March 14, 1945. Basically, the Instruction outlined a strategy for liquidating the Greek Catholic Church by pressuring priests and believers to join the coopted Orthodox. Among the measures it proposed was an "initiative group" composed of sympathetic or intimidated Greek Catholics who would advocate union with the Moscow patriarchate from within the Greek Catholic Church. Nikita Khrushchev, as Communist head of Ukraine, was also informed about the strategy. A note written on the draft a few days later said all that needed to be said: "Comrade Karpov: I agree with all the measures. Stalin."[34]

Propaganda also began against the Ukrainian Greek Catholic Church in particular and the Catholic Church in general. The most energetic and talented of the propagandists was Jaroslav Halan, who, according to Cardinal Slipyi, "early in 1945 [i.e., before or around the time of Karpov's strategy memo], was preparing a plan to destroy the church."[35] For Halan, Catholicism was "a Fascist form of Christianity," which was the tool of "American imperialism" and a "bastion of reaction." Pretending, as the Soviets always did in their antireligious campaigns, that his critique was not against religion per se, but only against its abuse, he wrote:

> Our Soviet State has inserted in its fundamental law inviolable and unbreakable words about freedom of conscience. It does not interfere with one's own religious conviction. But one cannot look on calmly, when the servants of the Uniate [i.e., Greek Catholic] Church exploit this freedom of religion in order to engage in criminal activities against the Ukrainian people, in the interests of Fascist Germany in the past [and] today for the glory and benefit of the Anglo-Saxon imperialists. Before the servants of the gods of the swastikas and trident there lies [only] one road — the road of treason against the people, the road of crimes, murder, monstrous frauds, lies, and deceit. This road will inevitably bring them to catastrophe. The people are merciless toward their mortal enemies, regardless of the clothes they wear.... The bloody activity of these criminals must be stopped decisively.[36]

As events were to prove, however, the kinds of outrages against the Ukrainian people that Halan listed would be perpetrated by the Soviets themselves, not the Church.

But his arguments, disseminated in large printings throughout Ukraine, had some effect. Halan was hardly a subtle propagandist: he called an article on the allegedly nefarious designs of the Ukrainian Church *With the Cross or with the Knife?* A book bore the blunt title *I Spit on the Pope*. Halan's misinformation was just the tip of a large iceberg of Soviet lies and propaganda aimed at portraying the Ukrainian Church as a Nazi tool whose wicked behavior and open exploitation of the people was leading lay people and good clerics to rise up and "demand" unification with the Orthodox for both political and religious reasons.

The culmination of this campaign followed shortly. On April 11, 1945, Slipyi was arrested along with all the other bishops after they refused to join the Orthodox Church. The sweep was comprehensive, reaching even outside Ukraine: a short time later, two Ukrainian bishops, Iosafat Kotsylovskyi and Gregory Lakota, along with their senior priests, who were not in Ukraine but in the Przemysl diocese (by then part of postwar Poland), were extradited by Polish Communist authorities to Kiev. Bishop Petro Verhun, apostolic visitator for Ukrainian Catholics in

Germany, was apprehended in Berlin, shipped to Ukraine, and charged with treason, even though he was a German citizen who had never lived in Soviet territory. The only Ukrainian bishop not in prison by the end of 1945 was Teodor Romzha. As we have seen, the KGB would remedy that oversight in spectacular fashion.

In the bishops' absence, the Soviets organized a *sobor,* or church council, under the surveillance of the NKGB, which, by a process guaranteed to arrive at the desired Soviet outcome, decided on union with the Orthodox. The council was, of course, invalid, since no legitimate bishops were present. They were all secretly tried and found guilty of having collaborated with the Nazis and promoted anti-Soviet attitudes. An official announcement claimed that ample documentation had been discovered to prove these charges and that the bishops had "confessed." The announcement ended with a veiled threat for any priest or other church member who could be accused of similar crimes unless they went along with the Orthodox reunion: "The criminal anti-Soviet activities of the accused have been confirmed by numerous eye-witness testimonies and by documentary data. The case of I. A. Slipyi, M. A. Charnetskyi, M. M. Budka, H. L. Khomyshyn, and I. Iu. Liatyshevskyi, accused of crimes under Articles 54-1 and 54-11 of the Criminal Code of the Ukrainian SSR, has been concluded and is being transmitted for trial by a military tribunal."

Even more outrageous than this standard show trial was the complicity in repression of the religious leaders designated by the NKGB to run the Lviv *sobor.* First, the *sobor* leaders sent fawning messages to Stalin and Khrushchev[37] and promised to send to Pavlo Khodchenk, plenipotentiary of the Council on Religious Affairs of the Russian Orthodox Church, "lists of all deans, parish priests, and superiors of monasteries who refuse to submit to the jurisdiction of the Initiative Group of the Greek Catholic Church for Reunion with the Orthodox Church."[38] This could not help but lead to persecutions, arrests, and deaths among the faithful clergy. Some managed to continue working underground, including some emergency apostolic administrators and vicars of dioceses, but many of these, too, fell to the Soviet instruments of repression.

The *sobor*'s ringleader, Havryil Kostelnyk, a renegade priest, later gave an interview to the Soviet news service TASS, clearly intended for purposes of international propaganda, in which he falsely characterized the *sobor*'s decisions as a voluntary liquidation of the Church and personal conversion of participating priests. But even worse, he lied about the well-known penalties imposed on "recalcitrant" clergy: "There were no arrests of the Greek Catholic clergy either before or after the Sobor." In fact, as he must have known, both before and after the *sobor*, there were many such arrests and some executions. Worst of all, however, he claimed that the rounding up of the whole Ukrainian hierarchy and several priests occurred not because of their status as Greek Catholic figures but "as citizens of the U.S.S.R., for their treasonous activity."[39] Kostelnyk quickly became disillusioned with the Soviets' failure to live up to their promises; within a few year he was assassinated by security agents.[40]

All the bishops received long sentences. Budka died during torture at the prison camp in Karganda, Kazakhstan. Khomyshyn did not make it even that far; he was brutally tortured to death in Lviv's Lukianavka Prison on December 28, 1945.[41] Bishop Lakota, tried separately, survived four years, ending his life in a forced-labor camp near Vorkuta. According to some accounts, the Soviets tried to use Bishop Kotsylovskyi for international propaganda purposes, freeing him so that they could claim religious liberty existed in Ukraine. He was released on condition that he accept the presidency of the phony *sobor* in Lviv. But he seems to have agreed solely because the Soviets told them they would kill his son, Ireneus, if they did not get what they demanded. In fact, Ireneus had escaped to the West. It appears that when Kotsylovskyi learned the truth, he reneged on the deal, was rearrested, and tortured to death.[42]

Bishop Liatyshevskyi spent ten years in the Gulag before returning to Galicia, where he did clandestine work in keeping the underground church alive. Bishop Charnetskyi was tortured terribly for many days and bore it with such courage and obvious sanctity that his tormentors were ashamed of themselves. One asked the bishop for forgiveness, calling himself a "scoundrel."[43] Charnetskyi also survived the prison camps and returned to Galicia to carry out duties in secret. Bishop Verhun died in the camps waiting for permission to return to his native Germany. In addition, Father Omelian Gorchinsky, who was elected vicar capitular in Lviv the very day he was arrested, perished in the Potma concentration camp over nine years after his arrest.[44]

Metropolitan Slipyi endured terrible tortures and almost twenty years in the Gulag, some of them spent with Charnetskyi and Liatyshevskyi. His behavior in prison was exemplary, though we have less than complete records about him because, for diplomatic reasons, he was restrained from speaking or writing about it as part of the deal with the Soviets which led to his release in 1963. Not only did he do pastoral work among the fellow prisoners, Christian and non-Christian alike, but he also kept alive the spirit of Sheptytskyi in trying to educate Catholics even in camp conditions. He lectured on medieval philosophy and wrote about the history of the Ukrainian Church.[45] This scholarly activity was clearly intended to prepare for the day when the Church would emerge again from captivity. In a courageous prison letter to Nikolai Podgorny, first secretary of the Ukrainian Communist Party, Slipyi reminds the powerful leader of eternal truths: "We ourselves shall die off, and all of you will die off too. But the Greek Catholic Church will endure in the catacombs."[46]

Slipyi also pointed out, as he had at his trial, that he had never held a position of responsibility during the Nazi occupation and was therefore wrongly accused of Hitlerism. He archly observed that Molotov, who had signed the nonaggression pact with Ribbentrop, had collaborated with Hitler far more than he ever had. Both Sheptytskyi and Slipyi had tried, in their role as nonpolitical pastors, to mediate between both extremes in Ukraine. Contrary to the claims of the Soviets, the Greek Catholic Church in Ukraine, as a particular instance of the Universal Church, had been under pressure from both Nazi Germany and Latin-rite Poland, not their political tools. But the Soviets could not understand religion as religion; they always reduced it to politics and economics. At one point during his interrogation, Slipyi was asked if he had ever been to Rome. Since he had studied at the Gregorian University there, the answer was obvious, and the interrogator shook his head, saying, "Rome, Rome!"[47] This otherwise comic reaction is only understandable in light of the Soviets' unwavering belief that the Vatican was the "bulwark of the world reaction"[48] and the pope the most potent international enemy postwar Russia faced.

Slipyi's captors tried repeatedly to coopt him, promising him freedom if he renounced Rome and placed himself under the jurisdiction of the Moscow Patriarchate. Joined with these offers were hints that he could be Orthodox metropolitan in Kiev and even a suffragan to the Moscow patriarch.[49] But Slipyi made it clear, even while he was in prison, that no one free to speak his mind, Catholic or Orthodox, believed the Lviv *sobor* to be valid. He forgave the leaders and begged God's mercy on them, but was far from thinking that freedom was worth the price of cooperating with such a travesty.

Conditions in the camps made such a principled stand costly. In his memoirs, Slipyi puts it delicately: "There were not a great many gentlemen." As in most prisons, the most ruthless inmates added to the ill treatment, stealing food and other goods, setting up networks of tribute.

The guards were little better. Slipyi describes his own repeated interrogations under extreme torture and the subjection of fellow inmates to "brutalities so horrible that prisoners were dying off like flies."[50] In one session, his hand was broken and he was threatened with even worse by guards carrying guns. Officially, nothing remained of normal, civilized life: "Every stage was a terrible cross from God, and the very act of describing it is a great torment. Surrounded by bandits, in the midst of hunger and cold, deprived of the possibility of taking care of my most fundamental needs, tortured by the guards, subjected to robbery, and the like."[51]

Unofficially, Slipyi turned his prison experience into great profit for the Greek Catholic Church. Close students of his later activity observe that, immediately on his release in 1963, he went into action with relief, educational, and spiritual programs that clearly show he had been meditating on them while still in the camps.[52] And despite the brutality, he manifested some spiritual presence that led people to him — Christians, Jews, and Muslims, as well as members of various small Protestant groups. Avrham Shifrin, a Jewish coprisoner and friend, described him as "a person who enjoyed an immense authority in the camps. By his sheer presence and with two or three words he knew how to get the attention not only of the prisoners who lived together with him, but of the officers."[53] The American president, the pope, and the Soviet premier negotiated his release in 1963, almost twenty years after he had been sentenced for crimes that, in few places outside the reach of Communism, would have been thought of as crimes at all. Many others, whose names and fates will probably never be known, were not so lucky.

Anything like a Ukrainian Catholic martyrology will have to await careful research into former Soviet archives. Those records are unlikely to be made available until most of those involved in implementing the various waves of repression have died — which might take decades. There are other problems in accounting for clergy and lay people who may have fled to other nations or simply gone into retirement in Ukraine on the one hand, or perished by various means of repression on the other.[54] We can say with certainty, on the basis of documents already released, however, that 344 clergy, meaning primarily bishops, diocesan priests, and members of religious orders, were officially recorded as having been "repressed."[55] Another half million lay people in Ukraine were imprisoned or sent into internal exile, some, no doubt, for religious reasons.[56] Assuming that the Soviets kept good records, a whole world of martyrs remains to be unearthed. But many martyrs who might have been confirmed by living memory may simply never be known as veterans of the camps die off.

We know only a few names, which, for the time being, will have to do duty for the rest. Father Volodymyr Sterniuk, who spent five years at a camp near Iertsevo in the Arkhangelsk region, notes that two thousand priests were imprisoned there along with most of the Ukrainian monks, nuns, and lay persons.[57] Over a hundred hieromonks (monks also ordained priests) of the Basilian order in Galicia were sent to prisons. Two died in the camps. Among others who succumbed to the terror was the Studite order superior, Archimandrite Klymentii Sheptytskyi, brother of the great metropolitan. He was appointed to administer the church in Slipyi's absence, but was arrested and died on May 1, 1958, in the Vladimir Prison. His successor as administrator, Redemptorist Father Joseph de Vocht, was also arrested and sent back to his native Belgium. Another Redemptorist, Father Ivan Ziatek, followed the route of the Archimandrite: prison, torture, death.[58] Similar fates awaited the Greek Catholic nuns. Basilian superior Mother Monika Teodorovych-Polianska was arrested for aiding the "catacomb church." She died on Christmas day 1951 in the Markova camp. Mother Venedykta Kaknykevych disappeared into Siberia. In Transcarpathian Ukraine, even before they moved against Bishop Romzha, the Soviets began intimidating clergy. They arrested ten priests. Romzha secured the release of nine, but one was executed.

During the 1950s, there was a brief respite as Khrushchev tried to distance himself from Stalin's heritage. The Gulag was partly dismantled and hundreds of priests returned to Ukraine, including Bishops Charnetskyi and Liatyshevskyi, who allowed their priests to work as Orthodox publicly while remaining Uniate in secret. Lavrentii Beria entered again into talks with Slipyi about normalizing relations with the Church and the Vatican. These came to a halt when Beria himself was arrested and Slipyi was resentenced to further internal exile and eventually rearrest. By December 1957, any hope that the Greek Catholic Church might be allowed to reconstitute itself was closed off by a public declaration of the coopted Orthodox leaders reaffirming that "the Union is a tool of the enemies of our Fatherland."[59]

In the 1960s, Khrushchev negotiated with Pope John XXIII for Slipyi's release and transfer to Rome. But this was clearly a tactical move:

Khrushchev not only was not open to the return of Catholicism to Russia, but he also closed many churches, monasteries, and seminaries of the very Orthodox who had been his instruments. Nonetheless, Greek Catholic underground bishops and clergy tried to test the limits of the Soviets in the 1960s. They held open masses and petitioned the government for recognition. Though doomed to failure, the pressure they exerted, together with the activities of Slipyi on their behalf in Rome, raised the visibility of the Greek Catholics, the largest persecuted Catholic body in the Soviet Union, throughout the world. That gain had its price: Bishop Vasyl Velychovskyi, who had been quietly named by Slipyi as his successor before he left the Soviet Union, was arrested with two underground priests and sent to prison and then to exile in the West.[60] Priests caught saying masses were given heavy fines.[61]

The Final Acts of the Helsinki Conference in 1975, which the Russians signed, enabled human rights groups to coordinate activities on behalf of the Church inside and outside the Soviet Union. But the greatest progress in defending the Ukrainian Catholics occurred when Karol Wojtyła, a Pole with knowledge of Communist tactics and the Ukrainian situation, was elected Pope John Paul II in 1978. He made careful diplomatic moves but also directly confronted Soviet policy by convening a world synod of the Ukrainian Catholic bishops in Rome. The Soviets sent one of their most trusted Orthodox agents, Metropolitan Yuvenalyi (KGB code name: ADAMANT),[62] to protest to the Vatican. When Yuvenalyi failed in his mission, he was relieved of his post as head of the Moscow Patriarchate's Department of External Ecclesiastical Relations.

These diplomatic threats triggered another wave of repression. In 1980, three priests were martyred; the following year, three more were imprisoned. But countervailing forces boldly moved into action. Yosyf Terelia, a fearless lay dissident who, along with several priests and monks, organized the "Initiative Group for the Rights of Believers and the Church," also began publication of *The Chronicle of the Catholic Church in Ukraine*. These initiatives responded to two perceived crises: the aging Greek Catholic clergy and the ongoing confusion among the faithful caused by the long period in which they had been forced into attending Orthodox services as clandestine Catholics.[63] The Ukrainian dissidents may also have sensed that, with the election of Mikhail Gorbachev, something was stirring within the Soviet upper echelons that might permit more open opposition.

But Gorbachev's Soviet Union still harbored various means of repression. In one wave of reaction against the new currents, militias in Lviv shot to death a nun, Maria Shved, on September 29, 1982. In December of the same year, Terelia and other leaders of the Initiative Group were arrested. As late as 1984, another nun was beaten to death by "hooligans" at the Lviv train station.[64] But the church dissidents began an energetic campaign of supplying Western human rights groups with evidence of popular support for the Church. A seemingly extraneous event — the 1986 nuclear accident at Chernobyl — helped fuel dissidence further. Even Ukrainian party members began to criticize Moscow's dominance and to lament their own lack of control over local policies.[65] And another, perhaps providential, spur to open action occurred when a young girl, Maryn Kizyn, reported in April of 1987 that she had seen the Blessed Virgin Mary standing on a church dome in the small town of Hrushiv. Whether authentic or not, it drew tens of thousands of pilgrims.[66]

By August of 1987 the time was ripe for a step that would have been suicidal earlier. Bishops Pavlo Vasylyk and Ivan Semedii, along with other leaders and lay people, announced that they would no longer operate underground and called on the pope "to promote by all possible means the legalization of the Ukrainian Catholic Church in the USSR."[67] Their stand received added visibility by the 1988 celebration of the Millennium of Catholicism in Ukrainian Rus' in various events at Rome. Millennium crosses were put up in plain view all over Ukraine. Despite Gorbachev's talk of *glasnost* and *perestroika,* however, public celebrations of Catholic liturgies were banned by new laws, and those who participated in public liturgies were subjected to the usual fines and penalties. But people turned up by the thousands for event after event, and the clergy willingly paid whatever fines were exacted.

The momentum for change had become unstoppable. Church leaders petitioned Gorbachev and Ukrainian officials directly, organized hunger strikes, and gained support from prominent dissidents from other churches, as well as human rights activists such as Andrei Sakharov. Ivan Hel, who replaced Josyf Terelia when the latter went into exile in Canada, organized massive public demonstrations: a hundred thousand believers turned out in Lviv and smaller numbers in smaller cities. The government began to concede that, even by its own laws, it had to recognize all churches equally. By the time that Gorbachev met with John Paul II in Rome on December 1, 1989, news sources in the Soviet Union were announcing that each congregation in Ukraine could decide whether it wished to be Greek Catholic or Orthodox. Though the Soviets tried to manipulate the process to favor the status quo, this opened up the possibility for major changes.

Change came quickly. Hundreds of "Orthodox" priests publicly became Catholics; over fifteen hundred Greek Catholic congregations formed. Intellectual and cultural leaders in Ukraine sponsored a conference in Lviv that demanded, among other things: full recognition and rights of the Church as an organization in union with Rome; an investigation into the way psychiatry had been made an instrument of repression;[68] and a formal governmental declaration that the 1946 Lviv *sobor* was a "violent, anti-constitutional act of Stalinism."[69] A quadripartite commission of representatives from the Vatican, the Ukrainian Catholic Church, the Ukrainian Orthodox Church, and the Moscow Patriarchate was set up to resolve disputes. Though it settled little, the way was open to final resolution. That came only as real, independent delegates began to be elected to government councils in the 1990s. The Church of the Transfiguration and the Cathedral of Saint George in Lviv quietly passed into the hands of Ukrainian Catholics. Surprisingly, the Church that showed itself after the fall of Communism had in place eight bishops, as well as somewhere around a thousand priests, twelve hundred nuns, and a half dozen religious orders that had survived underground.[70] Seminaries opened and hundreds of candidates for the priesthood were admitted. Though the situation in all parts of the former Soviet Union remains unsettled and, even at the dawn of a new millennium, still presents many problems for believers, the Ukrainian Catholic Church, after much suffering and not a few heroic martyrs, has arisen from near death to quite vibrant life.

## -FOUR-

# FRENCH PRODIGAL SON
## *Charles de Foucauld*

**O**N SEPTEMBER 1, 1916, at the height of World War I, one of the first great spiritual figures of the twentieth century was killed by a gunshot wound to the head administered at close range as he kneeled with his hands tied behind him. But the dead man had not met his last day on one of the fields of the great war. His end came in the middle of the Sahara Desert in a tiny village of "twenty hearths" named Tamanrasset, where he had lived for years as a hermit among the Tuaregs, an ancient nomadic people, of the Algerian Hoggar. The village lies on a plateau five thousand feet above sea level among stark granite peaks that rise to almost twice that altitude, under the brutal sun of the Tropic of Cancer. The scene is so desolate that local myths say that God formed mountains by throwing rocks at the Earth, but that when he grew tired of the game he threw down everything left on the Hoggar. It was from that desolation that Father Charles de Foucauld entered into eternal life.

The usual way of describing Foucauld's life is to say that he had deliberately chosen to work in obscurity among the Tuaregs in order to convert them. In a sense, that is true. But in another sense, the mission chose him. As he wrote to the Abbé Henri Huvelin, a well-known spiritual director in France, as he started out on his fifteen years in the desert:

> I was shown in my last retreats before entering the diaconate and the priesthood that it was my vocation to lead this life of Nazareth, not in the Holy Land that I love so much, but among the most sick souls, the most forsaken flocks.... In my youth I had explored Algeria and Morocco.... No nation seemed to me more abandoned than this, and I asked and obtained permission from the Prefect Apostolic of the Sahara to settle in the Algerian Sahara, to lead there, in solitude and silence, in holy poverty with manual labor, alone there or with other priests or lay brothers, a life that

was as closely conformed as possible to the hidden life of Jesus of Nazareth.[1]

The words here seem the language of conventional piety, but the man who wrote them lived one of the great Prodigal Son stories of the century in a turn from a wildly self-indulgent life to a life of zealous self-sacrifice — neither conventional nor pious, in the usual meanings of those words. And the path he took led to death, perhaps a death worthy of being called martyrdom, for the faith.[2]

Every human being deserves to be valued as an individual, independent of ties of time, family, and nation. We will examine Foucauld as an individual in the following pages. But it is also true that some people, as well as being remarkable individuals, seem to be emblematic of a whole cultural moment. Foucauld, by any estimate, belongs in that category. While Europe was tearing itself apart in the Great War and individual European nations were vying with one another for far-flung colonies, Foucauld represents a different, humbler current, emerging in Christian reaction to the larger events. France itself at the time had a socialist government that was closing religious institutions in ways less brutal but not unlike those that would soon appear in Mexico and the Soviet Union. But in figures like Foucauld, France was also returning to deep Christian roots.

While he was a young libertine, Foucauld embodied all the easy indulgence and irreligiousness of French fin-de-siècle decadence. Like many of the decadents, in the end he found that what he was really seeking amid his various small pleasures was God. Along the way, he became caught up in the West's expansive colonial thrust, which, at its best, eagerly mapped unknown continents, visited new peoples, and studied previously unknown languages, presenting them as a system. Foucauld played no small role in that historical development. But he also displayed unique characteristics that transcend the moral, religious, and cultural limitations of the turn of the century. His was a truly unique soul — and it showed.

Though he is now somewhat forgotten, Foucauld's spiritual writings made a big impression on people for several decades after his death. Thomas Merton said of his spiritual writing, "This voice rings in the ear of your heart after you have put the book away."[3] And Merton was so impressed with the whole story of the Prodigal Son turned contemplative that he tried to get Clare Booth Luce to read a biography of Foucauld in the hope of getting her help in making the story into a film.[4] Several years later, when he was thinking of moving out of the Trappist monastery into a hermitage, Merton invoked the example of Foucauld to a bishop whose permission he sought.[5] Foucauld had that kind of impact, despite his deliberately obscure life, on many who were to read about him after his death.

Much of what constitutes spiritual discipline in any age is a confrontation with the inevitability of death. As far back as the ancient world, some of the Greek and Roman pagan philosophical schools made it a rule to live each day as if it were one's last. This was not a license for self-indulgence, but a counsel to be recollected and self-controlled, and to make each day count. The Stoics were particularly emphatic about the importance of this attitude. As Marcus Aurelius, one of the greatest Stoics, observed: "Thou wilt find rest from vain fancies if thou doest every act in life as though it were thy last."[6] Instead of being a morbid obsession, as it might be regarded by modern psychology, this reality principle can liberate us from trivial anxieties and depressions. Charles de Foucauld took pagan and Christian wisdom on this subject a step further, perhaps a necessary step in the twentieth century. He wrote inside his breviary in capital letters: "Live as though you will die today a martyr."[7]

At first sight, it seems only common sense that the best that might be said of such a counsel is that perhaps it is useful for a given person or people in extraordinary circumstances, but it is too much for everyday Christianity. Jesus, however, who was not given to idle words, warned his apostles: "They have persecuted me and they will persecute you." The world always feels resentment toward or is threatened by authentic Christian faith and is not reluctant to let its feelings guide its actions. The history of the twentieth century displays a ferocity against Christians, even when they have not much entered into economic or political issues, which suggests that their deaths and sufferings are no mere accident. A real Christian should reflect daily on the fact that, like the life of Jesus, ours too can end unexpectedly in martyrdom. Since many of the things that led to the masses of martyrs in the century did not disappear on January 1, 2000, it is wise to prepare spiritually for what may still come.

Foucauld came to his own appreciation of that necessity by a circuitous route. He was born into a family of rare distinction in France. Over the preceding centuries, his ancestors had been at the heart of French religious and political struggles. Bertrand de Foucauld fought and died with Saint Louis in one of the Crusades; Jean de Foucauld witnessed the coronation of King Charles VII at Rheims with Saint Joan of Arc; Gabriel de Foucauld became the husband of Mary Stuart in Scotland; and there were many other more recent notables among members of the clan. Two of them were prelates, killed during the French Revolution for refusing to apostatize and declared martyrs and beatified in 1921. Several others, on both his father's and his mother's sides, rose high in the ranks of the French military. The famous French patriotic song the "Marseillaise" was first sung by its author in the very house in Strasbourg where Foucauld first saw the light on September 15, 1858. The family motto was the distillation of centuries of experience: *Jamais arrière* ("Never retreat.")[8]

But distinguished ancestors do not protect us from early sorrows, nor does nobility. Charles's mother died when he was only five. His father bore the patrician name François-Édouard, Vicomte de Foucauld de Pont-Briand, and died the year after his mother. Charles and his younger sister, Marie, lived after that with their grandparents, a Colonel de Morlet and his wife in the eastern city of Nancy. The old colonel had a soft spot for the children and spoiled them. He wanted Charles to pursue a military career. But he also introduced them to his own loves: science, archeology, and geography. Acquaintance with these subjects would serve Charles well in his later adventures in war, exploration, and religion. The colonel was also almost a caricature of a French military man's orderliness and attention to detail. Though Charles would end up in a way of life far from that ideal, it would be difficult to discount the later influence on him of those meticulous habits.

Foucauld had a rather typical experience of school and religious instruction in late nineteenth-century France. By the time he was fifteen, he had lost his faith, but was not particularly troubled to renounce it, once and for all, or look for it again, for over a decade. Like many people, he became indifferent and pursued various passing goals without larger ones in mind. He later remembered being troubled by doubts that a better Christian education would have shown him were adolescent confusions. But he never took steps to resolve such question under religious guidance. A strange indulgence of appetites came over him: he grew fat, soft, and lazy — vices that may have had a lot more to do with his religious problems and indifference than he believed at the time. It was not a beginning that augured well for future distinction.

Colonel Morlet wanted Charles to attend his old school, the École Polytechnique, as the first step toward a military career. Typical of the young Foucauld, Charles thought Saint Cyr, a similar institution but easier to get into, would be better. So the grandfather sent him to the Jesuit College in Paris to prepare for the entrance exams. Charles certainly did not take to the work or to Paris. He constantly begged for permission to go home to Nancy. The impasse was resolved when he fell ill and the Jesuits wrote the colonel that his grandson needed medical attention that they were not able to provide. In fact, this was a tactful and polite way to expel him, since he was not doing any work.

Surprisingly, at Nancy he worked hard with private tutors and passed the Saint Cyr entrance exam. But his weight was a problem for a military academy, and he almost flunked the physical exam. At Saint Cyr, there was initially no uniform big enough to fit the future ascetic and contemplative. He was forced to drill in regular clothes for the first few weeks ("Piggy" became his nickname). Nonetheless, Foucauld took to military education and was very happy at Saint Cyr, even if his grades reflected a certain lack of application. His classmates remembered him devouring *paté*, drinking champagne, and smoking custom-made cigars — a pleasant and amusing comrade, but self-indulgent and not particularly good at anything.

But even this fragile balance was soon upset. The colonel died in February 1878. Foucauld's grades and behavior dipped further. There were dozens of cases of disciplinary action against him; he finished the year number 333 out of 386 students. Somehow he managed to make it out of school that summer as a sublieutenant. It was an unfortunate coincidence that, as he was riding high from this very modest success, he turned twenty and received a substantial inheritance. The next step in military training required him to attend the lovely French cavalry school at Saumur, where he spent more time on oysters, sardines, wines, champagne, caviar, truffles, expensive dinners, rich desserts, and mistresses ("I rent by the day, I don't sign a lease,"[9] he told them) rather than on anything military — at least when he was not confined to quarters for infractions of discipline. He graduated from Saumur number 87, dead last in his class, without any knowledge of the sciences needed in a military career. The inspector general gave as his opinion: "M. De Foucauld has a certain distinction and has been well brought up, but is empty-headed and thinks of nothing but amusing himself."[10]

Foucauld received orders to report to Africa. He was delighted at finally seeing some action, but, of course, he also arranged for his current mistress, Marie Cardinale, to travel by ship with him as the Vicomtesse de Foucauld. They set sail from Marseille and made landfall in Bône, which had been known in classical times as Hippo, the diocese of Saint Augustine. It was only the first of many times that Foucauld would be connected with his great predecessor in self-indulgence as a youth and Christian repentance in maturity. Though he was shocked at the wretchedness of the Arab inhabitants, he was charmed by the lush beauty of Algeria, a land of fruits and vines with breathtaking mountains in the background. His ultimate destination, however, was Setif, an ancient Roman city. Outdoor maneuvers in that setting exhilarated him. But the French military and Foucauld's morals could not long coexist with one another. His superior told him to send his mistress back to France or else. Foucauld chose the latter and was put on inactive duty "for lack of discipline and notorious misconduct."[11]

Nevertheless, the Algerian natives — Arabs and Berbers — intrigued him. He began studying Arabic and the Berber tongues. It is difficult to say what spoke to his spirit in the North African landscape and the almost neolithic cultures of the minority tribes he gravitated toward. But whatever it was, it was quite powerful. Back in France he started regularly reading the newspapers for stories about Africa. He continued working at his Arabic, even reading the easier parts of the Koran in the original, and became so restless to go back to North Africa that he voluntarily gave up his mistress. His colleagues in the Fourth Hussars found him a new, more mature man. Something in the masculine religious submission of the Arab men and their total acceptance of everything as coming from Allah touched a chord in him. He had never encountered anything quite like it in the mostly feminine Christianity of turn-of-the century France. There were, of course, numerous examples of a manly Catholicism available. Foucauld had simply not bothered to seek them out.

An impulse toward the unknown began driving his spirit. First, it took a classic form of the period: he organized an expedition to map out a large portion of Morocco's *terra incognita*. This entailed another resignation from the military. His family was understandably alarmed at what seemed continuing erratic behavior and put his inheritance under the administration of Georges de la Touche. Foucauld's "judiciary counsel," as the administrator of an estate is known in France, found that his charge was not as wild as he was led to believe. Foucauld stayed on a strict budget and asked for extra funds only to buy exploration equipment: barometer, telescope, sextant, chronometer, and so forth. Not only had Foucauld lost his taste for the self-indulgent life, but he was about to embark on a demanding journey that no European had undertaken without dying from the rigors of the land or at the hands of exotic peoples.

Foucauld lined up support from the French Geographic Society. But who would help him through the mysterious challenges of the unexplored Moroccan interior? Curiously, he chose an old Jew, a Rabbi Mardochee, to be his guide; Foucauld himself dressed as a visiting rabbi to avoid attention. Jews were looked down on by the Maghreb Arabs, and Foucauld wrote: "It seemed to me that this, in degrading me, would permit me to pass unnoticed and would give me greater liberty. I was not mistaken. I kept to my disguise for the whole of my journey and never for a moment regretted it." [12]

He would need every advantage. The itinerary the Geographic Society suggested to him was supposed to take about half a year to complete. In fact, it would take almost a year, no small commitment of time for a formerly flabby young man of only twenty-four. Not only would he face natural and human hardships, but he would also have to make careful observations and keep meticulous records of the landscape. Presumably, the former gaps in his scientific training were remedied by his eagerness. His grandfather's interest in geography flowered in unexpected ways. Part of his interest arose in response to sheer beauty. In Chechaouen, high in the Atlas mountains, he recorded:

> Fields of wheat are spread out in amphitheaters up the slopes, and from the crowning rocks down to the deepest valley cloak them with a golden carpet; nestling in the wheat are a number of villages surrounded by their gardens; everywhere there is life, riches, freshness. Streams flow in on every side, tumbling in cascades amid ferns, laurels, figs, and vines growing wild along the sides. Never and nowhere else have I seen such an air of prosperity, such a generous earth, nor such hard-working inhabitants. [13]

However picturesque and industrious, the inhabitants were also a perpetual threat. Some of them, seeing his rabbi's disguise, said to him, "May God eternally burn the father that begot thee, Jew, son of a Jew." Even some of the Jewish communities were less than delighted to see Jewish strangers show up. But acquaintance with the Moroccan Jews had one important effect on Foucauld. He observed the strict regularity of their prayers, similar in its rigidity to that of the Moslems. The morals of both Jews and Arabs in Morocco also impressed him — but precisely because they left a great deal to be desired. Arabs lied chronically and mistreated women; Jews, perhaps in revenge for their mistreatment, exacted high interest for loans to Arabs. He had to fend off thieves by pretending that his scientific instruments were used to practice astrology. When robbers finally struck, they made off with his money and other goods, but left behind his notes and instruments as worthless trinkets.

Something in the Sahara Desert spoke to Foucauld, as it has to many natives and explorers, even more than had the lushness of the mountains: "In this profound calm, in the midst of this fairy-tale country, I had my first real taste of the Sahara. In the contemplation of these starlit nights one understands the belief of the Arabs in a mysterious night; *leila el gedr,* they call it, when the heavens open and angels descend to earth and the sea's waters become sweet; then the whole of inanimate nature bows down to worship its Creator."[14] Between the exoticism of the people and the overwhelming natural vistas, something immense and unusual was opening up in his soul as well.

The immediate result of all this exploration, however, was *Reconnaisance au Maroc,* a book surveying over twenty-five hundred miles of his trek and expanding the geographic knowledge of North Africa enormously. Foucauld has a place among those other great nineteenth-century explorers who both opened up Africa to outsiders and opened up the outside world to Africans. It was a remarkable achievement for a man who had never given any earlier indication of interest in, let alone capacity for, such a demanding enterprise. His book was used for years afterward by French military and political leaders and, even before it was written, his research won him a gold medal from the French Geographic Society. He himself returned from the journey lean, sunburned, sober, relatively chaste, self-controlled, wiser — an entirely different man.

But if this new man had self-possession, he still had no real goal. Foucauld became briefly engaged to a French woman, but let himself be dissuaded by his family. She was not of sufficiently distinguished background, they said, but Foucauld probably was beginning to realize that settled married life would never be for him. Instead, he returned to Algeria to compare the desert areas of that country to what he had seen in Morocco, and left three notebooks full of impressions. By 1886, he was back in France again. That year was the turning point of his whole life. Living with relatives in Nice who were cultivated and serenely Catholic, he compared their faith with the strong faith of the Arabs he had known in Africa. He admired both, but the differences between them seemed to suggest that religious truth as such was simply impossible.

Yet he began stopping in churches because he found himself "at ease only there." Inexplicably, he started praying — for hours at a time, on his knees — "My God, if you exist, make me know You."[15] A cousin gave him Bossuet's *History,* but he did not know what to think about its demonstration of the workings of Providence in time. He felt the need for a teacher. One soon arrived. Abbé Henri Huvelin, a famous confessor and spiritual director, visited the family. When someone remarked on how happy Huvelin always appeared, the abbé explained that it was simple to achieve: do not seek joys from the world or consolation from religion. Foucauld responded to this because it echoed what he had admired in the starkness of the African desert. He began giving away the exotic objects he had accumulated during his travels to the children: a helmet, military uniforms, a burnoose, scimitars, pistols, rifles decorated with ivory.

Given Foucauld's early life, it was fitting that, when he came to this religious quest, an answer came to him from the Church of Saint Augustine in Paris. (Even Augustine's escapades as recounted in his *Confessions* are nothing compared with the sheer pyrotechnics of vice in Foucauld's early life.) He went for confession to the Abbé Huvelin on October 28, 1886. The good abbé lived up to his reputation. When Foucauld entered the confessional and asked for instruction to resolve his difficulties, Huvelin replied that he did not need instruction. Just make your confession, go to Communion, and your doubts will be resolved. Foucauld did what he was asked, and the results exceeded anything than even the abbé could reasonably have expected. As Foucauld later wrote: "As soon as I believed there was a God, I knew I could not do otherwise than live only for Him." He wanted to become a monk immediately, even though he still had some doubts and occasionally even slipped Koranic prayers into his meditations.

Huvelin helped him get through his questions and wisely told him to wait a while on the question of a vocation. Chastity came to Foucauld unbidden. Later, when he was in a monastery at Nazareth, he writes in an Augustinian vein, "You had obliged me to be chaste, and chastity became sweet to me and a necessity of my heart."[16] Scruples over his past life did not trouble him. He quickly grew accustomed to a regime of daily Mass and Communion, prayer, study, and regular meditation. He finished up the manuscript of *Reconnaissance au Maroc* even though much was changing in his life, and he even planned future expeditions. The religious vocation seemed on indefinite hold.

Foucauld's family was amazed by what had happened to him. Like many average Catholic families, they were happy about the turnaround, but embarrassed by his public religiosity. His confessor suggested he go to the Holy Land as a way of clarifying his vocation. Foucauld immediately agreed, since it combined his new-found faith with his now-old love of Arab exoticism. He spent Christmas of 1888 in Bethlehem. But he was most moved by Nazareth and the Sea of Galilee, especially the hillside overlooking the water where Christ preached the Sermon on the Mount. Upon his return to France, he was determined to join a religious order. After retreats with four different groups, a Jesuit priest at Manresa finally convinced him that the Trappists, austere like his beloved Arabs, were the men for Foucauld. He applied, and they accepted him. On January 15, 1890, he departed for Our Lady of the Snows, the Trappist monastery at Ardèche.

Given the earlier turmoil of his life, it is no surprise that, grace notwithstanding, Foucauld's sense of vocation long remained unsettled. At Our Lady of the Snows, he was happy to be clothed in a white wool tunic and cape, which resembled the burnooses of North Africa. The rigorous fasting with no flesh or fats was no problem to a man who had crossed deserts on short rations (in fact, when the Trappist rule was later softened, Foucauld at first thought it too self-indulgent). Self-denial came as easily to him now as self-indulgence had years earlier. The strictly specified Trappist regimen seemed what his soul most needed.

But quite quickly he recognized that his particular vocation could not be satisfied in the hard but sure Trappist life. He was meant for greater obscurity and uncertainty. He began a hegira lasting several years to determine where that kind of life might be found. The first stop was another Trappist monastery, this time in Akbès, Syria, which was located in a high valley that required a two-hour climb on foot through a ravine to reach. Some of his words there give hints of the attitude he now had adopted. When cholera hit the monastery, but not him, he wrote a close friend, "I am not yet worthy to go and pray for you in Purgatory."[17] Survival as a sign of unworthiness is, to say the least, a rare view even among Christian ascetics.

Much about the new institution pleased him. For one thing, he had to do hard work, peasant work, in the fields: picking cotton, sawing wood, clearing land of stones, harvesting grapes and potatoes, in addition to indoor chores. He liked peasant work for two reasons. First, he thought it close to the kind of labor the Holy Family did in quiet obscurity during the thirty years before Jesus entered into his public ministry. This theme would grow in importance for him during his later life. But, second, he also found that such work allowed the mind freedom for prayer and contemplation so that the whole day, work time not excluded, could be constant prayer. By comparison, studying theology seemed to him something less than urgent. The Holy Family never studied theology but had been content with following the will of God in everyday workers' conditions. In addition, the priests in Syria were making hundreds of conversions; Foucauld admired the Arab peoples, but felt they needed to find the fullness of their rock-hard faith in the Catholic faith and a correction of their morals by French influence. As we shall see, this was no mere European prejudice.

Ultimately, even the Trappist life came to seem to him too opulent, too rich in human ways, if not necessarily materially abundant, for the vocation he foresaw. He began planning to live alone, away from the monastery in a nearby hermitage. He also toyed with the idea of founding a new, more austere order, like Saint Francis's early followers, without possessions, living by the work of its members hands, giving everything possible to the poor. "Your rule is absolutely impracticable," his spiritual director Huvelin wrote him, and repeatedly warned him in the following years that he was not a leader of men and should not try to put his rule into effect on other people. But the idea of living as the Holy Family did at Nazareth began to take complete hold on his imagination.

Foucauld saw humble heroism near to hand. In 1896, the Turks carried out a series of massacres against the Christians and the Kurds in the vicinity of the monastery. By the time it all ended, approximately 140,000 Christians had died within a few months by order of the sultan. In a nearby town, 4,500 Christians died in only two days. Foucauld wrote home to get money to distribute to those affected by the persecution. Though he had earlier resisted the notion of becoming a priest, something in the events of that time opened up his mind to the possibility. His Trappist superiors tried to encourage him in that goal. But he balked at the whole idea of remaining a Trappist; Dom Sebastian Wyart, abbot general, wrote Foucauld without knowing him well, ordering him to go to Staouëli, a town near Algiers, and await further instructions.

The Trappists were very flexible in dealing with Foucauld, recognizing his as an unusual vocation. But Dom Sebastian also became convinced that a few years in Rome studying at the Gregorian University might clarify certain questions in Foucauld's mind. Foucauld dutifully obeyed, though reading scholastic philosophy in Latin at that point in is life was a hard penance. When Dom Sebastian returned to Rome and finally met with Foucauld, however, he instantly realized that the young man needed to be released from his Trappist obligations to pursue the life to which he was being called. The most immediate way to do that was to follow the call literally, going to Nazareth to live the life of a poor worker.

Nazareth proved to be no more ultimately compelling than Syria or Rome for Foucauld. He talked his way into a job as a handyman for the Poor Clares in the town. But despite his saintliness, which the Poor Clares all soon recognized, he was not much of a handyman and his lack of mechanical skills cut against the grain of the life he wanted to lead. For a man who wanted to live the life of the Holy Family in the carpenter's shop at Nazareth, it was a bad sign that the simplest woodworking jobs were completely beyond him. He was too distracted by prayer even to make a good night watchman for the chicken coop. But if his manual skills were modest, his prayer life was spectacular. His spiritual writings at the time show real depth and the emergence of his particular charism: "Jesus, Mary, Joseph, I will learn from you to keep silence, to pass humbly on earth, like a traveler in the night."[18] He had drawn landscapes as an explorer; now he also began to draw great simple versions of scenes from the Gospels. Huvelin, back in France, tried to encourage him to remain at Nazareth, doing manual labor, which he regarded as crucial for Foucauld's stability.

Somehow, however, Foucauld got himself involved in another typically crazy venture in Palestine. One of his favorite Gospel sites, the mountain on which Christ preached the beatitudes, was about to be sold. Foucauld's inheritance was more than adequate for buying it and giving it to the Franciscans, who take care of many Christian sites in the Holy Land. But they were unsure they would be able to take care of and staff it. So Foucauld offered to provide for its expenses and live there himself during his lifetime. The negotiations, perhaps owing to Foucauld's impracticality, were haphazard. Another buyer appeared. Huvelin wrote from Paris that Foucauld should stay out of all serious financial transactions for obvious reasons. The plan came to nothing.

After these unsettled years in Nazareth, Foucauld decided that he needed to become a priest to serve God's people better. Though many believed in his sanctity, no bishop in the Holy Land would have him. So he returned to France. The Ardèche Trappists were generous enough to take him back for training. He made a quick pilgrimage to the shrine of Mary Magdalen, his patron saint. After that, he was determined. As if it would take a fresh new century for him to make the final transition from his previous life and its aftermath to some sort of tranquillity,

Foucauld was not ordained until June 9, 1901, by the local bishop at Viviers, who expected him to serve in the diocese. But a new idea had come to Foucauld in his prayers:

> I must live this life of Nazareth, which seemed to be my vocation, but not in the beloved Holy Land, but among the sickest souls, among the most abandoned of the sheep. The divine Banquet whose minister I was becoming must be offered, not to the relatives and to the rich, but to the lame, the blind, and the poor, that is to say, to souls lacking priests. In my youth, I had traveled all over Algeria and Morocco. In Morocco, as big as France, with ten million inhabitants, not a single priest in the interior; in the Sahara, seven or eight times as big as France, and much more inhabited than was thought earlier, a mere dozen missionaries. No people seemed to be more abandoned than these.[19]

Though he was forty-two by the time this realization came upon him, the explorer, the contemplative, the worker, and the missionary would all come finally together in this scheme, which made him world famous.

For his work in Africa, he needed the approval of the White Fathers, who conducted the missions there. Recommendations came from Abbé Huvelin ("You will find in M. le Vicomte Charles de Foucauld heroic devotion, limitless endurance, the vocation to work among the Moslems, a humble and patient zeal ... "), from Dom Martin of the Trappist Our Lady of the Snows ("I had never seen except in books such prodigies of penitence, humility, poverty, and love of God"), and from Dom Henri, prior of Staouëli ("the most beautiful soul I know.... There is in him the stuff of several saints").[20] But his approach to the Arabs would differ from that of the White Fathers. They built up the educational and economic infrastructure of the Africans as they conducted missions. Foucauld proposed to live like an Arab among Arabs, not even speaking of Christianity unless he was sought out by some neighbor. Since conversions by traditional methods were few among the Arabs, Jews, and Berbers, he would take a nontraditional approach.

This was a necessary step. Until then, missionaries in North Africa had been seen as agents of France or Europe. Christian behavior in Africa was far from ideal. Foucauld speculated in a letter: how would the French feel if Muslim missionaries showed up in their own villages in France preaching Mohammed? He would instead go down to the French garrison at Beni-Abbès, near a large palm forest on the banks of the Saoura River at the border of the vast sands, carrying the Blessed Sacrament deeper into Africa than anyone since Augustine's day. From there, he would also minister, alone and without protection, to French soldiers further south in the Sahara. Above all, he would live an isolated, contemplative life — like the Holy Family during the thirty hidden years of Christ's existence before his public ministry — that would not actively seek conversions but would preach by example. He would become a "universal brother," living among the desert peoples as they themselves did.

In the event, that was only partly what happened. Foucauld attracted people of many sorts, French as well as natives. One of his first chapels became a place visited by "a few officers, *many* soldiers, *many* Arabs, *many* poor to whom I give barley and dates, in so far as it is possible."[21] (Among these numbers, the group that surprised him most with its unexpected, if imperfect, piety was the soldiers.) The universal brother found himself in the midst of what he called the Fraternity of the Sacred Heart. The locals called it by an Arabic name, the *khaouia*, the fraternity. Without intending it, he became a kind of point of political exchange where the French and Tuaregs could communicate and also spy on one another.

Viewed from the outside — and perhaps from the inside by several actors in this desert drama — his presence might appear a relatively benign manifestation of colonialism. But if it was colonialism, it had noble aims. The various groups in the desert lived a life of constant warfare with one another, mutual betrayal, and banditry. As nomads, the desert peoples looked down on work, which they thought fit only for women and slaves, whom they acquired in abundance from Sudan. Slavery is a stubborn plant in Africa; at the end of the twentieth century, more than eighty years after Foucauld's death, Sudanese slavery in the form of Muslim dominance over southern Christians continued without letup.[22]

Foucauld tried a strategy that others down to modern times have also used: he bought slaves in order to set them free. A worthy effort in itself, it sometimes has the unintended consequence of encouraging slave owners to capture more poor souls in order to turn a larger profit. Foucauld's practice also annoyed the Arab masters and the French military: the latter in particular were under orders not to meddle in the affairs of the native peoples. Sometimes twenty black slaves a day would show up asking to be redeemed. Even the White Fathers, whom Foucauld begged for more ransom money, thought, from long experience in the region, that

his efforts would come to no good. The institution of slavery was too
entrenched and French influence too weak to allow for lasting change
at that moment.

The slavery question cured Foucauld of some illusions. When he first
visited North Africa and was enchanted by the place and the people,
he had believed that Moslems took good care of their slaves. Now he
learned differently. Also, French toleration of slavery contradicted everything he believed that France, at its best, might bring to the Sahara. In
a letter to home, he explained:

> Slavery continues here, in a painful fashion; and in permitting it, in
> supporting it we make ourselves despised, which is the natural fruit
> of injustice. The natives know we do not allow slavery at home and
> that we forbid it in Algeria; therefore, seeing us give in to it here,
> they say, "They are frightened, they dare not abolish it, they fear
> us," and therefore they despise us.[23]

The French, of course, had calculated that they could do little good and
much harm in trying to stamp out the practice. They were probably
right, humanly speaking; but Foucauld was right in every other way. His
efforts left little mark on the situation, but he was the first European,
and the last for a long time, seriously to try introducing basic human
decency into a widespread cultural evil.

Foucauld's failure to change French policy or local mores, however,
did not deter him from other plans for the civilizing and eventual conversion of his Tuaregs. On several of these points, he found no little help
among the French. For a dozen years before his death, he advised General Henri Laperrine, one of the remarkable and noble military leaders
in the French Sahara. Both of them tried to appeal to the inhabitants
by kindness, respect, and mutual efforts toward improvements. Laperrine admired Foucauld immensely and had a genuine desire to see his
evangelization efforts succeed, quite apart from what they might do for
the stability of the French presence. Like Foucauld, Laperrine believed
learning the local languages and customs was essential, and he ordered
newly arrived officers to do just that. It was Laperrine who encouraged
Foucauld's study of the Tuareg language, Tamashek, even though it was
spoken by only a few hundred thousand people at the time. Both of them
had a sense that keeping the local peoples away from stronger Arabic
influences would help politically, morally, and religiously. And both believed that this would be best for the people themselves, not just for
European interests.

With Laperrine as an escort, he started to make his way in 1904 deep into the desert. Foucauld was alert to every aspect of the landscape that might be turned to his purposes. He was the first European to notice and to call attention to Saharan rock paintings, which he thought might explain the origins of the Tuaregs and help to a better understanding of how to work with them.[24] Though Laperrine thought it was too early to establish a fixed base in the region, he let Foucauld go down into the lands of the Ahoggar Tuaregs with a Colonel Roussel. In just a few months they visited three hundred villages and covered over three thousand miles. During the trek, Foucauld worked on what was to become the first full-length book in Tamashek: his translation of the Gospels.[25]

Back at Beni-Abbès and his "fraternity," he found himself frazzled by all the visitors who now knocked at the door, dozens daily looking for a little food or encouragement. Though he had long made it a rule "to see Jesus in every human being and to act accordingly," he found the repeated distractions a burden. Lack of other laborers in the vineyard also weighed heavy upon him. But he turned this to spiritual profit: "Jesus chooses for each person the type of suffering which He sees is the most suited to sanctify that person, and often the cross which He imposes is the one which, accepting all the others, one would have refused if one had dared. The one He gives is that which one understands the least."[26] That was the spirit that would inspire his remaining work and led him to live a quiet life like a nomad among nomadic people rather than the quiet contemplative life he had once thought his vocation.

Yet it was part of his genius that he recognized that contemplation could go on even amid a relatively active life. A sort of interior silence could exist that words, in whatever language, could not disperse. And the fact that he did not "settle down" to a fixed form of religious life reminded him that there is no such thing as settling down in the world anyway, since all is passing. Besides, he wrote, everything in his past had been led by Providence to this step: "It is not for a poor humble sheep like me to give advice to my Shepherd."[27] The life of Nazareth meant literally accepting the humdrum little steps toward holiness:

My interior life is very simple. I see my path very clear before me. My work is to correct my innumerable faults and to do tomorrow the same thing I do today, but to do it better. It is peaceful, but mixed with a certain sadness arising from pride and self-love when I see myself at the evening of my life, so wretched and bearing so little fruit.[28]

Foucauld, like many saints, continued to have a sharp sense of his own imperfections. After years of a strictly ascetic life, he still wrote, "Je suis paresseux et gourmand," "I am lazy and a glutton."[29] Yet he had also learned that the sense of imperfection, which brought with it a feeling of separation from the Almighty, could be turned to good: "[If we always had a sense of God's love] earth would be Heaven. Let us be content with desiring and knowing that it is so; in this we have greater merit, if less sweetness."[30] And none of this, he realized, should be allowed to obscure the central, if humble, example he wished to give: "I must be the image of Our Lord in his hidden life; I must proclaim, by my life, the Gospel from the rooftops."[31]

There were outside circumstances that made the life to which he felt called next to impossible. He read in the Book of Daniel that Jerusalem had to be built up in *angustia temporum,* and he reflected that this is always the human condition, building the kingdom in spite of the problems of the age.[32] The problems were twofold. France was slipping from its Christian moorings, not only in dogmatic terms but in its daily life:

> After nineteen years spent out of France, what struck me most, in the few days I spent there, was that in all classes of society, even in very Catholic families, the habit and taste for costly and useless things had greatly increased, and I noticed an amount of worldly frivolity that was much out of place ... and seemed out of keeping with the Christian life. The danger lies in us, and not in our enemies. Our enemies can only make us win great victories. But sin has its source in ourselves. The only remedy is to return to the Gospel.[33]

The moral decay in national life had effects abroad. In 1912, he would observe: "If France does not administer her colonies better than she has done, she will lose them, and these people will relapse into barbarism, and lose all chance of conversion for ages."[34] Algeria, he thought, was "dying under Islam." And this offered opportunities, first among the Tuaregs, whom he called "a young, strong, intelligent people."[35] But it would take a long time to move even them: "It will go, then, little by little. Alms, hospitality, ransom and liberation of slaves, and, much better, the offering of the divine Victim, will reconcile hearts and open ways to open preaching."[36] But all this would take years, and he says with heartfelt simplicity, "Je sème, d'autres moissoneront," "I sow, others will reap."[37]

Foucauld was soon on his way back to the Tuaregs under the protection of Captain Dinaux, who was engaged in a much-needed pacification program among warring tribes. They struck a deal with a Moussa, a Muslim leader and *marabout* ("Holy Man"), who took to Foucauld right away. Foucauld also liked Moussa, though he judged even the best of the Tuaregs to be limited by inherited ways: "He is very intelligent, very frank, a pious Moslem, wishing to do the right thing as a liberal but at the same time — like Mohammed, the most perfect creature in his eyes — ambitious and fond of money, pleasure, honor. To sum it up, Moussa has the ideas, the way of life, the qualities, and the vices of a logical Moslem and at the same time is as open indeed as he can be."[38] Despite the distance between their ways of life, they recognized good will in each other and would remain close for the next decade.

Foucauld chose the stark, mountainous Tamanrasset as his base. Captain Dinaux wept as he left him there, saying, "Were there a third order in your fraternity I would like to join."[39] But Foucauld did more than just evangelize quietly. He kept his eye on the larger situation that might affect his main work. His greatest hope for the French presence was that it would put an end to the incessant warfare and banditry in the region, to introduce an orderly, peaceful system that would lead to a flourishing of the people and possibilities of conversions. He noted in his diary that one of the local chieftains, El Mahdi, "lives here by committing felonies." El Mahdi would be one of the figures responsible for Foucauld's death.[40]

In the meantime, Foucauld decided to do what he could for the inhabitants. He imported various vegetable plants from France and other places in North Africa that flourished in the Tamanrasset climate. He introduced a simple rosary made of olive pits. There were no conversions; social and intellectual conditions did not permit them. At one point, he began working less with the leaders and more with the average inhabitants. That, too, went almost nowhere. But he intervened where possible for the good of his "parishioners," providing food, fixing problems with the authorities, caring for the children. During a bad famine in 1907–8, he saved many lives, and the Tuaregs remembered it. When another famine occurred after his death, they told authorities that if Foucauld were still alive their people would not have died. But the only lasting fruit of all his efforts was that in the 1930s several orders were founded according to his rule to attempt similar work: the Little Brothers of the Sacred Heart and the Little Sisters of the Sacred Heart, followed by the Little Sisters of Jesus, which now have foundations around the world.

From Tamanrasset, he set up an even more remote post at Asekrem to follow his people into the mountains during the seasons when they migrated there. The countryside moved him more deeply than any other: "The very sight of it makes you think of God, and I can scarcely take my eyes from a sight whose beauty and impression of infinitude are so reminiscent of the Creator of all; and at the same time its loneliness and wildness remind me that I am alone with Him."[41] The sheer size of the regions led him to write down some advice to the French about how to administer the area, which was two and a half times larger than France, even though it contained only twenty thousand people.

Foucauld had set himself down amid a people who valued both war and poetry, and a rich literature of love and battles existed in oral form among them. Though their sexual morals were loose, and infanticide, slavery, and brutality marred their lives, Foucauld was enchanted by Tuareg culture. A proud people, the Tuaregs were not much impressed by French military might, but they were impressed by Foucauld. They told a French general after seeing Foucauld's example: "So you *do* have a religion and priests, and you don't just live like dogs!"[42] But the entrenched ways of the nomads stopped any evangelization efforts dead. After years, Foucauld realized that the more than thousand years since the Muslim conquest of North Africa would not be moved by him or anyone else for centuries. Yet he remained alone with his Tuaregs for nine years before his death.

The end came as a culmination of everything that went before. Some of Foucauld's closest Tuareg associates were bribed into helping plan his kidnapping. They had fallen back under the spell of a band of Muslim enthusiasts, the Senoussis, who were bent on driving French influence from the area. Foucauld constructed a kind of "fort" to wait out the turmoil. Other Tuaregs, including a village chief and a Muslim priest, offered to stay with him until the danger passed. But he sent them away. Somehow the rumor had spread that a large cache of French arms was hidden in the fort. The Senoussis arrived, some of whom he knew personally. He let one in and they tied him up. Then they began beating him, spitting on him, and questioning him about French intentions. Foucauld said nothing. An eyewitness, Paul Embarek, has given conflicting accounts of what happened next. In one version, Foucauld was pressured to abjure his faith by saying the *chahada,* the prayer that Muslims urge on those condemned to death so that they can commit themselves to Allah before entering eternity. If so, Foucauld was canonically a martyr, but the point remains disputed.[43] In the heat of the moment, with camels arriving in the village ridden by unidentified persons, the fifteen-year-old guard watching Foucauld shot him through the head. He died instantly.

Foucauld is one of the most important French figures in the recent history of Algeria, the Sahara, and Morocco. But even more importantly, he became an example for both Europe and the Arab world of how to live a Christian life and how to conduct oneself among another people with long religious traditions. Whatever might be said about his involvement in French colonialism, he took a real and deep interest in the humble tribes among whom he settled. At his beatification process, parts of the documentation included two volumes of Tuareg prose and two of verse he had compiled. A Tuareg grammar and a seven-hundred-page dictionary were left in scattered sheets on the floor of his hermitage by his fleeing murderers — the last entry he had made was the word *Ta mella (tas),* "to die a violent death." There are distinguished anthropologists who have produced less original material. Foucauld did it, not out of mere professional and scientific curiosity, but out of a love and care for his poor neighbors and a desire to explain them to the larger world.

This was not wholly lost among the tribes where he labored. The devout Muslims among them recognized in him something that bridged the wide differences of religion, culture, and experience that have long plagued interactions between Westerners and others. After his death, his friend Moussa wrote a letter to Charles's sister, heartrending both in its tenderness and unconscious savagery:

The one God be praised.

To her Ladyship Marie, our friend, sister of our Marabout [i.e., Holy Man] Charles, who was assassinated by the treacherous and deceitful people of Ajjer.

From Tebeul Moussa-as Amastane, Amenokal of the Hoggar. May great welfare surround the aforesaid Marie.

When I learned of the death of our friend, your brother Charles, my eyes closed and all grew dark for me. I wept many tears and I am in deep mourning. His death has caused me great sorrow.

I am now far from the place where the thieving traitors and deceivers killed him. That is to say, they killed him in the Hoggar and I am in Adrar. But God willing, we will kill these people who killed the Marabout until our vengeance has been fulfilled. Greet your daughters, your husband, and all your friends on my behalf and tell them this: Charles, the *marabout* has not died for you alone; he has died for all of us. May God have mercy on him and grant that we may meet him in Paradise.[44]

No man has ever inspired a more devout and heartfelt wish from a member of another culture who, in merely human terms, would otherwise have been a sworn enemy.

The cause for Foucauld's beatification was introduced in Rome in 1927. The Church, careful in its solemn proclamations, has not yet pronounced finally on him as saint or martyr. But it declared Charles de Foucauld "Venerable" on April 13, 1978. The title is formally right, but odd for a man who was not venerable in any normal sense of the term either in his early libertine years or in the eccentric religious forms his later life took. But the word "venerable" comes from the Latin word *Venus,* denoting the mythological goddess of love, and all those who are vener-able are, in the simplest sense, loveable. Foucauld in all his wild and madcap episodes is certainly that, as much for his exuberance in pursuing the good as in his willingness to die quietly for God — perhaps even without the posthumous compensation of officially being declared a martyr.

# – F I V E –

# SPANISH HOLOCAUST

I N MAY OF 1931, a Visitandine convent in Madrid dispersed its more than eighty sisters, disguised in street clothes, to their families and friends. Their problem was a common one among Spanish religious establishments at the time. Primo de Rivera's government had been dissolved a few days earlier, and rumors circulated that the convent was a target for burning by Spanish antireligious forces. The superior, Mother María Gabriela de Hinojosa, wanted to make sure that the women entrusted to her leadership, some of them over eighty, would not be harmed by the random and widespread violence breaking out. Things quickly quieted down — for the moment. But then another threat presented itself: the government started requisitioning empty buildings. In order to keep control over the convent without exposing the whole community to danger, the mother superior asked seven of the sisters to return. They did, as did the other sisters eventually, when that wave of danger passed. But a precedent had been established; whenever the nuns were forced to go into hiding because of persecution in coming years — a periodic necessity — seven would stay behind. It was a tradition that led to the deaths of seven modern Spanish martyrs.

Ironically, many of the nuns in the Madrid convent had chosen to return there from Mexico in 1913 when that country's revolution took place. At the time a Spanish convent seemed like a safe refuge. By 1931, the seven who were assigned to guard the building did not even dare to put their habits on or sleep in their usual cells. Instead, they slept in secular clothes on mattresses in a common room so that they could flee at a moment's notice. As things became worse in the next few years, they would rent an apartment as a precaution to make sure they had somewhere to flee to if the convent were overrun. These mostly contemplative, simple women had to learn the hard ways of the world and the practice of innocent deceptions to preserve their religious life. When war finally broke out, they had transferred the most precious objects of the convent — an altar, a tabernacle, some paintings, and a reliquary,

107

among other things — to their little basement apartment near the religious house. At night, they took turns in pairs to watch the streets for signs of trouble. During the day, they put on habits and showed themselves conspicuously at the windows to give the impression that the building was in regular operation. According to the people who met them, they felt themselves to be living "in some new catacombs of the twentieth century."[1]

But all their precautions were of little use against the storm that was about to break loose in the Spanish Civil War. Someone betrayed them to the authorities. The apartment was searched and the sacred objects were carted away. After another search, a sign was posted on the door: "This house has been registered." The nuns were summoned to the police station for questioning, but were released. Neighbors counseled them to leave. The sisters were torn between trying to save the convent and reaching safety. Not wishing to leave any one member of the order exposed to dangers the others did not run, they refused transport to the foreign consulates in Madrid that were providing sanctuary for some religious. Remaining united, they believed, took precedence over any physical peril.

Predictably, a truck arrived under the control of anarchist units. The sisters were loaded into it, and it set off. A few blocks later, it stopped abruptly at the end of Calle López de Hoyos. As soon as the sisters got off, shots were fired. All of the sisters — Teresa María Cavestany, Josefa María Barrera, María Inés Zudaire Galdeano, María Angela Olaizola, and María Engracia Lecuona — perished, except one, Sister María Cecilia Cendoya, who instinctively began running after feeling Sister María Gabriela, the former superior who had established the method of guarding the convent, slip to the ground. She was later apprehended by the police, declared herself to be a religious, and died a martyr as well. Seven Visitandine sisters had been martyred, and their convent burned, for no reason in the early days of the Spanish Civil War.

This little vignette is a microcosm of the wholesale murder of entire religious establishments during the Spanish Civil War. It is unrepresentative only in the relatively small number of those killed. We are accustomed to stories of atrocities and brutalities against large groups of people outside of Europe and North America. But in the early part of the century — in Spain, one of Europe's most staunchly Catholic countries — large numbers of Catholics were butchered solely for being Catholic. And unlike the martyrdoms in other parts of the world, they were often executions of whole sectors of the religious community as well as single individuals. The number of priests and religious martyred was at least 6,832, including thirteen bishops (from the dioceses of Sigüenza, Lérida, Cuenca, Barbastro, Segorbe, Jaén, Tarragona, Ciudad Real, Almería, Guadix, Barcelona, Teruel, and the apostolic administrator of Orihuela).

By one reckoning, the male religious orders martyred included 259 Claretians, 226 Franciscans, 204 Piarists, 176 Brothers of Mary, 165 Christian Brothers, 155 Augustinians, 132 Dominicans, and 114 Jesuits. The toll among the female orders was lower, but still shocking when we recall that these women could have had virtually nothing to do with the political struggle: 30 Daughters of Charity of Saint Vincent de Paul, 26 Carmelites of Charity, 26 Adoratrices, and 20 Capuchins, along with many others.

But perhaps the greatest fury fell upon diocesan clergy, though it varied a great deal from one place to another. Pamplona, a Nationalist and pro-Catholic stronghold, had no diocesan casualties. Barbastro in Aragón saw 123 of its 140 priests lost to Republican anarchists who were violently anticlerical. Elsewhere, too, the pattern reflected the fortunes of war. Seville was captured early by the Nationalists and therefore lost only four priests. But the other large cities that remained in Republican hands for the duration of the Civil War had far higher casualty figures: Barcelona, 279; Valencia, 327; Madrid-Alcalá, 1,118. In percentage terms, these represented 22, 27, and 30 percent of the diocesan clergy in the respective cities.

The savageness of the anticlerical fury can further be appreciated by considering that most of the murders were carried out in only the first six months of the Civil War, from July 1936 to January 1937, and that probably half of all clergy were, within a week of the uprising, protected in the relatively safe areas controlled by the Nationalists. Without the Nationalists, the slaughter could have been much greater. As it was, about a quarter of the male clergy in Republican-controlled areas disappeared.

Nor were lay people spared. One of the most impartial analysts of the Civil War has described their plight as follows:

> [In addition to the clerics] an incalculable number of lay persons were killed because of their religious associations, either as well-known church-goers, members of fraternal and charitable religious organizations, or as the fathers, mothers, brothers, sisters, and friends of clerics. Some were killed because they professed their faith by wearing some outward symbol of belief, perhaps a religious medal or scapular. Some were killed for acts of charity, for granting refuge to clerics attempting to escape the fury. It is impos-

sible to determine the number of these lay persons who were slain for their faith. Nor was the anticlericalism limited to killing. Thousands of churches were burned, religious objects were profaned, nuns' tombs were opened and the petrified mummies displayed to ridicule, and religious ceremonies were burlesqued. Indeed, practically any imaginable anticlerical act was not only possible but likely.[2]

Of the twentieth-century martyrs beatified by Pope John Paul II, it is no surprise then that the great majority resulted from the Civil War in Spain. In 1996, before the wave of beatifications and canonizations associated with the Jubilee year began, of the 266 he beatified, 218 were Spaniards. These included several large groups: 3 Discalced Carmelites, 26 Passionists, 8 brothers of Christian Schools, 71 Saint John of God Hospital brothers, 51 Claretians, 12 Scolopi religious, 17 sisters of Christian Doctrine of Mislata, along with several bishops, various diocesan priests, members of religious orders, and laymen and laywomen.

It has often been argued by supporters of the Spanish Republican cause that this antireligious slaughter reflected "symbolic" rage at the triumphalist Catholicism characteristic of Spain at the time. A famous photograph from the Civil War shows soldiers taking target practice at a statue of the Sacred Heart because, apologists for the outrages claim, it was the image of clerical dominance in education. Units of the Republican army are also said to have viewed religious images as symbols of antiprogressive forces. All this may very well be true. But just as there was no excuse for the Christians among the Nationalist forces who took vengeance for such acts by committing various brutal reprisals, so, all rationalizations notwithstanding, there is no justification for crimes against people who were, in the vast majority, innocent not only of any wrongdoing but of any substantial involvement in Spanish politics. Their deaths were the result of antireligious fanaticism that mars the record of Spanish Republicans.

These martyrs are usually overlooked in discussions of the Spanish Civil War because of a curious combination of circumstances. Since a large percentage of the martyrs fell in the first few months of the Civil War, it appeared to some observers who arrived later that the Nationalist claims of a hate-filled, anti-Catholic Republican government were exaggerations, if not outright propaganda. Some of the killings were carried out by mobs armed by the government, but outside of its immediate command, so-called "uncontrollables," when the conflict broke out. But the same governmental forces had allowed churches to be burned and clerics to be harassed even before the war. In 1931, i.e., five years earlier, Manuel Azaña, then minister of war, but later president of the Republic in the worst year, commented about a rash of church burnings: "All of the *conventos* [convents] in Spain are not worth the life of a single Republican."[3] The seven Visitandines and many thousands of others paid a heavy price for such statements. A weak man, Azaña may have only been trying to maintain popular support in certain circles, which he did by similar unscrupulous means throughout his tenure in office. But such remarks and the events to which they led might give Nationalist forces good reason to think that, even when they did not order the anti-Catholic outrages, the government ministers had no intention of stopping them — and the perpetrators knew it.

Even the best and most decent outside observers were basically blind to the antireligious injustices. George Orwell, whose novel *1984* is the twentieth century's classic fictional warning about totalitarianism of all kinds, went to fight with a Marxist POUM (Partido Obrero de Unificación Marxista, "Workers' Party of Marxist Unification") force in Barcelona in 1936 and gives an interesting account of his experiences in *Homage to Catalonia*.[4] But in those pages, Orwell, who is usually thought of as pitting common decency against political partisanship, falls into the very ideological blindness he so wonderfully denounces in others. For him, the Nationalists are all Fascists and the religious belong among various groups — landowners, military people, police, bourgeoisie, capitalists — who are the "objective" enemies of progressives. And the impression he gives is that, regrettable as their deaths may be, it was all inevitable, given the untidiness of any war for popular liberation.

In an essay written years after the Spanish Civil War, Orwell would observe that "what impressed me then and has impressed me ever since is that atrocities are believed in or disbelieved in solely on grounds of political predilection. Everyone believes in the atrocities of the enemy and disbelieves in those of his own side, without ever bothering to examine the evidence."[5] He describes the sheer delusions that had gripped the press and "eager intellectuals building emotional superstructures over events that had never happened."[6] But for all his desire to tell the simple truth, even Orwell falls prey to his own Republican sympathies and tries to argue that Nationalist atrocities were far worse. Recent scholarship disputes that. Even with plenty of blame to be distributed to all sides, the question remains for Orwell as well as others who allegedly were trying to do the right thing in Spain: the right thing means acknowledging the thousands of people killed, not for capital crimes they had committed personally, but simply for being members of the Catholic Church. The very anarchists-syndicalists with whom Orwell had the most sympathy and whom he thought had, at least at the beginning, a real chance of building a workers' democracy, were the worst offenders by far. That Orwell does not seem particularly bothered by this and even excuses it as a longstanding anarchist tradition to be anticlerical, suggests that political ideology played such a large, blinding role in Spain that even the best intentioned people could not see the martyrdom of the Spanish Church for the outrage and sheer injustice that it was.

The truth is that, despite atrocities, there was heroism and idealism on both sides, though the Republican sympathies of many writers and intellectuals have given the impression that only the Republican cause possessed any virtues. A notable exception, however, is Ernest Hemingway's fine novel about the Civil War, *For Whom the Bell Tolls*. Hemingway's protagonist, Robert Jordan, is an American, a professor of Spanish at the University of Missoula in Montana, who joined one of the International Brigades out of commitment to the Republican cause and opposition to Fascism. (The very good film of this novel with Gary Cooper and Ingrid Bergman faithfully captures much of the romance of the Republican struggle.) But Hemingway notes elements in the war that many writers, even those as generally fair as George Orwell, do not. First of all, he realizes that the Fascist vs. Communist characterization is a gross oversimplification. Robert Jordan has Communist interests and enjoys discussing Marxism with some of the Soviets who have come to fight in Spain. But even one of them, Karkov, tells him he has much to learn. For example, Calvo Sotelo, whose murder set off the conflict, was a "very good fascist; a true Spanish fascist. Franco [the general leading the Nationalist cause] and these other people are not."[7]

But perhaps because of his own complicated relationship to Catholicism, Hemingway notes the religious atrocities on the Republican side. Chapter 10 of the novel, which is almost entirely devoted to Pilar's account of the horrifying murders perpetrated by a mob in the first days of the war, includes the death of a priest (the movie version faithfully reproduces the mob scene, but squeamishly leaves out the priest's murder). Both Pilar, who tells the story, and Robert Jordan are sick at heart over the way their own people behaved, turning into an ugly and immoral mob that taunted, tortured, and eliminated people, very few of whom had done anything. In spite of his own Republican and Marxist sympathies, Robert Jordan thinks to himself during the story: "I've always known about the other, he thought. What we did to them at the start. I've always known it and hated it and I have heard it mentioned shamelessly and shamefully, bragged of, boasted of, defended explained and denied."[8] Unfortunately, in the heat of action, very few people in the Republican camp admitted as much. Hemingway's heroic characters, Pilar and Robert, are even more admirable for their rare admissions.

We have far fewer accounts of heroism on the Nationalist side. One unpublished memoir of José María Escrivá, the founder of the religious group Opus Dei, gives some of the flavor of what it was like to be a hunted priest at the time. Escrivá first hid at his mother's home in Madrid, but since he was known in the neighborhood as a priest, he soon departed disguised in civilian clothes. That, however, did not prevent the militias from violence. They captured a man who, unfortunately for him, looked a great deal like Father Escrivá. Probably as a kind of object lesson in terror, they hung the poor man from a tree in front of Escrivá's mother's house. In Madrid at the time, each block was under the supervision of a "control" person who kept an eye on what happened in every street. People were arrested for as little as wearing a religious medal.[9]

For these and other reasons, Escrivá and some of his early followers decided to escape from Madrid. Because of the array of forces, the only route of escape open to them passed through Valencia to Barcelona, one of the worst areas for religious persecution. On the way, they used whatever places of refuge became available. The Honduran embassy in Madrid, like other foreign embassies, provided cover for a while. At one point, Escrivá and his brothers stayed in a psychiatric hospital, where they pretended to be patients. Then they crossed from Barcelona into Andorra during the winter snows through high mountains and steep valleys, constantly threatened by Republican patrols with orders to shoot on sight. Even in the simple and pious form in which the *Remembrances* of that episode are written, the sheer pressure of events and physical challenges inject a Hemingwayesque romance into the story. In a curious coincidence, from Andorra the fugitives passed through France and then back into an area of Nationalist Spain made famous by Hemingway: San Sebastián, Pamplona, and all the northern area of Navarra, which were a Catholic, Carlist monarchist, and Nationalist stronghold. Some of the stories of the Carlist *requetés,* who all sides agreed were among the bravest and fiercest combatants in the war, possess similar romance. But compared with the many memoirs that have been written to document the Republican side in the struggle, relatively little has received wide attention from the Nationalist side.

To understand the reasons for this conflict, we must look briefly at some history. Spain in the first few decades of the twentieth century was suffering from a long historical hangover. One hundred years earlier, its largely corrupt monarchy had been gently deposed by Napoleon, who put his brother Joseph on the throne. Both brothers were themselves eventually deposed by European powers and the Spanish king returned. But an even more weakened Spain would soon lose its colonies in the New World to independence movements brought on by its chaos and corruption. In the middle of the nineteenth century, Spain tried to set up a republic. But social and political conditions were not favorable to this democratic experiment, and it reverted to a weak and largely inert monarchy. In 1898, Spain would lose Cuba and the Philippines, two island nations that had been under its control since the Age of Exploration. The humiliating loss was a harbinger of worse disorders about to come.

At the beginning of the twentieth century, Spain tried its hand at a republic again, but it would run up against further obstacles. First, like many other countries in Europe, it inherited the intellectual prejudice from France that the revolution could only be made against the Catholic Church. England and America had democratized without such radical measures. But on the European continent both church and state had to go through some mutual adjustments before they would settle into a relatively stable and amicable relationship. Spain in particular had some problems that would lead to an especially bloody explosion. First, its "republicans" were, as a group, really radicals having little in common with republican or democratic ideas as those are usually understood in other countries. Some were mildly socialist, but not a few were Communist or militantly anarchist, and atheist and violently anticlerical to boot. Socialist and anarchist unions swelled with the numbers of miserable workers who began to leave the countryside and arrive in the cities. In the agricultural areas, modernization and the concentration of large landholdings in a few hands caused unrest. And the Communist Party, though small in absolute numbers, was a larger percentage of the population in Spain than it had been in Russia in 1917 when the Soviet Union came into being.

By the 1920s, the country was in chaos, and a general, Miguel Primo de Rivera, staged a coup to restore order. Rivera's was a bloodless dictatorship, and he left power after a few years, allowing democratic elections to be held. But it was clear that the situation was highly unstable and the badly divided Spanish populace would not be able to settle its differences with mere elections. In 1931, elections were so unfavorable to monarchist candidates that Alfonso XIII went into exile in England and never returned. This led to a rapid series of political changes that set Spain on a self-destructive course. The Second Spanish Republic began with the king's departure. But unlike other modern democracies it had several authoritarian features, among them an animus against religion. Approximately one hundred church burnings occurred in 1931, and the government did little to stop them. In fact, it passed laws cutting off public funds to the Church, a proper move for a pluralistic democracy, other things being equal. But they were not equal. The government also proclaimed its right to expel religious orders, particularly the Jesuits, and to control all religious festivals, which are a traditional part of Spanish life. It also prohibited religious education. For these and other reasons, some military officers attempted a coup in 1932, which failed.

The next year, however, the government failed, and subsequent events revealed the deep rifts in Spanish politics. The next election gave a majority to rightist candidates, with a Catholic party (CEDA) leading all others in the number of representatives elected to the Cortes (the Spanish Parliament) under the guidance of CEDA's founder, José Gil Robles. The strongest opposition existed among the Socialists, under the leadership of Largo Caballero. Because of turmoil in the Cortes, the Spanish president dissolved it on January 7, 1936. Five days later, the socialist leader Caballero, often portrayed as a moderate, professed his belief that Marxist Socialism had to be built in Spain and even went so far as to state that, for the classless society he was seeking, "one class has to disappear." A few days after that, he remarked, "We are determined to do in Spain what was done in Russia." Language like this only fanned the flames of conflict.

When new elections were held on February 16, 1936, the nation was almost evenly split: according to the best estimates, the Right received 4,570,744 votes and the Popular Front (a Left coalition of socialists, anarchists, and Communists) 4,346,559. Other small parties got a few hundred thousand votes, and the Falange, the Fascist group, almost noth-

ing. But because of the peculiarities of the electoral system, the Popular
Front gained a large majority in the Cortes. Prudent leaders would have
taken note of the almost exactly divided national vote and tried to govern moderately. But the government had no intention of being careful or
even-handed. In March, several generals met in Madrid and decided that
they would lead a coup against the government if anarchy emerged, or
if institutions of public order like the police were changed in threatening ways, or if Largo Caballero were named prime minister. Ominously,
that same day, five churches, a convent, a seminary, and a Catholic school
were burned in Cádiz. Almost two hundred churches would burn and
several hundred Catholics were killed or wounded by the middle of the
year. The whole situation was a powder keg.

The spark that set off the explosion was the assassination of the rightist leader Calvo Sotelo on July 13, 1936. The generals decided to organize
an uprising on July 18 in Spanish Morocco, where most Spanish troops
were then garrisoned. The mainland Spanish uprising was to begin the
next day. General Francisco Franco, who would eventually come to lead
the revolt, was stationed in the Canary Islands, off the African coast, and
had to be flown in to lead the troops. Curiously, Franco, often thought
of as the mastermind of the coup, became the leader only because the
plane carrying the general that the others had chosen to lead, José San-
jurjo, crashed trying to bring him from Portugal into Spain. Much has
been written about Franco's alleged Fascism and brutality, but perhaps
the English historian Paul Johnson had summed up his character best:

> The Nationalists [the military coup's movement] won primarily be-
> cause of the capacity and judgment of Franco. Though Franco was
> an unlovely man and is unlikely ever to win the esteem of histori-
> ans, he must be accounted one of the most successful public men of
> the century.... The soldier-statesmen he most resembles is Welling-
> ton, a figure much admired in Spain.... Franco was never a Fascist
> or had the smallest belief in any kind of Utopia or system.[10]

By contrast, the Republicans attracted intellectual sympathizers who
publicized the cause. We have already seen the efforts by George Orwell and Ernest Hemingway. But "international brigades" of idealistic
progressives from various countries arrived to support the Republican
troops as well. Some knowingly embraced Communist principles at a
time when the 1930s Depression seemed to have cast doubt on the via-
bility — let alone justice — of capitalist market economies. And most
intellectuals, energized by a seemingly noble struggle to impose pro-

gressive thought on a backward and religious people, supported the Republicans in scholarly publications and popular journalism.

Implementing laws that had been passed earlier, in the spring of 1936, the Spanish government closed large numbers of Catholic schools and destroyed others. Members of the Catholic party in the legislature walked out in protest. But as with earlier instances of church burnings, political leaders seemed unmoved, either by the protest or by the actual violation of property rights and religious liberties. Hence, the Nationalists' perception that only a counterforce could keep the country from becoming a socialist outpost and unchecked persecutor.

The Nationalist forces have been much criticized since for seeking support from Hitler and Mussolini. Anti-Fascist writers and activists have portrayed this move as indicating some ideological similarity between the Spaniards and the German and Italian dictators. But this is a gross error. The Nationalists were largely Catholic, traditional, and, in some cases, monarchist. The German and Italian Fascists repressed religion, sought revolution, and certainly had no love for hereditary kings. Like the alliance of Britain and the United States with Stalin and the Soviet Union in World War II against Italy and Germany, the reasons for the partial alliance of the Nationalist Spaniards with less than ideal partners had less to do with similarity of views than with a lack of any other alternatives for conduct of a war.

Since the largest part of the Nationalist forces loyal to Franco were in Spanish Morocco, they had to be transported to Spain for the larger engagement. Transport by ship was impossible because the three ships available had fallen into Republican hands. Some of the southern ports were controlled by the Republicans. The only way to get Nationalist troops across the Straits of Gibraltar was by air. Spain at that period had few planes and the Nationalists only five of them. England was cautiously neutral. France had a more moderate Popular Front government itself. And the United States was still mostly isolationist; it would take the genius of Winston Churchill and the surprise Japanese attack on Pearl Harbor to get America to participate in World War II, and even then only in 1941, two years after the conflagration had begun. Germany and Italy were the only manufacturers of planes willing to give Franco and the Nationalists the means of transportation they desperately needed.

It was a marriage of convenience on all sides. Germany and Italy needed someone to oppose Communist forces. Spain needed planes. Much historical analysis since that time has mistakenly seen more in the connection than was really there. To argue that Franco was a Fascist like Hitler and Mussolini because they cooperated is similar to arguing that Roosevelt was a Communist like Stalin because they did the same. In fact, Franco, whatever brutality he may have used to achieve his ends, had very little in the way of ideological orientation except for his Catholicism and opposition to the revolutionary Republicans. The characterization of Franco as Fascist and the Republicans as engaged in an anti-Fascist struggle is a canard that has entered into many standard histories.

Far more ideological, however, were the Republicans. Though the Republicans included several different strands — anarchist, socialist, and others — they had strong financing and political backing from the Soviet Union. In addition, the leaders of various Communist parties in France, Italy, Hungary, and elsewhere began playing a serious role in the conflict. While it would be difficult to point to any clear sign of Fascism among the Nationalists, many clear indications of Communist sympathies were publicly celebrated by the Republicans, though this is often denied, even by contemporary Spaniards. A famous photograph from the 1930s, for example, shows mobs storming the Alcázar in Toledo carrying Soviet flags with the hammer and sickle.[11]

Amid these political complexities, it is easy to forget that, in practice, they led to the slaughter of many innocents like the seven Visitandines. By any just standard, the priests and nuns in Spain were far from participation in or responsibility for the political situation. But that did not protect them. As early as July 1936, they began paying a price, however, for the Republicans' view that they were "objective class enemies." On July 21 of that year, martyrdoms began. Three Jesuits and a Jesuit brother were captured and taken from a retreat house to anarchist headquarters in Barcelona. Anarchist crowds are reported to have shouted: "We are going to kill you because you are priests; not one of you will be left!" Like many of their co-religionists in the months and years to come, they were taken to a hill, absolved one another, expressed forgiveness for their captors, and were shot. Two days later in the same city, twelve nuns, four over sixty, were gunned down by the side of the road. Even a church organist, Jaime Busquets Xaubet, trying to prevent the mob from burning down a church, was murdered.[12]

The same day in Toledo Father Pascual Martín was shot in front of the Saint Nicholas Church and died shouting the slogan of the Cris-

teros in Mexico: *Viva Cristo Rey!* Father Pedro Ruiz de los Paños, the
head of the Brotherhood of Diocesan Priests, and Father José Sala, rector of the Toledo seminary, were shot and killed in front of a maternity
hospital. (Ruiz along with eight diocesan worker priests, who died in
various places on different dates, was beatified on October 1, 1995).[13]
On July 24, one of the most brutal atrocities of the whole Civil War
occurred in Madrid itself. Three Discalced Carmelite nuns, members of
the movement inaugurated by the great sixteenth-century Spanish mys-
tic Saint Teresa of Avila, were shot by militiamen in the street. One died
instantly, another was at first refused transport to a hospital by a bus
driver who wanted to "finish her off," a third wandered around dazed
until another band of militiamen executed her.[14] A priest later beatified, Dioniso Pamplona, was killed in the Plaza Mayor in Madrid with
twenty-four other people the following day. The day after that, fourteen
seminarians died in Lérida, but only after they had been tortured and
attempts were made to get them to show disrespect to a crucifix (one
was forced to try eating a rosary). On July 27, it was the turn of Bishop
Eustaquio Nieto in Sigüenza. On succeeding days a pattern emerged: several priests here, ten Christian brothers there. By the end of the month
(and the slaughter only started on the 18th), 124 priests were dead in
Madrid, 197 in Barcelona. Mass was publicly prohibited in Republican
Spain for the rest of the Civil War except in the Basque provinces. (The
Basques, staunch Catholics, had been promised autonomy by the Republican government, which, in return for their support, was willing to
allow them to determine their own religious policy.) Even allowing for
the fact that tempers were hot at that moment, this slaughter of three
helpless women, contemplatives shut away from the world no less, and
the public execution of a large number of harmless believers, constituted
repression on a scale not seen even in Mexico or the Soviet Union.

One of the ways that mob violence was stirred up against priests was
to accuse them, almost always falsely, of hiding weapons for the insurgents or actually participating in the fighting. That these charges usually
proved false did not mitigate the fury. Many churches and rectories were
ransacked for incriminating evidence and, when none was found, destroyed anyway, along with any priest or clergy who happened to be
nearby. That was the fate of the pastor of the Constantino church in
Seville, Father Manuel González-Semay Rodríguez, who also underwent
a three-day interrogation by a popular tribunal before his execution.[15]

Where these charges came from is harder to establish. Anarchists and
Communists certainly would not have balked at putting such rumors

into circulation. Other groups in the Republican coalition would probably have been more careful. But the results, whatever differences may
have existed among Republicans, were the same as if lawless murder of
Catholics had been an established policy. Indeed, no small number of
priests and religious were torn out of seminaries, hospitals, and nursing homes to meet death. Others were captured in schools and executed
along with young students. Still others were placed in front of popular
tribunals and given the opportunity to save themselves by renouncing
their faith. Remarkably, not one of them appears ever to have done so.

Indeed, the opposite seems to have happened: threat of imprisonment, torture, or death almost always led to serious recommitment to
faith. One such example provides a flavor of the kind of scene that was
repeated with variations in countless other circumstances:

> The parish priest of Torrijos, Liberio González Nonvela, for ex-
> ample, apparently told the militiamen who took him prisoner, "I
> want to suffer for Christ." "Oh, do you?" they answered. "Then
> you shall die as Christ did." They stripped him and scourged him
> mercilessly. Next, they fastened a beam of wood on their victim's
> back, gave him vinegar to drink, and crowned him with thorns.
> "Blaspheme and we will forgive you," said the leader of the militia.
> "It is I who forgive and bless you," replied the priest. The militia-
> men discussed how they should kill him. Some wished to nail him
> to a cross, but in the end they shot him. His last request was to die
> facing his tormentors so that he might die blessing them.[16]

There have been reports of actual crucifixions in Spain during the war.
They may have occurred, but, half a century later, no firm evidence for
any specific incident.[17] Crucifixion may have been the one outrage that
was not inflicted on Catholics in Spain.

But the brutal and blasphemous reenactment of the Passion described
above points to several truths. First, it has been sometimes argued that
much of the violence against the religious was actually a holy rage against
their failure to do what they should for the people. Whatever grain of
truth there may be in such an analysis, it is overwhelmed by the large
fact of truly blasphemous use of the Passion story to inflict unmerited
punishments. There is no point in trying to be oversophisticated about
this phenomenon. It was an antireligious and simply anti-Christian spirit
working itself out in largely illusory political categories.

Second, if this clergy had been as corrupt and attached to a comfortable bourgeois life style as is often asserted, we would easily have been

able to find many instance of priests and nuns who apostatized when their very lives were at stake. But there are few recorded instances of such apostasies; the Spanish clergy seem to have shared broadly all over the country a degree of virtue and outright heroism in the face of danger that has been rarely seen anywhere on earth for any cause.

Several, for example, faced the choice between breaking the seal of the confessional or death. Father Felipe Ciscar Puig, the chaplain of the Augustinian convent in Denia, Valencia, was imprisoned though he was seventy-one years old and hardly a threat of any kind. He heard the confession of Father Andrés Ivars, a Franciscan, in anticipation of the latter's execution. Their jailers put great pressure on Ciscar Puig to reveal what he had heard. He refused to dishonor the sacrament and, with Ivars, was shot on September 8, 1936. Other priests were offered a chance to marry as a way to save themselves. Andrés Molina, a twenty-seven-year-old priest in Granada, who decided against that escape, wrote a letter to his family, which has been preserved: "Dearest mother, do not be sad.... On the contrary, you must be very proud, because you are the mother of a martyr; and to you, brothers, I say the same: you are brothers of a martyr who will watch over you and all my beloved relatives from heaven."[18]

Sometimes the pressure to cave in understandably came from the relatives themselves. Francisco Sendra Ivars, a priest of the Valencia diocese, had to flee into his native town. He, too, was captured and offered freedom if he married. His own mother advised him to pretend to give in to save himself. After weeks of refusing both his mother's entreaties and the pressure from his captors, he was taken out, his genitals amputated as part of a slow torture, and, finally killed.[19] Others were subjected to crude attempts to break their vows of chastity. One, Brother Fernando Saperas, a Claretian from Cervera, Lérida, was exposed to all sorts of lewd provocations and then had even his manhood questioned in the worst Spanish *macho* tradition. He replied: "I am as much a man as you are. But I am a cleric, and my state does not allow me to do this. Kill me, if you want. But don't force me to sin. No, never that."[20] Even the prostitutes in Tárraga, whom the militias brought in for the purpose, balked at participating in such proceedings.

Clerics died merely because they refused to shout "Viva el comunismo!" instead of "Viva Cristo Rey!" Some of the militia involved in these dramas regretted that it forced their hands. Most probably did not know what Communism was well enough to give a reason why it should be opposed to Christianity. But it is one of the sad signs of the sinister tragedy being played out that these large-scale points of view were often a bone of ignorant contention while the life of an innocent man hung in the balance.

The relatively small Communist Party at the outset certainly sought the elimination of the Catholic Church. The Party's growing connections with the Soviets during the conflict indicated that, as in Soviet Russia, religion was perceived as a direct threat to ideological dominance of the country. In Madrid and the other large cities, the leftist political parties established *checas,* investigative committees deliberately set up in imitation of similar bodies in Russia, who pursued political enemies, including the religious. These groups were little more than armed mafias and even used a term they had learned from American films, "to take someone for a ride" (*dar un paseo*), to describe their form of justice.[21] Madrid's "dawn patrol" was infamous for its frequent, ruthless, early-morning visits to people chosen for elimination. Unfortunately, when the Republican government got control over the situation, many of the *checa* leaders found their way into the Republican police.[22]

Communist influence would also loom larger as the government relied more and more on the Soviets for war materiél and moral support. H. Edward Knoblaugh, an American journalist, observed that the influence was marked as early as late 1936, when the Nationalist government transferred its headquarters from Madrid to Valencia:

> The Russian influence was apparent everywhere in Valencia. Posters announcing Communist organization meetings were plastered on buildings and fences; oleos of Stalin, Lenin and Marx and bronze lapel-pins fashioned in the shape of a hammer and a sickle were on sale at every street corner; Marxist literature predominated at the book stalls; the only motion pictures were Russian propaganda films; sound trucks blared forth an unceasing stream of Communist propaganda in the plazas, and the Red flag vied with the anarchist black-and-red banners on public buildings. As in Madrid and Barcelona, streets had been renamed to conform to Marxist ideals. Directions were often difficult to find because the residents had not yet become accustomed to the new system of nomenclature. Saints' names, by which most streets in Spain are known, and names of former prominent political leaders were removed.

The new names included Via Rusia, Paseo de Lenín, Avenida de la Pasionaria...Plaza Rojo [i.e., "Red Square"], Avenida Thaelman, Avenida Libertarian and other names associated with the revolutionary theme.[23]

When George Orwell went to Barcelona at around the same time, he found a city that bore many of the same outward marks of Communist revolution.[24] Much scholarly debate, often obscured by ideological passion, has tried to determine how much Spain's Republicans were formally in the camp of the Soviet Union. The question is important, but perhaps this depiction of the social milieu gives a good idea of how close the two regimes at least seemed — or felt — at the time. Formal Communism, however, was only one of many factors in the anticlerical persecutions, which mostly came at the beginning of the conflict. The large anarchist movement was far more central. Despite opposition from some anarchists, the anarchist press, particularly *Solidaridad Obrera* ("Worker Solidarity") in Barcelona and elsewhere, called for anticlerical violence. The Trotskyist breakaway Marxist POUM Party did so as well.[25] Some historians have also pointed to virulently anti-Catholic masonic lodges in Spain as a source of the violence, but these were ambivalent, fearing that revolutionary violence would have bad results for their mostly middle-class membership and interests.

Another large portion of the anticlerical fury can best be described as the result of myth-making and propaganda. Some have seen the violence as a delayed response to the rigors of the Spanish Inquisition. But this seems clearly a literary rather than a historical explanation, since the Inquisition in any serious form was a long-past phenomenon. Nonetheless, it had a certain plausibility and provided a certain rationalization for those already inclined to murder. Republicans also believed that the clergy had secretly plotted with the generals who organized the Nationalist uprising. But there was never any real evidence for this at the time and the best recent scholarship indicates that it was highly improbable. The generals were quite careful about discussing their plans with anyone outside their immediate circle, and the idea that they shared them with the bishops or clergy has no historical basis. The Church's participation in the rising was, at most, minimal. But Republican propaganda did much to give the opposite impression.

The absurdity of some of these charges did not stop them from being believed. *Solidaridad Obrera* contended that priests were firing poison bullets on women and children, killing wounded in hospitals, and even eliminating children with poison bread, water, and candy.[26] Other press outlets claimed that priests were making hand grenades, groups of friars were attacking militiamen, and churches were being used as bases of operations. One probably typical article by a former education minister claimed in October 1936, as the worst of the atrocities were occurring: "The Government has confirmed that almost all churches had been converted into fortresses; that almost all the sacristies had been converted into arms depots, and most of the priests, curates, and seminarians into sharpshooters of the rebellion."[27] A moment's reflection might have raised doubts that priests and seminarians could have turned so quickly into sharpshooters, but reflection was in short supply. Churches did sometimes become the site of battles, but probably because rebels found their stony edifices a good place to put up resistance in chaotic towns and cities. One of the greatest historians of the Civil War states flatly, however, that, among the other propaganda misrepresentations: "Nearly all the stories of firing by rebels from church towers were also untrue."[28]

The truth is that these stories were concocted to justify murders and arrests carried out for other reasons. It was quite common for priests, nuns, lay Catholics, and other perceived "enemies" to be executed in retribution for some Nationalist military action. When the city of Irún fell to the Nationalists, for example, the Republicans retaliated by executing seventeen prisoners in Barcelona, six Claretians among them. In Madrid, twenty-three Adoratrices were taken to a cemetery and shot — on the odd charge that a Republican militiamen was killed on the street outside the apartment where they had fled after being driven from their convent. That same city witnessed the execution of twenty-four hundred prisoners, almost half of all those in custody, when it was feared that after the fall of Madrid they might identify their captors or become military opponents.

The campaign of destruction went hand-in-hand, from the outset, with a campaign of propaganda. For instance, the first bishop to be executed, Eustaquio Nieto Martín of Sigüenza, was portrayed in the most unflattering terms, often on manufactured charges, by the press. It was reported, and later embellished in various news accounts, that he had been apprehended with the diocesan strongbox containing 1,206,400 pesetas. The figure may be accurate, but it was hardly accurate to suggest that this sum represented wealth that the bishop had personally accumulated, as the stories implied. The propaganda was clearly intended to reinforce the notion that priests and bishops had exploited the people. But sober reflection might lead to the conclusion that a bishop running a large diocese with heavy expenses for churches, schools, hospitals, and other activities might need significant sums to carry out the very kinds of work among the population that the Republicans themselves thought necessary. The smear tactics even included rumors that the bishop had been taken "naked and in the act of abusing low women."[29] In fact, like many of his fellow priests and bishops, he was picked up at his residence, imprisoned, and soon thereafter shot.

Most of these priests and bishops could have tried to escape but showed a remarkable uniformity of action in deciding not to abandon their flocks. Even when they did, they often drew the line at any cowardly untruth. The bishop of Lérida, Salvio Huix, an Oratorian, refused a set of false identity papers, saying, "Oh no. I will always say that I am the bishop of Lérida." This was no small matter since, as he well knew, to admit as much to the militias meant death. In the event, that was just what befell him. After a brief period in prison, during which he heard confessions, celebrated Mass, and shared with the other inmates whatever food was sent him from the outside, he was killed in a cemetery with twenty-two other prisoners.

Several of the bishops saw their sacrifice as offered not only for the Church, but for Spain herself. Pedro Cruz Ocaña, the bishop of Cuenca, a man noteworthy for his widely attested simplicity of lifestyle and great energy, is reported to have said: "If it is necessary that I die for Spain, I will die happily." Earlier he had remarked at a suggestion that he flee: "I cannot leave out of fear of danger. My duty is to stay here, cost what it will."[30] At the same time, Cruz counseled his priests and others in the area to do what they had to in order to remain safe. As a bishop, though, he had a public role to fulfill. Others could prudently wait for a better time to return to their responsibilities. As his executioner later confessed, he fulfilled his duty: his mutilated and burned body ended up in a common ditch in the Cuenca cemetery.

Ironically, in several places, the government had arrested bishops, clergy, and others with the intention — often enough sincere — of "protecting" them from the passions of mobs. But whether by impotence or policy, the Republican government also allowed enormities unworthy of a civilized people. For instance, in a perverted and blasphemous parody, harkening back to the martyrdoms that occurred in the Colosseum during the early years of the Church, some priests were killed by animals in front of crowds. Antonio Díaz del Moral, from a small town near Madrid, was put in a bull ring where he was gored to death. Like the bulls killed in the Spanish *corrida,* he had his ear cut off after his death as a trophy. In some areas, priests' ears were cut off and handed around. According to other reports, monks had rosaries stuffed into their ears until their eardrums were pierced; people were compelled to swallow rosaries and crucifixes. In one instance a woman was made to do so solely because the she was the mother of two Jesuits. Bodies of priests and nuns were disinterred and mocked, often by putting them on display in front of churches with cigarettes in their mouths. Almost any imaginable profanation of persons and holy objects can be documented to have occurred somewhere.[31]

The religious destruction did more than eliminate people. It has been one of the long-held myths about the Spanish Civil War that the Republicans represented enlightenment and the Nationalists a murderous antihumanism. A Spanish democracy might have been a good idea after the departure of the last king. But the balance of the period shows no little antihumanist fury among Republicans, especially when it was linked to antireligious passions. Though the Republican government tried to safeguard artistic treasures, it did not always succeed against elements in its own coalition. There are many reports of people being required to bring their sacred books and objects to central bonfires. At an early phase in the conflict, several of the most prestigious Spanish names in the study of history, literature, philosophy, theology, Arabic, and other disciplines fell to "popular tribunals" composed of near illiterates solely because, in addition to being scholars, they were priests.[32] Often, their work in progress was destroyed along with them.

But it was not only people with private religious objects or scholars and scholarship that suffered. In Fuendetodos, Goya's birthplace, his earliest paintings, in the parish church, were destroyed. The library at the cathedral of Cuenca, which contained ten thousand volumes, was burnt along with a rare antique, the *Catecismo de Indias*.[33] In Ciudad Real, the bishop "was murdered while at work on a history of Toledo. After he was shot, his card index of 1,200 cards was destroyed."[34] The celebrated Spanish cellist Pablo Casals was put on a death list in Barcelona, but fortunately escaped execution; anarchists visited his home several times, however, looking for a rightist friend who had hidden there.[35]

Nor did the suspicion of the Republicans spare even those Catholics who generally agreed with their politics. In a notorious case, Father Pedro Gafo, a sociologist and Catholic labor leader, who has been described as "a highly significant figure in the Spanish labor movement and, furthermore, in the closest possible line within the Catholic camp to the large unions on the Left,"[36] met his end in a way embarrassing to the Republicans. Gafo was a Dominican priest who, between 1909 and 1919, had guided the formation of the Free Catholic Unions (Sindicatos Católicos Libres), which were introducing a type of democratic Catholic social thought common in the Vatican and the rest of Europe, but somewhat novel in Spain. Gafo and his colleague, Father Pedro Gerard, enjoyed a good reputation before the war among the very people who would later view them as enemies. His popularity among workers had gotten him elected to the Cortes as a deputy from Pamplona. When the war broke out, he was in Madrid. Within a short time, he was rounded up and sent to the Model Prison, where he was executed. This was so incredible to many people who knew the priest's sympathies that for a time they believed it was a trick of the government to keep him out of harm's way. But it was, unfortunately, true.[37]

To their credit, some Republican leaders rescued innocent people, including religious. Luis Companys y Jover, president of the Generalidad in Barcelona, helped protect the archbishop of Tarragona, Catalan Cardinal Francesc Vidal i Barraquer, from anarchist militiamen, and sent him into Italian exile. (Perhaps this generous gesture moved the cardinal to his somewhat unusual stance among the Spanish hierarchy of condemning the atrocities on both sides.)[38] The Catalan councillor of culture, Ventura Gassol, preserved the lives of the bishop of Gerona and many priests. Republican president Manuel Azaña y Díaz, though weak, as we have seen earlier, and disinclined, for political reasons, to protect church property, managed to rescue some of the Augustinian monks from his old school near El Escorial. Dolores Ibárruri, the famous female leader of the Republicans under the name La Pasionaria, saved nuns in Madrid from the Federación Anarquista Ibérica. And several others, including the socialist minister Juan Negrín, prime minister from 1937 to 1939, notorious for having sent Spain's entire gold reserve to the Soviet Union as finance minister in 1936, also acted honorably toward a few religious prisoners.[39] Despite the mixed records of almost everyone on both sides during the conflict, these acts or mercy and justice should not be overlooked.

The balance of this story, however, remains clear. Not one Western government supported the Republicans; Spanish anticlericalism paid no small part in that decision. Only the anticlerical government of Mexico, which we have already seen had committed and was continuing to commit massive atrocities of its own against its people, and the Soviet

Union, in much the same position, openly aided Republican Spain. Intellectual opinion, including some Catholic journals, at the time, however, ran much in the favor of self-described progressives of all kinds, and did not necessarily balk at alliances with Communists and other less than savory partners to pursue common goals. That view of the conflict became and remains quite common in intellectual circles.

Worried at how the conflict might appear outside Spain and in an attempt to clarify their own position, the Spanish bishops issued a joint pastoral letter on July 1, 1937, addressed to their fellow bishops throughout the world. Prior to the start of the conflict, there had been moderate bishops who sought to mediate between the two large camps and their several subsidiary formations. After the anticlerical fury, all supported the Nationalists, even those like Cardinal Vidal, who was one of two bishops who decided not to sign the joint letter. Vidal thought it more prudent to avoid reprisals by refraining from another public statement; he also believed that, in principle, the Church should remain absolutely nonpartisan.

But under the circumstances, and perhaps in any highly conflicted situation, it was impossible for the bishops not to take sides. Vidal himself had supported Catalan language and culture and regional autonomy when the issue arose earlier in the century. His stance was a proper one for a pastor concerned about his local flock. Yet as even his case illustrates, pastoral duties can never be entirely separated from public questions. It is an illusion of a certain kind of Enlightenment secularism that religion may be permitted privately, just so long as it has no public influence. In fact, real religion inevitably has a host of social implications. And the attempt to banish them from the public square is in effect to say that the state shall tell religious believers when their consciences can be engaged. But a religious conscience will often be engaged publicly, whether on "conservative" questions such as personal and social morality or on "liberal" questions of social justice.

It has sometimes been objected that the Spanish bishops' stance in the collective letter, while generally sound, betrays a certain simplistic reading of the conflict. Given the complexity of the situation, it is no doubt true that parts of the bishops' statement, nuanced as it is elsewhere by appreciation for men of good will and for the idealism that could be found on all sides, may appear simplistic. But it is no more so and a good deal less than the views of various intellectuals, some down to the present day, who see in the Nationalists and their episcopal supporters nothing but Fascist brutality and medieval obscurantism.

The letter responds in particular to the widespread charge that the clergy deserved their fate because they had blessed and even benefited from the economic exploitation of the people by the rich and powerful, held vast wealth for personal use, and were actively involved in the military effort in order to preserve their own privileges. In fact, as the letter tried to demonstrate, whatever the Church's position in the past, since the changes instituted during the nineteenth and early twentieth centuries, that was hardly the case. Ornate churches may have given the impression that the Church had vast holdings. It did not. In addition, the government salaries that had formerly been paid to clergy had stopped in the early 1930s, forcing no small number of priests to support themselves with menial jobs. The impression that the Church was not "doing enough" stemmed from the fact that, though endowments were largely used to help people, such endowments were not as large as most people assumed.

One special note in the letter is the need to forgive persecutors. Christians cannot regard even their persecutors as simply enemies to be defeated by any means. The bishops allowed that atrocities had been committed by the Nationalists and that not all Republicans endorsed the clerical bloodbath or other outrages committed on their side. The Spanish hierarchy sought a solution rooted in the Spanish tradition itself that would not be driven by "foreign models," a phrase that may hint at rejection, in the deepest understanding, of Marxism and Fascism alike.

The bishops clearly gave their support to the Nationalists, who had both protected the Church and allowed it some influence on education and culture. But it is necessary to be careful about what this endorsement did and did not imply. To begin with, it was not a blanket endorsement of Nationalists, Franco, "Fascism," Falangists, Carlists, or any other faction in the uprising. The Catholic social ethic, even in its somewhat anachronistic Spanish form, simply did not countenance brutality or summary action without due process of the law. The bishops have been criticized in hindsight for not remaining neutral and not being more pointed in criticizing Nationalist atrocities. Their collective letter, it is said, gave people the impression that they wholly supported every element among the Nationalists and harmed their reputation in the world.

Yet it is difficult to see how they could have done anything other than what they did. Some critics at the time, including Cardinal Vidal, feared that another wave of persecution would follow publication of the letter, and therefore opposed issuing it for that and other reasons.

Fortunately, another wave did not rise. Among progressive intellectuals, the letter certainly harmed the bishops' reputations. But most of those intellectuals already viewed Spanish Catholicism as effectively Fascist, with or without Franco. In the heat of the fray, with thousands of clergy dead in the first year of fighting and no alternative but the Nationalists, the bishops may be forgiven if their letter, intended to explain their case to the world, had the unintended effect of seeming to compromise them politically. The only other course would have been a weak neutrality that might very well have led, as it already had in the Soviet Union, to a regime that would have repressed Christianity and persecuted believers and nonbelievers for half a century. British historian Hugh Thomas, one of the most fair-minded analysts of the Spanish conflict, sums up its anti-Catholic dimension in harsh but just terms: "At no time in the history of Europe, or even perhaps of the world, has so passionate a hatred of religion and all its works been shown."[40]

# – S I X –

# THE NAZI JUGGERNAUT

**O**N NOVEMBER 9, 1942, Jakob Gapp crossed into southern France from Spain. He was traveling in a car with two friends who a few months earlier had asked him, a Marianist priest from Austria, to instruct them in the Catholic faith. In a complex covert operation, he was arrested by waiting guards of the pro-Nazi Vichy government in France at the Hendaye border post, interrogated briefly, and transferred to a prison in Berlin. The Gestapo debated briefly whether to put him through a process that would have sent him to Dachau, their camp of choice for arrested priests, but decided that he was a dangerous prisoner and had to be kept under "special protective custody." Later, a People's Court trial that lasted less than two hours sentenced him to death commenting: "He will forever be without honor."[1] The evening of August 13, 1943, thirteen years to the day that Gapp had begun his novitiate with the Marianists, he wrote his last letter to the superior of the order recalling the date and concluding, "Today I hope to begin the life of eternal happiness." Then, he went calmly to the execution shed of the Plötzensee prison and was beheaded, earning, not Nazi honor, but eternal honor.

The whole operation was eloquent testimony to the relentless surveillance and pursuit of troublesome Catholics by the Nazi regime. Unlike many priests, nuns, and lay people who succumbed to Nazi persecution on German soil, Father Gapp had reluctantly taken the advice of friends and gone into voluntary exile. After a particularly anti-Nazi sermon in the parish church at Wattens, Austria, he had managed to escape across Italy to the Church of La Madeleine, in Bordeaux, where William Joseph Chaminade had founded the Marianist order in the early nineteenth century. Even there his activities were monitored. Before long, his order reassigned him to Spain, where the German hand could not as easily reach. But it stretched to get him all the same.

Ironically, the Nazis used a Jewish ploy to apprehend Gapp. The two "friends" with whom he traveled to his arrest and martyrdom were, in fact, German agents pretending to be German Jews interested in converting. In the official minutes of his interrogation, Gapp openly admitted that one of the first things that got him into trouble after the 1938 Nazi annexation (*Anschluss*) of Austria had been his public statements opposing government encouragement of hatred and murder of Czechs and Jews as contrary to the "Christian-Catholic position."[2] One of Gapp's students remembered him as teaching that, even more broadly, the law of Christ demanded that "one must selflessly assist anyone, even one's ideological opponent, if he is in existential trouble or difficulty."[3] Father Gapp practiced what he preached. In addition to standing up for despised groups, he deprived himself of necessities like fuel for heating in winter in order to help the poor. Gapp knew that people who approached him for moral advice or formal instruction in the faith at several points might be Nazi agents, but decided early on that his status as a priest demanded he tell the truth whatever the consequences. He was beatified in 1995.

Most people today associate the rise of Nazi Germany with the attempted genocide against the Jews, who certainly died in droves for both religious and political reasons. A few celebrated Protestant figures such as Martin Niemöller and Dietrich Bonhoeffer are credited with authentic Christian witness against the Nazis to the point of martyrdom. But this standard account overlooks the many Protestants and Catholics martyred for expressing Christian views that challenged the Third Reich. Among German Catholic priests alone, the record is quite remarkable. In 1932, just prior to the Nazi rise to power, there were about twenty-one thousand Catholic priests in Germany.[4] Of these, more than a third (over eight thousand) clashed with the Reich,[5] and several hundred have been documented as having perished at Nazi hands.[6] No doubt many others, who will forever remain unknown, were eliminated as well.

Hitler and his minions were careful not to attack Catholics or Protestants in Germany as such. Indeed, it was one of their subtle and successful propaganda ploys to represent themselves as not concerned about religion or, at most, as representatives of a purer, Aryan, "positive" Christianity. But there is no question that their ultimate aims toward Christians were, if not physical genocide, then spiritual genocide and the total extinction of the traditional faiths through ever-expanding restrictions and terror. Shortly after taking power, Hitler explained to some of his closest collaborators in the Reich Chancellery that, like Mussolini, he would make a formal peace with the churches:

> Why not? That will not prevent me from totally uprooting Christianity in Germany and eliminating it lock, stock, and barrel. It

is, however, decisive for our people whether they have the Judeo-Christian faith and its flabby morality of sympathy, or a strong, heroic faith in god in nature, in god in one's own people, in god in one's own fate, in one's own blood.... One is either a Christian or a German. One can't be both.[7]

Instead of direct attack, Hitler planned — and carried out — a program of pretending that the Christians he arrested and executed were not being eliminated because of their religion, but because of illegal political activities or crimes. In private, however, he made it clear that he adopted this ruse only because he understood the power of an institution that had survived many regimes over two millennia. But he also expressed his intention to "crush [the Catholic Church] like a toad." Falsely believing that even the Catholics themselves would see that fighting Nazi power was useless, he expected that they would not risk a direct struggle. He had prepared a shrewd strategy in the unlikely event that Christians tried to challenge him: "If they do ... I'm certainly not going to make martyrs out of them. I'll stamp them as stupid criminals."[8] That is exactly what he did, thoroughly and ruthlessly, to the many Christian opponents in Germany.

Nazi persecution of Catholic clergy and resisters both inside and outside Germany was intense. Bedřich Hoffmann, a Czech priest who spent the years from 1940 to 1945 in Buchenwald and Dachau, vowed, while still in the camps, that he would document the extent of the persecution. At great risk to his own life, he interviewed prisoners, slipped into offices where official files were kept, and made brief notes. Even his necessarily incomplete survey indicates that Dachau alone — which was for some unknown reason the Gestapo's favorite camp for clergy, though priests were imprisoned in all the Reich's concentration camps — held, at one point or another, 2,670 priests from Albania, Belgium, Croatia, Czechoslovakia, Denmark, England, France, Germany, Greece, Holland, Italy, Luxembourg, Norway, Poland, Serbia, Slovenia, Spain, Switzerland, Yugoslavia, and other countries. Of these, almost 600 died in the camp; another 325 died during so-called "transport of invalids" to other sites, a euphemism for secret execution.[9] Two bishops — Michael Kozal of Poland (who was brutally tortured after being arrested merely as a potential anti-Nazi leader in his native Poland and has since been beatified for his saintly life) and Gabriel Piguet of Clermont-Ferrand in France (apprehended for having sent priests to hear the confessions of Resistance fighters) — also perished in Dachau.

Hoffmann's figures, as high as they are, are doubtless far lower than the actuality. By careful study of the numbers assigned to prisoners when they were arrested, he has been able to document that hundreds of priests designated for transport from Poland to Dachau in about a dozen large groups disappeared in transit or in unrecorded deaths at the camp. What this meant concretely can be glimpsed in the description of one such group: "The sixth shipment, one of the largest, came on October 31, 1941, from the Polish prisons at Konstaninow and Posen. The numbers were 28,026 — Stanislaw Owczarek — to 28,509 — Waclaw Frczionka. From this contingent there remained at the time of liberation only 130 (out of 483). The rest had been liquidated by a violent death."[10] Hitler's intention of exterminating the Polish "race" began with rounding up intellectuals and leaders, which included the priests. The Poles were the largest group at Dachau, numbering 1780 clergy. We can only speculate about the numbers who never arrived from Poland and other Nazi-occupied nations. Only careful historical reconstruction of the fate of these individuals by scholars in several nations may some day give us a sense of the true enormity of the crimes committed against them.

The Nazis gave various reasons for imprisoning these clergymen: stirring up the masses, spying, aiding prisoners, suspicion of treason, behavior unfriendly to Germany, support of Jews, insulting the Führer or National Socialism, or sometimes no reason at all. One was sentenced for telling schoolchildren "Love your enemies."[11] Twelve were rounded up after reading the "Lion of Münster," Bishop Clemens August von Galen's condemnation of euthanasia from the pulpit.[12] Father Otto Neururer arrived in Dachau "for hindering an Aryan marriage." He had opposed a young girl's marriage to a sixty-year-old with a bad reputation and died at Buchenwald for agreeing to instruct a fellow prisoner (really a spy) in the faith. According to some fellow prisoners, he had been crucified upside down for thirty-six hours.[13]

Father Karl Lampert, the pro-vicar of Innsbruck, was picked up and shipped to Dachau for "inciting the people" — by the mere fact of announcing Neururer's death, which the Nazis themselves had informed him about, without the gruesome details. He was released after a year, but rearrested on trumped-up charges. The president of the court that heard his case shot himself in the head rather than be an accomplice in the trial. Put into isolation, Lampert was interrogated brutally. At one point, his tormentors asked him which was more valuable, Hitler's *Mein Kampf* or the Bible? He said boldly: "*Mein Kampf* is the word of man and preaches the doctrine of hate; the Bible is the Word of God and preaches love."[14] A few of his letters expressing gratitude came to his comrades from Dachau. After that, Lampert was never heard from again.

As in most persecutions, the blow fell hardest, almost exclusively, on men. But there were great heroic female figures in this period as well. Though the Nazis did not execute many women, they regarded the Catholic nuns, who had played a central role in education in Germany and Austria as well as the countries occupied by the German army, as a prime source of resistance. Since Nazi strategy aimed at capturing the next generation by removing young people from Christian formation in their early lives, National Socialists moved quickly and effectively to suppress religious schools and disperse women's religious orders. Though forced to comply, the nuns were not submissive. An anecdote from one memoir from the period conveys the general attitude. After the *Anschluss,* an SS officer chided a nun that within ten years "you will be honoring Adolf Hitler on those altars where you now adore Christ." Unafraid, the sister replied: "If Hitler is prepared to die on the cross for his people and then rise from the dead on the third day, I'll change my habit for a Nazi uniform — but not before."[15]

The Nazis did not always take such sharp retorts kindly. A nursing nun, Sister Maria Restituta, was arrested as she left an operating room in Vienna for what the Gestapo called "dangerous language" — a common charge. A doctor had betrayed her to the authorities. During eight months in prison for mere expression of opposition to Nazism, she remained openly faithful to her political and religious beliefs: "I lived for Christ and I'll die for Christ." In the event, that is what the Nazis demanded of her. Sister Maria's name before entering the religious life had been Helene Kafka. But even the great writer with the same last name had never imagined anything more horribly absurd than her arrest, trial, and sentence, after which she was taken out and summarily shot.[16]

Another heroic woman religious came by a simple path to martyrdom at Auschwitz. Maria Cäcilia Autsch was born in German Westphalia to a modest working-class family who regularly practiced the faith. Though she was a very good and diligent student, the terrible economic conditions following World War I made it necessary for her to go to work at an early age. She took a position with a clothing company, where she was beloved by her fellow workers and customers alike. In the 1930s, after her mother's death and after helping other siblings to make ends meet, she decided to become a Third Order nun of the Trinitarian order in the Austrian Tyrol. As in her previous life, she proved herself to be remarkably modest and industrious. She undertook the running of a

Kindergarten, did embroidery, and helped out the priests and the local farmers with their fieldwork. As her vocation developed and she took perpetual vows in her order, National Socialism came to Austria.

After taking the name Sister Angela, she was made house stewardess. In that capacity, she wrote to the Spanish consulate, reminding them that the property of the order, which had been confiscated by the Nazis, actually belonged to the motherhouse in Valencia, Spain, which had founded the Austrian branch only in 1926. The Gestapo opened a detailed file on all her activities. The last straw came when, at a dairy in the town of Mötz, she remarked: "Hitler is a scourge for all Europe."[17] She was torn out of the convent and thrown into a police car on August 12, 1940. Her cellmate and fellow sisters describe her as showing a noble and brave soul throughout the ignoble treatment that ensued. She was sent to the women's camp at Ravensbrück.

Sister Angela was no pious milktoast. She told a fellow prisoner: "Maria, stop your ears. Don't let yourself be overcome. Think about a brighter day and hold on to what is better." The nun was often beaten for her resistance in prison. Yet she had a contagious good humor that often brought smiles to the other prisoners. One called her a "ray of sunshine in darkest Hell." This phrase, which might seem a mere truism, had concrete results. Some prisoners would have killed themselves, they said, without the relief she provided. Just to be near her, even in the terrible conditions of the prison, made you feel born again. Some who had no idea she was a nun felt uplifted by her help.

On her forty-second birthday, Sister Angela arrived at Auschwitz in the first transport of women prisoners. A Jewish doctor from Slovakia, Margarita Schwalbova, preserved a touching memory from her arrival. Dressed in a dirty old Russian uniform and wooden shoes, with close-cropped hair and feeling less than human that day, the doctor was touched deeply when Sister Angela came up to her and gently stroked her head. They became friends and amid the starvation, torments, and nightmares of the camp, Angela behaved in a way that later earned her the title "angel of Auschwitz." When Schwalbova was sick, Sister Angela took the doctor's hand in the evening and told her about the lives, deaths, and miracles of Thérèse of Lisieux and other saints, even though the doctor was an atheist. These were wonderful times and the doctor felt like a child listening to fairy tales from her mother. Sister Angela shared everything, including scarce rations, with all, even though it was strictly forbidden. In March 1943 she was transferred to Birkenau, where she worked in the kitchen and infirmary. There she cared equally for victims and their persecutors. She died taking care of patients during an air raid on December 23, 1944, and her body was burned in a crematorium only a month before the camp was liberated.[18]

The real "crime" of all these figures, trumped-up charges notwithstanding, was being Christian, which, in Nazi ideology, pitted them against the faith of the Reich, whether an individual did anything illegal under Nazi interpretations of law or not. During one interrogation, a Gestapo agent, losing his temper, characterized priests as "worse enemies than the Jews and Communists."[19]

Like other hated groups, the Catholic priests in the camps were treated brutally. Some died from exposure to sub-zero temperatures, others from overwork, starvation, or illness, still others as the result of medical experiments. (The infamous Dr. Klaus Schilling, who even after the Americans occupied Dachau could not believe he had been wrong in carrying out work for the Nazi Party, had made a point of using Polish priests as human guinea pigs in his "malaria station.") Flogging was a regular form of punishment as were sentences to isolation, naked, in concrete bunkers. Austrian priest John M. Lenz wrote an account of his own six-and-a half years at Dachau that provides chilling testimony to the experience of many lay and clerical prisoners who were not so fortunate as to survive. In the odd way of National Socialist ideology, at times the clerics got slightly better treatment as distinguished detainees and, at others, far worse treatment as particularly dangerous foes. Father Lenz learned this even before he arrived at Dachau. While he was still being dealt with in a Viennese prison, he and another priest were assigned to a section for the worst malefactors: "We had all sorts of criminals as neighbors — murderers, thieves, and firebrands, what the Nazis were fond of describing as the 'scum of society' — and we knew that in their eyes we priests ranked no higher."[20]

The notion that these men were scum is contradicted not only by their often heroic witness, but by their achievements in the world during peacetime. Among the "scum" who perished at Dachau were Agnello von der Bosch, a Franciscan who had founded the Belgian association for the blind; Titus Brandsma, a Dutch Carmelite priest and a journalist, whose fearless criticism of Nazism in his occupied homeland led to martyrdom in the camp; Father Viktor Dillard, a Jesuit and French professor of sociology; Josef Regout, a Dutch Jesuit and professor of international law; and Dom Ernst Vykoukal, a Czech who was abbot of the Emmaus community in Prague. The list of distinguished scholars, musicians, journalists, poets, art experts, and writers — to say nothing of the accomplished theologians, liturgists, and administrators — among the clerics at Dachau would be very long indeed. And these "intellectuals" to a man were happy to lend a hand in nursing the sick (even when typhus put volunteers in danger of death themselves), distributing what food and help they could find, performing menial tasks, and witnessing to the truth that brutality and hatred were not all-powerful, even in Dachau. Moreover, in the whole history of the camp, only one priest ever apostatized and betrayed his previous life. They were scum only insofar as their vocations were irreconcilable with the Nazi drive for total cultural mastery.

Like many of his fellow priests in Germany and other countries under Nazi sway, Father Lenz was arrested after an ordinary parishioner reported his off-the-cuff criticisms of Nazi ideology to the Gestapo. His behavior had not been illegal, but technically, like Jakob Gapp, he was a potential threat who had to be placed under "special protective custody." "Priest" and "dog" seemed to be equivalent terms for the guards who transported him to the camps. Priests were harassed at every stage of the process until they finally marched under gates with the inscription *Arbeit macht frei!* ("Work creates freedom"). After being stripped and shaven, they received their prison uniforms in a process that was meant to dehumanize the thousands who arrived: "It was some time before we could bring ourselves to raise our eyes and look at one another."[21] Quite a few prisoners were executed during transport.

Though Lenz makes clear that Dachau was not the harshest type of concentration camp — it was only a labor camp, not an extermination camp — his account is hair-raising. Rows of concrete "isolation bunkers" were immediately evident, a warning to any who resisted the camp regime. An electrified fence and moat surrounded the compound, and machine gun towers reinforced the threat to any who attempted to escape (despairing prisoners committed suicide by throwing themselves on the electrified fences): "The exit? For many thousands, if not tens of thousands, the 'chimney' — the crematorium — was the way out."[22] In addition, priests were automatically assigned to the "punishment squad," which also included prominent lay Catholics, Jews, gypsies, and members of Bible sects.

The punishment squad's commander was both an atheist and sadist. Even worse, however, were the "Capos," collaborating prisoners who did the dirty work for the commandant in return for favors. One of them came up to Lenz and informed him: "I'm your Capo. I may as well tell you from the start that I was human once, but I've been turned into a brute by all I've seen here. Who knows, I might turn human again if you work properly for me! And now get on with it, don't waste any more time."[23] A sub-Capo recognized Lenz as a priest from Austria and started a game with him:

> He filled an enormous wheelbarrow with gravel for me to carry across to the dump. I was totally unfit for heavy work like this. I wondered how it was to end. Very soon great blisters began to appear on the palms of my hands, but the man still drove me on, kicking me viciously from behind all the time. He forced me to run up the gravel hill with a full load and would then push me over the side at the steepest point so that I fell and rolled down some eighteen feet together with my load of gravel. This he did several times, running after me like an evil spirit in pursuit of his victim.[24]

Capos like this one drove many to death. (A few — a very few — struck in conscience, remarks Lenz, used their positions to help fellow prisoners by various subterfuges.) Father Lenz escaped being shot as a priest-saboteur the next day, only his second in the camp, when the SS officer who had taken out a revolver was distracted by another prisoner's escape attempt.

But another threat emerged that same day. "Jews and priests" were ordered to fall out of their columns: "Invariably we were coupled together, for in the eyes of the camp authorities we were the scum, the outcasts."[25] A thousand of them were put into a special block to prepare for transport to the hard-labor camp at Mauthausen. As Lenz learned later, the previous year 1,650 of the "scum" had been sent there and within a few months 950 were dead. Lenz made his confession to another priest to prepare for death. In August 1940, he and about a thousand others were shipped to Mauthausen in "a train, like cattle, intended for the slaughterhouse."[26] The torments of those he left behind at Dachau, and who survived, ended only with the arrival of the U.S. Army on Sunday, April 29, 1945.

The difference between a mere labor camp and a true hard-labor camp immediately became apparent. Prisoners were regularly worked to death. Trucks brought back the dead and dying every evening from the work areas. The bodies were disposed of unceremoniously, dead and dying alike tipped out into heaps inside the camp gates. Sick prisoners received no mercy. One old Polish priest, whose name has not been preserved, suffered from diarrhea and had collapsed. He was severely beaten for refusing to get up, and then ordered to stand in the hot sun for four hours. He collapsed again and died. Father Marcell Leeb, an old priest from the Austrian region of Carinthia, suffered a similar fate. The Poles, whose main story will be told in the next chapter, were especially singled out. During a "Polish massacre," when Capos were given special orders to eliminate Polish priests and intellectuals, over sixty perished. At one point, Lenz himself, after a bout of sickness that left him unable to complete his assigned tasks, was slated to be "disposed of" during a work detail.

Providentially, the believers at Mauthausen found quiet corners to pray. Father Lenz believes that "there can scarcely have been another concentration camp where so many of the prisoners prayed — and a great many of them were not priests either. Work, life, death — everything was accompanied by prayer, everything was consecrated by prayer. For all its horror, the 'death mill' of Gusen was a true community of prayer."[27] Groups gathered to listen to the Gospel on Sundays, when no masses were allowed. People who had been lax in their religious practice sought confession. Heroic solidarity emerged. Strangely, prisoners woke up to the beauty of nature in brief, startling moments. Lenz reports one of his own experiences of nature: "I well remember those still frosty November evenings, the dark sky sprinkled with stars. They shone down on us in our prison camp, a steadfast consolation. The stars, like the sun and God's fresh air, were things no one could take away from us. Timeless, ageless, unchanging, the stars proclaim how short this earthly life of ours is — and how soon our misery in this world is over."[28] By one of the paradoxes of the spiritual life, many prisoners — not only in Gusen, but all over the world in this century of blood — found a real humanity and divinity and joy for the first time facing the ultimate questions in extreme circumstances.

At every point in telling his story, Lenz remarks on the way he and others found Christ concretely in their own suffering: "I had penance enough to do anyway for my sins. God knew why He had sent me to this school, the hardest and most valuable of my life. Only when we are forced to endure the most profound suffering and hardship do we learn how to catch hold of God's hand in our misery — we learn to pray."[29] According to his experience, many died peacefully in the camps as a result.[30] Indeed, this remarkable man, who wrote his memoir only under orders from superiors, observes:

What we priests were forced to endure under the Nazi regime, especially in Dachau concentration camp, is no more than a cup filled from the vast sea of human suffering in the world today. It is not this suffering as such which is important. The important thing is to show those who have crosses of their own to bear in life just what the grace of God can do for those who follow faithfully in the footsteps of Christ the Crucified.[31]

He even confronted the ultimate question: "People have often asked me how God could permit such injustice.... One glance at the cross of Our Lord the Redeemer surely provides us all with the only true answer."[32] In most instances, this would be a stock response. Coming from a man who repeatedly found himself on the brink of death, this is heroic witness indeed.

Lenz's tale joins here with that of another priest imprisoned at Mauthausen. One of the most heartrending stories from this period involves the Carmelite priest Père Jacques (Lucien-Louis Bunel), whose heroism in protecting Jewish children in his church school in France was made famous in the film *Au Revoir les Enfants*. The film's director, Louis Malle, was one of Père Jacques's students at the Petit-Collège near Fontainebleau, and he based the story on some of his warm memories of the heroic priest. The film did not portray, however, Père Jacques's other activities as a Resistance figure, a man who harbored refugees and an organizer of a network of people looking to escape the Nazi forced labor (*Service du Travail Obligatoire*) and join the military resistance to the Germans, all of which lay outside Malle's personal experience.

Père Jacques was only one of a number of Catholic clergy and lay people in this work. His Carmelite provincial, Father Phillipe, collaborated with him and others at every step, even joining the board of the National Front for the resistance when it was clear that the risks were too great for the Petit-Collège if Père Jacques joined the resistance board. Père Jacques did join the regular resistance network, Vélite Thermopyles, as number R. X. 3289.[33] Other Catholics, too, were active in the French Resistance even before de Gaulle set up the Free French. The French Communists joined the struggle only later, after obeying party orders and refraining from attacking Germany, then an ally of the Soviets, until the Molotov-Ribbentrop Pact broke down with the 1941 Nazi invasion of Russia.

The Catholic opposition in Père Jacques's circle also included the Sisters of Notre Dame de Sion, especially the superior, a mother Maria, who was involved in finding Catholic families to harbor Jewish and other refugees. Père Jacques's novice master when he joined the Carmelites, Father Louis, was an admiral with de Gaulle's Free French. Père Jacques's confidence in those he was connected with extended to his students. When the three Jewish boys came to the Petit-Collège, Père Jacques took into his confidence the oldest three classes of students and told them to treat the clandestine students with special kindness. Not one student, despite their age and immaturity, betrayed the secret.

Père Jacques also prepared his charges in other ways for their responsibilities in Nazi-occupied France. He believed in gentleness in education, but also in preparation. "Culture and Will" became the school motto. Père Jacques instilled culture in his students with stimulating lectures and frequent outings reflecting his own love of French theater, music, and poetry. On the will side, he made sure all the boys got physical training and instructed them in the need for self-mastery. His older students were taken on nighttime maneuvers in the forest of Fontainebleau to prepare them for the hardships they might face later. Père Jacques's resistance was not merely abstract.

Indeed, this tender-hearted schoolmaster gave the lie to the Nazi claim that Christianity, by absorbing Jewish notions of humility and abasement before God, contradicted the heroism and courage of Aryan ideology. In the late 1930s, even as he was establishing the new Carmelite school in which his fate was to be sealed, he was called up for military service to defend France. Père Jacques did not object; he was humiliated by the Munich Accords, which allowed the Nazis to take over Czechoslovakia, and speculated, "How many [French citizens] no longer appreciate that death is preferable to dishonor."[34] This statement was for him a living creed that he argued was needed to live an authentically human life. Though he was not a chaplain but a mess officer in the French Army, he organized meetings, two a week: one on social issues, the other on religious questions. These impressed his fellow soldiers so much, believers and not, that when he volunteered for service in a French force to be sent to help the Finns stop an invasion by the Soviets, 105 members of his Twenty-First Artillery Brigade petitioned that he not be transferred.[35] There was something tough in this gentle Carmelite that impressed even soldiers in the field.

When the Maginot Line collapsed in 1940 and French freedom with it, Père Jacques spent five months in a prisoner-of-war camp, Stalag 152 in Lunéville. During that time, he occupied himself with his prayers, but also with another love: French literature. Even here, his courage was palpable. He slipped out of the camp in a truck one night, at great personal risk, to perform a wedding for a soldier who could not have a religious service in any other way. The Germans eventually allowed him to return to his school, but, as he would write to the alumni at Pentecost of 1942: "I am ashamed to belong to a generation that lost the war. I would have loved to belong to a generation that had left an example of self-sacrifice, even to laying down its life."[36] A chance for that came soon.

The film *Au Revoir les Enfants* ends with the priest and three of his Jewish students being taken away, but the story of Père Jacques's heroism was only beginning at that point. For all the risks he had willingly run, no word leaked out to the authorities until a former student, whom Père Jacques had helped to join the Resistance, gave them information under torture. Ironically, Père Jacques may have been the most tender-hearted of the victims of Nazism. A natural preacher and teacher, he had a knack for being compassionate and firm in the same breath. Born into a working-class family on the brink of poverty, he fought his way to academic and spiritual eminence, yet impressed everyone with his gentleness. Gentleness played a great role in his approach to formal education and the broader evangelization of a France losing its workers to Communism and Socialism. He says in his writings on education that "true gentleness is neither weakness, nor softness and timidity." Most descriptions of gentleness present a counterfeit. For him, though, gentleness was a "tranquil force."[37] That way of seeing gentleness as a firm element of character, which Père Jacques had clearly internalized, served him well in many different circumstances.

Not only was he kind, compassionate, and focused on the good of others while he was still at liberty, he probably became even more so under the difficult conditions of confinement. In his first prison at Fontainebleau, he was subjected to rigorous interrogation. Wilhelm Korff, the SS prison Kommandant, unable to break him, asked what he thought of the laws of the Reich. Père Jacques replied: "I do not know them; I know only one law, that of the Gospel and of charity." Korff was a hard man, later convicted of war crimes, but even he was impressed by the courage and dedication of Père Jacques: "He has only one defect; he is not a Nazi."[38]

After his arrest, Père Jacques discovered what might almost be called another vocation. When a fellow priest turned up one day with a large amount of cash concealed in his clothes in the hope of obtaining Père Jacques's release by a bribe, the latter gently refused the offer. He felt he could not go free while his fellow prisoners remained, adding, "There must be priests in the prisons." And there were. At the Compiègne prison, to which he was transferred, seven priests were among the twenty-five hundred French prisoners. At that point, they were still allowed to say Mass and had even been offered separate quarters from the other inmates. Characteristically, Père Jacques refused special treatment, explaining that "my place is with my comrades."[39] As happened with many religious in the camps, he radiated a contemplative serenity that comforted many, even nonbelievers.

He accepted the camp regime, but, at the same time, was not subservient to rules that impinged on religion. At Compiègne, he was required to submit the texts of his sermons for censorship. He did so regularly — but then gave completely different homilies from memory. That one act of dissent had serious repercussions. An SS officer marched up to him during one such performance and brought it to a halt. In retaliation, the camp officials transferred him to a notorious "death camp" at Neue Bremm in Germany. Père Jacques took this as an opportunity because, he said, "there were the men most in need of help." It was only too true. Of the fifty-one prisoners sent in Père Jacques's group, only seven were alive three weeks later.[40] Those who died quickly may have been the lucky ones. At Neue Bremm, sick prisoners were thrown into swamps to die, healthy ones were sometimes caged with savage dogs while crowds gathered. It was a spectacle of Christian persecution the likes of which had probably not been seen in Europe since the early martyrs were torn by wild beasts in the Roman Colosseum.

"Sexual deviants" were deliberately assigned to certain barracks, including that of Père Jacques, to harass prisoners. He was personally made to lead mock religious processions around the camp for hours. At one point, in mockery of the Crucifixion, the guards made him carry a large wooden beam around.[41] Disease was rampant in the camp. Père Jacques volunteered for the infirmary, which the camp administration thought might quickly put an end to him. Instead, he turned the poor facility into an oasis of gentleness, going so far as to give half of his own rations to the sick he believed needed them more. Perhaps because his behavior set the wrong kind of example in an atmosphere intended to degrade and humiliate, he was sent to yet another camp, the not very well known but vast complex at Mauthausen in Austria.

Dachau and Auschwitz are names famous as places of death. But Mauthausen accounted for around two hundred thousand victims during the war years. The air around the camp reeked with the smoke from the crematoriums. It was a labor camp, but the officials hardly cared for those who were shipped there to work. They knew there was an endless supply of replacements for those who perished and so did not much concern themselves about working prisoners to death. New prisoners were stripped naked, and their heads were shaved. Guards and prisoner-collaborators took turns sadistically torturing them. The camp administration made a game of pitting prisoners from various ethnic groups against one another and encouraging brutality and extortion among prisoners. Père Jacques's familiarity with the Carmelite tradition must have helped in physical conditions that embodied a kind of Dark Night of the Soul.

In those truly infernal conditions, a miracle of a sort occurred. According to Henri Boussel, a fellow prisoner who survived the ordeal, Père Jacques decided to accept his fate, but prayed to a fellow Carmelite, Saint Thérèse — no stranger to profound suffering herself: "I give you full liberty as to the manner I shall be received, but I dearly wish to have a sign that you receive me in this camp, a sign of your protection over me." The same evening, Boussel came looking for him. As a student of the Christian Brothers he was curious about the priest he had heard arrived, and there were few French among the many Polish prisoners in Mauthausen. They would share camp life until Père Jacques's death.[42]

They did backbreaking work in the stone quarry at Gusen I, one of the satellite camps. It was 1944, and the Allies seemed poised for a victory. Surviving the work in a weakened state until liberation, however, was their main occupation. A remarkable Austrian priest, Father Johann Gruber, had organized a little underground network by which fellow prisoners were able to get extra food and medicines for all sorts of ailments. Gruber was an energetic, nearly tireless, presence, helping others and teaching them, contrary to the overall ethos of the camp, to aid one another. A fellow prisoner recalled that he seemed to be everywhere trying to counteract various ills. He was occasionally beaten for his work, but never became discouraged in spirit or less intense in action. Father Gruber had even managed to send information to the outside world about what was going on in the camp. Unfortunately, owing to carelessness by an outside contact, the Gestapo discovered the operation. The camp commandant had him stripped naked and enclosed in a concrete isolation chamber for days. Beatings and dowsings with cold water followed, as the guards tried to make Gruber commit suicide. Breaking his spirit would have been a greater triumph in the context of the camp than mere execution. But Gruber resisted until his tormentors grew impatient. His family was told that he committed suicide.[43] But witnesses confirm that he was martyred, strangled at three in the afternoon on Good Friday, 1944, by Nazi guards, the perfect moment for such a heroic priest to go to his reward.[44]

Père Jacques, weak as he was, had to try to take Gruber's place as the spiritual leader of the group. It was a natural role for him even in such conditions, and he was a worthy successor to Gruber. He survived, and helped many comrades to survive as well, until the American Army liberated the camp in 1945, but just barely. The Nazi guards had plans to gas all twenty thousand survivors before the Allies arrived, but were caught unawares when a column of U.S. tanks showed up suddenly. They surrendered thinking the main force had already pushed through. In fact it was only an advance group. As often happens in war, a sudden miscalculation can mean lives — in this case, lives providentially saved from one last crime to cover countless others. Père Jacques led his men to a waiting area and then watched helpless as many of them, crazy with hunger after months and years of camp life, ate themselves to death. Though he himself weighed only seventy-five pounds at liberation, he controlled himself and survived. But it almost seems as if his will not to yield to the unjust oppressors came to its natural end at that point. Within a few days he caught pneumonia and died a free man on June 2, 1945.

The three Jewish boys he had tried to protect and Lucien Weil, a Jewish math professor he had taken in at the Petit-Collège, had not been so lucky. They were sent from the school to Auschwitz, where they died immediately.

Stories like all those recounted above were, of course, well-known to the Catholic hierarchy in Germany and in the Vatican, despite misinformation and difficulties of communication. The churches — Catholic and Protestant — had taken a cautious approach to National Socialism at the outset. Some religious leaders, including Catholic bishops and the heroic Protestant pastor Martin Niemöller, had even welcomed the movement early on as a remedy for the chaos and humiliation Germany had suffered after World War I and the disastrous policies imposed by the victors on their conquered homeland with the Versailles Treaty.[45] But they were quickly disillusioned. Despite attempts at working out a *modus vivendi* between the various Christian denominations and the regime, the Nazis would tolerate no Christian group that was not subservient to Nazi ideology. Hundreds of Protestant pastors, Catholic priests, and lay people of both denominations felt their wrath.

From the outset, it was clear to anyone who looked carefully at its theories that Nazism was utterly incompatible with the Catholic Church, or Christianity of any kind — at least as it has existed historically. But as is often the case in history, what, in retrospect, seems clear was not immediately apparent to everyone at the time, including some quite sophisticated and dedicated Christians. Despite the protests of Hitler that neither Catholicism nor Protestantism, which each had deep roots in German culture, were of any concern to National Socialism, in fact the whole thrust of Nazism was to undercut and eventually replace the traditional faith with something quite new. Typical of the subtle Nazi attempt to coopt while subverting was Hitler's public claim in 1934 that "National Socialism is neither anti-ecclesiastical nor anti-religious; on the contrary, it rests upon the basis of a real Christianity."[46] His private views, as we have seen, were something quite different and quite hostile, and, from his standpoint, quite rational.

Hitler's "real Christianity" was what the National Socialists often referred to as "positive Christianity" as opposed to the "negative Christianity" of the historic churches. In this view, Christianity had been distorted throughout its whole history by the "political Jew," Saint Paul, into a religion of submission, humility, mercy, asceticism, and slavery. Jesus himself, who in the labyrinthine reasoning of Nazism, was not of Jewish descent, did not teach the religion which Paul later grafted on to the Christian churches. Instead, Jesus taught liberation and, according to Alfred Rosenberg, the religious ideologist of the movement, the free assertion of the racially pure Aryan soul. All historical creeds and evidence of the Bible to the contrary, real, positive Christianity asserted that "the German People is the subject, not of original sin, but of original nobility."[47] This heritage authorized them to move mercilessly against all who opposed their divine spirit, especially the lesser races whom God had intended to be ruled by the pure Aryans.

Even at the time, the historical basis for these contentions was clearly nonsense. Both Catholic and Protestant scholars demolished the outrageous claims Rosenberg put forward in his *Myth of the Twentieth Century,* starting with its absurd premise that Jesus was not a Jew.[48] But like much in Nazism, positive Christianity was not addressed to the understanding of its audience, but to its will. Exploiting the resentments Germans felt between the two world wars over the harsh Versailles Treaty that had crippled post–World War I Germany and led to utter chaos, the Nazis portrayed the French as the external representatives of a Jewish conspiracy, which had to be eliminated. German Jews, many of whom were, like Edith Stein, assimilated into German culture and among the loyal defenders of the Prussian ethos, were the internal enemy. Of the religious influence of Judaism, Rosenberg argued, "Once for all, the Old Testament as a book of religion must be done away with" and with it "the unsuccessful attempt of the last fifteen hundred years to make us spiritually Jews."[49] Translated from the racial idiom into which it was cast, this meant that positive Christianity would do away with the whole tradition of the Christian churches, Catholic and Protestant, that had succumbed to Saint Paul's distortions. Church leaders understood this.

In addition to these ideological clashes, however, the Nazi leadership saw both the Vatican and the Catholic hierarchy as political threats, as they understood politics. In earlier chapters, we have seen how Communist leaders in Russia and Ukraine regarded the Catholic Church as a Fascist, pro-Nazi organization. That charge was absurd. But so was the Nazi contention that the Church, as it was often put, formed a "common front via Canterbury with Moscow."[50] Indeed, the fact that both Communist Russia and Nazi Germany, who regarded themselves locked in a struggle to the death with each other, could see the Church as a tool of the other side suggests that the Church did not support either movement and acted in a different dimension altogether than the political.

This did not stop the Nazis from reinterpreting theological thought into political terms. For example, the Church's protests against the Sterilization Laws and other violations of natural law were characterized by Hans Karl Leistritz as "an intellectual speculation used for political purposes under cover of faith," which the Nazi regime, though respecting religion, of course, was forced to resist. The heart of the conflict was that the Church believed in laws that transcended the Nazi identification of the will of the *Volk* with God Himself. Or as Leistritz complained, the Nazis objected to the idea of "the *lex aeterna* of the transcendent God," which was really a "speculative trick which enabled ecclesiastical interference in politics to present itself as a necessity."[51] Translated into concrete terms, this meant that any moral objections to Nazi practice derived from religious belief would be ruled out as illegitimate religious interference in politics. In the Nazi view "the People carries its own justification in its own innermost, which we call the living blood-stream."

Given such conflicting interpretations of what constituted politics and what religion, it is not surprising that, when the Church and the Nazi government signed a Concordat in 1933, it was doomed from the outset. On paper, the Concordat looked similar to previous documents seeking to define the Church's status within pluralistic, nonconfessional states. The Church and the state recognized each other's proper spheres. Pope and bishops had the right to publish pastoral letters and encyclicals, the Catholic press was theoretically free, religious schools had the right to teach the faith, churches and religious associations were at liberty to operate under their own rules. The only limitations on these operations were "the common laws of the land."

In a totalitarian state like Nazi Germany, however, which, in addition to its total political control claimed religious beliefs of a sort, the laws meant what the party, and more specifically Hitler himself, said they meant. The 1933 Empowering Acts clearly indicated that Hitler could selectively implement and even alter the Constitution.[52] He and his party were equally determined that the Concordat would be no limitation on the holy Aryan will. The exercise of religious rights, as those would have been understood in normal circumstances, was taken as illegitimate "political" activity by the Church. Bishops and the pope were accused of political meddling for spelling out Christian social ethics. Religious schools and presses were closed as incompatible with the Reich. When the Vatican's newspaper, *Osservatore Romano,* protested, the response from the Nazi minister for the interior removed all doubts: "We are not minded to put up with any more of that kind of sabotage of the laws of the Reich. . . . The Concordat does not free the Catholic Church from regarding as binding upon its members also those laws which are in force for all the state."[53] Of course, this meant that nothing, not even God's law, could stand above Nazi policy.

Within a few years, the official publication of the Storm Troopers, *Der S. A. Mann,* would argue, clearly with approval from Berlin, that the insistence of the Church on its rights and its resistance to full co-operation with Nazism placed in doubt whether it understood God's law. In Nazi theology, it raised the question "whether a Church so led can be of Christ, or a Christianity so misused can be accepted for the soul's salvation."[54] Statements critical of Nazi crimes by bishops and the pope were themselves crimes and an insult to the sacred Fatherland. Archbishop Michael Faulhaber of Munich, who had understood Nazi racial theories even before National Socialism took power and had denounced them from the pulpit before and after 1933, was repeatedly threatened.[55] The German bishops' annual conference in Fulda sent petitions and complaints to the Reich about euthanasia and anti-Semitic persecutions.[56]

The mutual charges of failure to live up to the Concordat show two main things. First, the Church had tried to defend itself with this legal agreement, but such a paper defense was useless against a state that claimed the right to constantly redefine its own scope. Second, the Nazis were right: the Church was not living up to its word — as that was understood by Nazism. The plain meaning of the Concordat would have given the Church room to operate in any decent country. Its clash with the Nazi understanding of what role "religion" ought to play was proof of an irreconcilable opposition.

Alfred Rosenberg, the Nazi's chief theologian, put the point well in 1937: "The Churches had the grand opportunity of putting their work at the disposal of Adolf Hitler, as the new state was being built up, and of marching with him. They have let the opportunity slip, and when one does not, or will not, recognize such chances of world-history, one has oneself spoken the verdict of destiny."[57] Rosenberg spoke truer than he knew. The churches' refusal to participate wholeheartedly in an anti-Christian regime speak of a destiny that is not limited to the kingdoms of this world.

An unfortunate and sterile debate has arisen over whether the Church, in trying to defend itself by way of the Concordat and a quiet diplomacy, was silent in the face of the Nazi Holocaust of Jews and — particularly during the papacy of Pius XII — perhaps even in favor of a Nazi triumph. This contention has set the agenda for discussion and made it appear that arguments to the contrary are defensive maneuvers by guilty Catholics. But at the time, the Nazis themselves had a different view. The mere visit of Cardinal Pacelli, later Pope Pius XII, to France revealed for them the dirty alliance between the Vatican and Moscow: "The ways of God are wonderful, but the ways of Cardinal Pacelli are unsavory."[58] For Jews and Catholics, two religious communities that suffered so much from a common enemy, this bad feeling is unseemly and, often enough, something less than divine. Continued arguments along this line keep alive the Nazis' stated intentions to divide believers in the Old Testament from those who embrace the New.

Not a few voices were raised early, if to little effect. One of the most remarkable and stunningly heroic was that of the German Jesuit Rupert Mayer. Father Mayer was a living refutation of the Nazi claim that the "negative Christianity" of the churches, with its humility, sense of sinfulness, and ascetic practice, was incompatible with the virtues Nazis admired, such as courage and boldness. Mayer was early attracted to the religious life in his native Bavaria. In World War I, as a chaplain to the German army, he distinguished himself by his fearless movements on battlefronts to administer the sacraments to the dying and in using his own body to shield wounded men. He was wounded so severely during a battle in Romania that he lost his left leg. Hans Carossa, an eyewitness to that event, was stunned by Mayer's courage as he lay bleeding: "The man lying there in his own blood maintained, even in the most wretched condition, the air of uncommon superiority over himself. . . . When people like us died, something not quite settled, not quite finished always remained. But this man floated like a sonata by Bach, conjured out of the darkness in clearly drawn lines and in a state of complete release."[59] Mayer was the first priest to receive the Iron Cross, first class, as well as other medals for valor.

It comes as no surprise then that, as National Socialism began its rise to power in Germany, Mayer was one of the few with both the perspicacity and courage to confront it head on. He spent long hours every day in a demanding round of hearing confessions, counseling the many people of all kinds who came to him, and collecting large sums for the relief of the poor. Realizing that the new situation called for new pastoral strategies, he set up masses on Sunday mornings in train stations so that the many people who wanted to spend the day in the country could hear Mass before they departed. Tens of thousands did so. But in the same pastoral vein, he also made it a point to attend political meetings that might have an impact on the faith in Germany. He did so not as a political activist but as a legendary, battle-tested priest who felt a responsibility to be a pastor over all dimensions of the life of his flock and had an enormous popular following. When twenty-one young people of the Catholic Association of Saint Joseph were massacred by marauding bands, for example, he took to the pulpit, counseling a firm response animated not by revenge, but by Christian love. One of his constant themes was: "If they feel our love, they will believe what we say."[60]

That Christian charity, however, did not prevent him from taking a firm line against all those then in Germany — Communists and National Socialists most prominently — who were preaching a different gospel.

At a Communist meeting in 1919, Mayer bumped into Hitler, who was then merely a political agitator. The priest rose to refute various points of the Communist speakers. Hitler stood up next and remarked that the priest had criticized Communism from a religious point of view; he, Hitler, wanted to do so from a political standpoint. That one and only meeting convinced Mayer that Hitler was a remarkably capable speaker. In subsequent meetings of the Nazis, which Mayer attended to offer a religious commentary, he became convinced that Hilter was "a fanatic of the first order."[61]

Understanding the various moral threats that Nazi views on nationalism, race, and the Bible presented, he became a tireless public exponent of the view that a Catholic could not in good conscience be a Nazi. At a political rally in Bürgerbräu to discuss that question, the pro-Nazi audience got so agitated before Mayer had said more than a few words that he had to be taken out of the room surrounded by bodyguards. His prominence brought him to the attention of the Nazis even before they took power. After they were asked to form a government, Gestapo agents came to his sermons and took notes. Mayer was not the kind of man to be intimidated: he spoke out without the least hesitation even though friends warned him that he was under surveillance.

Given his fame, however, the Nazis had to be careful not to make a martyr of him, which would have sparked a popular reaction in Bavaria. The German bishops, like the German political classes, were unsure how to deal with National Socialism. Some such as Cardinal Adolf Bertram of Breslau, remembering the persecution in the nineteenth century during Bismarck's *Kulturkampf* (culture war) against the Church, acted cautiously. Others such as Bishop Konrad von Preysing of Berlin and Bishop Clemens August von Galen, known later as the "Lion of Münster," believed the threat warranted direct confrontation. Mayer was firmly in the latter camp, and his judgment was that the Vatican should not have signed the Concordat in 1933 at least until the Nazis stopped their brutalities against the Church.

Pope Pius XI's 1937 encyclical on the German situation, *Mit brennender Sorge,* expressed regret that the Church had done so as well. Pius explained that he had signed the pact "despite many and grave misgivings" because he thought it would protect the Church and that the Church had an obligation to try to reach agreement with anyone who did not refuse a peaceful hand. By 1937, Pius said, it was clear that the Nazi regime had engaged in "intrigues, which from the outset only aimed at a war of extermination." Nazi interpretations of terms that had plainly different meanings in any other context had effectively abrogated the accord. In addition, Pius pointed out the absurdity of the national religion propounded by the Nazis, their racial theories, and their "aggressive paganism." Natural law with its universal norms governed all people and could not be abrogated by special claims about the German soul. Positive Christianity was a contradiction in terms: "Nothing but ignorance and pride could blind one to the treasures hoarded in the Old Testament." "There is but one alternative left," wrote the pope, "that of heroism."

Pius's words were prophetic. The Nazis banned publication of the encyclical, which nevertheless was circulated in clandestine fashion in parishes. A wave of arrests, trials, and persecutions followed. The Nazis also intensified a campaign against the Church that used seemingly legal channels to harass. Religious orders and other church institutions were often accused of having violated complicated currency laws when they sent monies to related institutions abroad. This was an unheard of charge at any other time and, despite the complexities of the law, clearly aimed at curtailing religious work. Huge fines sometimes ruined the religious institutions targeted. And deaths also resulted. Dominican priest Titus Horten died from lack of medical attention in prison after a trumped-up currency case. His cause for beatification was presented in 1984.[62]

An even more insidious campaign involved accusing religious of immorality, either in the corruption of children or in adultery. In Germany at the time, as there is at all times, there was of course a small group of clergy who could be justly accused of these failings. But the Nazi propaganda organs pumped up such stories — and many manufactured ones — to such an extent that in the daily press it began to appear as if priestly life were nothing but the corruption of youth and sly seduction. The first charge was clearly intended to help get young people out of Church schools and youth organizations and into the secular schools and *Hitlerjugend* that were inculcating Nazi ideology. Domination of the next generation through strictly regulated education was one of Hitler's strategies for breaking the hold of the Church on the people over time.

*Mit brennender Sorge* appeared in March of 1937. By June of that year, Father Mayer was imprisoned for the first time. Technically, he was arrested for a public denunciation of Nazi threats to Cardinal Faulhaber, but it was clear the Nazis wanted him out of action as they moved against the Church. A month earlier, they had sent him a note forbidding him to preach, then another. Since under the terms of the Concordat and in more general understandings of the relationship of church and state, the state had no jurisdiction over those the Church asks to preach, Mayer refused the order as prejudicial to religion. He was in and out of prison as church and state battled over their respective rights.

When World War II broke out in 1939 however, the regime arrested him and other potential opponents. Mayer was sent to the concentration camp at Sachsenhausen. His head was shaved and he was forced to follow camp discipline, but even in Sachsenhausen he was treated with no little respect. Still, he lost so much weight that the prosthesis for his amputated leg no longer fit properly and added to the trials of life in a concentration camp. Mayer was interrogated about his contacts with various people. He absolutely refused to discuss any of his conversations with anyone because, as a priest, he regarded them as confidential and secrecy as necessary for trust in the clergy. His accusers hinted that he was in touch with monarchists and other opponents of the Nazi government. Mayer would not even comment on such suggestions, either to confirm or deny them. Frustrated that Mayer's fame prevented them from pressuring him further, the interrogators relented.

Other German clergy who made the same claim were not treated lightly. Father Hermann Wehrle was approached by Major Ludwig von Leonrod about whether the Church allowed just tyrannicide. Though Wehrle answered no, he was later executed for not having reported the conversation to authorities.[63] Leonrod was part of the famous plot to kill Hitler directed by Lieutenant Colonel Klaus von Stauffenberg. Von Stauffenberg was a serious Catholic who, the day he carried the briefcase full of explosives into the room where Hitler was working, had sat quietly for a long time in prayer in a Berlin church. He had even sought moral advice about what he was about to do from Berlin's Cardinal Preysing, who put himself in danger merely by meeting von Stauffenberg. Preysing's opinion that there was no theological objection to the attempt could have brought him death as well. Fortunately, the Gestapo never learned of this pastoral visit in their investigation into the plot, or of Pius XII's flirtations with similar moves.[64]

The authorities at Sachsenhausen had a problem on their hands in Mayer. They could not brutalize the rock-hard priest as they did other prisoners. His very presence in the camp set a bad example. In a deal with church officials, they decided to send him to the monastery at Ettal, where he would be free but had to refrain from all public activity. It was a hard thing for Mayer to accept this compromise because he knew that people would be scandalized by his apparent acquiescence. But ultimately he was persuaded by the fact that he would cause trouble for the monastery, the Jesuits, and intercessors if he resisted the arrangement they had worked out. The pain this caused him was alleviated only when Allied forces liberated the monastery. Mayer immediately returned to his active life, but the imprisonment had taken its toll. He died shortly thereafter in the midst of a sermon. In 1948, when his body was transferred to its current resting place, thirty-five thousand people came to pay tribute to a man they admired. In 1983, the Vatican beatified him for heroic virtue.

As exceptional as Mayer was, there were many others who spoke out in various ways during the rise of National Socialism. Bishop Clemens August von Galen was the most vociferous among the German hierarchy. Von Galen's status both as bishop and scion of an old noble family made it difficult for the Gestapo to move against him directly. He gave many sermons criticizing various aspects of Nazi policy and boldly invited them to come and get him at his cathedral if they wanted, saying they could find him standing in the cathedral door in full vestments and bearing his miter and shepherd's crook. Even the Gestapo recognized that apprehending such a prominent man would be a bad move. But in private conversations, Hitler told his intimates what von Galen's outspokenness would mean, when the time was right: "A man like Bishop von Galen knows full well what I shall exact in retribution to the last farthing. And if he doesn't succeed in getting himself transferred in the meanwhile to the Collegium Germanicum in Rome, he may rest assured that in the balancing of accounts, no 't' will remain uncrossed, no 'i' undotted!"[65]

Von Galen's primary focus was the Nazi eugenics program that sought to eliminate "undesirables" such as the infirm, mentally deficient, and those of the wrong racial background, which included Jews, Gypsies, Slavs, and a host of other so-called lesser breeds. He also addressed pointed criticism against the *Hitlerjugend,* a movement that tried to replace religious formation with Nazi indoctrination. In one sermon at Saint Lambert's Cathedral, Von Galen emphasized parental responsibilities in the face of strategies that sought to seduce children away from family and Church. A party member in the congregation stood up during the sermon and shouted out: "What right does a celibate, without wife or children, have to talk about the problems of youth and marriage?" Von Galen immediately replied: "*Never* will I tolerate in this cathedral any reflection upon our beloved Führer!"[66] This witty riposte not only defended the Catholic clergy, but underlined the absurd incongruity of Hitler's propaganda encouraging good Nazi mothers to bear large numbers of pure Aryan children for the Reich when he himself was unmarried and childless.

Similarly, in Austria, figures like Jakob Gapp were not without support in the views of the hierarchy. In a 1932 Lenten pastoral, the Austrian bishops warned that while "some points of the [National Socialist] program allow the most varied interpretations in its explanation and in that way already cause confusion," on the whole, the movement presented some grave threats. In a pastoral early the next year, they were quite specific:

> One must point in particular toward National Socialism, which deteriorates into racial materialism and reaches its peak in the "blood myth." The National Socialist's point of view of race is totally incompatible with that of the Christian and therefore must be decidedly rejected. This is true with regard to the radical anti-Semitism that National Socialism preaches. Truly, there is nothing that is more opposed to Catholic Christianity than the nationalizing of religions.[67]

Though the Austrian hierarchy wavered on National Socialism as a political movement after Austria was occupied, its teaching about Nazism's ideological underpinnings was firm.

That Church leaders were unsure about their course is no surprise. Secular political leaders, both inside and outside Germany, were also unsure of how to deal with the Nazi threat. When British Prime Minister Neville Chamberlain went to Munich in 1938 to meet with Hitler, he struck what has ever since become notorious as a bad bargain: he indicated that he was willing, if France and his government agreed, to allow Hitler to annex the Germans living in the Czech Sudetenland. Chamberlain returned home triumphantly believing he had assured "peace in our time" through what he thought was a small concession. Many in Britain and elsewhere agreed at the time. Winston Churchill, one of the few exceptions, saw through Hitler's ploy and drily commented: "His Majesty's government had to choose between shame and war. They chose shame. And in spite of that, there will be war."[68]

Many religious figures were intimidated by Nazi tactics of arresting those who gave the slightest hint of opposition, an unfortunate lapse of courage. Given human nature, the same has occurred not only in Nazi Germany, but in everyplace where harsh and widespread threats have been institutionalized: the Soviet Union; the People's Republics in China, Vietnam, and Korea; in Cuba and Chile and El Salvador; and in various countries throughout Africa and the Muslim world. But quite a few others were outspoken and heroic, and paid the price for it. It is often claimed, for example, that there was no official response to such outrages as the Nazi terror against Jews during such events as *Kristallnacht* in the fall of 1938 because the Church wanted no trouble and only wished to preserve itself. This is not true. The complicated situation involving the Concordat, the Vatican's delicate diplomacy, and sheer confusion about how to deal with an unprecedented threat made effective action impossible. Secular opponents to Nazism found themselves in a similar bind. But it is wrong to say that there was no protest or that Catholics were unwilling to pay the price of witness. At *Kristallnacht,* to take only one example, Father Bernard Lichtenberg, the provost of Saint Hedwig's Cathedral in Berlin, publicly protested along with the cathedral pastor, Father Edward Winter.[69] Nazi authorities did not forget such public displays of religious opposition.

Lichtenberg was arrested a few years later because he prayed "for the Jews and the poor prisoners in the concentration camps, but above all for my colleagues" during an evening service at Saint Hedwig's. He died himself being transported to the concentration camp at Dachau. Lichtenberg had also written privately to the head of the Nazi Medical Affairs office that he and many others suspected and had publicly speculated that "undesirables" were being killed: "Even if the Ten Commandments are being publicly ignored, the Reich Penal Code still has legal force. Section 211 . . . states 'Whoever willfully kills a person shall, if he deliberately committed the killing, be condemned to death for murder.' " The same code, said Lichtenberg, designates it a crime if someone "fails to report same to the authorities."[70] Speaking up in this way, of course, was a Christian duty, even though Lichtenberg knew it would bring him no good. That he and many others were willing to do so, all the same, even knowing it would not help those they were concerned to protect, is proof of heroic virtue under immediate threat.

Nor was such protest carried out in merely personal ways. German Protestantism and Catholicism had a long history of conflicts with one another. They did not often collaborate before or during the rise of the Nazi regime. But in December of 1941, each church issued a formal protest against repression of the churches, treatment of Jews, and euthanasia of the mentally ill. Bishop Theophil Wurm spoke for the Protestants, Cardinal Adolf Bertram for the Catholic bishops. Though the impression remains that something more should have been done, the best scholars of religion in the Third Reich are doubtful whether any of the churches could have organized political, as opposed to moral and spiritual, resistance.[71] Indeed, under the circumstances, it is remarkable that they protested as they did. As late as 1943, the German bishops were bold enough to issue a pastoral letter arguing that "killing of innocent life — that is, of defenseless persons who were mentally impaired or ill, of 'incurable invalids,' of the 'genetically handicapped,' of unarmed prisoners and POWs, and of humans of foreign race and origin — is an attack against God."[72]

Many individual Catholic leaders were equally bold. Father Heinrich Feuerstein used to tell friends who, early on in the Nazi era, warned him that speaking out was not smart, "I would rather be reproached for stupidity than for cowardice."[73] Typical of many upright priests in Nazi Germany, however, Feuerstein was torn by the machinations of the Nazis. An ardent patriot, he had volunteered to fight in World War I, had received the Iron Cross for valor, and had served as an army chaplain later. But he would not be confused about calls for loyalty to the Fatherland. Indeed, he spoke in his sermons about the need to be willing to die for a different cause: "The martyr goes to a harsh death of his own free will. Greatness lies in martyrdom because it is an ignominious death, accompanied by the wild rejoicing of a spiteful mob. . . . In this day and age, too, we experience a return of martyrdom, in bloody and unbloody form. We greet them all, the martyrs of our age. . . . Hail to you in particular, you martyrs of Dachau!"[74] Feuerstein would take his place among the hundreds of priests and thousands of other believers whom he saluted, writing in his last moments of the providence and mercy that had led him to the "school of saintliness." He was murdered, probably on August 2, 1942, in Dachau.

Besides the priests, however, there was organized Catholic lay protest in Nazi Germany that, often enough, led to martyrdom. Perhaps the most notorious case is that of the layman Erich Klausener, who was the leader of Catholic Action in Berlin from 1928 until his death. In 1933, forty-five thousand Catholic people came to a rally he organized in a Berlin stadium that drew the concern of the Nazi regime. The following year sixty thousand Catholics attended a similar event in Hoppegarten. No swastikas appeared at either event. At Hoppegarten, Klausener closed the rally with a protest, drawn from Catholic principles, against Nazi pressures on the Church, anti-Semitism, and growing national arrogance. In spite of his open opposition, Klausener's talents were useful to the government, and he had been appointed to a high post in the Reich Ministry of Transport. But in 1934, the regime began intense elimination of potential opponents. In a wave of violence sometimes called the Röhm Purge, he was shot to death in his office by an SS officer who confessed to the deed at his postwar trial in Berlin.[75] Klausener's whole staff, including Baroness Stotzingen, his private secretary, were sent to concentration camps.[76]

We also know that several Catholic labor leaders such as Bernhard Letterhaus (Christian Textile Workers), Nikolaus Gross (Christian Miners), and Otto Müller (a priest who headed the West German Worker's Union), formed a group in contact with the famous Jesuit martyr Alfred Delp. (Delp would be executed in the Berlin-Plötzensee prison; Letterhaus and Gross died after time in the camps; Müller died in the Berlin-Tegel prison.) The Catholic activist-lawyer Josef Wirmer was executed in Berlin Plötzensee in 1944.

The Nazi sword fell on young as well as old and tried to make sure that the young would not grow up to be troublesome. Fred Joseph, for example, was arrested in 1934 when he was only twenty-three because he continued to organize a group of Catholic Scouts of Saint George. As must have been the case with many high-spirited people of his generation, he balked at Nazi orders that restricted Catholic youth organizations. Where such organizations were even allowed to exist, they were confined to strictly religious activities within the church. Arrested several times in his twenties, Joseph died at Auschwitz supposedly for being a "half-Jew."[77] Willi Graf, a Catholic youth organizer who went on to become a leader of the "White Rose" student group in Munich — a group that opposed National Socialism on the basis of Christian ideals — fell to the guillotine.[78]

Some older, distinguished figures took a similar path. Eugen Bolz, who had been president of the German state of Würtemberg, belonged to a group of Catholics who argued that the demands of the faith took precedence over mere politics, however much Nazi ideology tried to restrict religious activity. As early as 1934, Bolz argued in an essay entitled "Catholic Politics and Action" that a Catholic cannot allow primacy to state power: "Given that the commonweal, 'next to God the first and last principle in community of the state' [a citation from Pope Leo XIII], is the reason for and the objective of the government, the government's powers of authority and control can only apply to the extent it serves the commonweal.... When the public authority is blatantly and persistently abused, the people are entitled to defend themselves."[79] Put simply, this says that a lawless state is an illegitimate state. Bolz, therefore, saw participation in the Resistance as a moral and religious duty, making a martyr's argument: "Even if I die, my life is nothing where Germany is concerned." After a decade of resistance, he was arrested and executed, writing toward the end what was a virtual life's motto: "Only the soul is beyond the reach of all external powers."

No account of the Nazi martyrs can leave out the remarkable story of the Austrian Franz Jägerstätter. We know about him largely because the American sociologist Gordon C. Zahn happened upon an obscure reference to him, which did not even include his last name, in a book about Franz Reinisch, an Austrian priest martyred for refusing to take the loyalty oath to the Führer.[80] Zahn was intrigued enough to visit the small village of Saint Radegund, where Jägerstätter had spent his whole life, and to interview his widow, friends, and acquaintances. What he discovered about Jägerstätter underscores the way in which the faith can inspire heroic virtue that completely transcends cultural, social, and political conditions that, in the twentieth century, were confidently supposed to determine our behavior.

Jägerstätter's story is both simple and complex. He was born an illegitimate child in 1907 in a village that then still retained spiritual and agricultural roots going back centuries, perhaps as far as Roman times. His natural father, Franz Bachmeier, died in World War I; Jägerstätter received the last name by which he is known from a stepfather. His family and all his fellow villagers were primarily farmers. In some accounts of Jägerstätter's life, he is therefore described as a simple farmer who stubbornly refused to cooperate with the Nazis after the 1938 German *Anschluss* overran Austria. This is a true, but incomplete way of characterizing a man whose soul was of a quite rare kind, akin, in fact, to the great contemplatives and saints.

Franz Jägerstätter received only a basic education at the local school, a basic education, however, in which he developed good reading and writing skills. When in his mature years he became an ardent believer, he would take time out of his demanding work on the farm to read the Bible and spiritual works. By the time he was imprisoned, he was well versed enough in Christian history that he was delighted to find a copy of Saint John Chrysostom's sermons among the books provided for prisoners. As he wrote to his wife, "Although everyone here likes to read to kill time, they were perfectly happy to leave this book to me. A man first realizes the true value of our faith in a situation like this."[81] His clarity of understanding and lively response to his reading show an uncommon capacity to live what he understood, even if he had a limited formal education. As we shall see, this spirit also made Jägerstätter an almost classical writer in his lucidity.

The town myth is that Jägerstätter lived a wild life as a young man, but later got religion. There is some substance to this story. Franz was probably no more wild as a young man, however, than the average. He may have had an illegitimate child himself, though the record is murky. Some witnesses support the idea that he paid a woman support for a child that was not his. Others take a more conventional view that he had sinned and taken responsibility for it.[82] Jägerstätter seems to have come to some kind of repentance about his past life, particularly his illegitimate child, before he married in 1936. Some of the townspeople believe that Jägerstätter changed as a result of the piety of the woman he married; their subsequent honeymoon in Rome, they also think, changed him into a convinced believer. But the truth may lie in a different direction. The kind of woman he chose probably reflects his own already changed spiritual state, and their decision to make a trip to Rome — from a tiny village at a time when even people from cities in Austria almost never went abroad — must be the result of a spiritual impulse rather than its cause.

However we are to understand this, by 1936 Jägerstätter was a firm and active believer and began serving as the sexton in the local church. Around that year, he wrote to his godchild with the boldness of spiritual expression that was characteristic of him: "I can say from my own experience how painful life often is when one lives as a halfway Christian; it is more like vegetating than living."[83] And he poignantly adds: "Since the death of Christ, almost every century has seen the persecution of Christians; there have always been heroes and martyrs who gave their lives — often in horrible ways — for Christ and their faith. If we hope to reach our goal some day, then we, too, must became heroes of the faith."[84] As was always the case with Franz Jägerstätter, he was not merely writing pious words but describing a reality he himself would be willing to embrace.

In the meantime, he went about his business, much like other townspeople, but with important differences. He and his wife had three children and a farm to run, but Jägerstätter did not use family needs as an excuse to deviate in the slightest from his conception of what was right. He stopped going to taverns, not because he was a teetotaler, but because he got into political fights over Nazism there. Since he was a daily communicant, he had to fast every day until time for church, even while doing hard manual labor. And some of his neighbors say he always fasted until noon. At the same time, he practiced charity to the poor in the village, though he was only a little better than poor himself. The identification with the poor may have led to his decision to become a lay member of the Franciscan Third Order as well.[85] The usual practice in the village was to give a donation to the church sexton for his help in arranging funerals and prayer services. Jägerstätter refused these little payments, preferring to join with the faithful rather than act as a paid official. He had taken the path of prayer, fasting, charity, and even went to a Bavarian pilgrimage site just before his arrest.[86] The period of self-discipline prepared him for much more demanding sacrifices.

When the Nazis arrived, not only did he refuse collaboration with its evil intentions, which were quite well known to his fellow villagers as well as to Jägerstätter; he even rejected benefits from the regime in areas that had nothing to do with its racial hatreds or pagan warmongering. It must have hurt for a father, for example, to turn down the money to which he was entitled through a Nazi family assistance program for each of his children. And the farmer in Jägerstätter paid the price of discipleship when — after a storm destroyed crops — he would not take the emergency aid offered by the government.[87] Years before these questions were put before him, Jägerstätter had made his own view clear to his godson: "Though we must bear our daily sorrows and reap little reward in this world for doing so, we can still become richer than millionaires, for those who need not fear death are the richest and happiest of all. And these riches are there for the asking."[88]

As the Nazis began to organize Austria more thoroughly, Jägerstätter had to make the decision whether to allow himself to be drafted by the German army and cooperate with a regime that, he often stated, was persecuting the Church. Two seemingly good reasons were given to him, sometimes by spiritual advisers, why he should not resist. First, he was told, he had to consider his station and the responsibility he had toward his family. If he were taken away what would become of them? To this Jägerstätter replied: "I cannot believe that, just because one has a wife and children, he is free to offend God by lying (not to mention all the other things he would be called upon to do). Did not Christ Himself say, 'He who loves father, mother, or children more than me is not deserving of My love'?"[89] Obviously, this did not suggest any less concern for his family because of religious principles. In fact, when Jägerstätter thought about simply hiding in the woods, as many people did to escape Nazi supervision, he rejected the idea because it might bring reprisals against his family.

The other argument he was presented with was more complicated. Several priests — including Bishop Fliesser of Linz, whom Jägerstätter consulted[90] — told him what was quite true in Catholic social teaching: that he had a responsibility to obey legitimate authorities and give greater weight to his family's needs. The political authorities were the ones liable to judgment for their decisions, not ordinary citizens who could not be expected even to be in full possession of the facts about national life. Jägerstätter was equally vehement in rejecting this view. In normal times, of course, obedience to authority, especially democratic authority that can be changed by peaceful means, may be required even when we disagree on certain policies. But the 1940s in Austria were not normal times: to obey for obedience' sake would have been to do what Adolf Eichmann would later plead in his trial in Jerusalem: he was just following orders.

A third argument occasionally was offered to Jägerstätter: no bishop was requiring what he was doing. Strictly speaking, that was true. But some Austrian bishops resisted the Nazi embrace. Bishop Sproll of Rottenburg refused to vote for the Nazis, as Jägerstätter alone in his village had refused, because "I should have had to give my vote for, and express my confidence in, men whose fundamentally hostile attitude to the Catholic Church and against all Christianity has become more and more clearly revealed from year to year."[91] Jägerstätter would have agreed with every word, had anyone bothered to tell him about them. As a consequences of his stand, Bishop Sproll was the target of a violent demonstration by outside agitators who broke into his residence. Shortly after, he was forced to leave his diocese, having been branded "a permanent menace to public peace."[92]

The consequences of Jägerstätter's position were obvious: "Everyone tells me, of course, that I should not do what I am doing because of the danger of death.... I believe it is better to sacrifice one's life right away than to place oneself in the grave danger of committing sin and then dying."[93] The tone his correspondence takes on in these circumstances suggests a man inspired by the great Christian tradition more than it does the words of a "simple farmer." To begin with, he starts to sound themes that have resonated down the ages among the saints: "The important thing is to fear God more than man."[94] And there are indications that his prayer life has given him a certain intimate intercourse with the Divinity such as only contemplatives achieve: "I have faith that God will still give me a sign if some other course would be better."[95]

So with all the questions decided and no alternative remaining, Jägerstätter was sent on March 2, 1943, to the prison in Linz-an-der-Donau, the same Linz in which Hitler and Eichmann had lived in as children. According to the prison chaplain, thirty-eight men were executed there, some for desertion, others for stands similar to Jägerstätter's (no others have been positively identified, however).[96] His Way of the Cross would not be long. In May, he was transferred to a prison in Berlin. There his behavior during discussion with two officers of the military tribunal was so impressive, according to Jägerstätter's lawyer, that they literally begged him to accept noncombatant service. But even that was too much complicity with evil for the Saint Radegund farmer.

Some have raised the question of whether Jägerstätter was acting on principle or behaving like a religious fanatic, since the Church authorities themselves did not ask for such a stance. From all the evidence we have of those who knew him, right down to the two officers of the military court, everyone agrees that, despite the firmness and seeming irrationality of his position, there was nothing of the fanatic about Franz Jägerstätter. He did not accuse those Catholics who did not agree with him, solely observing that they had not been "given the grace" to see the truth yet.[97] His parish priest, his wife, and his lawyer all tried to change his mind. But it was useless.

Useless, though, only from a worldly standpoint. Jägerstätter is often thought of as a kind of patron saint for principled civil disobedience, especially when a regime is engaged in an unjust war. He is that. But he is also something more. Even the most successful civil protest is a limited thing; the next round of injustices will call for further resistance. Jägerstätter had not even that consolation. He went to his death knowing it would make no earthly difference in the Nazi death machine. His witness was known and accepted by virtually no one. No change in political circumstances would follow his sacrifice. In the end, he was a witness to the Christian virtue of a hope that must transcend time. His letters are full of tenderness to his wife and children, but his eyes are already turning toward something else.

A "statement of position," which he probably wrote a month before he was beheaded, seems like a newly found New Testament Epistle: "Neither prisons nor chains nor sentence of death can rob a man of the Faith and his own free will. God gives so much strength that it is possible to bear any suffering, a strength far stronger than all the might in the world. The power of God cannot be overcome."[98] Further down, he expands on what this means:

> The true Christian is to be recognized more in his works and deeds than in his speech. The surest mark of all is found in deeds showing love of neighbor. To do unto one's neighbor what one would desire for himself is more than merely not doing to others what one would not want done to himself. Let us love our enemies, bless those who curse us, pray for those who persecute us. For love will conquer and will endure for eternity. And happy are they who live and die in God's love.[99]

This is positive Christianity indeed, though perhaps not exactly what Alfred Rosenberg might have identified as such.

Yet despite this certitude, Jägerstätter reserves a touching message for his family at the end:

> All my dear ones, the hour comes ever closer when I will be giving my soul back to God, the Master. I would have liked to say so many things to you in farewell so that it is hard not to be able to take leave of you anymore. I would have liked, too, to spare you the pain and sorrow that you must bear because of me. But you know we must love God even more than family, and we must lose everything dear and worthwhile on earth rather than commit even the slightest offense against God. And if, for your sake, I had not shrunk back from offending God, how can we know what sufferings God might have sent us on my account? It must surely have been hard for our dear Savior to bring such pain upon His dear Mother through His death: what, then, are our sorrows compared with what those two innocent hearts had to suffer — and all on account of us sinners.[100]

On August 9, 1943, he completed his path of fidelity.

A Father Jochmann was the prison chaplain in Berlin and spent some time with Jägerstätter that day. He reports that the prisoner was calm and uncomplaining. He refused any religious material, even a New Testament, because, he said, "I am completely bound in inner union with the Lord, and any reading would only interrupt my communication with my God." Very few men could have made such a statement without seeming to be either in denial or mad. Father Jochmann later said of him, though, "I can say with certainty that this simple man is the only saint I have ever met in my lifetime."[101]

Jägerstätter was certainly a saint, and one who emerged from the German-speaking countryside of Austria almost solely because of special graces. There is no explanation that sociology or psychology could ever give for his revolt and steady adherence to his principles in spite of the apparent "foolishness" of his stand. He could not have anticipated that anyone outside a narrow circle of his friends and family would ever know his story, or that he was making a difference. But rare as Jägerstätter's case may have been, there were many similar heroic saints produced by the confrontation with Nazism. Accounts of two of the most remarkable among them — Saint Edith Stein and Saint Maximilian Kolbe — along with the martyrdom stories of many others, appear in the following two chapters.

# SEVEN

# MARTYR FOR TRUTH
## The Life and Death of Edith Stein

**T**HE TWENTIETH CENTURY witnessed an enormous expansion in our knowledge about the world and in technologies to control it. But our age has not been a century of truth. It inherited from the nineteenth century an assumption that philosophical and religious truth were dead and that, beside scientific truths, everything else was mere opinion. Darwin claimed that human beings were just another species, a branch of the physical forces of the universe that admitted of no "higher" or "lower" animals. Marxism asserted that morality, religion, and culture should be recognized for what they really are: a superstructure erected on material production. Building on these insights at the beginning of the new century, Freud believed that the human psyche was a mere byproduct of subconscious physical impulses, with which we wrestle. Perhaps Nietzsche was the single figure who summed up the whole movement; for him, God was dead and we had to create our own reason for living out of the meaningless universe that was left.

It is not too much of an exaggeration to say that the turbulent history of the twentieth century was an extension and reaction to this general line of thought. Marxist regimes pursuing international Socialism clearly tried to follow the materialist conception of human welfare, with disastrous results that produced corpses in the tens of millions. Nazism and Fascism, as nationalist forms of Socialism, reacting to what they regarded as the decadent rationalism of Marx and the bourgeois democratic societies, pursued their own bizarre theories about race and the primacy of power, contributing another wave of casualties numbering in the millions. Some of the century's most celebrated intellectuals joined, or at least flirted, with one or the other camp. In reaction, other intellectuals later in the century have sought to undermine all potential forms of modern terror by elaborating what they call postmodernism, which denies power to "hegemonic" theories by deconstructing all claims to

truth, leaving us without ideologies to kill for, but also without anything to live for. All in all, the human intellect was in a bad way during
the twentieth century.

It is a sign of hope, then, that one of the century's most distinguished
martyrs began her life as a modern intellectual locked in the struggles
of twentieth-century thought. She studied under some of the prominent
theorists of the early part of the century but gradually thought her way
to a position that not only embraced truth but convinced her to die
willingly for the truth. Her story is so unusual in an age that has virtually
abandoned human reason that she deserves a chapter all her own tracing
her slow philosophical growth, conversion from Judaism to Catholicism,
entrance into the contemplative life of the Carmelite order, and eventual
martyrdom at Auschwitz. For Edith Stein's story is a story of how one
intelligent, ardent, and dedicated soul picked its way through the rubble
of the age to a heroic death for the sake of truth.

Edith Stein was born on October 12, 1891, in Breslau, then part of Germany, today the Wrocław inside Poland. That location, poised between
the upheavals of Europe under the Nazis and the postwar domination
of Poland by Soviet Communism, is only one of the curious facts of her
early life. A great deal has been read back into her first years in light of
the seemingly fated nature of the later story. But even when we try to
sift out the merely accidental from the providential in her life, a large
number of remarkable "coincidences" arise that should give us pause.

Unlike most Jews in Germany at the turn of the century, the Stein
family was strictly observant of Jewish law, primarily because of the
energetic piety of Edith's mother, Frau Auguste Stein. This meant that
Edith Stein was exposed to a powerful personal example of religiosity
as well as a deep connection to ancestral traditions. Both shaped her all
along the way. In addition, there were specific elements in her life that she
and her mother believed had marked her out for special election.[1] Her
birthday, for instance, fell on Yom Kippur, the Day of Atonement, one
of the holiest days in the Jewish calendar. And the day of her death at the
Auschwitz concentration camp, August 9, 1942, is known among Jews as
*Tish'a B'Ab*, a day on which a "black fast" is observed to commemorate
the destruction of the First and Second Temples.[2]

Her great grandfather on her mother's side had been a cantor in the
synagogue. Because of their long history as People of the Book, like many

Jewish families in Europe at the time, the Steins had many generations of literacy behind them at a time when Christians might more typically have one or two. The concern with literacy spilled over into a serious family interest in education in all its forms. They felt themselves part of high German culture and participated in it actively. In this respect, the Steins are familiar from the vast Holocaust literature that has been produced about other Jews in similar social and cultural circumstances of that period. They remained Jewish, but constantly had to guard themselves against a loss of identity by assimilation and intermarriage. In the period prior to World War I, the status of Jews in Germany was higher than ever before, and Jewish contributions to German culture, science, and international prestige were considerable.

The Steins not only felt at home in Germany, they were deeply attached to their native country and showed no little patriotism during the tragic battlefield slaughters of World War I. Even in World War II, not a few Jewish families would distinguish between the Germany which they loved and believed themselves to be an integral and living part of, and the wicked Nazi mania that had usurped the government. Edith's own mother was astonished when she found out that, despite her family's long history in Germany and love of the country, some people thought of her and her family as *not German*.[3] Edith's father bore the deeply resonant German name Siegfried and ran a highly successful timber business. But Jewish success in Germany produced envy as well as admiration among the non-Jewish population.

Edith Stein was fortunate in her early life in that people in Germany in the last decade of the nineteenth century and first decade of the twentieth experienced a peace accompanied by a relative prosperity that inspired a great deal of affection for the values of the old Europe. In fact, she later remarked that people who had not lived through the period could never imagine the order and tranquillity of those days.[4] Subsequent events would change Europe beyond recognition, but it was not only a child's nostalgia that made her profoundly aware of the difference between the relatively idyllic world of her early years and the brutal totalitarian nightmare that followed.

From the very first, she showed a rare combination of qualities. On the one hand, she had a ferocious intellect and will, even as a child. In both respects, she resembled her mother. In addition to her strict piety, Frau Stein had a strong practical side. Edith's father died suddenly when she was only two years old. Frau Stein had to take over the timber business if the family was to survive. She quickly learned both the technical and

financial dimensions of the business so well that it remained a going concern until Nazi pressures to shun Jewish firms and her own death brought
the enterprise to an end. That tireless industry was also to be one the
characteristic features of Edith Stein's intellectual and spiritual labors.

She was the youngest of eleven children and was, therefore, both
spoiled by her parents and older siblings and driven to play a role in
a world of so many people older than herself. Her memory was prodigious and her early drive to learn so strong that she picked up a great
deal about German culture and literature even before she went to school.
In fact, she was so advanced that she refused to go to kindergarten after
she discovered that the other students were too far behind her. At the
same time, she was so deeply reflective that her older sisters characterized her, using apt biblical terms, as a "book sealed with seven seals."[5]
In that silence, which would eventually blossom into a vocation for
the Carmelite contemplative life, many things, spiritual and intellectual,
were emerging. At her graduation from grammar school, the headmaster was supposed briefly to sum up each student's achievements. For
Edith, he chose a German proverb: "Strike the stone [a pun: *Stein* means
"stone" in German], and wisdom will leap forth."[6] Many events would
strike that stone and prove the proverb true.

One of the early signs of her future path seems, at first sight, to contradict what followed. Around age thirteen, she stopped praying. As she
was later to admit, until she was almost twenty-one she found it difficult
to believe in God. The reasons for this difficulty were complex. In a way,
the whole episode was the beginning of a move away from the family, as
she started to find her own way toward the truths that would fulfill her
life. But a deeper reason behind her attitude was that she was embarking
on an intellectual journey that would take her far beyond unbelief. She
was interested in the truth and would soon begin pursuing it wherever it
might lead. Her own comment about this period sums it up best: "The
truth alone was my only prayer."[7]

But there must have been other things going on in her soul, though we
have no way of knowing now what they might have been. After years
as the brightest and most enthusiastic student at school, she abruptly
announced that she did not wish to continue. This may have been the
first of a series of periods of depression that, whether or not clinically
describable as such, seem to have preceded large new steps in her life.
After a brief rest with her older sister Else's family in Hamburg, the mood
passed. She returned to Breslau and entered the prestigious Victoria-
schule, where she encountered Latin: "It was like learning my native

tongue. Back then I had no idea that it was the language of the Church and that someday I would be praying in it."[8]

Edith began to study in a wide range of fields. And she also began to understand some fundamental things about herself: "I could not proceed with anything except on the basis of some inner drive. My decisions emerged from a level of depth which I myself was unable to clearly grasp. But once something had emerged into consciousness and taken on a definite shape in my mind, then nothing could hold me back. Then it became almost a game to accomplish the apparently impossible."[9] Powerful experiences like these of something moving in the depths of her own spirit foreshadow her later contemplative practice, but in the short run they led her to believe that she wanted to study psychology at the University of Breslau.

She was quickly disappointed. Psychology was still a young science in those days, but it was already showing some of the rationalist presuppositions that have made it, as usually practiced, a tool of only limited utility in the twentieth century. For Edith Stein, a full-blown psychology would be what the name implies, a study of the *psyche,* the Greek term for the soul. What she found at the University of Breslau, however, was a discipline dominated by quantitative measurements and reductive mechanical explanations. Something in her told her that what she was looking for in psychology could never be achieved by those means. But in her reading, almost by chance, she stumbled on a book that she thought spoke to her about her real concerns, the philosopher Edmund Husserl's *Logical Investigations.* Both the title of that book and the school of philosophy out of which it grew, phenomenology, seem at first sight hopelessly abstract subjects. But Edith truly discerned that behind the philosophical complexities lay a simple project: recovering the Spirit by an attempt to look at everything, all the "phenomena" in the world, as constituting the truth that precedes mere psychological processes. Among those phenomena are the experiences that have led to the historical development of religion and spirituality.

Practically speaking, Husserl and his students were responding to a set of problems that had plagued European thought for years. By focusing on inner experience, Descartes, Kant, and a variety of other modern philosophers had made it appear that there was little sure connection between our thoughts and the outside world. We could be sure of our psychological experiences, but what produced them, the "things in themselves," as Kant put it, were inaccessible to our minds. Descartes and Kant were seeking a way to preserve truth and the moral life. But the result was widespread skepticism, relativism, a psychology divorced from anything other than emotional and mental states, and the belief that science was the only form of real knowledge.

Husserl, as Edith correctly intuited, wanted to return to the main road of philosophy as a way to encounter reality, and his attempts to do so convinced her that the only way she could continue her studies was to enroll at the University of Göttingen under the tutelage of the man his students simply called "the Master." Stein's interest in his work turned into a passionate search that seems to have emerged as a replacement for her childhood faith. As one of her biographers describes it, for Husserl truth meant " 'luminous certainty' that something is or is not so, sharply distinct both from ordinary opinion and blind conviction."[10] This was no blissfully simple-minded psychology. Indeed, Husserl's students were encouraged to push beyond all merely subjective positions to reality itself, a goal, it has often been noticed, that has some similarities to medieval scholasticism. When Stein read Thomas Aquinas years later, she would recognize a spirit kindred to her former Master.

Husserl's approach also made it possible to speak again about the human person as a living whole, a subject that would fascinate Stein for years. Among the "phenomena" that Husserl encouraged students to examine was religion, and many did so, a large number of them becoming Catholics as a result of Husserl's undogmatic approach to studying all phenomena. The Master himself went through a long period of uncertainty about religion before making a profession of Christian faith before he died. Yet even at this period he recognized the powerful religious effects he was having on his students, joking that he ought to be canonized by the Church for leading so many of his students to Catholicism.[11]

It would take several years for that to happen to Edith Stein. She got her mother's permission to go to Göttingen, arriving there appropriately on Easter Sunday 1913. Within a few semesters, she had decided on a dissertation topic that combined her generous impulses with the search for truth: an essay on how empathy for another human being is possible. The Master was somewhat skeptical of this eager-beaver student and warned her to take some time before tackling this huge question. In the meantime, two other professors were to affect her in ways that were not strictly speaking philosophical, as the term is usually understood. But their influence was the kind of phenomenon that the wide embrace of phenomenology encouraged students to examine.

Max Scheler was a Jewish convert to Catholicism, and Adolf Reinach, a convert to Lutheranism. Scheler was a fascinating lecturer who attracted crowds of young students with his spiritually bracing views. He is often thought of as a kind of Catholic Nietzsche. For Scheler, God, with his transcendent attributes and fullness of being, was necessary to man, even in this world, so that religious faith made human beings more themselves. His enthusiastic lecturing did not appeal to Edith Stein's more sober approach to the intellectual life. But she later remarked that the way he spoke of the perennial reality of religious experience removed the rationalist blinders she had been wearing. Phenomenology was, if anything, an attempt to reason dispassionately and to record faithfully all human experiences. That the religious sense was a major human experience, Stein could not deny. She even began, characteristically, to think about whether the presence of the "Eternal" could be detected in the everyday world.

But it was Reinach, or rather his death at the battle of Flanders Field during World War I, who turned some of her new thoughts into living reality. Reinach is little remembered today, but he was so talented that he was Husserl's personal assistant and *Privatdozent* in Göttingen. His early death probably also truncated what could have been great contributions to modern philosophy. Yet Reinach had another side than the merely intellectual. By all accounts, he was the kind of teacher who touches the lives of his students deeply. Stein's account of their first encounter reflects the impression he made: "Never before could I remember meeting anybody so absolutely good-hearted. Naturally, I expected that love would be shown me by my relatives and close friends. But here was something entirely different. It was my first glimpse into a totally new world."[12] Reinach also had the steadiness and seriousness of character that she found missing in Scheler.

The experience may have been somewhat heightened because Stein was going through another bout of depression, which also seems to have had elements of a religious crisis. She was happy enough when busy, but when she was alone or idle she even had thoughts of suicide. Overwork may have been a factor. The only recreation she seems to have allowed herself was weekend backpacking with her friends in the Harz Mountains. Also, Germany was going through World War I during her university years, and Stein was a strong German patriot — indeed, naturally inclined to the virtues of duty, hard work, neatness, and a certain sternness that made up the Prussian ideal. Under the circumstances, she felt she was not doing enough for Germany as a student. She volunteered in April 1915 to be a nurse in the military Hospital for Infectious Diseases at Mährisch-Weisskirchen. Though she was back at her studies in September, she remarked later that in Reinach and the hospital experiences she encountered phenomena which were hard to ignore or rationalize away. Prominent among these was the lesson that it was good to be smart, but even better to do good.

Reinach was killed at the front in 1917. Stein dreaded having to see his wife, with whom she had also become close. Yet the encounter produced a surprise. Instead of a despairing widow, Stein found his wife full of Christian hope in the afterlife and actively comforting the others who had come to offer their condolences. Stein's account of this incident is pregnant with the future:

> It was my first encounter with the Cross and the divine power that it bestows on those who carry it. For the first time, I was seeing with my very eyes the Church, born from its Redeemer's sufferings, triumphant over the sting of death. That was the moment my unbelief collapsed and Christ shone forth — in the mystery of the Cross.[13]

(Reinach's widow later became a Catholic and his daughter entered a convent.)

For Stein, the meeting with the Reinachs and the whole subsequent story was providential. So, too, were other developments. In 1916, she finished her doctorate, which was awarded *summa cum laude*. Her accomplishments and easy demeanor so impressed the great Husserl that he asked her to become his research assistant and accompany him to his new position at the University of Freiburg. The relationship would be an uneven one because Husserl was almost entirely lacking in the human warmth Stein had found in Scheler and Reinach. Furthermore, he was terminally disorganized and, at least at this period, seemingly incapable of finishing the work that he had before him. Yet Stein's sense of humor shines through even at the moments of highest exertion. She joked to Roman Ingarden, himself a significant figure in modern philosophy: "The Master's [i.e., Husserl] latest prognosis for the production of [his great work] *Ideen*: first of all, I am to stay with him until I marry; then I may only accept a man who will also become his assistant, and the same holds for the children." Even supposing she could find a man to put up with her, she says, it is "essentially impossible" that any man could work with the demanding Husserl.[14]

Her labors were so heavy that they temporarily turned her into a "semi-imbecile" as she put Husserl's notes in order. Nonetheless, she became mesmerized by the work, so much so that she remarked that she hoped "to remain at such scholarly work totally and forever,"[15] and told her mother that all she needed was a lifetime income from somewhere. At the intellectual level at which she was being asked to work, it is not surprising that she had doubts about her philosophical gifts, even going so far as to wonder whether she had a right to neglect other, more practical work. Ironically, given the way Germany eventually treated her, she again felt guilty that she was doing nothing "for the fatherland," a nation so great that she thought it could not be defeated; she even compared it to the great powers of the ancient world, Sparta and Rome.[16]

Yet her contribution was an indispensable aid to German thought in moving Husserl's great work forward. She recognized that she had a sense of the overall architecture of the Master's thought that perhaps he himself did not. And, though humble about her own talents, she understood that she was a kind of intellectual midwife to Husserl in trying to get his work into publishable shape — something that without her would probably never get done. At the same time, by 1918 her old spirit of independence was rising again and she was chafing at the arrangement. She had to do at least a little something "original on the side" and be treated as a collaborator rather than as a mere subordinate. Also, it seems, there began to emerge a philosophical and spiritual distance between the two. She had originally thought Husserl provided a path away from the inward-looking idealism of German philosophy in the direction of reality. But the Master seemed to be slipping back, perhaps unwillingly, into the old trap. Other things were beginning to summon her energies. She left Husserl's service and returned to Breslau.

The dark devils that had bothered her the previous year now came out in full force. A kind of dark night of the soul ensued. She wanted rest, rest from the overwork for Husserl, but also rest of a different order. She was acutely conscious of being unable to think or truly love. Yet she also began "resting in God," patiently waiting for what Providence willed. And she found that mystical energies are stirred up in the soul by doing so. As she was to write in an essay published in 1922 about this development:

> It came in the wake of an experience which had overtaxed my strength, drained my spiritual resources, and robbed me of the ability to act. Compared to that inertia, arising from a lack of vital

energy, "resting in God" is something entirely new and distinct. One is a kind of "stillness of death," whereas the other is marked by a sense of tremendous activity ... which to the degree I give myself to it, fills me with life.... This invigorating flow of energy appears to be the result of activity other than my own.[17]

After the childhood experiences of something powerful moving in the depth of her soul, after the encounter with the consolations of the Cross in Reinach's widow, here was Edith Stein with a personal experience of the earliest beginnings of contemplation. It was the kind of psychology she left home to find. And she comments further: "This inner sphere is not only beyond the reach of all external influences, it is also beyond the attempts of the self to mold it. Therefore, when a change occurs within this sphere, it cannot be considered the result of some 'development' but a transformation accomplished by some transcendent power, a power outside the individual and the entire nexus of natural circumstances."[18]

But who was this transcendent power, other than a vague deity? A transformation was about to happen within her, one that would not obliterate the natural virtues and talents she had shown all her life, but it produced an unmistakable shift in her very being nonetheless. She read Kierkegaard. She was unmoved by a faith that was only an "existential leap," lacking a foundation in truth. Instead, in the summer of 1921, as was her custom, she went to visit her friend and fellow philosophy student Hedwig Conrad-Martius and her husband at their farm in Bergzabern. They, too, were having a religious crisis. The group held tightly to one another as they traversed unfamiliar spiritual territory. The Conrad-Martiuses would eventually resolve their difficulties by becoming Lutherans. Edith took a different path.

Looking for some nighttime reading, she came upon Saint Teresa of Avila's *Autobiography* on one of their bookshelves. From the first page, she was riveted by what she found in it. After passing the whole night reading, she remarked the next morning: "That is the truth." It is not easy to say exactly what in the Spanish saint's account of her life particularly moved Edith Stein, but it would not be a stretch of the imagination to say that she may have understood that the "psychology" in which she had always been interested is deeply and exhaustively explored in Teresa's humanly moving and eminently practical description of the soul's intercourse with God. The two women were in other respects quite different. Teresa a feminine and outgoing woman with little education; Edith a "masculine" intellect of world-class training. Yet that, too, may have been an attraction; perhaps Edith intuited that some shadowy side to her own personality needed development. At least that is what later happened in her single-minded devotion to contemplation.

Never being a person to waste time, Stein bought a catechism and missal and studied them. It is indicative of her sense of the faith that she did not buy books of theology and philosophy; conversion for her meant an intimately personal commitment rather than an intellectual solution to a problem. One day, sitting in a church, she was deeply struck by the palpable piety of a simple woman who came in to make a visit to the Blessed Sacrament. Stein asked the local priest to be baptized. After briefly examining her and discovering her solid knowledge of the faith, he agreed, but set January 1, 1922, as the date. When Edith told her mother, the reaction was worse than a fight: her mother simply wept at what she thought was the abandonment of the family faith. Edith, however, still went with her mother to the synagogue on Saturdays and took a deep interest in the readings as she never had before. For her, they were now the soil out of which the Jewish Savior would spring.

There are some indications that she was already thinking about becoming a Carmelite. But it would have been too early after her conversion for any prudent convent to accept her. And her spiritual director at the time, a Canon Schwind, discouraged her for two reasons. First, her mother was still smarting from Edith's conversion, and the two, for all their disagreements, were still unusually close. Second, he believed she had a responsibility to use her intellectual gifts in the service of the Church. Finding out how to do so remained to be settled. So in the meantime, he recommended her for a post as a teacher at Saint Magdalena's, the Dominican school in Speyer.

Though teaching German in a school might have become a disappointing end to such bright academic promise, in fact it led to a wider intellectual world. Edith Stein always brought a great deal of life to whatever she did, and she impressed the students by her intellect and quiet power. In fact, the concentration that people detected behind her calm exterior intimidated quite a few students. By all indications, her prayer life was growing by leaps and bounds. She would spend hours, motionless, in front of the tabernacle. Anyone who has tried to pray knows that the human animal cannot easily spend hours praying without extraordinary love for prayer itself or extraordinary outside graces, or both. The experience seemed so natural to her that she remarked in response to queries about how she did it: "I cannot understand how prayer can make one tired."[19] For such a normally sensitive women, the comment suggests an almost blinding experience, since most people recognize how difficult prayer is. Incredibly, with everything else she was already committed to, she began working with the poor. But as often happens with people who have other large talents, Providence did not let them go to waste.

Almost by chance, she met the distinguished Jesuit scholar Erich Przywara at Speyer, who recognized her potential and encouraged her not to abandon her intellectual work. He convinced her to translate into German John Henry Newman's *Letters and Journals,* which she did quite quickly and professionally. Then he made an even more momentous suggestion: she had spent so much time studying phenomenology, perhaps she could profit from translating Thomas Aquinas's treatises, *Quaestiones Disputatae de Veritate (Disputed Questions on Truth).* The old Jesuit was a crafty bird. He must have understood that Edith might find some things on the philosophical level in Aquinas that she had missed, but had been seeking, in Husserl.

That was exactly what happened, though it took remarkable self-discipline for Edith to do a little Aquinas every day in between all her other duties. In addition, she began to see how faith could sharpen the intellect, direct the intellect to love (a virtue higher than knowledge), and reconcile the seeming contradictions between the life of scholarship and the life of contemplation. When the great modern philosopher Martin Heidegger, another student of Husserl's, asked her to contribute an essay to a 1929 Festschrift in honor of the Master, she submitted a late-night dialogue between Aquinas and Husserl. Heidegger convinced her to turn this into a regular article, but a manuscript of the original version still exists to attest to her lively sense of a possible exchange between the two great minds.

Though she was teaching at a Dominican school and had made the acquaintance of Aquinas, the great Dominican friar-philosopher, her initial attraction toward the austerities and devoted prayer of the Carmelites also began to grow. A letter she wrote to a friend during the 1920s lamenting that Husserl had not made a religious commitment expressed her conviction that "prayer and sacrifice, in my opinion, are much more crucial than anything we can say."[20] It is important to remember in reading words like these, which might be mistaken for conventional piety, that the writer was a first-rate intellectual and had been grappling with intellectual, moral, and spiritual questions during these years in ways that can only be imagined. She deeply felt the impulse to offer sacrifices for others and would soon come to include many people in that generous impulse.

Perhaps Przywara best understood her. He remarks that she was growing into a double nature in her spiritual being: "large feminine receptivity and companionship coupled with severe masculine objectivity."[21]

In addition, she was "saying" a great deal at the time. Thanks to Przywara, Stein was invited to lecture at Catholic institutions all over Germany. Many of these lectures had to do with the position of women in modern societies. Though deeply conservative in a cultural sense and even politically, Edith Stein thought that modern circumstances made it important to recognize, simultaneously, that women have a special role as mothers, but that they would increasingly have to find their way into the larger society as well. She had earlier demonstrated in favor of women's suffrage when it was a fringe and highly eccentric position, usually taken up only by radical leftists. She and her university friends were eccentric both in terms of a society that had not yet recognized female claims but also in terms of the feminist radicals. Stein and comrades were conservative feminists, a contradiction in terms according to the usual categories.

Her power as a speaker is widely attested, but it was not a power derived from rhetorical force or passion. In fact, what seems to have most struck the majority of her hearers was the delicate, almost quiet way in which she spoke, which was combined with a spiritual purity and depth that made her seemingly simple statements powerful. The entry of women into the professions, she knew, would present temptations, especially in light of the modern tendency toward agnosticism and even atheism in public life. So she proposed to her listeners: "More than anything else today, what is needed is the baptism of spirit and fire. This alone can prepare those who shape human life to take their rightful place at the front lines in the great battle between Christ and Lucifer. There is no more urgent task than to be constantly armed and ready for this battle. For, 'If the salt loses its savor, how can it be restored?' "[22] This placed added burdens on women, who would not only enter the workplace as workers in the male mold; they would also have to bring maternal concern and a deeper perspective to bear in order to restore dignity and spirituality to work.

Though Stein was quite successful in this lecturing, she wanted to put her own words into practice and teach at a university. In the German system, this requires a second doctorate and the writing of a second dissertation, the *Habilitationsschrift*. So in 1931, after spending Easter at the Benedictine convent at Beuron, she left her teaching post and applied to become a *Privatdozent* at Freiburg, Husserl's university. While she

waited for a reply, she returned home to live with her mother and got the
latter's permission to take a Catholic post at the University of Breslau,
if one was offered. Meanwhile, she was already working at her new
dissertation. She wrote several hundred pages of a dense philosophical
argument excavating the similarities and differences between Aquinas
and Husserl without wholly committing herself to either of them. It was
called *Act and Potency* at this stage, two terms drawn from Aristotelian
and Thomist philosophy. (It would later be developed fully and published
under the title *Finite and Eternal Being*.)

But despite her evident industry and productivity, the way to a university career was blocked by two factors: first, phenomenology and
Catholic scholasticism were not in the mainstream of German university
studies, and the fact that these were being done by a woman did not
help the candidacy; second, growing anti-Semitism in Germany made it
difficult, if not impossible, for even a converted Jewish woman to expect
employment.

It was good for her to be back in close contact with her mother. But
her sister Rosa, who had decided to become a Catholic herself, only de-
laying out of respect for their mother, felt isolated in a non-Christian
environment and needed her presence as well. Duty beckoned again,
however. Edith was offered a lectureship at the Catholic Educational Institute in Münster. She did not reply immediately, wanting to continue
on with her dissertation and see if a university professorship would come
through. But by the spring of 1932 she decided to accept. Becoming a
Carmelite was still in her mind, but her spiritual director, the Benedictine Dom Raphael Walzer, convinced her that she was meant to make
contributions to Germany outside the cloister.

Edith Stein took a great interest in educational questions, especially
for women, and not only because she had been teaching for over a decade. One of her central worries was that women would be unprepared
for the new responsibilities the twentieth century had thrust upon them.
She was particularly distressed at the way she believed Hitler came to
power, in part by playing on the emotions of German women.[23] Also, she
believed that sex was becoming too prominent in all dimensions of culture and life and that it needed to be actively curtailed by presenting its
true place in the Christian life, within marriage. These and other weighty
reasons made her appointment to this Catholic Educational Institute one
that she thought might bear important fruit, especially since the Federation of Catholic Teachers and the Association of Catholic Women
Teachers were closely linked to the Institute.

She brought to this work the accumulated effort she had made since her university days at developing a "philosophical anthropology." The term was used by many philosophers at the time to distinguish between the kind of anthropology normally practiced, which treated human beings as essentially an extension, if not members, of the higher primate species, and an anthropology that would recognize all the differences in human beings that cannot be accounted for by comparative studies with animals. Yet something in her work at this time made her feel a misfit in both the Institute and the Catholic philosophical circles in which she was beginning to move. Despite all the lectures she was giving, she remarked: "It is always one small, simple truth about which I speak; what we can do to live close to the Lord."[24]

It may have been that she was beginning to sense that philosophy or even thinking itself could not much help with the situation in which Germany more and more found itself. As early as the first few years of the 1930s, she recognized that the Jewish people were threatened, and she identified herself with them in their precariousness. Her friends and spiritual director thought she was exaggerating. So strong was the conviction, however, that she wrote to Pope Pius XI, requesting a private audience in the hope that she could persuade the pope to avert catastrophe by an encyclical in defense of the Jewish people. He sent a blessing for her and her family, but his schedule was too full to see her. Nonetheless, her request may have made a modest contribution to the apostolic letter Pius published in 1937 with the German title *Mit brennender Sorge* ("With Burning Concern").

One sign that her premonitions were truer than the calmer opinions of her friends was that she was quietly asked to leave the Münster Institute until the anti-Semitic wave passed. An offer of a teaching position in South America arrived in Münster. Though she considered it, finally she decided it was not for her. Instead, as she was praying on April 30, 1933, she asked whether she could now in good conscience enter the Carmel; when she rose to leave, she believed that God had communicated to her that it was precisely what he wanted her to do.

Her decision to become a Carmelite meant she would have to face her mother, who, she knew, would think of the move as a final separation from the family. Though Edith spent almost a month with her mother before entering the convent, it was a time when two strong-willed women, attached to each other both by their similarities and differences, grappled one last time. In a dialogue that perhaps could only occur between a quintessential Jewish mother and her brilliant Jewish, but also Christian daughter, the mother asked, "Why did you have to get to know him?" that is, Christ, without, of course, mentioning the name. "He was a good man — I'm not saying anything against him. But why did he have to go and make himself God?"[25]

It did not helped the situation that the Jewish people were increasingly facing persecution at the time. Yet to Edith there was no opposition between being a Jew and being a Christian. In fact, they both had a special place for her personally. As she remarked years later to Father Johannes Hirschmann: "You don't know what it means to me to be a daughter of the chosen people — to belong to Christ, not only spiritually, but according to the flesh."[26] The great Carmel in Palestine, which stands near the caves where Elijah once dwelled, and the personal experience of reading Saint Teresa of Avila became for her a kind of living symbol for the way Judaism branched into Christianity. But none of this was understood by her mother. Frau Stein saw the deep piety in her daughter at prayer, but still could not accept what was about to happen. When Edith left on October 12, 1933, her birthday, her mother did manage at least to spit out: "May the Eternal One be with you."[27]

Deciding to enter the Carmel at Cologne brought its own rigors. By this time, Edith was in her early forties and had the formed habits of a middle-aged adult. She threw herself into trying to adapt to the unusual life of the Carmelites. She had never done much manual labor before, and all novices had to help with the work of the community. From needlework to scrubbing floors, there was a lot of it to do. She had always worked hard, but with her brain and not her hands. And she had always been very good at intellectual work; at Cologne, for the first time in her life, she was asked to do work at which she was decidedly *not* one of the best. Characteristically, Stein said she never laughed so much as during this period when her inadequacies were revealed for all to see. Later she would remark that living in community, as opposed to the mostly solitary life she had led earlier, was useful in that it uncovered faults that otherwise would have remained hidden. But for a person who liked to give herself wholly to and excel at whatever she did, there must have been a great deal of unexpected humiliation in these early times. It was a bit like a middle-aged professor having to take basic training to join the army.

The years of individual prayer and contemplation deepened Stein's sense that something larger than her own personal story was beginning to unfold. Before she entered the Cologne Carmel, she mentioned to the prioress during their first conversation together that, given the situation in Germany: "Human activity cannot help us, but only the Passion of Christ — my desire is to share in that."[28] And in some of the things she wrote soon after entering the convent, she hints at what she may have meant in that interview. In an essay on prayer, she notes what she regards as the real motive forces of history:

> In the hiddenness of the quiet chamber of Nazareth, the power of the Holy Ghost came upon the Virgin praying in solitude, and brought about the Incarnation of the Savior. . . . In the solitary conversation of consecrated souls there are prepared those widely visible events of the Church's history that renew the face of the earth. . . . The official historians are silent about these invisible and unaccountable powers. But they are known to the trust of the faithful and the patiently examining and carefully weighing judgment of the Church. And our own time, seeing that all else fails, finds itself more and more urged to hope for ultimate salvation from these hidden sources.[29]

It may have been the external threats that led her to observe that the mystery of the Incarnation and the mystery of iniquity are closely related: the existence of the latter requiring God's action by means of the former.

During this period events outside and inside the Carmel seem to be coming together for her into one single act. The very day of her profession, a friend expressed relief that, at least, she would be safe in the convent. But the now Sister Teresa Benedicta of the Cross had chosen her religious name because she believed that she was blessed by the Lord's suffering. She anticipated that she would have to share in that Passion. About her supposed security, she replied: "Oh no, I do not think so. They [i.e., the Nazis] will surely get me out of here. In any case I cannot count on being left in peace here." And according to the friend, "It was clear to her that she was going to suffer for her people, that she was meant to bring many home."[30] Sister Teresa Benedicta was aware that remaining faithful to this calling would require trust in God: "To be a child of God, that means to be led by the Hand of God, to do the will of God, not one's own will, to place every care and every hope in the Hand of God and not to worry about one's future. On this rests the freedom and the joy of the child of God. But how few of even the truly pious, even of those ready for heroic sacrifices, possess this freedom."[31] When in April of 1936 she lost her right to vote because of Nazi anti-Semitic legislation, she wrote to a friend: "Please do not worry about it. For a long time, I have been prepared for much worse things."[32] Edith Stein was so literally truthful that we can take this as a sure sign of the long spiritual preparation that would eventually enable her to meet her end not only with dignity but with concern for the others with whom she made the final journey.

In a sense, she is providing an answer in these remarks to a political question that could not be solved by mere politics or philosophy. She observes in an essay on Christmas that the King of Kings came in a very different way than a political reading of the history of Israel led many to expect: "The Romans remained masters in the land, high priests and scribes continued to oppress the poor. Whoever belonged to the Lord carried his Kingdom of Heaven invisibly within himself."[33] It was what the Jewish Virgin in Bethlehem had begun that had led her to becoming the Mother of God and the Church. Several people have remarked that Sister Teresa Benedicta started to become more maternal in the Cologne Carmel during this time, perhaps by reflecting on such truths.

Meanwhile, her own mother neared her end. Sister Teresa received news that her mother was sick, for the first time in her life. That alone was ominous. The cloister made it impossible for Teresa to be with the dying old woman, a cross in itself. But a remarkable thing happened that, given the emotional bond between the two, seems entirely plausible. The Feast of the Exaltation of the Cross, September 14, is the day when Carmelites habitually renew their vows. On that day in 1936, Sister Teresa was making her third such renewal. When her turn came, "my mother was with me. I distinctly felt her presence."[34] This phenomenon, duly recorded and mentioned to a friend, received an uncanny confirmation: later that day a telegram arrived at Cologne informing Sister Teresa that her mother had died — at the very hour the Carmelite was renewing vows.

Motherhood and the maternal were much in her mind at this period. In her book *Finite and Eternal Being*, finished just a few weeks before her mother's death, Sister Teresa confronted one of the burning questions of the existential movement that was emerging from Husserl and Husserl's student Heidegger: how can we, transitory beings that we are and exposed to so many threats to our existence, live without anxiety? Her answer came from sources other than the merely phenomenological:

> The undeniable fact that my being is transitory ... and exposed to
> the possibility of nonbeing is matched by the other, equally unde-

niable fact that, notwithstanding the transitoriness, I *am* and am *kept in being* from one moment to the other, and embrace a lasting Being in my transitory being. I know myself held, and in this I have peace and security — not in the self-assured security of a man who stands in his own strength on firm ground, but the sweet and blissful security of the child who is carried by a strong arm — considered objectively a no less reasonable security. Or would the child be "reasonable" who lived in constant fear that its mother might drop it?[35]

With Frau Stein dead, the way was open for Edith's sister Rosa to be received into the Church. She was baptized on December 15, 1936.

But otherwise the situation was worsening everywhere. Sister Teresa remarked on the deaths of the Spanish Carmelites, then experiencing persecution from the Republicans in the Spanish Civil War. By Easter of 1937, even the eminent Husserl had been driven out of his position at Freiburg because of anti-Semitic passions and had taken up asylum, with his wife, at the convent of Saint Lioba. Husserl had long remained ambivalent about God. But he wrote to Sister Teresa after her entrance into Carmel that he was happy for her. He then made a remarkable statement about his life's work: "I wanted to reach God without God. I had to eliminate God from my scientific thought in order to open the way to those who do not know Him as you do, by the sure road of faith passing through the Church."[36] Husserl also admitted that he took a great risk in using this approach, but professed that he was bound in the depth of his heart to God, and even hints at belief in Christ.

On Good Friday 1937, the Master had a powerful experience; near death, he saw some kind of vision, at first of something frightening from which he recoiled, then a powerful light. He had another vision the day he died, but before he could describe it, he passed away. After a lifetime of patient investigation of the fullest possible truths, the old man dying in a Catholic convent on the border between Judaism and Christianity, driven there by one of the century's most evil regimes, presents a moving image. External circumstances and internal developments seemed to be coming together for many people caught up in the persecution that was more and more clearly threatening not only Jews but any Christian who tried to resist the new Nazi order and spirit.

Indeed, in her *Life of Edith Stein*, the prioress of Edith Stein's Cologne Carmel made the point about the common threat by 1938: "The principles of National Socialism and the Government of Hitler had so clearly proved hostile to Christ and God, that even the most unsuspecting German could no longer be in doubt about the goal at which they were aiming." Religious houses were being closed and the ones that remained open were under serious pressures. The very choice of a celibate life was looked upon as unpatriotic, contrary to the Nazi ideology of being fruitful and bearing large numbers of Aryan children for the Fatherland.

Under these circumstances, the Cologne Carmel faced some terrible decisions. When the 1938 elections were held, the sisters had to debate how to vote; since the "secret" ballots were not secret any longer, Hitler would win, of course, whatever the real vote. So several sisters argued that it would be a pointless and dangerous gesture to vote against him. Typical of Sister Teresa Benedicta, she vehemently opposed this infidelity to the truth, even for the best of motives, whatever the consequences. In 1938, the sisters were not even allowed to go to the polling places. Nazi election officials showed up at the convent and collected the ballots. When they found out that "Dr. Edith Stein" was a non-Aryan, they made a note of the fact and left.

Dr. Stein was familiar enough with the ways of the world to know that she was now a danger to the whole Cologne community. The other sisters thought she was exaggerating the danger. But she immediately began making efforts to be transferred to the Carmel in Bethlehem. Unfortunately, Nazi authorities were by then denying visas to German Jews who wished to go to Palestine, and the plan came to nothing.

In 1938, Stein wrote to Mother Petra of the Ursulines, who had befriended her earlier, using imagery from the Jewish scriptures that Edith had meditated on since her youth: "I firmly believe that the Lord has accepted my life as an offering for all. It's important for me to keep Queen Esther in mind and remember how she was separated from her people just so that she could intercede for them before the king."[37] Separation of a kind soon followed. On November 8, 1938, the outbreak of attacks on Jewish businesses, homes, and synagogues known as *Kristallnacht* made it obvious that Jews were threatened everywhere in Germany. The beast was now out in the open, and Sister Teresa Benedicta observed: "This is the shadow of the Cross falling on my people. This is the fulfillment of the curse that my people has called down on itself. Cain must be persecuted, but woe to him who touches Cain. Woe also to this city and this country, where God shall revenge what is today done to the Jews."[38] Several of Edith Stein's siblings managed to emigrate to the United States and elsewhere. The prioress of the Cologne Carmel, seeing that Jewish Christians were no longer safe in Germany, sent Edith to the Carmel in Echt, Holland, on December 31, 1938.

Echt had been founded in 1875 when another group of sisters had been expelled from Germany during Bismarck's *Kulturkampf* against the Catholic Church. So it was a fitting place for refuge from a new threat. When she arrived, Sister Teresa made a point of visiting the graves of the German nuns who had come to Echt during the persecution. She seems to have had many premonitions, however, that, as welcoming as Echt was, it would not protect her from the storm about to break over all Europe. Her last Testament, written during her first year there, eloquently states:

> I joyfully accept in advance the death God has appointed for me, in perfect submission to his most holy will. May the Lord accept my life and death for the honor and the glory of his name, for the needs of his holy Church — especially for the preservation, sanctification, and final perfecting of our holy Order, and in particular for the Carmels of Cologne and Echt — for the Jewish people, that the Lord may be received by his own and his kingdom come in glory, for the deliverance of Germany and peace throughout the world, and finally, for all my relatives living and dead and all whom God has given me; may none of them be lost.[39]

On Passion Sunday that year, she wrote the prioress with a remarkable request: "Please may Your Reverence allow me to offer myself to the Heart of Jesus as a sacrifice of expiation for true peace: that the reign of the Antichrist may perish, if possible without a new World War, and a new order may be established. I should like to do this today, because it is the twelfth hour. I know that I am nothing, but Jesus desires it, and He will certainly call many others to this in these days."[40] The hidden mysteries which she had earlier spoken of as the driving force of history, emerge here in concrete terms.

It is easy to read words like these with knowledge of what was to happen soon after and categorize them as what is only to be expected of a martyr and saint. But it is important to recognize the near prophetic quality of the statement and the universal fidelity to God, vocation, people, nation, and individuals, which are all interwoven together into what finally appears a special mission. Edith Stein did not know that she would become Saint Teresa Benedicta of the Cross. It was the purification of the will, represented by words like these, that transformed her from one to the other.

In 1940, her sister Rosa managed to make her way to Echt and seeming safety. The two sisters at least had the consolation of facing the future together. Sister Teresa Benedicta was devoting seven hours a day to prayer and rapidly learning Dutch. But that same year, the Germans invaded Holland and brought danger close to hand again. As she had at earlier periods of stress, Edith Stein believed it was important to go on with duties, not letting the turmoil in the outside world gain further victories by frightening souls into abandoning their given tasks. Ironically, she was ordered by the Echt prioress to write a study of Saint John of the Cross, an assignment she regarded as a great grace. It was the last writing she would do. *The Science of the Cross* appeared posthumously.

It has sometimes been asked whether Edith Stein was actually a martyr or whether she was just incidentally destroyed by the Nazi juggernaut. The Church has decided that she was, indeed, a martyr, and the circumstances supporting that decision are quite persuasive. In addition to her numerous prayers offering herself up for reparation, Stein had several chances to escape from the whole situation. She had been offered a teaching position in Latin America earlier, but refused it out of a desire for solidarity. Hers was no blind sacrifice, however. She sought asylum for herself and Rosa in the Carmel at Le Pauquier, in Switzerland. For Stein, this was following a biblical principle; she even carried around with her next to her heart a piece of paper on which was written Matthew 10:23: "When you are persecuted in one town, take refuge in another. In truth, I say to you that you will not have finished all the cities of Israel before the Son of Man has come."[41] Tragically, though the Swiss convent had room for Edith, a professed member, it was already too crowded to take Rosa. Since leaving her sister behind was out of the question, Edith stayed in Echt.

But a second reason to regard her as a martyr also appears in that her lifelong vocation to the truth was the final reason for her fate. She could have tried to save herself and Rosa by going into hiding, either in another convent or in a private home. Many Jews did so in Holland, and some survived. A priest suggested that course. The Dutch populace were by and large quite heroic in risking their own lives and well-being to do what they knew was right. But Edith Stein did not think it was right for several reasons. First, it would bring reprisals against the Echt Carmel. Though these would probably have been of a limited duration, she was not willing to risk others on her behalf. Second, she was reluctant to do something "illegal," a stance reminiscent of the Greek philosopher Socrates' refusal to escape from prison, despite his innocence. Characteristically, she also mentioned that Protestants in Germany were always slandering Catholics for lying. And she would not provide any public pretext for the charge of being untruthful.[42] In the final account, we have to say that, for multiple reasons, she refused an ignoble way of saving herself and as a result fell afoul of the Nazi machinery. Given the fate this moral purity meant, we can only regard it as martyrdom, pure and simple. On October 11, 1998, Pope John Paul II officially declared: "*A young woman in search of the truth* has become a saint and martyr through the silent working of divine grace.... Now alongside Teresa of Avila and Thérèse of Lisieux, another Teresa takes her place among the host of saints who do honor to the Carmelite Order."[43]

But like many stories of the martyrs in the twentieth century, Edith Stein's trails off without definite conclusion or much detail. We know a few facts about her last days, but almost nothing more. By 1942, Nazi intentions for the Jews were clear. Even in Holland, their days were numbered. To their credit, Dutch Christians of all denominations objected to the German outrages. Some wore the yellow Star of David out of solidarity. Others engaged in open protests against deportations "to the East." The leaders of both the Catholic and Protestant churches sent a joint telegram to the SS officer responsible, Reichskommissar Seyss-Inquart, recording their disapproval of treatment of Jews within Holland, which effectively deprived them of participation in national life, as well as the ominous shipping of Jews to far distant camps. The church leaders made a final point of objecting to Nazi treatment of Jewish converts to Christianity, which prevented them from exercising religious liberty.

The telegram gained a brief respite for the "Jewish Christians," but the deportations of other Jews continued until almost all of them were gone. Church leaders planned another public protest. But the Reichskommissar, alerted to their plans, forbade it. A few leaders complied with his order, in some cases out of fear, in others out of a prudential calculation that it was the best way to avoid reprisals. Among those who refused to comply was the Catholic Archbishop of Utrecht. He ordered a pastoral letter to be read in all the parishes of Holland on July 26, 1942, which read in part:

Dear brethren, let us begin by examining ourselves in a spirit of profound humility and sorrow. Are we not partly to blame for the calamities which we are suffering? Have we always sought first for God's kingdom and his righteousness? Have we always fulfilled the demands of justice and charity toward our fellow men?...When we examine ourselves, we are forced to admit that all of us have failed....Let us beseech God...to swiftly bring about a just peace in the world and to strengthen the people of Israel so sorely tested in these days....[44]

It was a bold gesture but had disastrous results. The German authorities began considering whether to nationalize some of the Catholic charitable institutions in Holland because of the bishops's interference. (It has sometimes been suggested that Pius XII was hesitant to make too open a criticism of the Nazis out of concern that, given the Dutch example, he might provoke even wider retaliation. At the time and after the war, his quiet exertions on behalf of Jews earned him widespread acclaim from figures like Einstein and the chief rabbi of Rome, who converted to Catholicism with his wife in gratitude. Today, his prudence is unfortunately often considered a moral failure.) The Nazis could not attack the Church directly, so, in retaliation, a week later on August 2, they rounded up all the Catholics of Jewish background.

As a result, Edith and Rosa Stein were among those ordered to pack a few belongings and proceed with the SS to the Roermond police station. The departure was heartrending. The streets were filled with Dutch anti-Nazi protesters. But the two sisters were quickly taken to the station, where it is reported that Edith said upon entering, "Praised be Jesus Christ." It was not a statement likely to win her friends, and the police were not amused. She had made a practice of doing the same thing every time she was called in by the police because she thought it made it clear that what was occurring was the "age-old fight between Jesus and Lucifer."[45]

All the prisoners were then forwarded to the main holding camp at Amersfoort. Edith Stein showed great peacefulness throughout this sudden plunge from the tranquillity of the cloister to the brutality of the Nazi final solution. The years of abandonment to the Cross paid dividends, and not only for her. Numerous witnesses confirm that she was not at all self-absorbed amid the anxious circumstances but a radiant island of consolation and confidence for many others, especially children.

But things moved fast now. The whole group, over a thousand, was shipped by train to Westerbork, the central detention camp. One survivor reports that while Edith was still calm, she displayed a profound sense of sorrow at Westerbork, "a Pietà without the Christ"; another immediately judged from her preternaturally calm demeanor in such awful conditions that "here is someone truly great."[46] They stayed at Westerbork only four days, August 3–6. Somehow, Stein was able to communicate with the sisters at Echt. She wrote them a note during these few days saying: "I am content about everything. One cannot acquire a *scientia crucis* [science of the cross] unless one begins by really suffering the weight of the cross. From the very beginning I have had this inner conviction and I have said from the bottom of my heart, *Ave crux, spes unica* [Hail to the Cross, our only hope]." On August 7, all but a handful of the internees were put into freight cars, those who had been taken out of religious institutions still wearing their distinctive clothes.

Those religious habits are responsible for the last two bits of information available about Edith Stein's journey toward death. When the train stopped at Schifferstadt, the stationmaster was asked by someone in dark clothing on one of the cars whether he knew the family of Canon Schwind. He did and, in fact, Schwind had just left the station. The woman asked him to convey Edith Stein's greetings to Schwind and his family. The only other fact to emerge came, sadly, from Breslau, Stein's home town. According to a man working as a mail deliverer, he was on a train being refueled on one track when a freight train pulled into a parallel track at the Breslau station. His eye caught a woman in a nun's habit who said, "It's terrible. We don't even have containers to relieve ourselves." And then: "This is my home; I'll never see it again." Years later, when he read about Stein, he felt sure she was the one he had glimpsed. But we will never know for sure. According to Nazi records, Sister Teresa Benedicta of the Cross died on August 9, 1942, in an Auschwitz gas chamber. Only a week earlier, she had been a cloistered sister in the contemplative stillness of the Echt Carmel, seeking to live the truth.

# -EIGHT-

# SAINT MAXIMILIAN KOLBE AND SOME POLISH VICTIMS OF NAZISM

**A**T AUSCHWITZ, everything was designed for death, even the desire for life. If a prisoner succeeded in escaping from the extermination camp, the guards retaliated by killing ten or twenty of the six hundred or so prisoners remaining from his cell block. The usual procedure was to make the executions as humiliating and excruciating as possible: the prisoners selected were stripped naked, virtually buried alive in a lightless underground bunker, and given no food or water. All this was quite familiar to the Auschwitz prisoners. So anyone who sought freedom and life by flight did so with no little guilt. The whole system was set up to punish the slightest human impulse with a response that was as degrading, dehumanizing, and destructive as could be imagined.

Even without specially sadistic punishments, life in the concentration camp was already intolerable. Prisoners were worked, starved, or beaten to death, shot in the back of the head, driven to suicide on the electrified fences; those who might hang on from day to day did so in a constant atmosphere of overwhelming fear. Within a few months of organizing the concentration camps, the Nazis began setting up a great death machine in which millions would be gassed, their bodies cremated in great ovens or merely tipped in heaps into common graves. It was entirely understandable that anyone who got the chance would try to flee as fast and as far as possible. But there was a very high price: the diabolical machinery exacted retribution in the blood of others for anyone who tried to elude its death grip.

On July 31, 1941, a prisoner from Block 14 escaped. The camp guards set up roadblocks for miles around and the German shepherds were put on the trail. That night, the other prisoners in Block 14 were interrogated about the escapee's plans and whereabouts. Already emaciated from months of heavy work with short rations, they received no dinner. The next day, they stood at attention in the hot sun without food or water as the Nazis searched. By evening, the deputy commander at Auschwitz, an officer named Fritsch, announced in no little irritation to the "Polish swine" that ten of them would be chosen to go to Block 13, where they would pay in the usual way for their friend.

In some ways, it did not much matter who was chosen. Death was near for everyone. The Auschwitz Kommandant Rudolph Höss or one of his subordinates used to announce to each arriving trainload of prisoners: "Let me tell you that you have not arrived at a health spa, but a German concentration camp. You will find only one exit — the crematorium chimney. If you don't like the sound of this, you can leave at once by throwing yourself on the electric fences. If any of you are Jews, you have the right to live no longer than two weeks. Priests one month. The rest of you three months."[1]

We are familiar with the Jewish victims of Auschwitz from the vast literature that has grown up around this unspeakable horror. The thriving Polish Jewish community of over three million souls emerged from the war reduced to under a hundred thousand. But at the time of this particular escape, the Final Solution had not yet been put into full effect. Jews at Auschwitz at the time were about 10 percent of the total, roughly their proportion in the Polish population. The first transport specifically dedicated to Jews would begin seven months after these events, in March 1942.[2] Less known, however, is that fact that three million Poles, almost all of them Christians, also perished at Auschwitz. Among those three million, one-fifth of all Polish priests died, along with several thousand religious brothers and nuns, and virtually the whole intellectual and political leadership of the nation. For the Nazis, *die schweinerischen Pfaffen,* "priest swine," were hated second only to the Jews and treated accordingly.

But even if all these groups were vilified and marked for death, some deaths were worse than others. As in battle, a gunshot or electrocution was, given the alternatives, at least a quick passage to the next world. Other punishments like back breaking labor or starvation were a slow slide into the darkness. But nothing was more fearsome than the Starvation Bunker under Block 13. No one ever returned from there. A virtual tomb, prisoners selected for that death went into total darkness and were only in touch with the outside world when, once a day, the guards came to remove the bodies of the dead. No food, no talk, no mercy. Yet the worst of these trials was the lack of water. Prisoners drank their own and each other's urine. When that dried up, they underwent what doctors know to be one of the most hideous ways to die: the slow collapse of the system from thirst with all the physical and mental agonies it entails. Many went mad in the sadistic conditions; they were meant to.

The ten from Block 14 chosen for the Starvation Bunker were selected the same way previous groups had been: by the whim of the Kommandant. Fritsch clearly enjoyed drawing out the suspense and displaying his power over life and death. As he went down the lines, supposedly examining the health of each individual, indicating one, then another, then another, the prisoners were frozen in terror. The men selected were immediately hurried off to their fate, often leaving last, brave words: "So long friends! We'll meet again up there, where real justice is meted out!" "Long live Poland! It is for her that I give my life!" In this group, however, one man, prisoner 5659, a Sergeant Francis Gajowniczek, broke down, crying: "My poor wife, my poor children. Goodbye, goodbye!"[3]

It was a scene that had probably occurred countless times. But before the group could be herded off, something unprecedented happened. Prisoner number 16670 began to walk up to the Kommandant, a bold act in itself since any unauthorized moves by prisoners usually got them shot on the spot. Later, survivors recounted that nothing similar had ever occurred. Miraculously, 16670 went up to the officer without incident and, in German, said, "I would like to die in place of one of these men." Even more miraculously, the brutal and sardonic Fritsch did not dismiss the ragged prisoner out of hand. "Why?" he asked.

It was a delicate question. Anything resembling heroism, defiance, or a show of spirit would have brought instant consequences. Prisoner 16670 cited a Nazi principle: "The sick and the weak must be liquidated," and added, "I am an old man, sir, and good for nothing. My life is no longer of use to anyone...."[4] Fritsch inquired as to whose place he wanted to take. The one with the wife and children. And who are you? A Catholic priest. A less crude man might have sensed that this meant a heroic act was being performed in front of men who were being deliberately stripped of all human dignity. But Fritsch was only aware of the fact that he had one of the despised *Pfarren.* There is no other human explanation for his immediate acceptance of the priest's offer. Fritsch ordered his assistant, Palitsch, to cross out number 5659 and add 16670, Franciscan Father Maximilian Kolbe, to the death list.

In that instant, it might be said, the whole machinery of death was broken and reversed by the free act of one man giving his life for another. (Gajowniczek would live another fifty-four years, dying in the 1990s; during his life he believed he had been miraculously cured of spinal tuberculosis, contracted at Auschwitz, by Kolbe's intercession.) The harsh conditions in Auschwitz usually set men to fighting with one another over a scrap of bread or some small relief among the heavy burdens. The conditions enforced the most rigorous of zero-sum games: what was taken by one person came at the expense of another. But Kolbe's act, a Christian act, introduced something that did not — could not — fit into the savage bestiality of Auschwitz. He had shown the greatest heroism and human dignity in the face of the worst torture and degradation the camp held. So far as is known, no other prisoner followed his example. But the ones who witnessed that act never forgot it, prisoners and SS officers alike. One of the reasons we have such relatively good information about the whole matter is that nothing in Auschwitz could obliterate it from their memories.

Nor was the choice to die for another the last noble act in Kolbe's memorable life. There was more, much more. Bruno Borgowiec, a Pole who served as interpreter and a kind of undertaker for the Starvation Bunker, has provided stunning accounts of what happened next. They were all ordered to strip naked before going into the bunker. No doubt Kolbe thought of Christ being stripped of his garments. The guards shoved them into the dark hole, which already contained prisoners who had spent several days there. *"Ihr werdet ingeben wie die Tulpen!"* Borgowiec recalls a guard's ominous threat: "You will dry up like tulips!"[5]

They all died, of course, but not quite like flowers that bloom one day and are gone the next. Thanks to Kolbe they died like men. Good men. As Borgowiec later described the astonishing change: "It doesn't even seem like the Starvation Bunker.... When I go down there, it's like descending into the crypt of a church." Kolbe had organized prayers among the men along with the singing of hymns and recitation of the rosary: "Sometimes they would be so absorbed in prayer that they would not even realize the guards had come for the daily inspection and had opened the door of their cell. Only when the SS began shouting at them would they stop praying."[6] It was as if, even in the darkness of an Auschwitz isolation cell, they were already living in another, better world.

A few men died almost immediately. Kolbe kept up the courage of the others and, remarkably, was the last of them to grow weak. He had suffered from tuberculosis for decades and was effectively operating with only one lung. Just a few months before, he had spent some time in the camp infirmary because of his health problems. But his behavior in the Starvation Bunker was only an extension of his behavior earlier in the camp. He showed superhuman patience and forbearance under terrible treatment. One prisoner who knew him remembered:

> One day when we were working with the manure, a member of the SS hit him savagely in the face several times and then ordered his dog to attack. The dog went at him repeatedly, biting him and tormenting him. Father Kolbe bore all this with dignified patience, and then he climbed back down into the ditch and we continued to pitch the manure. He had not complained once as he was being struck, and even afterwards he did not utter a single word against that savage guard.[7]

Another prisoner, Henry Alexander Sienkiewicz, tells how Kolbe advised him to put himself under the protection of Mary Immaculate and to be fearless in bringing things back into the camp after his work detail outside. Sienkiewicz not only brought in food, but money, religious objects, and a few Communion hosts that allowed Kolbe to say Mass twice for about thirty prisoners. How Sienkiewicz was able to do this is not clear in merely human terms. The guards frisked him carefully after every outing and, even though he was sometimes carrying large two- and four-pound loaves of bread, he was never caught.[8]

Prior to his last days, Kolbe had noticeably tried to help others who, he felt, needed it more than he did. One of his fellow prisoners later remarked: "After all the acts of love he performed in the barbed wire enclosure of Auschwitz, I'd have been more surprised if he hadn't made the supreme sacrifice than I am by the fact that he did."[9] Even allowing for some later exaggeration, the record seems indisputable. Kolbe's meager rations were quietly reduced further as he gave to people he thought especially needed it. One of the Polish doctors, Rudolf Diem, noted that Kolbe several times suggested putting off his own admission to the infirmary so that others could be treated. Since on any given day there was usually a line of four hundred to five hundred sick prisoners waiting to see the doctors, it entailed no little inconvenience to come back again: "He was serene, completely in control, psychologically sound in every way."[10] In fact, Diem's own Evangelical faith had been shaken by Auschwitz, and he asked Kolbe how he could still believe in God's providence or even in God's existence. Kolbe did not argue with him. What impressed Diem was that "without the slightest gesture of hatred toward the invaders responsible for so many atrocities, he would assure me that one day I would believe again.... though every day I dealt with hundreds upon hundreds of prisoners — priests, religious, professors, noblemen, artists, men from every social stratum and walk of life, I'd like to emphasize: I was attached to that Camp from January 1941 to January of 1945 and I never saw such a sublime example of love of neighbor."[11]

Kolbe did all this and more, without complaint, all the way to his end in the Starvation Bunker. Even the guards noticed at the end. When they came for their daily inspection to remove the dead, they always found Kolbe either standing or kneeling in serenity. The others were usually sprawled in one place or another. One of the guards said in Borgowiec's hearing: "That priest is a real man. We never had one like that here before."[12] In fact, the "real man" and three of his fellows wore out the patience of the guards. The cell was needed for other prisoners. So on August 14, 1941, the vigil of the Feast of the Assumption, they ordered Doctor Boch to inject the surviving men with carbolic acid. It was astonishing that they had all lasted two weeks without light, air, food, and water on top of the months of abuse in the camp, but even more so that the chronically ill Kolbe had also survived.

He could no longer stand or kneel, and sat propped against the wall. Boch came in and injected the other three men. The poison worked quickly and within seconds they were dead. He turned to Kolbe, who was praying. Without interrupting his prayer, Kolbe offered his arm to the executioner. Borgowiec got so emotional at the sight that he made an excuse and went outside. When the doctor and the guards emerged, Borgowiec knew it was all over. Most of his account of Kolbe is quite sober, but even Borgowiec was moved to a kind of dark poetry by what he then saw: "When I opened the iron door, Father Kolbe was no longer alive. His face had an unusual radiance about it. The eyes were wide open and focused on some definite point. His entire person seemed to have been in a state of ecstasy. I will never forget that scene as long as I live."[13]

Ironically, this priest, who had given so much to others during his time in Auschwitz, received a rare luxury after his death. Borgowiec and another prisoner put his body in a washroom. Then the next day they placed it in a makeshift wooden coffin. Apparently, some kind of funeral service was held briefly and furtively. Kolbe's body was one of the few, perhaps the only one, to enter the cremation ovens in a kind of casket. But the place where he died, the Starvation Bunker, went on to even greater enormities. Less than a month after his death, it was used as the first experimental mass gas chamber at Auschwitz: 600 Soviet prisoners of war and 250 patients from the infirmary died in this test run.[14] It was the beginning of the mad drive to extinguish whole segments of the European population who did not fit Nazi politics or notions of racial purity.

The story of Kolbe's heroic sacrifice has often been told and is well known to people who follow the lives of recent saints. Less known, however, is where this extraordinary man came from. It is one of the commonplaces of theological reflection that grace and the virtues it imparts are a free gift from God. Put that way, it is a rather abstract and difficult to understand truth. But if there is any martyr in the twentieth century who shows how that truth may be understood — and in an open, clear, and not at all conventionally pious way — it must be Raymond Kolbe, the future Saint Maximilian. He was born in the small Polish town of Zdunska Wola, on January 8, 1894. Poland was at that time partitioned among three great powers: the Austro-Hungarian empire, Prussia, and Russia. Zdunska Wola stood in the Russian sector in 1894, so Kolbe was born under the jurisdiction of Czar Nicholas II.

This fact, which seems a mere accident, actually had two large effects. The Kolbes were ardent Catholics and resisted attempts to make Russian Orthodoxy the religion of all the people under the czar. They were also ardent Polish patriots, a stance which was inextricably intertwined with their Catholicism. Polish Catholicism centered on the Virgin Mary as Queen of Poland, especially as Our Lady of Częstochowa. All these features formed the Kolbes to be confident, independent, and somewhat militant about the faith in a Marian vein. Without a strong sense of identification with the Church, they might slowly have slipped into indifference or an easy acceptance of the political and spiritual domination of Russia.

But that was not to be, even though the Kolbes were very poor. Zdunska Wola was a small town in the general vicinity of the industrial city of Lodz. Everyone in it, male and female, usually going back generations, was a cloth weaver. To be a cloth weaver in those circumstances was no rural idyll; workers put in long, backbreaking, fourteen- and sixteen-hour days to be able to earn a living selling their products to the merchants who arrived from Lodz. The future Father Maximilian's parents, fortunately, were industrious and sober people. His mother, Maria Dabrowska, actually would have preferred to become a nun, but circumstances (including the Russian closing of several Catholic convents) made that impossible. She was outgoing, a hard worker, and a strong influence on the family. By contrast, Julius Kolbe, Maximilian's father, was a shy, rather retiring person. He, too, was industrious, neither smoked nor drank, and was deeply religious. In fact, both father and mother were Third Order Franciscans, lay members of the order that Saint Francis of Assisi had founded to serve God in the joy of holy poverty.

Raymond (Maximilian) Kolbe and his brother Francis were born two years apart in a poor one-room house that was rich in things of the spirit. Both boys were lively, and it became clear that the house was too small for the family. So they began a series of moves to several towns seeking a better place: Lodz, Jurzkowice, and Pabianice. The last was poor, but a slight cut above their previous places of residence. It also offered several new opportunities. Their cottage was large enough that they could rent part of it to another weaver. Maria opened a second-hand shop and Julius tended three vegetable patches to supplement their income from weaving. Besides having three more children of her own (only one, Joseph, survived), Maria also picked up the skills of a midwife. She must have had an instinctive talent for tending the sick because she quickly was much in demand as a practical nurse as well. The Kolbes were never afraid of work and, all in all, their industriousness bore fruits.

The boys, too, soon showed talents. The future Maximilian had a notorious gift for numbers that he carried with him his whole life. He began working in the second-hand shop. Francis, the older brother, was being gotten ready to be "sent to school," a phrase with much more meaning then than now. It meant opening up a much wider world for the few lucky enough to be able to afford it. Though the other two children could not be spared from the family businesses, all three children were taught to read and write, and learned their catechism and a little Latin from the local priest, Father Waldimir Jakowski. The Church and the world, however, may never have had Saint Maximilian Kolbe without the providential intervention of one man.

Raymond was sent to the pharmacist, a man named Kotowski, one day with a prescription. When he ordered some *vincon greca*, the pharmacist was amazed that he knew the Latin name. In fact, he was so impressed by the boy's obvious intelligence that he offered to tutor him, free of charge, so that he would be ready to go to school the following year, like his older brother. The offer was gratefully accepted; both Kolbe boys attended a local school for a year. But it was a less than ideal situation because of the political and religious conditions under the czar. Fortunately, in 1907, when Kolbe was thirteen, some Conventual Franciscans gave a mission at their local parish. Both Francis and Raymond were interested in joining the Franciscans and, given the piety of their parents, they were thought good candidates. The Franciscan school in Lwow (present-day Lviv in Ukraine) provided room, board, and tuition. It operated in the part of Poland then controlled by the Catholic Hapsburgs. Kolbe's father smuggled the two boys, disguised as farmers, across the border and enrolled them.

All the Kolbes had a natural sympathy for the Franciscans. But Raymond had had a special experience that he confided only to his mother when he was about the age to make his first confession and Communion. He was acting wild, the way healthy boys do, and his mother, like many mothers before and since, thought out loud: "My little son, I don't know what's going to become of you!" For some reason, the remark struck home. Kolbe went and prayed intensely to the Virgin Mary to ask what would become of him. According to Maria, he later told her: "Then the Virgin Mary appeared to me holding in her hands two crowns, one white and the other red. She looked at me with love and she asked me if I would like to have them. The white meant that I would remain pure and the red that I would be a martyr." Kolbe said he wanted them both: "Now anytime I go to church with you and Daddy, I imagine it isn't the two of you but Saint Joseph and Our Lady with me."[15] Whether this was a true vision or the imagination of a particularly religious boy is impossible to say. Maria stated, however, that after the vision, he was completely different and she was certain that he would end his life as a martyr.

Kolbe would claim to have leadings from the Virgin at other crucial points in is life. The fact that these make up the usual pious hagiographies should not lead us to think that they were unreal. The whole of the Old and New Testaments is full of such visitations of the divinity and of holy figures. It is only a modern prejudice, even among believers, that such appearances cannot occur in our own time. Those selected for this special help need not be unusual persons, either. Many of the people who knew Kolbe during his life say they often feel his presence watching over them. If the communion of saints means anything, it must leave open the possibility that these visitations come from somewhere else than our own subconscious or other psychic sources. But whatever we are to make of all this, if we can know people by their fruits, the influence of visions on Kolbe was prodigiously fertile.

A strong Franciscan spirit was taking possession of all the Kolbes. Mother and Father decided to pursue the religious life themselves in the ways open to them. Maria took the youngest son, Joseph, to Lwow, where he later went into the Franciscan minor seminary himself. She became porteress to the Felicians, a Franciscan order. Julius joined a friary for a while, and then opened a religious goods store at Częstochowa. But when World War I erupted, he fought for Polish independence. How his life ended is not entirely clear, but it appears that he was captured by Russian forces during the war, declared a traitor because he had been born in Russian-controlled territory, and executed.

In the Franciscan seminary, Kolbe distinguished himself as a brilliant student, especially in mathematics. His devotions were fervent and his imagination, even at this stage, began leading him on to larger things. All his life, Kolbe would combine piety with a fascination for the ways new technologies might be used to help evangelize. He took an almost entrepreneurial attitude toward such developments. Hollywood films are immoral? Then we have to make them Christian. Science is leading people away from God? Kolbe conceived that out in space it might be possible to recapture images and sounds from Earth's past with the goal of seeing and hearing how Jesus and the Virgin Mary looked and spoke. Some of these ideas are schoolboy dreams, though perhaps technically possible; others, like interplanetary travel, radio, publishing, and the plans he drew up for a defense of Lwow from the Russians, had practical value.

As is the case in other parts of the Catholic world, the best students were selected to be sent to Rome for further study. Kolbe, of course, was sent there in due course. By November 1915, at the age of only twenty-one, Kolbe received a doctorate in philosophy from the Gregorian University. Four years later, he earned a doctorate in theology from the Franciscan International College in Rome. In between, on April 28, 1918, he was ordained a priest. Only one shadow fell over the Rome years: during a school soccer match Kolbe began spitting up blood. He had contracted tuberculosis. Though he kept it hidden from almost everyone then and in later life, it would dog his steps everywhere. Father Stephen Ignudi, rector of the Franciscan College, summed up Kolbe's sojourn in Rome with a simple list of degrees achieved and date of ordination, and then ended simply: "A young saint."[16]

But perhaps the most far-reaching of Kolbe's activities during his stay in Rome was his founding of the Militia Immaculatae, the Army of Mary Immaculate. The immediate inspiration came to him on January 20, 1917, the day that the seventy-fifth anniversary of the apparition at Lourdes was celebrated in Rome.[17] This simple group devoted itself to evangelizing under the aegis of the Virgin as Christ's immaculate mother.

It was approved by Kolbe's superiors in Rome when it still consisted of only six members, plus Kolbe. By the time he was arrested by the Nazis twenty years later, Kolbe would have enrolled tens of thousands of members in his little army from countries all around the world. Though the group's name sounds conventionally pious and somewhat odd to modern ears, those who collaborated with Kolbe on this and his other projects did so with wild dedication and enthusiasm — and fun. Like his patron Saint Francis, Kolbe seems to have had a gift for doing humble work, organizing large enterprises, and practicing poverty with a rare spirit of joy that communicated itself to large numbers of people.

Some have described his gift as naivete combined with deep spirituality: others, more charitably, as a deep simplicity that recognized no limitations on what he felt he was called upon to do, not even when the objections came from other Franciscans who thought Kolbe's activism a disturbance to traditional Franciscan life. He returned from Rome to Cracow to become a professor of church history at the seminary he had once attended. But academic life was not a full enough challenge for a man with Father Kolbe's talents, energy, and dedication. Soon he was engaged in spreading the word of salvation to the world. As he later described his mission: "The earth needs to be flooded with a mighty deluge of Christian and Marian literature, written in every language and reaching every country, so as to drown in the waves of truth all those voices of error that have been using the printing press as their most powerful ally. The globe must be encircled by words of life in printed form, so that the world may once again experience the joy of living."[18]

Awash in the glut of information generated by the ease of desktop publishing and access to the Internet, we may find it hard to appreciate Kolbe's achievement and how it appeared to his contemporaries. But it is worth looking at carefully. He formed Marian "focus groups" in Cracow for university students, women, and soldiers. He wore himself out giving lectures to groups and taking the time to talk with unbelieving individuals — with astonishing effects. But he soon felt the need of a publication and, therefore, a printing press. His Franciscan superior did not oppose the idea. In fact, he thought it a good one, "but only on the condition that you raise the necessary funds yourself, because the community is too poor to help you."[19]

So in the great tradition of the *poverello* of Assisi, Kolbe went out and begged for the money to start up his enterprise. The first issue of *The Knight of the Immaculate* came out in January 1922, even though the country was going through an economic crisis that forced the closing of established publications. Kolbe had big dreams, but he was honest with his readers: "Due to financial difficulties, we cannot guarantee that our readers will receive the magazine regularly. The magazine relies on free offerings."[20] Indeed, owing to a sharp devaluation in the currency, he did not have enough money to pay for the second issue. His Franciscan superiors could not help; in fact they more or less chided him "we told you so." Kolbe went and prayed in front of the statue of the Virgin. Whether by miraculous intervention or coincidence, when he returned later he found an envelope on the altar with the exact amount he needed marked, "For you, my Immaculate Mother." In similarly uncertain fashion, five thousand copies of *The Knight* wound up in print every month for two years.

Kolbe decided he needed a printing press of his own. Many of the Franciscans believed owning such machinery, even for good purposes, was contrary to Franciscan poverty. Their job was to pray and care for the poor, not to build publishing houses, however modest. But another providential help to Kolbe's enterprises came at this very moment. An American Franciscan, Father Lawrence Cyman, was traveling through Poland and stopped at Cracow. When he heard Kolbe's plans, he offered one hundred dollars toward the press. Kolbe was allowed to buy a rickety old machine that had to be cranked by hand. But to remove a potential source of distraction, the Cracow Franciscans also suggested that Kolbe move the whole operation to another friary in the distant city of Grodno.

It moved and turned into an enormous success. If the work was grueling — writing and turning the press crank for long hours — it paid off, at least in terms of influence. Subscriptions increased with every issue. But because Poland was experiencing runaway inflation, Kolbe actually lost more money, the more subscriptions he got. Still, he was successful because he appealed to common Poles in common language. Sometimes he made the arguments easier to follow by casting them as dialogues among several characters. Something in the formula must have touched a nerve among the Polish population. By 1936, *The Knight of the Immaculate* had a circulation of eight hundred thousand and had given birth to two related publications, also with large circulations. And an almanac he published for the Holy Year in 1925 was such a financial success that he bought another, more modern press.

Kolbe not only attracted subscriptions, he attracted vocations among people who wanted to collaborate with the publishing projects. In part, these resulted from his personal charisma and the energy that was evident in the enterprise. But at one point he got a big boom in applications when he published pictures of the monks working in the Grodno facilities. To Poles living in poor cities or on farms, it looked like the monks were involved in a highly advanced, even "modern" enterprise. Many of them wanted to be part of it. It did not take many years for the various activities originated by Kolbe to outgrow the facilities at Grodno.

He started looking for a new piece of land where he could establish a "City of the Immaculata," *Niepokalanów.* He found a spot outside of Warsaw on the Teresin plains that was perfect, but the price was far too high. When Kolbe informed the owner, Prince John Drucki-Lubecki, that they would have to forget the deal, the prince unexpectedly made him a gift of the land. In 1927, the friars started to arrive in the fields along with building helpers and machinists to help set up the presses, to the great astonishment of the local peasants. Their beginnings were quite modest; a few shacks were all that existed for years. But Kolbe had big plans for Niepokalanów. Not only was it to become a city; it would have the most up-to-date scientific equipment in order to carry out its work. For one thing, it would have an airfield to enable the Friars to spread the word to the furthest corner of the globe. Two Franciscans were soon in training as pilots.

But even these various activities did not satisfy Kolbe. They exhausted him physically; he went through several periods of enforced inactivity during serious flare-ups of his tuberculosis, some of which were life-threatening. For a man like him, inactivity was probably a worse cross than work is for other people. Yet at the beginning of 1930, he took a leave of absence for a different reason. He had met several Japanese tourists in Warsaw, and it put an idea into his mind that was confirmed during his time of prayer. He went to Rome to get approval for a new enterprise and stopped in Lisieux on the way back to pray at the tomb of Saint Thérèse. When he returned, he informed his brothers that he was going to found another "City of the Immaculate" in Asia. Four set out with him, first to Rome, then to the port of Marseille, then on a seven-week sail to the Orient.

They stopped in several places along the way: Port Said, Saigon, Hong Kong and Shanghai. China was their original goal, but the bishop there did not like the idea. Finally, they disembarked at Nagasaki. At first, the local ordinary, Bishop Hayasaka, gave them a cool reception. Then they made a deal: since Kolbe had doctorates in philosophy and theology, the bishop would allow the Franciscans to set up shop if Kolbe agreed to teach in his seminary. A month later, ten thousand copies of the first issue of the Japanese *Knight of the Immaculate (Mugenzai no Seibo no Kishi)* came off the presses. Eight thousand went to the Catholic parishes. The friars sold the remainder to passersby, observing the Japanese etiquette for such matters. It was considered impolite in Japan to send someone a copy of a magazine, even a free copy. But if you met and exchanged cards, it was allowed. The friars, though they knew little or no Japanese, were able to distribute the whole press run.[21]

On the face of it, it was a mad idea, but perhaps mad in just the way that Francis of Assisi, who went to Palestine in the hope of converting the Saladin, would have appreciated. Kolbe wrote each issue in Italian and then had it translated into Japanese by a native Japanese Methodist named Yamaka, who eventually converted to Catholicism. Yamaka participated in the enterprise because, like most Japanese, he appreciated boldness and heroism in the face of hardships. Conditions were so bad that the building where the friars lived had no furniture and let in the snow while they slept at night. Kolbe's experiment also appealed to Japanese intellectuals who had abandoned traditional beliefs and were looking for something to replace them. Buddhist monks were moved; Kolbe started to gain vocations to the work among native Japanese. He saw all of this as rebuilding the faith in a country that had once had a flourishing Christian community thanks to the early Jesuit missionaries, but had seen it virtually wiped out by the persecutions three centuries earlier. Letters expressing appreciation came to the journal from all over Japan.[22] The success gave rise to even larger dreams: "When our work has really taken root here in Japan, then I want to go to India, and afterward to the Arabs in Beirut. I plan to publish the periodical in Turkish, Persian, and Hebrew. A billion readers! Half the world's population!"[23]

But first he had to travel back to Poland for a provincial chapter. The friars there, quite prudently, thought the whole thing madcap and foolhardy. In the end, though, the spirit of the "holy fool" of Assisi prevailed. Kolbe was sent back to Japan with the acquiescence, if not the full blessing, of the chapter. When he arrived, everything was a mess. The old press was not moving. His collaborators were discouraged. Kolbe decided to relaunch the whole enterprise. First, he bought another patch of six acres on a distant slope of Mount Hikosan, above, but facing away from, the city of Nagasaki. (When the United States dropped the atom bomb at the end of World War II, this seemingly inconvenient location insured that the complex survived with only minor damage and no injuries.) There he set up another city, *Mugenzai no Sono,* "The Garden of the Immaculate." By 1931, of the Catholic journals produced in non-Christian countries, his had the largest circulation.[24]

Five years later, just as the Nazi menace was becoming palpable, he returned to Poland for another provincial chapter. This time, he was asked to take over the leadership of the other city he had founded, Niepokalanów, which by that time had grown to five hundred religious and another two hundred who wished to join.[25] But Kolbe was not a man to rest on past achievements. He drew up a new plan for the city to make it more effective both as a spiritual center and as a public apostolate. In 1938, *The Knight* reached a circulation of 800,000. Two subsidiaries — *Young Knight* and *Little Knight* — sold 170,000 and 30,000 copies respectively each month. He was sending out 15,000 copies of an international quarterly in Latin for priests. A "mission bulletin" sought to reach non-Catholics. The city itself published a weekly paper, and soon a daily national Catholic paper, *Maly Dyiennik* ("The Little Journal") was arriving at 135,000 homes during the week and 225,000 on Sundays. On the Feast of the Immaculate Conception, December 8, 1938, a radio station went on the air, and Kolbe was making plans for producing Catholic films.[26]

That would remain one of Kolbe's few unrealized dreams. The Nazis invaded Niepokalanów the following year. For reasons of safety, Kolbe had dispersed almost all his flock back to their families before the Nazi arrival. The rest were taken to the Amtitz concentration camp. Kolbe's parting words to his people before they went off to face various threats and uncertainties was: "Do not forget love."[27] For some unknown reason, they were all released, again on the Feast of the Immaculate Conception, in 1939. Kolbe returned to Niepokalanów with his friends and told them: "Let us pray. Let us lovingly accept all our crosses, and let us love every neighbor, whether friend or enemy, without distinction."[28] It was a twofold rule that Kolbe had lived by all his life, both accepting others as neighbors and accepting all crosses as manifestations of God's will.

These principles were soon put to the test again. Because Kolbe had a German last name, he was offered a Satanic bargain: if he adopted German citizenship, he would be spared any further trouble from the Reich. He refused on both religious and Polish patriotic grounds.[29] Shortly, the SS arrived and were greeted with Kolbe's "Praised be Jesus Christ!" This time, they sent him to another, infamous camp at Pawiak. There he was abused and beaten for wearing a crucifix, but did not protest. Before long, he was transferred to Auschwitz. One sign of the impact

Kolbe had on Poland through his various activities was that it was noticed when his name was read upon arrival at the camp. Many people, of course, knew about him and were upset that the Nazis had arrested so eminent and benevolent a figure. But his presence gave courage to the others. One later said, "We were glad to have such a real man, a fighter — a fighter for truth — with us."[30] But fighter for truth or not, like all the other prisoners, he had his head shaved and his warm clothing taken away, and put on the rough, striped prison uniforms at Auschwitz.

In the camp, he behaved as he had always done. As we have seen, Jews and priests were special targets of the guards, receiving the heaviest, most murderous jobs and taking the most abuse. A Jewish survivor of Auschwitz, Eddie Gastfriend, remarked about their situation: "Those of us Jews who came into contact with priests, such as Father Kolbe (I didn't know him personally, but I heard stories about him), felt it was a moving time — a time when a covenant in blood was written between Christians and Jews."[31] Sigmund Gorson, another Jewish survivor of Auschwitz who knew Kolbe well there, said he lost his faith under so much evil, but that "Kolbe gave me that faith back." As many others who knew Kolbe attest, he had a motherly heart inside his masculine and highly entrepreneurial head:

> He knew that I was a Jewish boy. That made no difference. His heart was bigger than persons — that is, whether they were Jewish, Catholic, or whatever. He loved everyone. He dispensed love and nothing but love.... For someone to be as Father Kolbe was in that time and place — I can only say the way he was is beyond words. I am a Jew by my heritage as the son of a Jewish mother, and I am of the Jewish faith and very proud of it. And not only did I love Maximilian Kolbe very, very much in Auschwitz, where he befriended me, but I will love him until the last moments of my life.

Given such clear personal testimony by people who knew Kolbe, it is unfortunate that in 1982, around the time of Kolbe's canonization, a firestorm of controversy erupted over his alleged anti-Semitism, which, it was argued, helped prepare the way for the Nazi takeover of Poland and the subsequent Holocaust of over three million European Jews.[32] Just prior to the canonization date, John Paul II received Yasser Arafat at the Vatican as "a sign of good will and concern ... for the Palestinian people." The story spread through the media — including some Catholic periodicals[33] — that Kolbe had expressed virulent anti-Semitism in his journalism, and that the pope intended to make him a saint anyway because the Catholic Church, complicit in the success of Nazism and Fascism, needed an Auschwitz saint as vindication. The canonization and the Arafat meeting were uncritically interpreted and read together as a "lack of sensitivity in dealing with Jews and Judaism," in the words of an American rabbi.

On the face of it, the charges are wildly inaccurate. Many Catholics died at the hands of Fascists and Nazis, proponents of two ideologies hardly compatible with Church doctrine. At Auschwitz itself, Catholic deaths probably equaled the number of Jewish deaths. The specific charge — that Kolbe promoted hatred of the Jews — seems contradicted by everything we know about the man, especially his repeated statements that he wanted to love everyone without limits, even his persecutors. More moderate voices, some of them Jewish, soon were raised to try to dispel a scurrilous charge. But the attack had its effect: Kolbe still remains tainted, in some eyes, as associated with anti-Semitism.

The facts, however, paint a different picture. A careful review of all his journalism and letters suggests that, to begin with, there are only a handful of instances in which he even mentioned Jews.[34] Kolbe did accept that there was a "cruel clique of Jews," as presented in the spurious *Protocols of the Learned Elders of Zion*, engaged in what he called a "Jewish-Masonic" conspiracy. He also noted that the Talmud in places "breathes hatred against Christ and the Christians."[35] He was wrong in believing the *Protocols* to be authentic, but many were deceived by the forgery in Poland and elsewhere at the time. Kolbe drew no conclusions about public policies even from that document. Indeed, he told his collaborators, "I devote great attention not to stir up accidentally nor to intensify to a greater degree the hatred of our readers against [Jews]." Jews who were involved in a conspiracy, he thought, were "relatively few."[36]

Many defenders of Kolbe have argued that his actions were even more forceful than his words. As Jewish refugees from the Nazi advance began arriving at Niepokalanów, he practiced the "love without limits for all" that he had espoused. Somewhere between several hundred and two thousand Jews were sheltered at the City of the Immaculata. Kolbe worked among all groups, including Jews, without regard to who they were. He organized New Year celebrations for Christians and Jews, a kindness that moved some of the Jews to tears.[37] And he told one of the women, Rosalis Kobla, who lived near the friary, that she should feed the Jews just as she did the Christians "because all men are our brothers."[38] At no time did Kolbe contradict this steady principle incarnated in his whole life and preach hatred against anyone. The charge of anti-Semitism has withered away, though not entirely, in the face of this undeniable evidence.

But Kolbe is larger than and invulnerable to any slanders against him. He believed in this invulnerability on special grounds. Not only did he constantly place himself under the protection of the Immaculata, but he had a living conviction that anything that happened to him was willed by God. As he wrote back to the friars from his first imprisonment at Pawiak: "All the Brothers must pray very much and well. Work with fervor and don't worry too much about us because nothing can happen to us without the permission of God and the Immaculata."[39] Kolbe was sensitive and responsive to all those around him. Jan Szegidewicz later recalled that, when Kolbe learned that he was a Tartar Moslem, the priest went out of his way to comfort him within the teachings of Islam.[40] He even instructed those around him to pray for the Nazis since "no one's conversion is impossible,"[41] as one of his fellow prisoners at Auschwitz, John Lipski, has reported. Henry Sinkiewicz remembered him as the kindest confessor he had ever known and as saying there after cruel treatment by the Auschwitz guards, "Hank, let's offer all this suffering for the Mother of God. Let them see that we are her servants."[42] A fellow priest, Father Conrad Szweda, took particular comfort from Kolbe's instructions, which in their simplicity provided him with great strength: "Take Christ's hand in one of yours and Mary's in the other. Now even if you are in darkness you can go forward with the confidence of a child guided by its parents."[43]

It was part of Kolbe's power all his life to speak in such simple human terms — and live out the implications himself — in circumstances that others approached with many worries and, therefore, found overwhelming. In Auschwitz, where objective conditions were, by human standards, certainly overwhelming, his simple tenacity overcame everything. Joseph Stemler, an intellectual who had served as head of the Polish Education Department prior to being sent to Auschwitz, testified that he was torn between a desire to live and a despair that made death appear attractive. Kolbe calmed him and instructed him to return good for evil, which understandably repelled and troubled Stemler. But the advice helped him survive.[44]

Mieczyslaus Koscielniak, an artist and intellectual who drew some tiny holy pictures for Kolbe at Auschwitz and later tried to portray some of the events of Kolbe's life in larger formats, commented: "He made us see that our souls were not dead, our dignity as Catholics and Poles not destroyed."[45] Alexander Dziuba records an even greater effect: "When he spoke to us of God, we had the impression that the speaker was someone not of this earth." Dziuba went to Kolbe for confession three times and listened to Kolbe's talks: "Thanks to what he taught me in those conferences and to the three confessions I made to him, I changed my life for the better. I can say that after each confession I was not only relieved in soul but *I saw the world differently*."[46] These would be nearly miraculous effects in normal times; in Auschwitz, they represent something beyond human description.

All these testimonies, however, agree in portraying a man with highly masculine endurance of suffering and a highly feminine, almost motherly, heart. His special devotions all his life to the Virgin must have had something to do with this unusual balance. Kolbe is reported to have said at Auschwitz: "If I have to die, I would like it to be on the feast of Our Lady."[47] In fact, he received the fatal injection on August 14, 1941, the vigil of the Feast of the Immaculate Conception. Friends recalled later that he had said years before entering Auschwitz, "I would like to be ground to dust for the Immaculate Virgin and have the dust be blown away by the wind all over the world."[48]

On August 15, 1941, the Feast of the Immaculate Conception, Kolbe's body was placed in the ovens and his ashes passed into the air through the chimney of an Auschwitz crematorium.

It has been noted that an unusually large number of the people who survived Auschwitz knew Kolbe. In some ways, that is not surprising. The kind of moral and spiritual strength he instilled in people fitted them to endure hardships. But during the process for his canonization reports arrived at the Vatican from people in Nagasaki injured by the atomic bomb and from various parts of the world claiming Kolbe had helped them survive or heal. Many of these people attended the beatification in Rome on October 17, 1971, including Polish Cardinals Wyszyński and Wojtyła (who as John Paul II would canonize Kolbe), a host of other dignitaries, and Francis Gajowniczek, the man Kolbe replaced in the Starvation Bunker. A short time later, a Mass in Kolbe's memory was celebrated at Auschwitz, where a crowd of more than a hundred thousand braved bad weather to honor him. On October 10, 1982,

Kolbe was proclaimed a saint in Rome with Gajowniczek and many other concentration camp survivors among the crowd.

But Kolbe, great a figure as he was and is, was far from being alone in Nazi Poland. In June of 1999, Pope John Paul II, who had witnessed Nazi persecution as a young man in Poland, proclaimed 108 other confirmed martyrs of the Nazi era during a pilgrimage to his homeland. The official number was small given that almost three million Polish Catholics had died in the death camps and in other ways during the Nazi occupation. But the Vatican is quite careful in officially declaring anyone a "martyr." The 108 themselves were selected from several hundred other potential candidates. As the official documentation pointed out, the diocese of Włocńawek alone lost 220 clergy and religious (52 percent of all religious in the diocese) during the Nazi persecution. And the Vatican had waited for the fall of Communism in Poland so that the beatifications and declarations of martyrdom would not be misunderstood: "The political climate . . . created in Poland after the war and that lasted until the end of the 1980s, with persecution of the church in various forms, promoted by the atheistic Soviet system, certainly did not allow for the drawing up of the cause of martyrdom of such a scope without political pressures or the risk of instrumentalizing the cause on the part of the regime then in power."[49]

But however late, the account is powerful. Many of the priests and nuns declared martyrs were simply shot after refusing to abandon their churches and convents. The Dominican priest Michal Czartoryski was killed for ministering to the wounded and dying during the Warsaw Insurrection.[50] A Dominican nun, Julia Rodzińska, fell victim to typhus at the Stutthof concentration camp after providing charitable services to Jewish prisoners.[51] Capuchin Anicet Kopliński died in an Auschwitz gas chamber after refusing to use his German origins to save himself. And the Marianist Antoni Leszczewicz was assassinated along with 380 others when he would not leave them without a priest when they were in mortal danger.[52] Sisters of the Immaculate Conception Maria Ewa Noiszewska and Maria Marta Wołowska were shot because they had provided sanctuary to Polish Jews at the hospital and religious house in Słonim.[53]

Others were tortured, subjected to medical experiments, gassed, hung, strangled, guillotined, or killed by other means simply for refusing to

commit blasphemies or renounce their religious vocations in the concentration camps at Dachau, Sachsenhausen, Auschwitz, Działdowo, Gusen,
Ravensbrück, Majdanek, Mauthausen, Bergen-Belsen — a virtual roster
of all the principal and secondary Nazi death camps — or in local jails.
One, Father Zygmunt Pisarski, pastor of the church at Geszyn in the diocese of Lublin, was executed "because he had not wished to turn over
Communists even though shortly earlier they had persecuted him."[54]

Perhaps the most striking stories from the 108 are those who, like
Kolbe, offered their lives for others. Marianna Biernacka, a laywoman,
volunteered to be imprisoned in place of her daughter-in-law, who
was then pregnant. Her sacrifice saved her grandchild and daughter-
in-law, but her fate was to be shot at Naumowicze, near the city of
Grodno.[55] The Claretian-Capuchin Maria Teresa Kowalska offered herself for the liberation of other religious women at the concentration camp
in Działdowo, where she later died. Father Grzegorz Frackowiak, a Ver-
bite, willingly substituted himself for a group of prisoners at Jarocin and,
as a result, was later decapitated in Dresden. Eight others are known to
have offered their own lives directly, in one way or another, to save the
lives or the faith of others. We do not have nearly as much information
on these humble figures as we have on Kolbe, who was an internationally known personality before he died. But it is certain that heroic virtue
of the kind they displayed must have been formed over a long period
of prayer and self-discipline.

All in all, three bishops, fifty-one diocesan priests, two seminarians,
twenty-six priests of religious orders, eight professed brothers, eight religious sisters, and nine lay people made up the new group (plus Bishop
Michael Kozal, beatified in 1987). In the nature of things, these numbers are only the tip of a much larger iceberg. So many priests, religious,
and lay people perished in Nazi-occupied Poland that the official Vatican proclamation explicitly adds that, working with diocesan bishops
and the heads of religious congregations, it limited itself to "only the
most representative cases, whether in how they gave witness in their sufferings and death, inflicted *in odium fidei*, or through the message they
transmitted by their lives. We have taken into account that there were
people of various walks of life who gave special, indeed heroic, Christian
witness, ending, during the persecution, in the sacrifice of their lives."[56]

One large group left out in the 108, but whose cause was presented to
the Vatican in September 1991, involves eleven sisters of the Holy Family
of Nazareth who were executed as an entire community by the Nazis on
August 1, 1943. Secular historians have made a point of keeping alive

the memories of large groups of lay people executed in a similar fashion, such as the twenty thousand murdered in the Katyn Forest by the Soviets in the spring of 1940. But smaller numbers of religious, who suffered no less abuse, have remained almost invisible. In this case, the eleven may be taken to represent other groups similarly subjected to a brutal attempt to stamp out religion.

Everything about the sisters' end has larger echoes. They died outside the town of Nowogródek, which was then part of Poland but today lies within Belarus. Nowogródek was a small municipality, undistinguished in modern times, but it had a legendary history. In a way it was the site of the entry of the Catholic faith into Northwest Poland and Lithuania. One of the first churches in the region was built on a hilltop there, according to legend above the very place where a temple had stood to Perkuna, the chief of the pagan Lithuanian gods. In 1422, Władysław Jagiello, one of the famous noblemen of early Polish and Lithuanian history, who gave his name to the Jagiellonian University, married his wife Sonka there.[57]

But even more important for the emergence of modern Poland, the great Polish poet and patriot Adam Mickiewicz was born in Nowogródek in 1799, where he studied with the Dominicans. Mickiewicz is not much known outside of Poland and Lithuania. Indeed, he was exiled by various foreign occupiers for a large part of his life even from those countries. But he is perhaps the single most eminent patriotic poet of his people. In his poem "To a Polish Mother," he writes of the sorrow and martyrdom of those who have genius and feel the call of Polish nationhood:

> Though people, powers, and schisms a truce declare,
>   And though the whole wide world in peace may bloom,
> In battle — without glory — must he share;
>   In martyrdom — with an eternal tomb.

As always seems to be the case for Polish nationalism, the fate of the nation seems to Mickiewicz intertwined with the Redemption:

> A child in Nazareth, our Savior mild
>   Fondled the cross whereon he saved mankind:
> O Polish mother, I would have thy child
>   Thus early learn what playthings he will find.

For Mickiewicz, hidden martyrdom, usually connected with human betrayal, was the common lot of Polish heroes and their only compensation was "For glory — but a woman's tears, soon spent, / And fellow patriots' whispered words by night."[58]

A century later, during World War II, that was the pattern that the eleven sisters would follow. They fell after the Nazis broke with the Soviets, whom they had earlier allied themselves with by means of the Molotov-Ribbentrop Pact. In the middle of 1942, however, the Nazis thrust their way into Nowogródek. Soon they began arresting the professionals and leaders of the town. Two priests, Michal Dalecki and Józef Kuczyński, were among those arrested. A few weeks later, without any judicial proceedings, both were shot near the Nazi barracks along with several other men. But numbers of those arrested remained alive to attest to the memory of those who did not survive.

The eleven sisters, first individually, then as a group, began praying that, "if sacrifice of life is needed, let them kill us rather than those who have families," as the prioress, Sister M. Stella Mardosewicz, told a priest at the time.[59] It was a gesture, in its way, like Maximilian Kolbe's even if less open. Remarkably, the Sisters of the Holy Family of Nazareth were relative newcomers to the town, having arrived only in 1929. At first, they were even looked upon with some suspicion by the inhabitants. But gradually they earned trust and affection. The nuns did manual work and performed the usual corporal and spiritual works of mercy. Perhaps most important, they opened a school, which was instantly oversubscribed, to help prepare young people for a better life.

But this quiet attempt to improve the local prospects was struck by a double blow. First the Russians moved in. Many of the Poles in the town were deported to far off Kazakhstan. Then the Nazis arrived. They immediately executed about fifty Jews and left the bodies in the town square as an object lesson. Then other elements of the town, also despised in Nazi ideology, were arrested. On Saturday, July 31, 1943, the sisters were told to report to a Nazi command post. Both they and the townspeople thought it a good idea to obey the order: at worst they expected some of the sisters would be sent to work camps in Germany. They were never heard from again.

From reports of those tangentially involved, however, their fate is clear. Only an hour after the sisters came in, they were loaded on a truck and driven out of town toward a wooded area. But at that hour on a Saturday evening there were still many people tending cattle and working in the fields. The presence of so many potential witnesses temporarily thwarted the Nazi plan. The nuns were put back in the truck and locked in the basement of a church on one of the hills. The basement was so small, according to an eyewitness, that the nuns had to take turns standing and sitting. All prayed. In the middle of the same night, about 3:30 a.m., the truck was loaded again and the cargo driven to a stand of pines and birches. It returned empty.

It was not until March 1945 that the bodies could be exhumed. When they were, they were mostly intact, but all the faces were disfigured. Presumably, the soldiers had shot them, one by one, either in the face or the back of the head, and dumped them in a previously prepared mass grave. A painting of the original event exists (see the photo section following p. 230). It is overemotional. The nuns are angelic; the soldiers look like animals. But the heroic martyrdom and witness of these simple women were real, and they were beatified on March 5, 2000. Sentimentality aside, the portrait is a fitting, humble, and powerful memorial to all those who, like Maximilian Kolbe, sacrificed to preserve life beyond a system intended to produce only death.

# -NINE-

# A BRIEF INTRODUCTION TO THE MARTYRS OF EASTERN AND CENTRAL EUROPE

O N OCTOBER 19, 1984, Father Jerzy Popiełuszko was returning from some pastoral work in the town of Bygdoszcz to his parish, Saint Stanislaw Kostka, in Warsaw. Three state security officers stopped his car without much bothering to hide what they were doing. They tied him up, beat and tortured him to death, and then threw the body, weighted down with stones, into the Vistula River. When he did not turn up at home at the time expected, everyone feared the worst. Since 1982 he had been repeatedly accused of crimes, harassed by police, and subjected to intimidation. After a bombing attempt, workers from the Huta Warsawa steel mills had to take turns protecting him. Popiełuzsko was under regular police surveillance and was arrested twice in 1983. In the first half of 1984 alone, he was interrogated thirteen times. It was still a shock, however, when ten days later his body turned up as the authorities dredged the river.

The Popiełuszko case also stunned the world because, contrary to official announcements claiming the priest had been kidnapped by unknown persons, everyone familiar with the situation in Poland knew the murder was the government's work. In the mid-1980s, the Polish Solidarity movement, ten million strong, was in the midst of the peaceful, but effective, resistance to the Communist regime that would eventually free Poland and, in conjunction with other forces, lead to the breakup of the Soviet empire. The young priest had become a kind of pastor to the workers' movement. Popiełuszko's death confirms how seriously the Polish regime and its Soviet masters took the Catholic opposition. A few years earlier, in 1981, Mehmet Ali Agca, operating under Bulgarian and Soviet instructions, had tried to assassinate John Paul II in Saint Peter's Square. Unlike their earlier, cautious treatment of a powerful national

216

Church, authorities had turned desperately to violence in the waning days of Polish Communism.

In 1982, just before John Paul II was scheduled to return to Poland on a visit, about twenty thugs attacked the Saint Martin's Church in Warsaw and beat the volunteers working there for the Primate's Aid Committee.[1] Around the same time, Fathers Tadeusz Kurach and Jan Borkowski were arrested for "hooliganism," several other priests were beaten, and two, Bishop Kazimierz Kluz and Father Honoriusz Kowalczyk, died in "accidents." Wrocław archbishop Henryk Gulbinowicz's car was bombed. Father Tadeusz Zaleski had a corrosive chemical thrown at him and his clothes set on fire for his work with Solidarity.[2] On another occasion, he was beaten unconscious and almost strangled with a wire. As late as 1988 and 1989, five priests died under mysteriously violent circumstances.[3]

Unlike many other places of persecution in the twentieth century, these desperate attempts to stop growing Catholic resistance resulted from the weakness rather than the strength of the Communist regime. Indeed, Father Popiełuszko, who had presided over many public masses during the rise of Solidarity, had constantly urged his listeners to show the maturity and humanity of their cause by their refusal to be goaded into violence:

> Do not struggle with violence. Violence is a sign of weakness. All those who cannot win through the heart try to conquer through violence. The most wonderful and durable struggles in history have been carried on by human thought. The most ignoble fights and most ephemeral successes are those of violence. An idea which needs rifles to survive dies of its own accord. An idea which is imposed by violence collapses under it. An idea capable of life wins without effort and is then followed by millions of people.[4]

It is no wonder that this eloquent soul was appointed by Cardinal Wyszyński as chaplain to striking steel workers in Warsaw and then naturally gravitated toward becoming a kind of unofficial spiritual advisor to the Solidarity movement. The nation was grateful. Estimates vary, but it is believed that at his funeral four hundred thousand Poles showed up to honor him.

As great as Popiełuszko was as an individual, in many respects he was the culmination of several decades of spiritual and social maturation within the Polish Church that made it a formidable moral force by the 1980s. Those developments were all the more remarkable in that the Church in Poland was hard hit by Nazism during World War II and had to contend with another serious threat in the form of Communism as soon as the Nazis were driven out. As we saw in previous chapters, Polish priests formed a significant portion of the prison population at Dachau, and Polish Catholics died in the millions at Auschwitz.[5] In sober estimates, 3,646 Polish priests wound up in Nazi concentration camps; 2,000 of them along with 170 monks, almost 300 nuns, and 113 seminarians died.[6] No one knows what happened to the 1.5 million Poles deported by the Soviets to Siberia in 1939.[7] Poland had been partitioned in 1939 between the Nazis and the Soviets until the former broke the Molotov-Ribbentrop Pact in 1941. The Polish government was in exile in Paris and then London, but it never returned. Instead, a Provisional Government of National Unity was set up by the Communists after the war, and the Yalta and Potsdam Conferences, which brought Churchill, Roosevelt (Truman, after Roosevelt's death), and Stalin together to decide the future of Europe recognized the new regime. Similar Communist governments would follow all over Eastern and Central Europe.

Ironically, the redrawn boundaries of Poland made it about 95 percent Latin-rite Roman Catholic. Earlier it had had a larger Orthodox minority; but many Orthodox were placed under the jurisdiction of the Soviet Union. Its Protestants, almost two million, were mostly transferred to other nations. The Jews, almost 15 percent of the prewar Polish population, had been reduced to about eighty thousand. Despite its weakened state, the sheer size of the Church in Poland made it difficult for the Communists to pursue their usual tactics. From the end of the war in 1945 until 1947, then, the regime was hostile and sometimes rough with the Church, but also cautious. Still, about a hundred priests — the most active and influential — disappeared in those two years, probably martyred, through the machinations of the State Security Bureau.[8]

After staged elections in 1947, the Communists started a more typical pattern. Church property and publications were slowly confiscated; religious schools were laicized; Catholic hospitals, orphanages, and other charitable institutions were transferred to the state. As the Polish primate, Cardinal Augustus Hlond, objected at the time, it was obvious that the government intended to restrict Catholic activity to churches and slowly wean young people and the whole society away from the faith. Protests against government misbehavior brought the charge that the Church was fomenting political opposition. By the fall of 1948, four hundred priests were imprisoned, and one, Boleslas Stefanski had been sentenced to death on the pretext that he had turned his students into a "secret gang."[9]

The usual murderous lies and propaganda campaign had begun. Several bishops, including the auxiliary bishop of Częstochowa, were falsely accused of having been Nazi collaborators. Communion with the Holy See was characterized as siding with a vicious foreign threat. Morals charges were brought with increasing frequency against clergy. The government signed an agreement with the Church that, on paper, seemed to establish reasonable spheres for church and state to operate harmoniously with each other. In fact, like Hitler's Concordat with the Vatican, the party who got to define the borderline between what was political or not could turn the document to opposing aims. The Polish regime left no avenue unexplored. It even started setting up "patriotic" Catholic organizations and supporting the small number of clergy who collaborated with the government in national and international action under the auspices of the Pax movement. A shrewd observer of Poland has remarked that Pax did not delude the Polish people, perhaps because during the Stalinist era it was "almost more Stalinist than the Party."[10]

But despite these vigorous measures, the Communists in Poland were not as successful against the Church as they were in other nations in Central and Eastern Europe. The Church's resistance owed a great deal to the well-formed Catholic laity that resulted from steps Catholic leaders took to thwart the worst threats to the faith. Hlond's successor, Cardinal Stefan Wyszyński, in particular hewed to a strong line that combined confrontation, as necessary, with a vigorous program of building up alternative sources of social formation within the Communist system. He asserted that Poles had demonstrated "in Dachau and the Warsaw Uprising that we have learned how to die for the Church and for Poland." But Wyszyński believed that his people should embrace "martyrdom only as a last resort." Instead, he wanted to find a way, despite all odds, that the Church in Poland could live and flourish.[11] By a combination of bravery and shrewdness, he and the rest of the Catholic leadership managed to minimize outright martyrdom and the worst dimensions of persecution even as they faced tremendous pressures and threats. Though the Church signed accords with the government, these were not merely the prelude to capitulation. Rather, Wyszyński and his colleagues utilized them to open a way to a better future. In the short run, there were definite setbacks. Bishop of Kielce Czesław Kaczmarek, a strong opponent of the regime, was subjected to a rigged legal process and sentenced to twelve years imprisonment. Wyszyński himself was arrested, along with eight other bishops and nine hundred priests, in 1953.[12] By the end of that year, at least eight bishops and nine hundred priests had been detained. Two years later more than two thousand clergy, religious, laity, and Catholic social activists were rounded up. But by 1956, powerful unrest within Polish society convinced Communist leaders that they had to come to terms with the Church.[13]

Partly, the social crisis stemmed from Khrushchev's denunciation of Stalin's crimes at the 1956 Twentieth Party Congress. In Poland, fifty thousand workers demonstrated against the Soviets after the revelations. Polish Communist leader Władysław Gomułka approached Wyszyński in prison for help with the social chaos he faced. The cardinal extracted concessions for the Church as the only conditions on which he would agree to be freed. The regime had no alternative. From that moment, the Polish Church began a reconstruction that would lead to the miraculous liberation in 1989. The cardinal immediately planned a Great Novena of nine years, from 1957 to 1966, in preparation for celebrating the millennium of Catholicism in Poland. A massive popular outpouring of support followed him wherever he went during those years. The Black Madonna of Częstochowa toured the country evoking immense spiritual emotion while the Church organized study sessions and a variety of other activities to bolster both theological and social awareness. The movement grew so powerful that the government had to put a stop to the Black Madonna's circulation by "arresting" the icon. The Church sent the empty frame throughout the country; it still drew masses.

By 1966, something unprecedented in Communist-dominated countries had occurred. There was a powerful element of independent civil society in Poland linked directly with the Church. The Church had such great credibility in Polish society that Polish intellectuals — traditionally anticlerical — as well as labor leaders, journalists, historians, all came to regard Polish Catholicism as central to the basic moral reconstruction of the nation. The philosopher Leszek Kolakowski characterized the situation, as did many others, in striking terms: "It is not possible with internal repressive instruments to destroy the most powerful crystallizing force of social consciousness to resist the Sovietization process and the most powerful source of moral authority, viz., the Catholic Church."[14] It is no surprise then that when the first Polish Pope, John Paul II, came to Warsaw in 1979, the crowds in Victory Square chanted: "We want

God, we want God, we want God in the family circle, we want God in books, in schools, we want God in government orders, we want God, we want God."

The Polish case most graphically demonstrates that there were wide differences in persecution and martyrdom in Eastern and Central Europe under Communism. Some of the countries subjected to the Soviets experienced persecution as great or greater than any in all of Christian history. Albania, Lithuania, and Romania were particularly hard hit: their stories are briefly described in the following chapters. Poland suffered no small numbers of deaths even in its relatively better circumstances. Workers were killed during strikes; troublesome priests were isolated. Even Father Jerzy Popiełuszko's celebrity could not entirely protect him.[15] Poland's story is well known and has been told many times. In other Eastern European countries that had large Catholic populations and were historically close to the West, persecutions were lighter than in more religiously mixed and distant countries. Czechoslovakia and Hungary, for example, went through awful repressions, but their martyrologies are not quite as long as some of their neighbors.

The fate of the Church in Hungary exhibits a regrettable soft tragedy. Historically, the Church there had always been close to the government. When the Communists came to power after the Second World War, many within the Church thought it prudent to continue the traditional pattern. Only the Hungarian Primate, Cardinal Joszef Mindszenty, archbishop of Esztergom, resisted vigorously. The cardinal was from a simple peasant background, but was not about to relinquish any of the privileges of the Church to dedicated atheists. As a result of his heroic and lonely stand, he was tortured for forty days straight and then, weak and unable to resist any longer, forced to make public statements supportive of the regime. Six hundred priests went to prison with him. All were threatened with deportation and forced labor in Siberia.[16] With their confinement, virtually all heroism in the Hungarian Church disappeared and, over the decades, the Church settled into a more or less compliant relationship with "goulash Communism."

The price of that compromise was high. All church schools were confiscated. Religious orders were all but banned with ten thousand monks and nuns forced to find other ways of living. Of them, two thousand fled the country; many were arrested and died. Hardly any records of their fates exist. Despite the slow acquiescence of Hungarian society in a soft form of Communism, the Hungarians were among the first to revolt against the Soviet system in 1956. Russian tanks and troops restored power to the regime. But subsequent leaders, particularly János Kádár, who had been tortured by his own party earlier in the development of Hungarian Communism, worked to prevent a repeat of the uprising by seeking to bring all elements of the society into the government. Since Catholics formed almost two-thirds of the Hungarian population, they had to be accommodated, but also carefully tamed. In the very year of the uprising, Mindszenty was freed and asked for asylum in the American Embassy in Budapest, where he remained for eighteen years, dying in 1975. Some of his supporters organized small clandestine Catholic "base communities," but their influence on the larger society was marginal.

As a result, the Church virtually lost its prophetic voice in Hungary's soft despotism. Communists deferred to the hierarchy, as long as it was loyal to the party line and government officials were able to ensure that appointments satisfied their requirements. Mutual advantages resulted, but at the price of truth. Hungarian Christians faced far less physical danger than in other European countries, but only because they became a tame, almost bourgeois force within the Communist system. More vigorous Christians often speculated why Catholics and other believers did not speak out against the slow evaporation of their witness in Hungarian society since the threats were minimal. Church and state converged in a lukewarm embrace. Though the government retained its anti-Christian aims, by 1980 it was allowing the reading of the Bible in state-sponsored schools for its literary and cultural importance.[17]

Quite a few base groups sprang up — four to six thousand in some estimates, involving sixty to one hundred thousand people — which sought to revitalize what had become a rather uninspiring Church. One priest in particular, Father György Bulányi, often arrested for his activism, tried to restore the Church's prophetic voice. But he and the movement he spawned were caught between a conformist hierarchy and a Vatican that did not know what to do to galvanize real Catholic action. Though Hungary after the first few years of Communism had few physical martyrs, it is clear that the regime shrewdly killed off the moral and spiritual witness that might have made the Church potent during the Communist years. Since Communism's fall, indifference to the Church has been the most prominent feature of Hungarian society. One anonymous protester described this as "pioneering new methods of persecution" that did not have to employ the crude means of the other Communist nations in Eastern and Central Europe.[18]

Among those nations, Czechoslovakia had a somewhat strong Church in place after the defeat of Nazism, particularly in Slovakia. Catholic priests participated in the Czechoslovak People's Party as the nation sought to rebuild itself. Though the Church took no formal part in politics, it was clear, even to the Communists, that they needed Catholic backing to govern effectively. When Klement Gottwald was named president after the Communists seized power, the Czechoslovak primate archbishop of Prague Josef Beran offered formal prayers for the new government without endorsing any of its positions. The government invited some priests to participate in various ministries, but it became clear that this was an attempt to coopt rather than cooperate with the Church. After consultation with the Vatican, the Czechoslovak bishops, to the annoyance of the government, announced that priests could not exercise political office unless their superiors approved.[19] Minister of Information Václav Kopecky replied angrily: "We leave nobody in doubt that traitors will not be suffered and spared, even if they wear sacred garments.... We note after all, that patriotically feeling Roman Catholic priests do not agree with the hateful attitude of the Vatican against Czechoslovakia."[20] The battle was joined.

From the very first, the Czech regime tried to infiltrate and use the moral prestige of the Church for its own purposes. In June 1949, for example, it initiated a conference in Prague, led by fellow travelers, who set up a Catholic Action group subservient to the government. Priests who opposed the group were arrested.[21] Though propaganda efforts were used to make it appear that Catholic Action represented patriotic and independent Catholicism, the people were not deluded. The move was so badly handled — one prominent member, Václav Brezny, turned out to be a Protestant — that the real Church gained in the exchange. Though the Catholic press and Church schools were curtailed and silenced, most believers understood and rejected the onslaught.

When the archbishop issued a clandestine letter laying out the real needs of the Church in order to negotiate with the government, he was arrested. Beforehand, anticipating the lawlessness common in Communist countries, he warned the faithful not to believe any confessions or retractions that might be issued in his name if he were imprisoned. Beran knew well what might happen: he had spent three years in Dachau and other concentration camps for his anti-Nazi stance. Government agents attended his Sunday Mass at the Saint Vitus Cathedral and shouted during the homily so that he could not be heard and had to stop. When the archbishop returned to his residence, State Security was waiting to take him into custody. All churches were placed under surveillance after the incident. Minister of Justice Alexej Cepicka portrayed the crackdown as the State protecting the religious freedom of believers: "We shall not permit that the personal or the religious freedoms be restricted in any way by the Church hierarchy. Everyone who should feel threatened by the Church dignitaries will be fully protected and supported."[22] Cepicka would become president of the State Office for Church Affairs and the fiercest of the Church's persecutors.

Show trials began. Father Oto Mádr was convicted of "spying" and sentenced to death. After a year expecting the worst everyday, his sentence was commuted to life imprisonment. He served fifteen years. In Bratislava, the Slovak capital, Bishop Michael Buzulka was sentenced to life imprisonment and fined; in Presov, the Greek Catholic bishop Pavel Gojdic received the same sentence and was to die, still in prison, in Leopoldov in 1960; in Spisske Podhradie, Bishop Jan Vojtasak only got twenty-four years and a fine.[23] The other bishops, including Archbishop Beran, were removed and replaced by subservient figures through "administrative" measures. A few took a loyalty oath to the government to prevent the whole Church from being put into disloyal hands.[24]

In 1950, the government also moved to eliminate religious orders by subtle and not-so-subtle means. In effect, several monasteries and convents were turned into concentration camps, where religious were interned and made to do forced labor. Others were simply converted to secular uses. Schools were closed and priests who organized cultural activities for young people were sentenced for spreading an "inimical ideology." When this process began there were 15,200 religious in Czechoslovakia; three-quarters of them along with nearly half of the 7,000 priests and thousands of lay people were condemned to prison camps amounting to virtual slavery. Some were made to dig in the Ostrava mines, but the regular miners regarded the enslaved clergy as martyrs and anti-Communism spread further among them. An average sentence lasted five years, but the leadership of the religious orders and other prominent Catholics typically were not released until the 1968 "Prague Spring," a brief period of liberalization brutally crushed by Soviet tanks. In the meantime, many perished from malnutrition, overwork, and diseases.[25] Such real Church activity as continued had to go underground.

But martyrdom still occurred. We have few detailed stories of the martyrs of this period, but one is very touching and may be taken as an example of many others still unknown. Zdenka Schelingova, a Holy Cross sister, has been proposed for beatification on the basis of what she suffered in the early years of Communist rule in postwar Czechoslovakia. Sister Schelingova was born on Christmas day 1916 in Kriva Orava, a town located in northeastern Slovakia. At fifteen, she already knew she wanted to be a religious and studied to become a nurse during her period of candidacy with the Holy Cross order. By all accounts, she radiated a spiritual calm and human warmth as she cared for patients.

At the hospital in Bratislava (the Slovak capital) to which she was assigned, she was given responsibility for a sick priest. As they talked, Sister Zdenka learned that the priest was to be sent to the Siberian labor camps as soon as he recovered. She helped him to escape from the hospital and was arrested herself and given a twelve-year prison sentence. Helena Kordova, a fellow prisoner, recalls that Sister Zdenka was terribly tortured in a Prague jail. She was repeatedly hung upside down and beaten relentlessly. Since the regime did not want to create any public martyrs, the prison released her in so weak a condition that she died three months later on July 31, 1955. All her fellow prisoners agree that she never complained and retained an obvious spiritual focus during the ordeal. The Holy Cross Sisters presented her cause in 1998.

Though the regime was generally careful not to be as openly bloody as in the Soviet Union, the Czechoslovaks pursued a hard Stalinist line. Priests who remained free had to obtain state licenses, meaning their ministries could be suspended for any infraction. They and recalcitrant intellectuals could be forced into terribly straitened circumstances requiring them to take menial jobs. Until the 1968 liberalization, many clergy were required to join the Catholic Peace Priests, a group sponsored by the regime and intended to make clergy take orders from the government rather than Rome. After 1968's brief opening, the clerical organization was reorganized as the Pacem in Terris movement, a so obviously compromised crew that the people gave its members the disdainful name "pax terriers." Its news weekly, *Katolické Noviny*, was known to refuse articles from the cardinal himself, and it held so little interest for average believers that stacks of the newspaper frequently remained in the back of churches after Mass.[26]

Anti-Catholic measures struck Slovakia, where Catholicism was both strong and claimed about 70 percent of the population, especially hard. By 1977, only 30 percent of children were receiving religious instruction, despite their parents continued adherence to the Church, because to be a known believer could close off opportunities for higher education. Teachers were given bonuses for convincing students not to study religion. Pressure on school children who openly engaged in religious activity could become so severe that two children reportedly committed suicide after bitter taunting.[27]

The regime was not above open persecution to the point of martyrdom. After a return to a hard line after 1968, the government went after prominent members of the hierarchy. Bishop Jan Korec, a national hero for his defense of the Church, had been secretly consecrated a bishop. He spent twelve years in prison when the truth was discovered, and was released in 1974 only to be forced, in spite of poor health, to work in the Slovak capital Bratislava as a street sweeper, factory worker, and luggage handler. That same year, Cardinal Štefan Trochta was arrested for refusing to allow members of religious orders to be banned from his diocese. He was interrogated by the police for six hours and, as a result, died.[28]

These and other violations of human rights led many intellectuals, activists, and Church members to sign Charter 77, a public statement requesting that the government respect the human rights provisions of the Helsinki Final Act of the Conference on Security and Cooperation in Europe. They also set up the Committee for the Defense of the Unjustly Persecuted (VONS). A brave priest, Father Václav Malý, emerged as a prominent leader in both groups. From 1979 on, he suffered terrible retribution: frequent arrests, beatings that broke his nose and jaw, weekly interrogations, and death threats. The government gave him a chance to emigrate on four separate occasions. Remarkably, he refused to leave the struggle despite the persecution.[29]

But by the late 1970s, Father Malý's was not a lone voice. After the 1978 election of John Paul II, the Czech Cardinal, Frantisek Tomasek, a man who earlier had been quiet about persecution, found new courage and began to speak publicly with a strong voice. At the same time, the underground Church, though small, began to exert a powerful influence. In Slovakia, the underground and official Church were, for all intents and purposes, the same organization.[30] Elsewhere, it became an important *samizdat* publishing arm: from 1977 to 1981 it issued over seven hundred works of philosophy, theology, and lives of saints. Two underground periodicals, *Informace o Církvi* ("Information on the Church") and *Teologické Texty* ("Theological Texts") provided news and spiritual formation that the official Church organs did not. These activities were risky: when the government discovered one underground publishing operation it arrested Fathers Frantisek Lízna, Rudolph Smahel, and Josef Zverina along with eight lay people. After a 1981 raid on another operation, three elderly nuns died in police custody.[31]

The regime seemed especially concerned not to allow the resurgence of religious orders, especially Franciscans, who had strong appeal, particularly to young people. In 1982, Franciscan Father Jan Bárta was arrested for running a clandestine seminary and died. Another secret monk and Slovak underground leader, Father Premysl Coufal, was found dead in his apartment in February of 1981. Though his body bore signs of torture and mutilation, the official inquiry concluded that he had committed suicide.[32] Augustin Navrátil, an outspoken defender of justice though a father of nine, wrote a letter to Czech president Husák with information on Coufal's death. He himself was arrested, attacked by Gypsies under the pay of the government, and sent to a psychiatric hospital.

Though all this pressure against dissident groups and underground publications was terrifying, the forces that led to Czechoslovakia's "Velvet Revolution" were emerging without letup. Perhaps the most remarkable spontaneous display of religious commitment and public opposition to a Communist government, outside Poland, occurred in 1985 in the Slovak city of Velehrad. Velehrad is the traditional burial place of Saint Methodius, who together with his brother Saint Cyril, brought Christianity to the Slavs and introduced the Cyrillic alphabet used in much of Eastern Europe. The eleven hundredth anniversary of Methodius's death fell in 1985, and the Church organized a celebration. Cardinal Tomasek invited the pope, but the government imposed conditions for the visit that the Vatican could not accept.

Despite alternative events scheduled by authorities on the same day to divert attention, somewhere between 150,000 and 250,000 Czechoslovaks attended the celebration. A few months earlier, the cardinal and about a thousand priests — a third of those active — together with some monks conspicuously wearing their habits had gathered in Velehrad. John Paul II had proclaimed that Cyril and Methodius along with Saint Benedict should be honored as the fathers of European monasticism. Since the government was particularly worried about the return of religious orders, the whole affair presented a sharp challenge. The cardinal read a message from the pope encouraging the Church in Czechoslovakia: "in the spirit of Saint Methodius to continue intrepidly on the path of evangelization and testimony, even if the present situation makes it arduous, difficult, and even bitter."[33]

The next day the government raided homes all over the nation of those believed connected with the event. For the eleventh centennial itself, authorities refused visas to English cardinal Basil Hume as well as to French cardinal Jean-Marie Lustiger and Austrian cardinal Franz Koenig. At the event, government officials tried to open the proceedings by characterizing them as a "peace festival." The crowd replied spontaneously, "This is a pilgrimage!" After other attempts to recast the celebration as a reaffirmation of national culture, which drew boos, people chanted, "We want the pope! Faith, Faith! We want the Mass!" Other public demonstrations erupted, inspired by the first one. In the fall of 1985, twenty thousand people — mostly young people and Franciscans in habits — made a pilgrimage to a shrine in Šaštin, where they chanted: *Christus vincit, Christus regnat, Christus imperat!* ("Christ conquers, Christ reigns, Christ rules!"). Two years later, another 120,000 went to Velehrad again at an event led by the cardinal.[34]

Public expression of opposition through religious channels had broken wide open. In March 1988, during a special Mass at Saint Vitus Cathedral in Prague to celebrate the upcoming canonization of Blessed Agnes of Bohemia, and the inauguration of a decade-long program of spiritual renewal, crowds demonstrated outside the church chanting: "We want bishops! Bring us the pope!" Other demonstrations followed. After one in Bratisalva, riot police unleashed dogs on peaceful believers and used water cannons and tear gas to disperse the crowds. Bishop Jan Korec commented: "Not even the most narrow-minded of policemen could have thought that girls with rosaries and candles in their hands posed a threat to Bratislava or Central Europe."[35]

A short time after, the forces unleashed by Gorbachev's *glasnost* throughout the Warsaw Pact, together with internal resistance centered around the Church and other dissident groups, led to the "Velvet Revolution," which ended fifty years of Communist rule and installed Václav Havel as president. Though it took decades for these witnesses to truth to find their public voice after the initial defeat by the regime, they ultimately proved the power of the human spirit. As Havel wrote during his own time as a dissident:

A single, seemingly powerless person who dares to cry out the word of truth and to stand behind it with all his person and all his life, ready to pay a high price, has, surprisingly, greater power, though formally disenfranchised, than do thousands of anonymous voters. . . . It is becoming evident that wholly personal categories like good and evil still have their unambiguous content and, under certain circumstances, are capable of shaking the seemingly unshakeable power with all its army of soldiers, policemen and bureaucrats.[36]

Though the return to truth since the fall of Communism has been slow, occasionally even some bureaucrats in Eastern Europe have accorded justice to martyrs. In the fall of 1999, the Supreme Court of Bulgaria, a country with a small Catholic population that was ruthlessly persecuted under Communism, admitted that Bishop Eugene Bossilkov, who was executed on November 11, 1952, for supposed spying activities had been the victim of an injustice. Bossilkov was beatified by John Paul II on March 15, 1998, but in the early 1950s he had been sentenced to death because foreign postcards and parts of an old record player, which the regime called an apparatus for the clandestine transmission of State secrets, had been found in his home. He had "confessed" to anti-Communist crimes after torture.

A stone tablet has been placed in the prison where the bishop died to commemorate his martyrdom. Vassil Gotzev, the Bulgarian minister of justice, refused any credit for allowing this step:

> Permission to place a stone in memory of the martyr in this jail is not the merit of the Ministry of Justice. Rather, the Ministry is at fault for not ordering until today the placing of the names of all those killed in the struggle for liberty and democracy in this and other jails. . . . What I can say as Minster of Justice of a democratic government is that we are doing all that is necessary; may God bless us in achieving this, so that we will never again allow the jailing of persons of a different ideology, that those detained will never again be mistreated, and that there will never again be people who must endure sufferings because of their ideas. When the society we are building achieves all this, Blessed Bossilkov will be satisfied because he is among us.[37]

This admission is a good beginning that should be repeated in several Eastern and Central European nations.

Everyone knows that Christianity suffered horrifying persecution under the Communist regimes in the region. A few people in the persecuted nations have blamed the churches, with some justice, for not taking a more active role in defense of human rights. A synod of the Romanian Orthodox Church which met in January of 1990 after the departure of that country's longstanding dictator Nicolae Ceauşescu, for example, went so far as to apologize for its clerical and lay leaders "who did not always have the courage of martyrs." An apology of this kind acknowledges a real fault, but it also makes clear that it would have taken a willingness to be martyred in any Communist country to confront heavily armed and ruthless regimes.

A more balanced reading of the history of Eastern and Central Europe after the Communist takeover would have to take into account that, at least in the early years, many believers were martyred for their faith and for their opposition. Whatever the subsequent behavior of the churches, their activities must be judged against a background of the many who died. To oppose Communism effectively, the Eastern churches would have had to organize or to participate in multiple revolutionary wars. There are serious questions about whether that would have been prudent or the proper role for a faith that more closely follows the way of its Founder by accepting suffering, persecution, and death, even as it seeks to preserve the truth. In the end, Eastern Europe's martyrs and confessors may have achieved something that could not have been accomplished by direct confrontation.

The following three chapters will look carefully at martyrdom in the rather distinctive churches of Albania, Lithuania, and Romania.

*Miguel Agustín Pro, S.J.,
stretches out his arms
in the form of a cross,
a traditional Mexican
posture of prayer, as he
faces the firing squad.
(Courtesy of CNS)*

*The Austrian Marianist
Fr. Jakob Gapp,
apprehended in France by
the Nazis and executed in
Germany for criticizing Hitler.
(Courtesy of the Marianists)*

*Edith Stein before she
entered the Carmel and
became Sister Teresa
Benedicta of the Cross.
(Courtesy of CNS)*

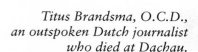

*Titus Brandsma, O.C.D.,
an outspoken Dutch journalist
who died at Dachau.*

*An unidentified priest just prior to his being shot at Dachau, the preferred Nazi detention camp for priests. (Courtesy of CNS)*

*Saint Maximilian Kolbe, O.F.M., who gave his life for a fellow prisoner at Auschwitz. (Courtesy of CNS)*

*A painting of the eleven sisters of the Holy Family of Nazareth slaughtered in what is today Belarus. (Courtesy Sisters of the Holy Family of Nazareth)*

*Father Jerzy Popiełuszko, the fearless chaplain to Polish Solidarity, brutally slain by government security forces. (Courtesy of CNS, from KNA)*

*Archbishop Oscar Romero,
shot by paramilitary forces
during Mass in San Salvador.
(Courtesy of CNS, from KNA)*

*Bishop Juan Gerardi,
killed by unknown assailants
shortly after issuing a lengthy report
on human rights violations
during Guatemala's civil war.
(Courtesy of CNS)*

Bishop John Joseph of
Islamabad, who died in
suspect circumstances after
protesting the repression
of Christians in Pakistan.
(Courtesy of CNS, from
UCA News)

Bishop Ignatius Kung,
who survived more than
thirty years in Communist
Chinese prison camps.
(Photo by Bill Pritchard,
courtesy of CNS)

*Swiss Father Maurice Tornay,*
*killed by Tibetan Lamas*
*for his missionary work.*

*Patrick J. Byrne, M.M.,*
*Prefect Apostolic of*
*Kwangju, who disappeared*
*and was executed early*
*in the Korean conflict.*
*(Courtesy of CNS)*

*A bombed-out Catholic Church in Southern Sudan.*
*(Courtesy of William L. Saunders)*

# -TEN-

# THE FIRST ATHEIST STATE
## *Albania*

ALBANIA IS A SMALL COUNTRY that prides itself on its fierce national identity and long Christian history. The faith first came to the areas that make up the modern state by way of the missionary journeys of Saint Paul and the other early leaders of the Church.[1] Bishops from the region were prominent in some of the early church councils. Albania claims among its distinguished sons and daughters Saint Jerome, the scholar who first translated the New Testament into Latin; Pope Clement XI; and Mother Teresa of Calcutta, a Yugoslavian (Gonzhe Bojaxhiu) of Albanian background. Albania suffered under Fascism, as all nations subjected to the Axis Powers did, during World War II. But its worst horrors were reserved for the period after the war when the new Communist People's Republic of Albania was created in January of 1946. Initially, Communism promised relief from the terrors that Fascism had inflicted. Indeed, the Communist Constitution of Albania contained guarantees of freedom of speech, conscience, and religion. But as in all Communist states, these rights existed only on paper. In hard reality, it was only the witness of those who resisted the daily violation of their rights and beliefs, including many Christians who were persecuted to the point of martyrdom, that kept the most basic of human ideals alive during a period that did everything in its power to stamp them out.

Albania has had a complex history. It was a Christian nation until its subjection by the Ottoman Turks in the fifteenth century. Various waves of political turmoil have sent Albanians into several other countries, including Greece, the Balkans, and Italy (Gian Francesco Albani, a descendent of an Albanian refugee family in Italy, became Pope Clement XI in the eighteenth century). Over a million Albanians live in parts of the former Yugoslavia and almost as many in modern Turkey. Albania's long ties with Italy have led to almost a third of a million refugees living in that country. Turkish dominance over half a millennium created a Mus-

231

lim majority, primarily for political, economic, and social rather than religious reasons. Today, about two-thirds of Albanians are Muslims, 19 percent are Orthodox Christians with long ties to Byzantium, and about 13 percent, mostly in the north, are Roman Catholics.

It was not until 1913, after various arrangements, that the Great Powers in Europe recognized an independent Albania. World War I put even that precarious agreement in jeopardy, and it was largely owing to the influence of the American president Woodrow Wilson and Pope Benedict XV that an independent Albania emerged, in reduced size, after the war.[2] In 1920, Albania joined the League of Nations. Unlike other nations in the region, however, Albania did not immediately come under German influence during World War II. The long Italian connection made an invasion by Mussolini's Fascist armies easier and more acceptable to other world powers. Resistance to Fascism came from many sources, not least the Albanian Catholic Church. The Franciscans published a newsletter, *Hylli i Drites* ("Morning Star"), that was highly influential.[3] A Franciscan priest, Father Anton Harapi, distinguished himself in those years for his outspoken opposition to Fascist oppression. Harapi had been a leader in education and caring for the sick during the years of Albanian independence. Ironically, he would be executed after World War II by the new Communist government as a traitor. According to reports, he told the tribunal that condemned him: "If to suffer for the people and with the people and fight for the Faith and Fatherland are considered weakness and treason, then, not only myself but all the Albanian Franciscans deserve the great honor of being shot."[4] He died blessing and forgiving his executioners.

Communist resistance forces in Albania played a cruel game against those who wanted a different future after the war. At first, Communist organizations refrained from attacking Germans while the Molotov-Ribbentrop pact between the Soviets and the Nazis was in force. When that pact dissolved in 1941, they went into action against not only lingering Fascist and Nazi forces but other Albanian currents as well. In 1944, Enver Hoxha, who emerged as the Communist leader, announced that other nationalist, anti-Nazi forces should be "exterminated without pity."[5] Aided by British and Yugoslav materiel and training (both nations would soon regret the involvement), the Communists followed the retreating German forces with bloody "purges." But in northern Albania, with its high concentration of Catholics and a strong ecclesial structure, they met with a great deal of opposition.

As early as 1945, Hoxha, who would continue in power from the

1940s until his death in the 1980s, paid indirect homage to the Albanian Church even as he described the party's goals:

> The Catholic clergy is influential in [the ancient northern capital of] Shkodra and the surrounding region. Its influence cannot be eliminated by merely administrative measures. The Catholic clergy is a well-organized body, with strong traditions and close links with the Vatican. Therefore, we should confront its organization with our better organization, confront its policy with our political line, and oblige it to fight on our ground, and not on its own.... We must find the right method of struggle and appropriate tactics to use against the Catholic clergy.[6]

That struggle, it would soon become clear, would involve persecution, expropriation of property, the wholesale slaughter of the Catholic leadership, and an attempt to create "the first atheist state on the planet."

The Communist party began with its usual "tactics." In the first election after the war, it received 93 percent of the vote, in a race that permitted only Communist candidates. The Soviet Union and other Eastern bloc nations officially recognized the new government. But Great Britain and the United States, seeing the direction in which Albania was heading, withdrew their diplomats before a year had passed. Those two nations, along with Italy, even prepared an invasion to free Soviet-dominated Albania, but the effort failed when the Soviets learned of the plan ahead of time through their later notorious mole in British intelligence, Kim Philby. The invaders were quickly captured and their families and friends were subjected to arrest and persecution.

Yet even the ties to the Soviet Union were not sufficiently radical for the Albanian Communist leaders. When Nikita Khrushchev took power in 1953 and maneuvered opinion against the "crimes" of Stalinism, his stance caused problems for leaders who had followed — and wished to continue — the Stalinist line. Albania switched its primary allegiance from the Soviet Union to the new Communist regime in China, which took a different, more hard-line tack under Chairman Mao than did the new Soviet leaders. It was Albania that proposed Communist China for membership in the United Nations and a place on the Security Council. When the Chinese implemented the Cultural Revolution in the 1960s, Albania followed suit and began a reign of terror against all opposition groups, especially the Catholic Church.

Unfortunately, this particular history left the victims of Albanian Communism without a strong voice in the free world. An estimated thirty-five thousand people were executed and forty thousand were given life sentences in the process.[7] More Albanians died at the hands of the Communist government in peacetime than had died in World War II. Anti-Soviet Albania was not an issue in Cold War negotiations with Russia; and Communist China was not important enough to the West until the 1970s to make it worth trying diplomatic tactics on behalf of Albania. Left in total isolation, with little information about their plight leaking to the outside world, Albanians of all denominations, but especially the Catholics, suffered truly terrible persecutions. The Holy See, speaking boldly through Vatican Radio, was one of Albania's few defenders in the free world. Even the Greek Orthodox Church and the Islamic League were silent for political reasons.[8] The Vatican was denounced by the regime as Fascist for its witness; Albanians caught listening to Vatican Radio could find themselves with stiff prison sentences.

The Albanian Communists had good reason to pay attention to the Church. In addition to a strong ecclesial structure, Franciscans and Jesuits had played a major role in modern Albanian culture. The Franciscans may have arrived as early as Saint Francis's return from Syria in 1219, and they made their presence felt through the education of Albanians of various religious backgrounds and through publishing projects of a scholarly and popular nature. The Jesuits did not arrive in Albania until the nineteenth century, but they helped promote the teaching of Albanian and, as a byproduct, Albanian nationalism in a nation still heavily influenced by the Ottoman empire. The Jesuits soon organized the seminary that trained all Albanian priests and the College of Saint Xavier, one of the premier institutions of higher education in Albania. They also carried out a vigorous publishing program. Other orders — Salesians, Servites — established communities of nuns who ran hospitals, kindergartens, and trade schools. In sum, the religious orders were integrated into the very heart of national life.

In standard Communist fashion, this historic role was suppressed in the textbooks produced by the new regime. Small countries like Albania usually have a tiny intellectual and political elite who serve multiple functions as diplomats, politicians, writers, and journalists. In Albania, those who had performed those tasks in the previous hundred years were either priests — many of them contributed to the Renaissance of Albanian culture earlier in the century as poets, ethnologists, historians, and composers — or had been trained by Catholic institutions, which also accepted Orthodox and Muslim students. And in the longer vistas of Albanian history, it was the Church that loomed as the largest cultural factor in the nation. In addition, in the heavily Catholic north, missionaries labored to end the Sicilian-style vendettas common among the tribal peoples. They improved the status of women, long relegated to subordinate roles by Islamic influence.

Ismail Kadar, a non-Catholic and Communist collaborator who was one of Albania's best known twentieth-century writers during the worst periods of Hoxha's dictatorship, observed, "Our culture has been in large part founded on the Catholic tradition and even the Turkish invasion could not remove that impression.... Here in Albania, all the great writers, with very few exceptions, have been Catholic, while Islam, despite centuries of occupation, has had an influence that may be passed over in silence."[9] To eliminate all these figures from national history was tantamount to obliterating Albanian culture. The regime filled the void it created with portrayals of itself as the only guarantee of national identity and with charges that earlier periods were marked only by Italian imperialism, priestly collaboration in Vatican machinations, and "Fascism" and "Nazism" of various stripes. The lies were large and absurd, but they were the only information formally available to Albanian students for almost two generations.

The Albanian regime would also try to obliterate all record of its crimes against the people, not least against the Church. But enough has remained through living memory and sporadic written records that the long, and perhaps unmatched, suffering of the Albanian Catholic Church can be reconstructed in its large lines, if not in great detail. From the outset, Enver Hoxha's new regime practiced a two-track policy toward the Church: harsh treatment followed by invitations to apostasy. Even before the formation of the new government, persecution began in earnest. Catholic publishing houses were closed and journalists were silenced almost immediately. Catholic Action and other Catholic groups were branded Fascist and broken up. One bishop was expelled as an "undesirable" and the apostolic delegate was arrested, mistreated, and deported back to Italy. Catholic kindergartens, schools, orphanages, and hospitals were confiscated. Teaching of dialectical materialism became obligatory. Even the College of Saint Xavier had to accept Communist professors. Two Jesuits who protested, Father Gardin and Brother Vata, were arrested and sentenced to forced labor. Amid these initial pressures, Hoxha met with the Albanian archbishops and offered better treatment in exchange for their definitive break with Rome and the transformation of Albanian Catholicism into a national church subservient to the government. The Albanian hierarchy refused the offer.

The sequel was terrible, but it is doubtful whether even such a betrayal of their vows and Albania's history would have saved the Church much suffering. The Albanian Communists had early decided on a crusade to eliminate religion in the country. To be able to carry out this mission without witnesses to the outside world, they rounded up and expelled foreign clergy, mostly Italians. In 1945, the regime outlawed the Jesuit order and all its institutions. In 1947, the Franciscans were banned. Propaganda campaigns, of course, were mounted to make it appear that all of these steps were taken for justifiable political reasons. The religious orders were allegedly involved in plots, servants of foreign tyrannies; they sought to wreck the socialist future of Albania — all the usual Communist lies. Though the ploy was transparent abroad, it worked to a degree in many non-Catholic areas of the country, primarily because the government controlled all media and other sources of information.

In the first years of the new government, the number of acts of persecution started a steep climb. Summary executions and torture became an instrument of terror. Judicial proceedings, when they took place, were often merely show trials. At times, they were broadcast live over the radio.[10] One such broadcast went awry in 1948 when Pierin Kchira, a former member of the Sigurimi, the Albanian Secret Service, blurted out:

> You are the most wretched people in the world! I have received orders from you to torture the people, to fabricate slander against the Catholic clergy. I, your blind instrument, as cowardly and criminal as you, have done all that was in my power to carry out your orders.
>
> You commanded me to go, at night, to hide arms in the churches and monasteries, so you would have a pretext to eliminate the clergy and to destroy the Catholic Church. I confess to the entire Albanian people that I have carried out your orders with great diligence and secrecy. . . . My personal disgrace is not important to me. Instead, I detest having been a vile instrument in your hands and of having betrayed the blood of so many innocent members of the Catholic clergy.[11]

The radio crew managed to cut off the transmission at that point. When the station came back on the air, Kchira was receiving a death sentence. According to reports, he was immediately executed and his body was thrown into the same common graves as the priests he had betrayed.

Two Franciscans (Lek Luli and Anton Harapi) and two secular priests (Lazer Shantoja and Andrea Zadeja) were summarily executed. Shantoja was so badly tortured before he died, his forearms and leg bones broken, that he could only "walk" around on elbows and knees. His own mother asked his captors to kill him rather than continue the torture.[12] Before the new government was even officially formed, several Jesuits were given long sentences to hard labor. Others were rounded up on the flimsiest of pretexts. Jesuit vice-provincial Gjon Fausti (an Italian seriously wounded while getting people into a church for sanctuary during the earlier Nazi occupation), the seminary rector Daniel Dajani, and the Franciscan editor of *Morning Star,* Gjon Shllaku, were accused of subversion and "Fascism" and executed. (In a perverse show of impartiality, the Albanian government also arrested and executed the Muslim lawyer Muzafer Pipa, who had chosen out of conscience to defend many of the Jesuits and Franciscans.)

One of the most notorious instances involved Vincent Prendushi, a Franciscan who had risen to become archbishop of Durres. Father Prendushi had been a student of Albanian folklore and published several collections of traditional songs. He wrote poetry and translated into Albanian some of the best poems of other European languages. But his cultural contributions and religious eminence only hastened his arrest in 1947 by the fledgling Communist regime. Sentenced to twenty years hard labor, he was also subjected to beatings and savage torture in prison. At one point, he was tied up and hung from the prison bathroom ceiling. The archbishop was sixty-five-years old at the time.

As if this were not enough, one day he was forced into a work detail carrying logs up a hill. Guards loaded his shoulders with a burden he obviously could not carry. He fell repeatedly, while the guards and director laughed at him. He remained silent. After various episodes of mistreatment, his health failed and he ended up in the prison hospital with heart problems and asthma. A fellow prisoner records that he spent his final several months gasping for breath with little medical attention and only a limited amount of fuel allotted to stay warm.[13] Those who were with him at the end, however, felt that something they had seen in him alive bore witness to an immortal element that survives the death of the body.

Around the same time, Bishop Frano Gjini and Ciprian Nika, the Franciscan provincial, were machine-gunned along with about twenty other clergy. Bishop Gjini had already braved serious threats when he was appointed abbot of the church in the Mirdita region during political and social turmoil there in 1929. With the creation of the Communist regime, he was again asked to undertake a dangerous task when he replaced Leone De Nigris as substitute apostolic delegate for Albania.

Since Mirdita was a heavily Catholic region, it resisted the imposition of Communist rule, and the Communists blamed Bishop Gjini. Enver Hoxha tried to pressure him into convincing Catholics to join with the government and break with the Vatican. It was a tactic bound to fail with the man whom the other Albanian bishops had chosen to be their official link with Rome.

Bishop Gjini issued a statement protesting official slanders against the Church and persecution. He knew in advance what the response would be. After his arrest, they tied him up and administered electric shocks. Then they got serious. He was cut in various places and the wounds were irritated with salt, wood splinters were driven under his finger and toe nails. Finally, he was shot and dumped in a mass grave, without any proper judicial review.[14] As has often been the case in periods of direct persecution, instead of intimidating the Catholics of Mirdita, his brutal, but heroic, death inspired the people to greater resistance against growing tyranny.

Cyprian Nika fell in the same wave of repression. In the fall of 1946, he was accused of hiding arms in a Franciscan convent. The charge was obviously false and the arms planted. One of Father Nika's fellow prisoners, who survived the camps, reports that they were often taken for torture and interrogation. During the whole period, Nika maintained deep spiritual and emotional tranquillity. One of the guards' favorite pastimes was to "discuss" the existence of God with Father Nika during the torture sessions. Though he and the other prisoners knew it was only intended as a mockery of religion, he took it as his duty to make the case for the Creator. In one of the final sessions, a guard told him, "My God is Enver Hoxha," just before Nika was beaten unconscious. He was shot shortly after.[15]

Another bishop, George Volaj, of the diocese of Sappa, had the distinction of becoming the youngest bishop in the world in 1940 (at only thirty-six) and the youngest bishop to be martyred seven years later.[16] So obviously talented a man quickly drew the attention of the Communist government. His carefully nuanced criticisms of the regime's abuse of human rights led to his being forbidden to participate in religious events and to house arrest. When the restrictions were relaxed, he preached, notably at the Sanctuary of the Madonna of Shkodra, a favorite place of pilgrimage for Albanians (it was destroyed by the Albanian Red Guards in 1967), asking all Albanians, Catholic and not, to be witnesses to the truth in their various homes. Soon he too participated in the familiar pattern. Arrested and tortured, he was shot on February 3, 1948. It seems clear that the government had planned to liquidate the Catholic hierarchy from the first; by March 1948 one bishop was left alive outside of prison, Bernardin Shllaku, and he probably survived because he was hiding in the northern mountains.[17]

Ordinary priests felt the persecution as well. An even more brutal fate awaited Father Nikoll Gazulli, a pastor in the Shkodra archdiocese. Gazulli fled to resistance forces in the mountains when the Communist persecution became too heavy. He was tricked into returning to administer Extreme Unction to a dying villager. Betrayed by an informant, he was shot in the back, though not mortally. As an object lesson to people in the area, he was hung, still alive, in front of the village church for several days.[18] Another priest, Father Jak Bushati, was arrested and tortured: he, too, was hung up as a warning, but upside down, repeatedly, for several days at a time, before he died.

But the terror did not only involve clergy. Many lay people were tortured and occasionally executed for their failure to make public declarations against the "crimes" of the clergy. (In an unprecedented show of fidelity and courage, whole parishes of Albanian Catholics asked to be arrested in place of their priests. They also met to say the rosary on Sundays in the priest's absence.)[19] Others were condemned, rightly or not, for alleged collaboration with anti-Communist forces, which might mean anything from political opposition to involvement in providing food and medical care to guerrilla forces. Elena Shllaku, a devout laywoman accused of collaborating with the anti-Communist resistance, underwent the usual tortures; then she had her hair pulled out and was bound with barbed wire. Her end is unknown. Another laywoman, Bianca Krosaj, only twenty years old when she was arrested, suffered all the same torments and also had all her teeth pulled out. Maria Shalaku, from Kosovo, was pronounced too depraved for quick execution by a firing squad. Her tribunal ordered that she and other companions "be slowly burned alive to ashes."[20]

In the meantime, nuns were beginning to be expelled from convents and forbidden to wear religious habits. The few remaining religious went virtually underground to administer the sacraments. Before 1949, many Catholic properties throughout Albania were confiscated and turned into public facilities such as theaters, cafes, courtrooms — and prisons. The cathedral at Shkodra became a basketball court. Sacred vessels were profaned and sold off. By the end of 1949, all religious groups — Muslim and Orthodox included — were required to submit constitutions for state approval. All but the Catholics ceded control to the state.

In retaliation, the government appointed as minister of the interior General Mehmet Shehu, who had become notorious for the relish with which he attacked clergy during a period as a volunteer fighting with the Republican side during the Spanish Civil War.[21] He had one of the bishops beaten and forced the Church to sign an agreement removing Albania from Roman institutional control, but permitting a "spiritual" link. When the agreement was published, however, it had been revised without consulting the Church — effectively subordinating it to the state. According to the agreement, schools, churches, and seminaries were supposed to receive state support. Naturally, they did not, and were slowly strangled.

In the prisons camps, the slow torture took many different forms. One Jesuit survivor recorded in his journal the variations in torture inflicted on inmates:

> Most of them were beaten on their bare feet with wooden clubs; the fleshy part of the legs and buttocks were cut open, rock salt inserted beneath the skin, and then sewn up again; their feet, placed in boiling water until the flesh fell off, were then rubbed with salt; their Achilles' tendons were pierced with hot wires. Some were hung by their arms for three days without food; put in ice and icy water until nearly frozen; had electrical wires places in their ears, nose, mouth, genitals, and anus; burning pine needles placed under fingernails; forced to eat a kilo of salt and having water withheld for twenty-four hours; boiled eggs put in their armpits; teeth pulled without anaesthetic; tied behind vans and dragged; left in solitary confinement without food or water until almost dead; forced to drink their own urine and eat their own excrement; put in pits of excrement up to their necks; put on a bed of nails and covered with heavy material; put in nail-studded cages which were then rotated rapidly; a cat and a mouse put down the bodice of a nun; sisters forced to disrobe and walk naked through the streets.[22]

The sorrowful litany shows an inventiveness in torture surpassing the punishments that Dante, one of the great human imaginations of all time, displayed in writing his *Inferno*.

As resistance to this arrangement mounted, the state struck back even harder. In the late 1950s and early 1960s, more than a dozen priests were martyred: "Titular bishops and vicars were forced to clean the streets and public bathrooms wearing clown outfits with paper signs across their chests saying, 'I have sinned against the people.' "[23] In 1967

Enver Hoxha started a cultural revolution in imitation of his Communist Chinese allies and called on the Albanian Red Guard to exterminate religious superstition. They burned, vandalized, and razed to the ground churches, monasteries, and mosques, and harassed clergy. Toward the end of that year, on November 22, 1967, the government completely outlawed religion, thereby becoming the first officially atheist state. By the end of the rampage, 2,169 religious buildings had been closed or destroyed, and few clergy of any denomination remained free.[24]

It would be almost twenty-five years, after the Berlin Wall fell in 1989, before the situation would improve. Clandestine religious activity, of course, continued in secret gatherings and in private homes. But the risk of such activities was high. For example, Father Stephen Kurti, an Albanian born in what later became the Yugoslavian province of Kosovo, was killed in 1972 merely for baptizing a child in a prison camp.[25] In typical fashion, the Communist government justified the murder, when it became known internationally, because, the government alleged, the seventy-four-year-old was a Fascist and Nazi as well as a "despicable agent of the Anglo-American espionage network, a spy and an informer, and a subversive agent of the Vatican."[26] There were some astonishing leaps of logic among these and the other charges against Kurti, beginning with the assumption that to adhere to the Vatican was the equivalent of backing Mussolini, with whom the Vatican had had a tempestuous struggle in Italy. Kurti had already spent sixteen years in jail after allegedly "confessing" espionage activities after the war. When he was released, said the government, he had engaged in one of the cardinal anti-Communist sins: "trying to disrupt and sabotage production." It was for crime against the people — not for baptizing a baby — that he was executed. The statement even justified the earlier closing of all religious institutions on similar grounds: "All the priests, whether Catholic or Orthodox or Muslim, were forced to go to work and earn an honest living."

Yet religious instruction, masses, ordinations, and even the secret consecration of bishops continued under these daily threats. In fact, the regime remained irritated throughout its decades of misrule that Party members were not zealous enough in stamping out "superstition." The primary means by which religious instruction continued was the family. As elsewhere in Communist countries, the Albanian government declared the family "reactionary" and tried to get children to inform on whether their parents were giving them religious instruction at home. It forbade parents to give children "religious" names. A family saying the rosary together, at home, could get five years in prison; teaching a child the sign of the cross might bring a similar penalty. The mere possession of religious literature could lead to a death sentence.[27] Surprisingly, many families still celebrated Christmas and Easter, continued to pray, and transmitted their Catholic identity quietly to the children. The youngest, who might be tricked into divulging information by teachers, had to be exposed only slowly and at the right age to these clandestine ways of keeping the faith alive. Miraculously, this worked in most cases, though the government had succeeded in introducing worries about Communist spies into the very heart of family life.

The proof that not only clergy but ordinary lay people remained faithful is that when the first public religious services were permitted again in 1990, they immediately became events where thousands gathered. Part of the Albanian spirit can be glimpsed in the way that Albania's only cardinal in two thousand years of Christian history returned to his duties. Cardinal Michael Koliqi (dubbed "The Ironman" by the nuncio) returned to rebuild his cathedral at Shkodra and to begin publishing his weekly paper *Kumbone e së Dielës* with a naturalness as if he had been away a weekend. Koliqi had been forbidden to perform any public services for fifty-six years, thirty-seven of which he spent in prison and camps.[28] The government agreed to return religious properties in 1991, the same year that Mother Teresa made a brief visit and opened the first convent for nuns in Albania since 1967. In 1983, the regime had compared John Paul II to Mussolini; in 1993, it received him as a distinguished world leader who had spoken out in defense of the Albanian people for fifteen years.

The Albanian people and the Albanian Church triumphed — at a high price. Out of 156 priests before the persecution began, 65 were martyred and 64 died during or after imprisonment. Tens of thousands of common people died for religious or other reasons. Basic knowledge of the faith also perished in large segments of the population for lack of teachers, and paganism, superstitions, and indifference grew in the absence of church structures. The ultimate effect of all this on Albania remains to be seen. But there is no people on earth who passed through a worse time of testing in the twentieth century. In the nature of things, few people know about the history of Communist Albania. But many ought to. As John Paul II has told the Albanians: "History has never seen before what happened in Albania.... Dear Albanians, your drama must interest the whole European continent: *Europe must not forget.*"[29]

# -ELEVEN-

# A STEADY LIGHT IN LITHUANIA

ON SEPTEMBER 8, 1970, Nijole Sadunaite was sitting in a courtroom in Moletai, Lithuania. She was not the accused. A priest friend, Antanas Seskevicius, was being tried for the crime of having taught religion to children. The "trial" mostly consisted of children and their parents being pressured to testify and — when they refused to give the right answers — being threatened themselves with prison. For these remarkable people, the threat was not as serious an evil as a sin. Many volunteered that they themselves had taught their children about religion and if anyone should go to prison, they should. The priest had only tested the children's knowledge, they maintained. Frustrated, the officials removed all potential witnesses from the room, but made a special show of detaining Sadunaite: she had hired a lawyer from her meager earnings as a factory worker (the only kind of job a regular churchgoer could hold) to defend Father Seskevicius.

We know about this incident only because Sadunaite, though sentenced herself to the Lithuanian Gulag, survived and published an account of her life that has been described as a Catholic equivalent of the *Diary of Anne Frank*. Her autobiography had to be smuggled out piecemeal from Communist Lithuania, the names of those who had helped with the process carefully concealed, so that it could appear in Western nations while Communist control over information entering and leaving Lithuania was all but airtight.[1] Sadunaite came by her courage in a common and honorable way during the persecution: her parents were accomplished professionals and committed Catholics who refused to deny their faith in the slightest in spite of all the blandishments and pressures the regime brought to bear on them.

But it was not only her parents' example that had formed Sadunaite. As a young girl, she had seen the prison clothes of the martyr-bishop Vincentas Borisevicius, at times soaked in blood, at other times foul with excrement from humiliations and tortures. The bishop's sister, Maryte, would bring them home to wash after visiting her brother in the KGB prisons. Canon Kemesis, the priest who had baptized Sadunaite in the town of Dotnuva shortly after she was born, had also been arrested and tortured and had died in a Soviet prison. Neither had given an inch to the torturers.

Sadunaite was equally adamant when she was charged with "anti-Soviet agitation and propaganda" under section 68 of the Lithuanian SSR Criminal Code for having been caught typing an underground, or *samizdat* (in Lithuanian, *savilaida*), copy of the *Chronicle of the Catholic Church in Lithuania,* an invaluable source of information about abuses in that country. Those abuses, little noticed by the Free World at the time, constituted a terrible crucible in which — despite the daily harassment, prejudice, and mockery that believers suffered, even when they did not fall into the hands of the KGB — they manifested a heroic witness to the faith in the twentieth century.

Nijole Sadunaite even succeeded in turning the tables on her captors, a rare feat in the Soviet Gulag. They accused her of mental illness since she was unrelenting in "slandering" the regime. But when she maintained her self-composure for months, they offered her freedom for just one statement that would incriminate her acquaintances. She replied:

> If you gave me eternal youth and all the beautiful things in the world for one statement which would cause some trouble, then those years would turn into hell for me. Even if you kept me in the psychiatric hospital all my life, as long as I knew that no one had suffered on my account, I would go around smiling. A clear conscience is more precious than liberty or life. I do not understand how you, whose conscience is burdened by the spilled blood and tears of so many innocent people, can sleep at night. I would agree to die a thousand times rather than be free for one second with your conscience.

At this retort, Major Vyatautas Pilelis, a notorious KGB agent who was questioning her, "blanched and hung his head."[2]

Pilelis quickly regained his composure and months later was back at the old game of calling her and her fellow believers "fanatics." Though he seemed to have a strange fascination with Sadunaite, he promised her a prison sentence worse than that for murderers since "you know too much." But she gave him another searing response: "[Fanatic] fits you, yourselves best... because you try with all your might to make us atheists, but believers love all people because Jesus Christ said, 'What you do for anyone, you do for me.' We fight only against evil. For you we fell sorry, and if necessary, we would give our lives for you. You know that!" And she stung Pilelis again when she told him Communists were worse than Fascists because, though the Fascists committed great crimes, at least they were open about who they were killing and why.[3]

Six soldiers guarded this brave and eloquent woman on her way to the trial (murderers usually had only one or two). The guards were young Russians, deliberately chosen because they did not understand Lithuanian and could not be later called as witnesses to the proceedings. Even at that point, Sadunaite's captors were willing to release her if she remained silent; she would not. Sadunaite refused the help of a lawyer, who, she knew, would probably only get into trouble defending her. So she defended herself, citing international human rights conventions, signed by the Soviet Union, and Lithuanian decrees on the separation of church and state that guaranteed religious liberty. She characterized her captors' behavior, which included denying spiritual consolation to the dying, as "spiritual hooliganism."[4] And she warned them: "Your crimes are propelling you to the garbage heap of history at an ever increasing speed," while calling on them to release all those unjustly imprisoned.[5] The effect on the judges was so obvious that the young Russian guards, who had understood none of the discussion, asked her after, "What kind of trial was this? . . . You were the prosecutor, and all of them were like criminals condemned to death! What did you speak about during the trial to frighten them like that?" Despite appearances, she was sentenced "to three years loss of freedom, to be served in strict regime labor camps, and to three years of exile."[6] Unlike the many others who traversed the same path, she survived.

Nijole Sadunaite was perhaps an unusually courageous and talented believer, but it is difficult not to think, reading her autobiography, that through her the spirit and ethos of the whole Lithuanian people under Communism finds a voice. Thousands of Lithuanian Catholics endured persecutions and martyrdom similar to the treatment believers suffered in the other Eastern and Central European countries. But perhaps no people, with the exception of the Poles — a nation long linked with Lithuania — manifested as much poise and eloquence under repression as did the Lithuanians. Sadunaite is, in that perspective, only the best known of a remarkably heroic nation of believers.

To most outside observers, the vast areas of Eastern Europe, stretching into the even greater expanse of Russia, seem populated entirely by peoples of Slavic linguistic and ethnic background, historically connected to Orthodox Christianity. Poland, with its potent Catholic faith, made even more visible by the unexpected 1978 election of the first Polish pope, John Paul II, appears the sole exception. But the region contains an equally fierce Catholic nation, with an ancient non-Slavic people, who suffered brutal repression and notable martyrdom during the twentieth century: the small, but distinctive nation of Lithuania.

Lithuania has a unique history extending back to around 18,000 B.C. Traces of the ancient migration of an Indo-European people who became the modern Lithuanians have been discovered by archeologists and ethnologists. The Lithuanian language has remained so pure a descendent of the Indo-European mother tongue that lies at the roots of most Western languages that it has close affinities with the Sanskrit in which the archaic religious texts of the Hindus were written. The great modern Polish-Lithuanian-American poet and Nobel laureate Czeslaw Milosz remarks in an essay about his youth that, prior to the attempts by totalitarian powers beginning in the 1940s to stamp out Lithuanian culture, institutions of higher learning in Lithuania, most of them founded and run by Catholic religious orders, set up departments of Sanskrit studies as a way of deepening understanding of modern Lithuanian.[7] These and other historical factors gave Lithuanians a special identity that even the totalitarians were unable to erase.

For much of their history, Lithuanians were largely forest-dwellers and agricultural people. Lithuania boasts over three thousand glacial lakes, called "the eyes of Lithuania," and rich forests with two-thousand-year-old oaks. In ancient times, it was one of the sources for the precious amber that made its way along the Amber Route on the eastern edge of Europe. It produced food and materials — cotton, beetroots, potatoes, beef, milk, and fish — in abundance, and its bounty helped the country to become a European power in earlier ages. Lithuania was the last major European nation to be converted to Catholicism, but the faith quickly became an integral part of national identity. We have already seen in the chapter on Poland how that country and Lithuania became unified in the fifteenth century under Prince Ladislaw Jagiello, with Lithuania retaining its own autonomy as a Polish Grand Duchy. Saint Hedwig, a favorite of Edith Stein's, worked vigorously to strengthen Catholic belief and practice in Lithuania.

Despite a pagan past lasting thousands of years, Lithuania became fertile soil for the Church. Lithuanians were prominent in the early resistance to the Ottoman Turks and fought with Jan Sobiewski in the 1683 Siege of Vienna, which put an end to the Turkish threat to Europe. After that Lithuania weakened and started to fall prey to various outside interests. Russia tried to stamp out its distinctive language and Western-oriented Catholicism. At times, Scandinavian influence fell over the national territory as Sweden and Russia sparred for influence in the region. The nation was partitioned, like Poland, between Germany and Russia. Along with his fervent Polish patriotism, the great poet Adam Mickiewicz championed Lithuania, especially the capital city, Vilnius. Given its rich history and popular traditions, it is no surprise that Lithuania surfaced as an independent nation whenever circumstances in Europe or Russia allowed.

By 1940, when the modern persecutions began, just under 85 percent of the population was Catholic. Thirty-five years later, after decades of Nazi and Soviet invasions and harsh repression of the Church, the Catholic portion of the population was unchanged, even though a million Lithuanians had fled into North and South America, Australia, and Western Europe. Perhaps another 1,250,000 Lithuanians "disappeared" in purges and forced labor in the Soviet Gulag, reducing the population so much that it was not until 1963 that there were as many Lithuanians in the country as had been there in 1940, before the turmoil began.[8] Yet despite all hardships, the Lithuanian people remained remarkably faithful to Catholicism.

Their fidelity is all the more noteworthy in that the Soviets made it their settled policy from the very first to gain control over the Church because of its longstanding contributions to Lithuanian national identity and popular feeling. A noted scholar of Lithuania has remarked that "the Kremlin considered the containment of the Catholic Church only very slightly less important than the seizure of the state apparatus or the control of the armed forces."[9] During World War II, the Soviets had allied themselves with the Church through a popular front strategy to expel the Nazi invaders. But the Vatican had seen similar moves toward Uniate and Roman-rite Catholics in other countries. The papal nuncio, Luigi Centoz, asked for and received special emergency powers. But within a few weeks, the Soviets ordered him to leave and attacks on the religious rights of Lithuanians began in earnest.

Religion disappeared from schools, military chaplains were dismissed, private educational institutions, mostly run by religious orders, were confiscated by the state. On July 16, 1940, the school of theology and philosophy at the University of Kaunas was "suspended and the professors fired."[10] All publications in Lithuania had to be licensed, which meant the many Catholic journals were effectively closed. Religious weddings were declared illegal. Religious holidays were abolished in October of 1941. Religious literature was destroyed. Though the Church owned little land (about 3 percent) in Lithuania, even that was slowly transferred to state jurisdiction. To anyone familiar with the usual Soviet tactics, each step was ominous.

Clergy soon came under surveillance and persecution. By best estimates, during the scant twelve months in which the Soviets temporarily controlled Lithuania, every priest in the country experienced either arrest, prison, or interrogation. Many were tortured; several died. Among them, 150 priests, about 10 percent of the 1450 then active, were interrogated and pressured into changing their ministries or collaborating, but none apostatized.[11] This was at a time when Lithuania was a bone of contention between Nazis and Soviets. The Molotov-Ribbentrop Pact meant that, at least nominally, the two great powers had conceded to each other spheres of influence. In fact, the pact soon collapsed, and Lithuanians were divided about which regime would be more brutal. On the whole, opinion seemed to favor the Soviets as having softened somewhat in their ideological crusades. The Soviets shrewdly attempted to divide "progressive," i.e., pro-Soviet Church leaders, against traditionalists. Events soon revealed the meaning of these maneuvers.

When Lithuania came under regular Soviet rule, it brought to the fore a much harsher system than the interim government had been. N. G. Pozdniakov, who became a kind of proconsul in the new government, warned Bishop Vincentas Brizgys to find another line of work because "what was achieved in Russia in twenty years will be accomplished in Lithuania in two or three," and that "neither Hitler, the Pope, nor Roosevelt will be able to wrestle you away from us."[12] Though the Soviet Lithuanian constitution protected personal rights, freedom of conscience, and equal citizenship (in articles 99, 96, and 95) and the bishops claimed protection under those clauses, the standard practice of ignoring law in obedience to unwritten directives effectively began to appear everywhere, closing off religious practice. Priests were not allowed to visit prisons or hospitals to administer the sacraments. Teachers were pressured to teach atheism. Seminaries were closed.

When the Nazi invasion came in 1941, thirty-four thousand Lithuanians had been arrested and sent to labor camps in the Soviet Gulag. The retreating Soviets perpetrated mass murders against the Lithuanians. For three years (1941–44), Nazi Germany and the Soviet Union battled over Lithuania. By the end of the war, another sixty thousand people, many professionals and the most educated parts of the country, had escaped to Germany to avoid a new period of Soviet dominance. The Soviets shrewdly allowed the Lithuanian Church a tranquil period in which it helped rebuild the country. Then it began applying outrageous taxes on church buildings. Meetings of church officials were disrupted, as were religious services. The bishops protested, asking to be allowed their own freedom of action, which they proclaimed they would not abuse by entering into the politics, the proper sphere of the state.

The Communist regime, of course, rejected this simple compromise, which has worked tolerably in many nations around the world. It began painting the clergy as reactionary, anti-Soviet, servants of a "bourgeois nationalism." (The Soviets apparently had no wish to learn of Lithuania's long ethnic and religious nationalism, which had long predated any social development that could remotely be called bourgeois.) Juozas Žiugžda, a propaganda specialist for the regime, turned out a 1948 volume entitled *Reactionary Catholic Clergy — Eternal Enemy of the Lithuanian Nation.*[13] This and the flood of anti-Lithuanian Catholic propaganda that would follow in subsequent years had remarkably little effect on a people who knew their real enemy.

But violence against the Church had great effect. One of the first figures to fall was Bishop Borisevicius of Telsiai, whom Nijole Sadunaite had known as a girl from the evidence of his tortures. The details of his death, even its location, are unknown; both lacunae probably represent the KGB's desire to cover up an atrocity. Borisevicius had opposed the Nazis and rescued several Jews from their clutches. Two other bishops, Pranas Ramanauskas, auxiliary of Telsiai, and Teofilis Matulionis of Kaisiadorys, were imprisoned and exiled, as was Matulionis's replacement, Bernardas Suziedelis. Even the archbishop of Vilnius, Mečislovas Reinys, a philosopher who had written against Nazi racial theories and aided Jews fleeing death, found his way into the Gulag. The one remaining active bishop, Kazimieras Paltarokas, seems to have survived because he was willing to praise Stalin publicly and condemn Western militarism.

These moves essentially decapitated the Lithuanian Church and they were followed by the arrest of priests, the closing of monasteries and convents, and the imprisonment of the heads of the religious orders. On September 20, 1947, the Lithuanian Catholics addressed a letter to Pope Pius XII, which was smuggled out of the country and delivered to Rome. Among many charges, the letter detailed massive atrocities by the occupying Soviets: "In the month of June 1941, in three days, the Soviets arrested forty thousand Lithuanians: men, women, children, aged persons, and deported them on cattle cars to Siberia. We have seen with our own eyes the corpses thrown alongside the roads." Even worse, they remarked:

> The Russians have destroyed our cities and our villages; they have taken from us not only our lands, our houses, but also our liberty of thought and action. For us, the slavery of the spirit is the worst of all. They want to force us to believe and to repeat that Russia of the Soviets is the paradise of the earth, that outside its confines there is only misery and deceit, and meanwhile our children no longer know what sugar, meat, and butter are.[14]

Among the specific religious abuses, the letter points out the pressure to create a national church severed from Rome, the summary arrest and disappearance of priests who refuse to become informers for the regime, widespread surveillance over religious activities, and the suppression of Catholic associations, the press, schools, seminaries, hospitals, charitable works, and much more. The arrested were subjected to torture (many went insane), the withholding of food, and interruption of sleep; the "kindest" sentence was ten years in Siberia. Those who survived the month-long trip to Siberia with little food or water did not last, as a rule, more than five years. By these direct and indirect, but always carefully hidden means, the Soviets were able to do away with many clergy and lay people without creating well-known martyrs.

Even decades after the events, it is difficult to reconstruct specific cases. The few names that we have may be taken to represent a vast number of similar ones that we do not. Some come down to us only as names. In 1941, Fathers Benediktas Šveikauskas Stasys Baltrymas, and Vladas Didžioks were murdered by the Soviets. Torture and deportation began in earnest during the late 1940s and early 1950s: Petras Liepa, Antanas Reuba, Kazys Čiplys, Balys Beionoravičius, Petras Margevičius, and Anatanas Žakevičius perished in the process.[15] Still others survived the camps only to die shortly thereafter from the rigors they had suffered, like Bishops Matulionis and Suziedelis. Their stories may have no literary interest, simply being a repetition of an evil that occurred over and over again for decades, but every one of them deserves recognition for heroism and fidelity. The *Chronicle of the Catholic Church in Lithuania* became a painful thorn in the side of the regime because, beginning in 1972, it not only documented the ongoing nature of this and other forms of repression; it published constant reminders that the *Chronicle* and others had not forgotten those who had died for the faith.

During most of the 1970s, Nijole Sadunaite was in the Mordovia Female Political Prisoner Strict Regime Concentration Camp until she was sent into exile in Siberia in 1977. She and her fellow prisoners of conscience, mostly Catholic Ukrainians and Orthodox Russians, were considered the equivalent of murderers and other dangerous criminals in the threat they posed to the Soviet system. The Orthodox women complained repeatedly of the compromises the Orthodox leaders were making with the regime.[16] They called themselves the true Orthodox and openly prayed and sang hymns in the camps. These women were brave in their resistance, like Sadunaite, and did not hesitate to tell officials to their faces that they were part of "a Satanic government." Many of them died during the harsh conditions of the forced labor camps or, weakened beyond recovery by years of spoiled food, overwork, and mistreatment, in the exile that often followed prison terms.

Their martyrdom may not have been spectacular, but it was real martyrdom all the same. Little is known of this vast number of victims, neither their names nor their ends. One of the most painful discoveries about prison life was that it was riddled with informers, themselves prisoners, who betrayed their fellow sufferers into solitary confinement and sometimes death for better rations and slight reductions in their sentences. Many people, therefore, suffered not only under the evils of the system, but because of the weakness of its victims. Their experiences, when rightly borne, however, seemed to Sadunaite to turn them into spiritual giants.

Sadunaite survived hard labor, if barely, but had a heart attack as she was being transported by train to Siberian exile. She was not yet forty, an age when heart attacks are quite rare in women. Since she was almost entirely without fear, the attack had to be the result of overwork and mistreatment. Despite her poor health, the KGB decided to send her out, however, to the *taiga* to cut timber with the men, a fate worse than prison. It would have almost certainly have led to her immediate death. For most women, it did. Providence had other plans for Nijole Sadunaite. By an odd set of coincidences, she wound up as a cleaning lady in the school at Boguchany and, though the work was hard even there, recovered her health to a certain extent. Soon she was shifted to a hospital to work as a nurse. She had earned a degree in nursing in Lithuania and was finally allowed to practice by the Soviets, if only in prison.

Even in Siberia the KGB slandered her as a fanatical and seditious believer. Russian Baptists, who were also harshly persecuted, took this as a sign that she was worth getting to know. Paradoxically, the very religious repression the Soviets imposed led to ecumenical outreach. Before long, she was slated to be sent to a dairy farm in Irba sixty miles from Boguchany to work as a milkmaid in temperatures around fifty degrees below zero. There was no feed for the cows, the "workers" were perpetually drunk, and they fought and killed one another endlessly. But because Sadunaite's case was by then known abroad—packages arrived for her from more than twenty foreign countries, which she mostly passed on to other prisoners—the KGB feared sending her to her death.

She was freed in July of 1980. Like many other martyrs and confessors, she attributed her survival to the strength God had given her and counseled others that "fear is the beginning of betrayal."[17] Resignation to the divine will, which she had learned from reading Saint Thérèse of Lisieux, kept her at peace. But not being able to get at her directly, the KGB, under Yuri Andropov's government, went after her brother and his wife. Her brother ended up in a "psychiatric hospital," where the regime seems to have been intended to induce rather than cure madness.

The authorities were furious that the *Chronicle of the Catholic Church in Lithuania,* which they had been trying to stop since before Nijole's arrest in 1974, was still operating vigorously and informing the outside world of persecution a dozen years later. Many lives had been willingly given up to torture, prison, or worse to keep that channel of information open. Sadunaite herself was visited again by the militia with an arrest warrant, but miraculously, they left quietly when she did not open the door to them.

During the next few years she was forced to live as a virtual fugitive. She worked in a church as a cleaning lady, continued contributing to issues of the *Chronicle,* and visited those who needed help, but somehow never was apprehended. Assassins assigned to finish her off failed again and again. An outsider might regard all this as just an extraordinary stroke of good luck. But the mathematical chances of her survival were so small that it seems more believable to attribute it to the source she credited: God's oversight and the prayers of Lithuania's other martyrs.

Around the time of her release, the regime let loose another burst of violence against Catholic priests. Father Leonas Sapoka was tortured to death in his home in October 1980.[18] The following May, Father Leonas Mazeika and his groundskeeper were murdered. Both were active in protesting religious repression. Many other clergy were threatened, beaten, attacked, and left for dead, but survived. In a notorious 1981 case, Father Bronius Laurinavicius, sixty-eight years old, was the victim of a highly suspect accident. A truck struck him on November 24, 1981, in the streets of Vilnius, the Lithuanian capital. In 1979, Laurinavicius had become a member of the Lithuanian Helsinki Association, a human rights group. The secret police had him under constant surveillance. His death was all the more odd in that he had arrived in the city the very same day he was killed, after having lived a long time in Adutiskis, about fifty miles northeast of the capital. According to the reports of two eyewitnesses, a woman and a student, four men grabbed the priest by his arms and threw him in front of the truck. The driver was never charged. Lithuanians, familiar with secret police methods, immediately proclaimed Bronius Laurinavicius a martyr.[19]

Events like these forced clergy into alerting parishioners in advance not to believe unusual "accidents" or apparently documented charges. For instance, Father Ricardas Cerniauskas was arrested and beaten by the KGB in the summer of 1981 for having led a retreat for young people. The retreatants themselves were detained, interrogated, the boys maltreated, the girls threatened with rape. In a sermon, Father Cerniauskas had stated that the police had warned him to keep quiet or face an "extraordinary death." The priest continued: "There are people ready to kill me, hang me, testify that I am suffering from venereal diseases, simulate my suicide, or send me into a psychiatric hospital. You will know where that comes from. . . . I became a priest to speak the truth and I want to talk about God, not only in church, as the police command me to, but wherever I am."[20] Like a good part of Catholic Lithuanians, Cerniauskas succeeded in keeping truth alive amid the threats.

As late as 1986, just a few years before the entire Soviet Communist network collapsed, Lithuanian chekists were still applying strong repressive measures, at times resulting in death. In October of that year, Father Juozas Zdebskis received second- and third-degree burns from chemical devices put in his car, presumably by Lithuanian security forces. Not content to wound Zdebskis physically, the KGB tried to harm him morally as well: they asked the emergency room personnel to say that the priest was suffering from a venereal disease. The medical workers honorably refused to obey the order. Zdebskis was really suffering because he was a member of the Catholic Committee for the Defense of Believers' Rights, not because of sexual or other misbehavior. On February 6, Father Zdebskis had an "auto accident," in which he died—another roadside martyr.[21]

But by the late 1980s, it was evident that the Soviet system could not stamp out the faith in Lithuania, whatever subterfuges and brutalities it employed. Indeed, the exemplary behavior of so many Lithuanian believers in such terrifying circumstances is one of the many reasons for hope in the human future at the end of a bloody century. The fall of the Soviet Union brought democracy and religious liberty to all of Eastern Europe. But in Lithuania, the triumph was not merely the result of the Soviets' failure: the Lithuanian Church endured crucifixion, and thereby earned resurrection.

# -TWELVE-

# THE CALVARY OF ROMANIA

CHRISTIANITY FIRST CAME TO ROMANIA in 106 A.D., when the armies of the Roman emperor Trajan conquered the region then known as Dacia, bringing the new faith with them. Though Romania, situated in Eastern Europe, naturally came under Slavic influence over the centuries — most importantly the Bulgarian invasions of the sixth and seventh centuries — it retained a deep connection to Latin civilization. Even today, almost two thousand years after the Roman conquest, Romanian is classified by linguists as a basically Romance language. Over the long history of Romanian Christianity, the population has divided into Orthodox, by far the largest denomination with about 87 percent of the population, Catholics at 6 percent, and Protestants with 5 percent. Though census figures in Romania are not entirely reliable, this means that, in concrete terms, there were about 1,560,000 Catholics in Romania before the advent of Communism in 1948. (By contrast, the Communist Party in Romania had no more than a thousand members when a Marxist regime was imposed on the nation through internal machinations and Soviet pressure.) But after fifty years of one of the worst persecutions of the century, there were still over a half million Catholics in Romania.[1]

Romanian Catholics mostly fell into two large groupings. A Latin-rite Roman Catholic Church was located primarily in Timişoara (a large city in a region whose Catholics were predominantly German by background) and Transylvania (an area of sizeable Hungarian Catholic concentrations). This Latin Church, though hard pressed, proved surprisingly resistant to the persecutions of Romanian Communism, perhaps owing to its distinctive ethnic composition. This was not true, unfortunately, for the Romanian Greek Catholic Church. As occurred in Ukraine under the Soviets, Romanian Communist authorities organized an illegitimate synod of this church, which no Romanian Catholic bishop, even under torture and other pressures, agreed to attend. The synod was forced to declare that it was the will of the faithful to be-

255

come Orthodox, though Romanian Orthodoxy had been available as an option for anyone who wanted to convert for centuries. In October of 1948, the Greek Catholic Church was liquidated, its thousands of churches confiscated and converted to Orthodox use. The date was intended to rub in a point: it was the 250th anniversary of the Church's 1698 declaration of unity with the Vatican. The justification for this act was typical propaganda: the Greek Catholic bishops had "distanced themselves from the people to serve imperialist interests, obeying the Pope of Rome."[2] There were six authentic Greek Catholic bishops in Romania at that point. All were arrested at the close of 1948. Five died in prison (Ion Suciu, Valeriu Traian Frențiu, Alexandru Rusu, Vasile Aftenie, and Ion Bălan). The lone survivor, Cluj-Gherla Bishop Iuliu Hossu, spent the next twenty-two years in prison and under house arrest before he died, still under detention.[3]

Two bishops' secretaries were also imprisoned: Fathers Alexander Rusu and Foisor. But the sweep went much further. Security forces apprehended Blaj Vicar General Victor Macavei, Canons Victor and Nicholae Pop, Ion Moldovan, Dumitru Neda, and Ion Folea, together with the theology professors Septimius Todoran and Eugen Popa. The whole of the Bucharest Chancery was arrested: Archpriest Liviu Chinezu, Ion Chertes and Mare Vasile, and many others. Elsewhere those detained clearly were chosen in order to decapitate the Catholic leadership: in the city of Cluj, Father Joseph Bal and Canon Dumitru Manu; in Oradea, Canon Iuliu Hirtea; and in Lugoj, Father Vasile Teglasiu.[4] Ion Ploscaru, consecrated a bishop in 1948, was also imprisoned the following year.

At the beginning, all the bishops were held in Dragoslavele, the summer residence of the Orthodox patriarch. Patriarch Justinian visited them often and urged them to become Orthodox. The government put out propaganda that the bishops had gone on a "spiritual retreat."[5] The regime needed at least one bishop to apostatize in order to claim that their unification of the Catholic Church with the Orthodox was licit. No bishop obliged them. When gentle persuasion failed, the bishops were separated and sent to different locations. By May 10, 1950, Vasile Aftenie, after suffering terrible tortures in the Vacaresti prison, went mad and died, even though he was a relatively young man and had been in good health.[6] The fates of the other bishops were soon sealed in similar fashion. Of the clergy, six hundred were imprisoned, about a third of them in the Soviet Union; only half survived.[7] Pope Pius XII reacted to this slaughter with a moving statement in his March 27, 1952, apostolic letter *Veritatem Facientes:* "We desire to kiss the chains of those who, unjustly imprisoned, weep and are afflicted because of the attacks against religion, the ruin of sacred institutions, for the eternal salvation of their people, now in peril, more than for their own suffering and lost liberty."

Unfortunately, about a quarter of the Romanian Greek Catholic clergy gave in and became formally Orthodox during the persecution, fearing repercussions on themselves and their families. Since there were ample opportunities prior to the advent of the Communist regime for these men to have become part of the majority Romanian Orthodox Church had they so wished, there is no reason to believe that even a single one of these allegedly "voluntary" conversions was sincere. (Many later recanted.[8]) The means needed to convince them testify to that. One priest was thrown into a sewer full of rats for two days. He relented. Another was cast into a quagmire, with similar results. In the town of Oradea, a Father Damian was subjected to torture by fire and electricity until he surrendered. In Sibiu, a Father Onofreiu miraculously survived being hung when the rope broke. He still refused to accept Orthodoxy but was declared insane and released — temporarily. It is easy to understand why a quarter of the clergy, subjected to such treatment in so many different places, were not hardy enough to withstand it.

But the Greek Catholic people did not acquiesce easily in this forced change. Bishop of Oradea Ion Suciu, prior to his arrest, appealed to his people for financial support after the government suspended payments to Catholic schoolteachers. The parishes responded vigorously: the bishop received more than he needed to keep his schools in operation.[9] As the anti-Catholic attacks became stronger, so did the defense by lay people. When agents of the Securitate, the Romanian secret police, sought to arrest the entire Basilian monastery at Bixad, the local townspeople forced the security detail to withdraw. A few days later, however, fifteen truckloads of agents returned and rounded up the remaining monks while holding the people at bay with machine guns. The monks were beaten and told to renounce the pope. They refused. One of the Securitate group shouted: "These idiot monks care more about the Pope than God and the Church. Let's see if after they are shut up the Pope comes to save them."[10] Orthodox priests, monks, and nuns were forcibly installed in this and other monasteries, convents, and churches. Wherever there were resisters, they were arrested and sent to jail. But the people often boycotted the new religious regime.

The cathedrals at Blaj, Oradea, Cluj, and Lugoj were "reconsecrated" as Orthodox by collaborating Orthodox bishops. At Lugoj, the faithful had to be forced out. One of them, observing that the police were seal-ing the doors, cried out: "Seal all you want, gentlemen; the Jews too sealed Christ's tomb, but on the third day he arose."[11] Needless to say, Orthodox doctrine does not permit forced conversion or confiscation of churches of a different denomination. Seventy-six brave Orthodox priests refused to take over confiscated churches and participate in this political and religious abuse of power. They were, in turn, arrested.[12] And at least one Orthodox bishop who refused to collaborate with the puppet bishops, Bishop Nicolas Popovici, was arrested and died — perhaps after being poisoned — in 1958.[13] But on the whole, the Orthodox leadership was responsible for no little injustice toward the Catholics.

The Orthodox suffered themselves, however. The old Orthodox metropolitans, Mihălcescu and Criveanu, who were not sympathetic to Communism, were replaced with "people's prelates" by the government. To achieve this end, the regime and those prelates slandered the old leaders and pressured church institutions to remove them. Metropolitan Mihălcescu himself probably died a martyr's death. After his replacement and exile to a monastery, where he was allowed only limited freedom, he appears to have been poisoned.[14]

Ironically, some of the Catholic figures who were marked to suffer had been generous toward the Orthodox when the situation had been reversed. From 1940 to 1944, Hungary occupied parts of Romania, and Bishop Iuliu Hossu had defended the rights of Jews[15] as well as the Orthodox, particularly Orthodox bishop of Cluj Nicolae Colan. When the Communist regime came to power, however, this same Bishop Colan confiscated and reconsecrated the cathedral of the bishop who had been his benefactor.[16] Understandably, events like these and others listed above would leave a deep rift between Orthodox and Catholics all during the Communist government and years into the post-Communist period.

In Paris, the Romanian archimandrite Stefan Lucaciu wrote the pope to pray for abundant grace to be given to the persecuted Catholics. In another letter, he deplored the treatment of Greek and Roman Catholics in Romania, warning: "The religious opportunism which the Communist regime displays today will tomorrow turn furiously against the Orthodox Church, which it intends to transform shortly into a political platform for achieving its political aims."[17] In fact, the Romanian government was soon persecuting all religious groups: Jews, Orthodox, Catholics, and Protestants. One of the most moving accounts of this persecution from the period is Protestant pastor Richard Wurmbrand's widely acclaimed *Tortured for Christ*.[18] The chief rabbi of Romania, Alexandru Safran, was summarily deposed and exiled. The anti-Catholic campaign, because of the special social and religious place of Catholics in Romania, was particularly virulent.

Yet the harsh campaign was not wholly successful. In 1949, Stoian Stanciu, the minister of cults, complained in a public speech of the pro-Catholic feelings among some intellectuals.[19] "Pro-Catholic" here may mean either actual support for the Church or a general sympathy for wronged Christians. But in either case, some serious secular opposition to religious policy clearly had endured. There was historical precedent for pro-Catholic leanings among Romanian intellectuals. I. C. Bratianu, Romania's leading democratic political figure in the nineteenth century, had converted to Catholicism on his deathbed. And Iuliu Maniu, the head of the National-Peasant Party, the most important democratic and anti-Fascist politician in the nation, was a devout Greek Catholic (he died in the 1950s in a Communist prison). Among the Orthodox leadership, however, governmental pressure and long-standing belief that Greek Catholicism was illegitimate in Romania led to shameful acts by Christians against fellow Christians. The distinguished Romanian scholar of religion Mircea Eliade expressed the sympathy of all Romanians at the time for their Catholic brothers and sisters and lamented that "we have not heard that a single Orthodox bishop has publicly stated his disapproval of the violence."[20]

The Romanian patriarch Justinian played a particularly unsavory role in this process. After the fall of Communism, his name was remembered with much fondness by Romanian Orthodox for his energetic efforts on behalf of the Orthodox Church.[21] But Eliade pointed out that the patriarch was playing with fire: "Today in the world, Christianity in its entirety is being attacked without mercy, it is attacked by those who long ago condemned it to death, and these same people are the ones who have given arms to Justinian. . . . Today or tomorrow the Orthodox bishops will join their brothers in prison and exile. They too will be martyrs, but after having been compromised and degraded in the eyes of all the faithful." Allowing that no one has the right to demand that another become a martyr, Eliade appealed to the bishops to recognize that without the willingness to become a martyr for the truth, the bishop's staff becomes mere wood and metal.

Whatever historical rationalizations against the legitimacy of the Romanian Greek Catholic Church might be used by Orthodox leaders, they could not use the same arguments against the Romanian Latin-rite Roman Catholic Church. The Roman churches were mostly located in Transylvania and Moldavia, and they were linked with ethnic minorities historically in union since the twelfth and thirteenth centuries with Rome. These churches were flourishing, with about 1,200,000 adherents before the advent of Communism. Yet their full rights could not be acknowledged without running the risk of opening up the claim that the Greek Catholic churches, too, deserved state recognition. Recognizing either church was never a real possibility. Communist Party Secretary Gheorghiu-Dej announced peremptorily in February 1948 that the sole obstacle to "democracy" in Romania was the Catholic Church.[22] And he continued: "The new constitution of Romania will not allow Catholic citizens to be submissive to the directives of a foreign ruler; it will not allow Romanians to be tempted by the American golden calf, at whose feet the Vatican wants to bring its faithful."[23]

When the Roman Catholic churches insisted on official recognition, the Romanian Communist regime adopted a dual strategy of silencing them and encouraging a schismatic Roman Catholic Church subservient to the state, all under the legal cover of stopping "agents of imperialism" and protecting "state security." Two bishops were accused by name of anti-democratic attitudes: Aron Marton of Alba Iulia in Transylvania and Anton Durcovici of Jassy in Moldavia. Covert means began to be used to weed out recalcitrant clergy. In June of 1949, Anton Bisoc, the Franciscan superior, received a telegram, apparently from Bishop Durcovici, asking him to come to see him at once. Bisoc set out and was never seen again. His assistant, Father Herciu, went to look for him. He, too, disappeared without a trace.[24] The message was clear: a recalcitrant Roman Church would be dealt with in the same way as had been applied to the Greek Catholics.

Bishops Marton and Durcovici were soon under arrest. The other four dioceses, with their bishops, had already been suppressed on a cunning legal technicality: the government required a diocese to have at least 750,000 faithful in order to be recognized — no problem for the Orthodox, but a virtual suppression order in all but a few Catholic centers. Durcovici was so mistreated in prison, that when he was thrown naked into a cell, he was unrecognizable. A short while later he disappeared never to be heard of again. Father Rafael Friedrich, a priest-prisoner who was passing by his cell, heard him groaning. Saying "Laudetur Jesus Christus" ("Praised be Jesus Christ") to let the bishop know he was a Catholic, the priest heard the reply: "Hic Antonius moribundus" ("Anthony is dying here"). By June of 1949, there were no Roman Catholic bishops active in Romania. Almost all churches were closed. Roman Catholics were specially marked as such on their identity cards. In the

Jassy diocese, 106 parishes were occupied by militias. During one of the occupations at Faraoani, the militias and the people got into a fight. Shots were fired. One person lay dead and four badly wounded on the church steps.[25] Similar scenes occurred elsewhere.

In 1950, all the Communist nations were using their churches to support the antinuclear movement centered around the Stockholm Appeal. In strict terms, opposition to nuclear war was something every Christian could support. But in fact, the appeal was turned into an ideological weapon against the West and an international prop for the Soviet Union. The Romanian Roman Catholic Church held special importance in this propaganda campaign. If its leaders supported the government, it could be plausibly argued that they had repudiated the Vatican and the allegedly pro-Western policy of the Holy See.

The Romanian government transported about a hundred priests, lay people, and parish leaders of the Latin rite to a Congress at Targu-Mures to induce them to sign the appeal and to accept the position within Romanian society that the government wanted them to occupy. They refused, but under extreme threats finally yielded. After that, they were told to get the approval of the vicars who had replaced the bishops as the leaders of several dioceses. This failed. But in the Church's weakened state, the government tried another ploy. It prepared a church statute, in effect a kind of concordat, that appeared to grant the Roman Church everything it wished: the pope was the supreme moral and dogmatic head of the Church, the bishops were sovereign in their own dioceses, as well as concessions on other contested points. The last article of the statute, however, stipulated that the exercise of the earlier rights could be carried out only with government approval, effectively annulling everything that went before. Furthermore, contact with the Holy See could be undertaken only through the Ministries of Cults and Foreign Affairs. It was clear, even to the remaining Catholic leaders, that it was impossible to sign such a document. In May 1950, the government made the final move. The vicar general of Alba Iulia, Louis Boga, was arrested. Marcu Glasser, vicar of Jassy, was imprisoned, tortured, and died on May 25.[26]

The Romanian Communists also banned all contact with the Vatican. (Even in the 1960s, no Romanian Catholic bishops were allowed to attend the Second Vatican Council, and priests were still being arrested.[27]) The government began the break with the Vatican by expelling the papal nuncio, Monsignor Gerald O'Hara. O'Hara, who happened to be an American by birth, was branded a CIA spy and an agent of American imperialism. Under orders from Pius XII, O'Hara consecrated several bishops and apostolic administrators in secret. These men — Ion Ploscaru, Ion Dragomir, Ion Chertes, Iuliu Hirtea, and Alexandru Todea (later named a cardinal) — faced tremendous challenges; almost all survived the persecution, showing that Pius XII's strategy was successful. They provided a certain continuity for the Church when it reemerged after the 1989 fall of Communism. Furthermore, before O'Hara was forced out, Latin- and Greek-rite Catholic bishops had issued a joint statement protesting to the government that "three million citizens are being treated as if they were enemies of the people." Two hundred priests were arrested under that charge. Though the government moved slowly against the Latin-rite Catholics for fear of provoking a reaction from the nations — Hungary, Germany, Croatia, Slovakia, and Bulgaria — from which these largely ethnic-minority Catholics were drawn, it moved steadily to eliminate Catholicism. Every one of the loyal Catholic priests listed with the nunciature wound up in prison.[28]

We may form some idea of the remarkably harsh treatment Catholic prisoners received in Romania from the accounts of those who survived to tell their own stories and those of their fellow internees. One of the most prominent among these, Father Tertullian former vicar general of the Cluj Diocese, was arrested in the earliest waves of repression in 1947. His crime, according to the judge who sentenced him: "There is no evidence against you, but since you are in prison, it is because you are guilty, guilty of having been arrested."[29] Given the regime's understanding of justice, it is no surprise that he was only released seventeen years later, after accumulating a wide range of experiences in the prisons.

Like many who survived such injustices, Father Langa returned to freedom believing that "I was arrested in order to fulfill a plan intended to bring about the sanctification of my life." He was able to comfort and ultimately convert many fellow prisoners and learn something about the sufferings necessary to the Christian life: "Prison for me was the seminary that I had never experienced." And his seventeen years there were "the most beautiful and productive years of my existence."[30] Obviously a man who could speak in such terms is someone special, and the terrible things he witnessed on the way to reaching these conclusions make his declaration all the more remarkable.

One of the most brutal punishments involved what the prisoners called the "marathon." This consisted in making prisoners run or march while a dog, specially trained to leap on them if they stopped moving, followed their every step. The ordeal would last so long that, at times, Father Langa began having hallucinations. During one episode, "I seemed to be walking on diamonds, but in fact the soles of my feet had become completely swollen. Then, I started to see, as if I were looking through the cell's walls, a beautiful garden, an orchard with apples.... Then I fell, unconscious, hitting my head on the wall." Naturally, the dog attacked and the pain revived him. He began running again without knowing what he was doing. "Later, the guard told me that I had been running and walking fifty-nine hours straight. It seems unbelievable, but why would the guard lie?"[31]

In another sadistic exercise, the prisoners discovered that prison authorities had been ordered to kill them all by exposure to the cold. Their only defense against freezing to death was to keep warm by walking briskly without stopping. A neighbor, the prisoner in the cell next to Langa's, stopped one day. Langa roused him and started him moving again. The man resented being awoken from a beautiful dream: "I prayed to God, falling on my knees, to bring the moon into my room and he heard my prayer. He sent me the moon and I was in the process of eating it when you woke me." The next morning, the man's body was carried away. His fellows believed that perhaps his dream was sent to him as a consolation, a Eucharistic symbol, before he left this world.[32]

Many others succumbed as well. Father Langa partly attributes his survival to the "spiritual masters" he was fortunate enough to know as a young man. These included Father Iosif Pop, Ion Miclea (a philosopher and friend of Jacques Maritain), and Monsignor Vladimir Ghika, all of whom became martyrs or confessors. Langa also provides information about some of the church leaders who disappeared early in the persecution. Vasile Aftenie, the vicar general of Bucharest, was the first bishop-martyr in Romania. As usual, the Communist authorities tried to coopt him, offering him the Orthodox episcopal see of Moldovia immediately, and with a promise to make him Orthodox patriarch in Bucharest later, if he broke with Rome. Aftenie refused saying, "Neither my nation nor my faith are for sale." The sequel was foreordained: "He was subsequently tortured to death. His body was disfigured, the dislocated arms were no longer connected to his trunk."[33]

Equally bold was Bishop Ion Suciu, a young energetic man, who, before his arrest, had publicly proclaimed at a speech in the Latin-rite Cathedral of Saint Joseph in Bucharest: "We must have the courage and dignity to be Christians in the very face of the Communism and atheism that have come." When the Soviet Procurator Vychinski learned of this pronouncement, he replied: "That mouth must be shut." The Romanian authorities quickly did just that. Another bishop, Liviu Chinezu, secretly consecrated as bishop, died in 1955[34] in the Sighet Prison, a notoriously harsh institution which was the preferred place of detention for Romanian political and religious leaders. The prison commandant, Vasile Ciolpan, apparently wished to make it seem that the bishop died of natural causes. He ordered the window in the bishop's cell to be left open in frigid mid-January weather. Chinezu froze to death.[35] In a five-year period, at least fifty-two Sighet prisoners are known to have died, and probably many more unknown perished as well.[36]

These early deaths were only a foretaste of much greater atrocities. In the early 1950s, approximately 180,000 were sent to prison camps, often the very camps set up earlier by the Nazis.[37] The Romanian Communists pioneered brainwashing techniques in Eastern Europe, often giving them a satanic cast. The typical prisoner was forced to denounce everything that he held most dear: "friends and family, his wife or girlfriend, and his God if he was a believer."[38] The Romanian jailer Eugen Turcanu created a special approach for seminarians: "Some had their heads repeatedly plunged into a bucket of urine and fecal matter while the guards intoned a parody of the baptismal rite. One victim who had been systematically tortured in this fashion developed an automatic response that went on for about two months: every morning, to the great delight of his reeducators, he would plunge his own head into the bucket."[39]

But even this degradation of religion apparently was not enough:

> Turcanu also forced the seminarians to take part in black masses that he orchestrated himself, particularly during holy week and on Good Friday. Some of the reeducators played the part of choirboys; others masqueraded as priests. Turcanu's liturgy was extremely pornographic, and he rephrased the original in a demonic fashion. The Virgin Mary was called "the Great Whore," and Jesus, "that cunt who died on the cross." One seminarian undergoing reeducation and playing the role of a priest had to undress completely and was then wrapped in a robe stained with excrement. Around his neck was hung a phallus made of bread and soap and powdered with DDT. In 1950 on the Saturday before Easter the students who were undergoing reeducation were forced to pass before the priest, kiss the phallus, and say, "he is risen."[40]

Turcanu would eventually be arrested himself and executed for "crimes against humanity which discredited the Communist regime in the eyes of the people and world opinion."[41] In fact, he was carrying out orders from higher up, probably from a General Nikolski, to conduct a brainwashing experiment. A thousand young men, all believers, were rounded up and subjected to the "Piteşti" system. According to one account: "They were tortured in such a manner that all — absolutely all — students became informers, so that they were robbed of their manly natures and became simple robots in the hands of political officers. They were depersonalized."[42] In perhaps the most brutal form of mind control techniques ever applied in the century, the boys were tortured, physically and morally, into abandoning their former beliefs. Worse, once they had been put through the process, they were ordered to carry out the same brainwashing on another crop of students, fearing all the time that the least display of weakness would land them back among the tortured. The pangs of consciences this must have produced are easy to imagine.

The brainwashing followed a Pavlovian method. The students were first asked to recant their former beliefs or be tortured. When they refused, as most did initially, they were beaten, forced to clean floors with a rag between their teeth, and made to eat like animals from bowls in which they also defecated. At night, an already "reeducated" student sat at the foot of the bed of another student still being processed. The moment the new student fell asleep, the other beat him on the feet with a rubber hose. The pain inflicted was intended to condition the young men to have an unconscious negative reaction to everything that had earlier been regarded as good.[43]

After these reflexes had been established, the brainwashing moved on to religious beliefs. Sacrileges such as those described above were required. The subjects were forced to admit monstrous crimes and sexual deviance so frequently that, confused by the beatings and sleep deprivation, they began to believe them and lose touch with the truth. At this point, they were introduced to new loyalties to the Communist regime and their very torturers. They were made to become torturers themselves, thereby demonstrating their sincerity, but under the constant threat of being returned to torture: "The great obstacle . . . was the haunting fear, locked into every fiber of the unmasked victim, that any day the terror might be resumed."[44] It appears that the experiment stopped only to give the experimenters a respite to assess its effectiveness. One of the young men who survived to tell of it, Roman Braga, eventually became an Orthodox priest. He described the experience in stark terms: "I think that there is no other mind than Lucifer's capable of imagining the Piteşti system that kept man suspended between to be and not to be, at the limits of madness and reality, tortured by the idea that he might disappear — no, not as a physical entity, but as a *spiritual person.*[45] Though the tortures were carefully calibrated not to kill the young men, about fifteen died during their reeducation.[46]

Amid so much suffering and blasphemy in the prisons, it was remarkable that there were also points of great light. One of these centered around a towering figure, Monsignor Vladimir Ghika, whose cause for beatification is underway. Ghika was the grandson of the last prince of Moldavia and also obtained the martyr's crown. His dedication to the Catholic cause was unshakeable. He had converted to Catholicism years earlier because, he believed, that to be Catholic was "to become even more Orthodox."[47] A man of immense culture and intelligence with many international contacts, he chose to remain in Romania after World War II, even though he knew the risks it meant for someone with his familial and religious background. In Romania, many people in the 1990s still attested to the fact that they "owed everything" to him, including their resistance to Communism, their vocations, and their faith itself.[48] In the prisons, he was responsible not only for the return of many to belief, but for people who went from nonbelief to ardent vocations. Tragically, he ended his life in prison in the midst of this work.[49]

Another heroic church leader was bishop of Alba Iulia Aron Marton. As we have already seen, he was arrested early and spent from 1949 until 1955 in prison. He was gravely injured in an "automobile accident" staged by government agents, but survived that as well. Protests by his people got him released to house arrest. But his courage and activism, despite all threats, made him a much-loved figure. Marton assisted the Greek-rite Church as much as he was able, an unusual move for a Latin-rite bishop. For decades before he finally died in 1980, he had to carefully thread his way through government-imposed restrictions, censorship, the presence of potentially compromised priest-spies, and a host of other difficulties.

Father Alexandru Ratiu, a survivor of sixteen years in the Romanian prison system, from 1948 until the general amnesty for political prisoners which occurred in 1964 when Nicolae Ceauşescu took over the leadership of the country, remarks that prison had an unexpected effect on priests and other believers, as well as former atheists: "In prison one either goes mad or becomes a saint."[50] For many who suffered imprisonment, it was usually the first time in their lives that they were forced to rely solely on prayer and God's support: "We were never so happy.

We never felt the presence of God so intimately; and we never prayed more seriously, confidently, and successfully than in those prison barracks."[51] After Ratiu's harrowing account of the tortures, deaths, and sadistic treatment all prisoners experienced, these are not words to be taken lightly. It was, of course, a terrible path to piety and virtue. But so many people in so many different countries, even under differing regimes like Nazism and Communism, have reported similar experiences, that it may be that their experiences will ultimately have some spiritually stimulating effect now that several portions of the world have been freed to practice religion again.

As late as April 1982, however, murders of priests occurred. According to reports, Father Ion Ecsy, rector of the Seikenburg Marian Church and an energetic pastor, died in that year under mysterious circumstances.[52] His funeral was carefully controlled, lending further reason to believe that something had occurred in his case that worried authorities. Many reasons could have led to his death. Romanian priests were subjected to lengthy interrogations if they met with foreigners. By law, they were supposed to report such contacts within twenty-four hours. Congregations, too, were infiltrated, and priests had to be very careful what they said in or out of the pulpit. Teaching of the young was prohibited until age fifteen and any number of obstacles was erected for other religious and charitable activities. Even a pastor saving money to repair a church building could be arrested, as happened to Father Michael Godo in 1979. Surprisingly, Mass attendance among Latin-rite Catholics nonetheless remained high: about 80 percent.

Unfortunately, little of this material was given much attention during the period of persecution, even though a great deal of it was known. In the struggles of the Cold War, the free world rarely pressed for justice toward the many people, religious and secular, who suffered and died in Romania. Prominent among the resisters were Neo-Protestants who, beginning in the 1980s, doggedly confronted all attempts by the regime to force them into conformity. Though their role in the eventual fall of Communism is partly known, much still remains to be uncovered about these brave dissenters. One of the heroic Romanian bishops, Iuliu Hirtea, remarked before he died in the 1970s: "It is not we who keep silence here. It is not we who are the Church of Silence, but the members of the Church in the free world who are the real Church of Silence, for they do not speak on our behalf."[53]

In the late 1970s and early 1980s, Romanian Catholics benefited from the fact that Karol Wojtyła, a Pole with a good understanding of the

machinations of Communist regimes in Eastern Europe, became pope.
John Paul II was able to appoint some interim bishops and to loosen the
straitjacket on the Church somewhat. Two seminaries were reopened,
but the government reserved to itself the right to approve those to be
ordained, often keeping them waiting years to discourage them. In addition, textbooks were not allowed to be printed. Lectures had to be
dictated and old books shared by several students. Catholic books in
general were not allowed until the late 1970s. And seminaries were often
"infiltrated" by government agents looking to capture promising future
religious leaders. Under President Nicolae Ceauşescu the Church was
never given much room to maneuver. Rectories were bugged, and their
telephones were tapped; mail was frequently opened and read by security agents. Romania was the only Eastern bloc nation that did not send
a representative to John Paul II's installation as pope.[54]

After the complicity of the Romanian Orthodox Church in the persecution of Catholics, the situation since the fall of Communism calls for
some special reconciliation. The Orthodox, of course, suffered terribly
themselves in these years, forced to take positions and operate in a way
that an independent church would never have done willingly. And no
small number of Orthodox wound up in prisons themselves, where they
and their Catholic brothers and sisters learned ecumenism by working
together in a very hard school. Since the fall of Communism, there have
been steps taken to remedy past hurts, but conflicts remain. Some Romanian Orthodox resent the Catholic Church's attempt to recover all
its lost institutions and faithful, a restitution in justice that should be *in
integrum* (i.e., total). Orthodox Archbishop Corneanu of Timişoara has
distinguished himself for his generosity in returning Catholic churches.
Obviously, there are some delicate situations that need to be resolved
where Orthodox parishes have been operating in Catholic buildings for
over fifty years now. A further sore point is that Catholic evangelization
is being successful, particularly among those Romanians who believe the
Orthodox Church collaborated all too readily with the Communist government. John Paul II, however, has counseled: "Brothers who shared
for some time the same suffering and trials should not pit themselves
against one another today, but should envisage together a future that
will open up toward signs promoting hope."[55]

The story of Romanian persecution and martyrdom is virtually without equal in the twentieth or any other century. As the *Osservatore
Romano* wrote in 1948, when the persecution was only starting: "No
similar story of moral violence, of persecution, of the *Via Crucis* of lib-

erty, of personality, and of human dignity can be read in all the pages of history."[56] Given the two millennia in which the Church has existed, these are strong words indeed, but probably no more than just. Perhaps this terrible Romanian example will encourage all people of good will to try to make sure that the pages of future history will never again bear such infamies.

# –THIRTEEN–

# MURDER IN THE CATHEDRAL
## *Archbishop Oscar Arnulfo Romero of El Salvador and Some Latin American Martyrs*

ON MONDAY, MARCH 24, 1980, AT 6:25 P.M. in the chapel of the Divina Providencia Cancer Hospital, where he lived in a small house, Oscar Arnulfo Romero, archbishop of San Salvador, the capital of the Central American nation El Salvador, was killed during his homily by a gunman who fired one well-placed bullet through his heart. Romero's martyrdom came in the midst of terrible civil strife that would become even worse during the 1980s until it was finally resolved by a 1992 peace accord. As was often the case in the twentieth century, Romero was martyred even though he had taken neither side in the conflict, but had tried to maintain Christ's own position of asking the warring parties to forgo violence and hatred, and to seek a reasonable compromise and reconciliation with one another. Like the Master, he was put to death for his teaching.

In more immediate terms, as later investigations have revealed, he was murdered by figures connected to the highest levels of the Salvadoran military. During the protracted guerrilla warfare of the late 1970s and 1980s, religious figures in El Salvador were subjected to various forms of repression and intimidation, supposedly because they were playing into the hands, wittingly or unwittingly, of Communism. The Cold War was entering its final phases with various proxy wars being fought between the United States and the Soviet Union on several continents. El Salvador was one place where to speak in favor of peace or social reform was regarded by the government as tantamount to calling for Marxist revolution. Romero had repeatedly disputed this interpretation and denounced violence by rebels as much as by the government. But the day before his death was a Sunday, and during his homily at the cathedral, when he often reviewed the "events of the week" (*hechos de la semana*) not reported on by the official news sources, he had urged his listeners:

270

"In the name of God, then, and in the name of this suffering people, whose screams and cries mount to heaven, and daily grow louder, I beg you, I order you in the name of God: stop the repression." For the Salvadoran military forces, who often operated independently of their own government, it was the last straw.

So assassins acting with the support of the Salvadoran military carried out the act; at his funeral, thirty-nine people died when a bomb exploded and gunfire was exchanged. That same year, four American churchwomen working in El Salvador were brutally raped, tortured, and murdered. (In 1998, the four former Salvadoran national guardsmen who had been convicted of the crime confessed that they had been told that the order had come "from higher levels, and nothing is going to happen to us.") At the other end of the decade (1989), six Jesuits, their housekeeper, and her daughter at the University of Central America in San Salvador were killed by army units. The Romero assassination and massacre of the Jesuits frame an entire decade of violence against religious figures in Central America. And the violence spilled over into the 1990s as well, and will probably continue into the new millennium.

Yet from these deaths something came to life. Not long before he died Romero remarked, "If they kill me, I shall rise again in the Salvadoran people."[1] In another man, the indirect comparison of himself with Christ might have seemed presumptuous. In Romero's case, it was neither more nor less than the truth. Peasants composed poems and songs about him; his reputation both inside and outside El Salvador grew as the situation itself became worse. His memory could not stop the conflict or lead to an immediate solution. But it kept a spirit alive that provided a crucial limitation on government repression and riveted the attention of the outside world on a small country that had little geostrategic importance.

Romero's predecessor as archbishop was Luis Chávez y González, who had assumed leadership almost exactly forty years earlier, in 1938. Yet, contrary to the stereotyped image of the Church in Latin America, Archbishop Chávez himself had been no mere supporter of the status quo. His archdiocesan offices defended the rights of peasants to organize, even during a period when the two main peasant unions, the Christian Federation of Salvadoran Peasants (FECCAS) and the Farm Workers' Union (UTC), were branded as un-Christian agitators and potentially subversive Marxists. As one observer describes them: "To the landowning oligarchy, they were Lenin and Satan in one."[2] Though the archdiocese was careful to avoid official involvement in such political movements, it unequivocally supported the right of these illegal (i.e., nongovernment controlled) workers' organizations to exist. Needless to say, even nuanced stances like these caused charges of subversion to be made against the Church itself and entailed no little risk in the troubled atmosphere of 1970s El Salvador.

The seventy-five-year-old Archbishop Chávez thus bequeathed to his successor a strong but careful tradition of reform. The logical choice for his replacement would have been Arturo Rivera y Damas, an auxiliary bishop in the archdiocese with views similar to Chávez's. (Rivera y Damas would become archbishop after Romero's assassination.) But elite opinion in San Salvador ran strongly against more of the Chávez approach and strongly favored Romero, then bishop of Santiago de María, who appeared to be mildly conservative in his views of Catholic social teaching. More than forty people consulted by the papal nuncio from various elite sectors — business, government, the military — all favored Romero.[3] Consequently, Paul VI named him archbishop.

At all stages in his development as a pastor, Romero made a point of including all the Salvadoran interest groups in his comments. He wanted to be a centrist who pursued justice. The Catholic clergy, he remarked, had a vocation that was primarily "religious and transcendent." At the same time, a priest's concern for the common good and social justice should not be automatically branded as subversive.[4] These remarks can be read with different emphases and were probably crafted to allow just that. Given Romero's relatively quiet past, however, most Salvadorans had the impression that, whatever he might say, he probably would not rock the boat very much. Most of his priests were not keen on his being chosen over Rivera y Damas, as he knew, and he tried to appeal to them as brothers as well.

But all this appeal to moderation and centrism soon bumped up against Salvadoran reality. In February of 1977, even before Romero was installed as bishop, the country was racked with protests over a fraudulent presidential election. Romero had invited the nation's priests to his installation in the San Salvador cathedral on March 7. But Plaza Libertad in the capital was the scene of angry demonstrations toward the end of February, which were finally broken up by government forces at a cost of somewhere between eight (the official figure) and three hundred lives. Priests, many of them foreign, were deported, others arrested and beaten, still others targeted for intimidation through bombings and death threats. The date for the installation was postponed and Romero would formally receive his office in a quiet and almost private ceremony at the diocesan seminary. The archbishop-to-be occupied himself with setting up an information service to keep track of the situation and correct any misstatements from official sources. Willingly or not, Romero had been thrown into the heart of the fray.

One of his first proposals was that the Church had to make a candid statement about what was happening, not only to the clergy, but to all Salvadorans. In a meeting of the episcopal conference, some of his fellow bishops worried that alienating the government might lead to even worse repression. Romero replied that this was not his intention; rather, he merely wanted to go on record with the truth, which, as pastors, they were obligated to speak. Besides, the people expected this from the Church. This seems to have convinced the doubters and, surprisingly, Romero took out a text of a formal statement he had already prepared for publication. After a few points had been worked on by the group, Romero asked that it be read in all the churches of El Salvador on Sunday, March 13. Though he had some doubts after giving the directive, he read it himself at the cathedral and it was carried over the radio. The letter called both for a cessation of human rights abuses and, the more basic issue, social justice reforms to correct large disparities in wealth, property, and living standards. The bishops even used religious language about the situation: "This is the basic sin to which we, as shepherds, must call attention."[5]

But even before it could be read, another earthquake struck. Father Rutilio Grande, a Jesuit working with the poor, was killed as he was riding toward a small village to say Mass. El Salvador is a deeply Catholic country and, despite a violent history going back to pre-Spanish times, murdering a priest for political reasons had been unheard of. A new chapter in Salvadoran history had opened. It was the Saturday evening before the bishops's letter was to be read. Salvadoran president Arturo Armando Molina, who had been elected in the fraudulent voting of the previous month, called Romero to offer condolences. The archbishop told the president that a full and fair investigation had to be made. Molina agreed. Romero went out the same evening to pray over the bodies of the priest and two *campesinos* who had been traveling with him. In the aftermath of that sad and shocking episode, Romero gave, by all accounts, a very heartfelt reading and commentary on the Gospel prescribed for Sunday Mass the following day.

On Monday morning, the papal nuncio performed the funeral services for the three dead. Romero gave the homily and recalled the personal influence Grande had had on his own life. But he put the deaths in the larger context that the bishops' statement had tried to get at, observing that it was a time "to gather from this death a message for all of us who remain on pilgrimage."[6] And the message, he said, quoting Pope Paul VI's encyclical *Evangelii Nuntiandi,* is that without the fullness of faith, the inevitable result would be continued injustice, strife, instability, and violence. For Grande's murderers, who had incurred excommunication by their act, he offered pardon if they would repent. And he quoted the Bible verse that appears so often around scenes of martyrdom: "Father forgive them, they know not what they do." Under the circumstances, it was an astonishing display of deep foresight and temperate Christian charity that achieved remarkable balance.

The question of justice, however, remained. At least one doctor believed that the types of wounds on the bodies suggested the kinds of weapons used by the police. In an exchange of letters with Romero, President Molina hinted that rebel elements might have murdered the priest and his companions in order to discredit the government, to inject greater chaos into Salvadoran society, and to further revolutionary aims. But whatever might be thought about Molina's words — and it must be admitted in fairness that such tactics were unfortunately not unknown among the guerillas in El Salvador — Molina's actions were highly suspect. The government took hardly any measures to identify the killers or even to gather evidence. If the president had been truly disturbed about the event and thought revolutionaries were behind it, it is doubtful that he would have let the opportunity slip to make his case.

Under the circumstances, Romero and his fellow bishops felt it was important for the whole Church in El Salvador to make a strong statement. The Sunday message of the bishops had been read from most pulpits but, owing to censorship and fear of reprisals, had not been carried in newspapers. The bishops and a large number of the nation's pastors conferred with one another; they decided on several concrete steps to publicize their position further:

1. Holy Week would be celebrated only in the cathedral so that all Catholics would understand that the Salvadoran Church was protesting the various forms of repression.

2. Catholic schools would be closed for three days, but students and their parents would be provided with material to reflect upon having to do with the situation.

3. The Church would be careful about giving the impression of supporting the government through participation in the presidential installation and other large official functions.

4. All available church media including parish bulletins, radio, etc., would continue to provide independent information about events.

Both the papal nuncio and various elite groups within El Salvador warned Romero that these measures might lead to even worse reaction by the government. The nuncio raised questions about whether, for example, Canon Law permitted the Mass restrictions for Easter. Some people began saying that Romero had been misled by "Communist priests" into imprudent confrontation. Others hinted that several pastors and bishops disagreed with his intended course, even though large majorities of both — amounting to virtually unanimity on several issues — had supported him during the consultations. In fact, all the bishops of the various dioceses were unconcerned about any possible reaction given the need for the Church to adopt a strong position. The general view among the clergy was that the measures would send a message to the government that the Catholic leaders were united and willing to adopt quite prophetic attitudes to end violations of basic human rights and to promote justice. Romero, therefore, did not waver. About a hundred thousand people filled the square and streets outside the cathedral for the single Mass he had authorized, one of the largest religious demonstrations in Salvadoran history.

But even before this event, Archbishop Romero realized he needed to have stronger backing than he had already obtained within the country. Consequently, he quickly arranged a trip to Rome, where he had studied for six years, to speak with various individuals in Vatican offices. He prayed at Peter's tomb and the tomb of Pius XI, who had been pope during Romero's seminary years, which included the times when the Church had to face Hitler and Mussolini. Though he had had doubts about the Salvadoran Jesuits in the past, believing they betrayed Marxist leanings, he made a point of meeting with the Jesuit superior general, the Spaniard Pedro Arrupe. Everywhere he went, he explained the circumstances of the Jesuit Rutilio Grande's murder. Important media outlets such as Vatican Radio and the *Osservatore Romano* were briefed about the Salvadoran situation. Some of the Vatican offices were less than entirely convinced about the wisdom of his course, but Paul VI met with him privately after the regular audience and remarked: "Courage! You are the one in charge!"[7] With this encouragement and generally good reaction in Rome, he hastened back to San Salvador in order to be present during Holy Week.

At the urging of the other bishops, he issued a pastoral letter at Easter, which he entitled "The Paschal Church." It is an interesting window into his heart and mind. While he emphasizes that vast injustices exist in Salvador, he sees the renewal of Christian commitment, both in its Easter hope for the world to come and in Christ's victory over the evils of this world, as the basis for national reform. But like the risen Christ himself when asked by the apostles whether he was about to assume the kingship of Israel (Acts 1), Romero did not promise achievement of the kingdom on earth. Instead, he puts forward a vision for the archdiocese that he sees as the true message of the contemporary Church: "Let there be seen in Latin America the ever brighter face of a church authentically poor, missionary and paschal, disentangled from all temporal power, and daringly committed to the freedom of the whole person and of all persons."[8]

This lofty vision of the Church in theory was difficult to follow in practice. In the ensuing months, Romero was constantly embroiled in disputes with the government over priests arrested without due process, the government's slanders of reform-minded clergy and laity as dangerous radicals, and ongoing terrorism by government and rebels alike. His evenhandedness was clear both in his forceful defense of innocents to the government and a similar stance toward the rebels. When the latter kidnapped Mauricio Borgonovo, the Salvadoran foreign minister, Romero publicly and repeatedly called on all sides to forgo violence and negotiate. The rebels demanded the release of some of their jailed members; the government, understandably, rejected this blackmail, as most governments do in similar circumstances, because to agree almost always leads to further kidnaps. Unhappily, Borgonovo's body was found within a few days. At the funeral Mass, Romero once again defended the Church's desire for justice, and repeated that, like Christ, it rejected violence: "It has said so a thousand times, and none of its ministers preaches violence."

This eloquent plea, however, seems to have fallen on deaf ears. The same day, a self-described White Warrior union killed a priest and a young boy, they said, as revenge for Borgonovo. Romero was back in the pulpit officiating at a priest's funeral the next morning. Amid the proliferating deaths and reprisals Romero held firm to his message: "This is not the hour, brothers and sisters, to be divided between two churches. It is the hour to feel ourselves one church that strives for Christ's resurrection, that brings redemption not only beyond death but here on earth; to strive for a world more just, more human; to strive for a social sensitivity that makes itself felt in every setting; to struggle against violence, against criminality."[9] He was exactly right. But words alone were powerless to calm the passions that had been set loose.

Segments of Salvadoran society that unreservedly backed the government often invoked the traditional values of the Church against clergy preaching reform. Yet they themselves had lost sight of the deeper values that had given rise to the Church's social teaching. The developed doctrine of the Church, for instance, has always favored private property. Thomas Aquinas himself had given strong reasons why property was necessary to the proper working of individuals, families, and whole societies.[10] Yet property, as Aquinas also stated, is not an absolute right. Questions of justice, to say nothing of the demands of charity and mercy, always qualify property rights. The destitution of the large masses of Salvadorans did not mean property had to be abolished, *pace* the socialist elements. Rather, it meant that a better distribution of property was required by the Church's own traditional norms.

The Salvadoran bishops issued a statement at the time that addressed some of these points. They rejected Communism and pure laissez-faire capitalism and continued: "We would be false to our mission as shepherds if we were to reduce evangelization to mere practices of individualistic piety and disincarnate sacramentalism." It is worth noting that the bishops did not oppose either personal holiness or the sacraments; they were making the point forcefully that these are not all there is to the Christian faith. To the traditionalists they remarked: "To cling more and more to one's own advantage, ignoring the cry of the dispossessed, is to create a favorable climate for totalitarian violence."[11] These were prophetic words. As national security became a catchall excuse for government forces, violence would spread even more widely.

The outrages were not merely directed against radical clergy. In another incident soon after the statement, government forces moved into the town of Aguilares, killing peasants and arresting innocent persons. But they also used the village church as a barracks, treating it in ways reminiscent of the sacrileges perpetrated in Mexico and Spain decades earlier. According to reports, the soldiers shot up the tabernacle, which resulted in the consecrated hosts falling all over the floor. These soldiers did not even have the excuse of the radical Mexicans and Spaniards of being anti-Catholic. Romero wrote to President Molina: "I do not understand how you can publicly declare yourself a Catholic by up-bringing and conviction and yet allow these unspeakable outrages on the part of the security forces in a country that we call civilized and Christian."[12] The answer may be that those who lose respect for the commands of charity to their neighbor also lose respect for the traditional and sacramental elements of the faith, which they claimed to protect.

Romero's criticism of Catholics from a Catholic standpoint needs further clarification. At times, it has been suggested that he favored the so-called *iglesia popular* ("popular church") over the traditional hierarchy. This is to project on a troubled Central American pastor intellectual battles that are more common in the First World. Romero cared about his people, and he believed that the hierarchy, as guarantor of Christ's word, could cooperate with the local initiatives in El Salvador in fruitful ways. In the immediate aftermath of Romero's death, his outspoken defense of human rights and social justice was viewed as a large change of heart from his earlier views. Some who knew him, however, dispute the claim, as did Romero himself.[13] The ongoing and growing civil war in El Salvador gave both sides reason to exaggerate Romero's stance, the government to deplore it and those sympathetic to the rebels to champion it. But there was a great deal of continuity in Romero's position all along. The most conspicuous changes in his attitudes and behavior had to do with the immediate circumstances in which he found himself as archbishop.

Indeed, it would have been quite surprising if Oscar Romero, a man of humble background who had spent the early years of his priesthood in quite modest pastoral duties, would have behaved any differently. Romero was born on August 15, 1917, in a small mountain town called Ciudad Barrios, in the eastern department of San Miguel only a few miles from the border with Honduras. At the time of his birth, the town was not easily accessible from other parts of the country. So the young Oscar spent much of his youth among an isolated, small population of mostly mixed Spanish and Indian blood. Romero's father, Santos Romero, ran the telegraph and local post office; but those duties were not onerous in a small town. Santos spent most of his time growing cacao and coffee on a twenty-acre hillside plot that his wife, Guadalupe de Jesús Galdámez, had inherited. Oscar and the other Romero children delivered letters, learned how to run the telegraph, and did farm chores, including milking cows.

The family was not particularly pious, though Oscar remembered his father as having taught him the Ten Commandments and how to pray. Nor were conditions in Ciudad Barrios likely to produce a future archbishop of San Salvador. The local school had only three grades. So the Romeros had to pay a private teacher to instruct the children until they were twelve or thirteen. After that, Santos Romero thought it was better to learn a trade. Oscar became a carpenter's apprentice. The future archbishop's father was not an unaccomplished man: he apparently taught the children to read music and play the bamboo flute. But Oscar Romero's first dozen years seemed to destine him to take part in the simple round of work and other duties in a small, typical Latin American village.

Somewhere amid this early activity, Romero conceived the idea that he might want to be a priest. He was a serious boy and above average in intelligence. According to some accounts, the town mayor urged the seminary on him.[14] In any event, in 1930, when the diocesan vicar general happened to be in Ciudad Barrios, Oscar talked with him. His father did not like the idea. But soon Oscar Romero was making the seven-hour trip on horseback to the minor seminary in San Miguel. Over the next seven years, his vocation continued to grow, and he was quite successful in his studies, so much so that in 1937 he was sent to the major seminary in San Salvador and, by the middle of the same year, to Rome to study at the Gregorian University. It was a meteoric rise for a twenty-year-old from an obscure town.

He lived at the Latin American College in Rome, where he was noticed for his brains, speaking and writing ability, and solid self-discipline in the various ways priestly formation requires. As wonderful as it must have been for him to be in Rome, the period had a dark side. By 1939, Europe had erupted into World War II; the Italian government was aligned with Hitler's Germany. Ironically, Romero and the other seminarians had to take shelter as Allied planes began bombing in an attempt to invade Italy and deprive Hitler of one of his important props. Despite the distractions, Romero received a licentiate in theology *cum laude* in 1941. Canon law at the time required any candidate for the priesthood to be at least twenty-four. So while he was waiting, he began studying for a doctorate in ascetical theology. He was not to finish it, however. Ordained on April 4, 1942, he was called home a little over a year later. His bishop assigned him to Anamorós, a town quite similar to the one where he was born, in the department of La Unión.

In most of Latin America, the priest shortage requires clergymen to occupy several posts simultaneously. After his Roman training, Romero could not be allowed merely to work as a country pastor. Within months, his bishop appointed him secretary of the San Miguel diocese and pastor of the cathedral. Romero manifested an enormous amount of energy. Not only did he direct the final work of building the cathedral; he carried on various charitable activities and directed more than a half-dozen Catholic organizations ranging from Alcoholics Anonymous to the Knights of the Holy Sepulcher. He personally visited prisoners, oversaw catechism classes, preached often, and managed to juggle a dizzying number of other commitments. Remarkably, he kept all this up for twenty-three years, perhaps because he made a point of regular daily practice of some of the ascetical exercises that he had begun to study in Rome. Though he would be emotionally troubled as an adult, something grew in him over these years that made him into a strong and steady personality at the deepest level.

In 1967, however, just as he was turning fifty, he was called to San Salvador to become secretary general of the Salvadoran Bishops Conference. It is only one sign of the good work he had done in San Miguel that many people there signed a petition asking him to stay. But other duties were now required of him. He did them so well that the bishops noticed and, within a year, he was asked to serve as executive secretary of the Central American Bishops Secretariat in addition to his duties at the Salvadoran Bishops Conference. Administrative offices such as these, however necessary to the life of the Church, are often a Cross to be borne. It is a tribute to Romero that, as his diaries show, he maintained his focus on spiritual progress during this period. Such progress usually brings both doubts and gains; he had an abundance of both when Archbishop Chávez, who had known him almost thirty years, asked him in 1970 to become an auxiliary bishop of San Salvador.

By 1970, the Church had begun the uneven process of renewal mandated by the Second Vatican Council. In addition, the Latin American bishops were starting to conceptualize the various ways that the council might be fruitfully implemented in their own region. At their 1968 meeting in Medellín, Colombia, they took the first steps toward trying to integrate spiritual renewal with Christian social witness. Out of that meeting came a phrase that was to provoke much discussion in following decades: "the preferential option for the poor." In its more traditional meaning, the preferential option restated the Catholic principle that the poor and the marginalized had a special claim on the attention and resources of Christian individuals and societies. In more radical forms, it seemed to mesh with actual proposals for political and economic policy drawn from Marxist or quasi-Marxist literature and pointing toward Socialism. Given that, globally, the Cold War was at its height and that, regionally, Latin America was trying to find its way toward true democracy and economic development, the introduction of Marxist analysis into the situation made many nervous — some because of genuine concern about the threat of Marxism, others out of a desire to protect vested interests.

The very week after Romero's installation as auxiliary bishop, the Salvadoran Church held a "national pastoral week" to examine how to apply Vatican II and Medellín to local circumstances. Romero had chosen as his episcopal motto *sentire cum ecclesia,* "to think and feel with the Church." It was clearly a statement of principle meant to reflect his attitude about a variety of issues. In terms of the pastoral week, it meant that he was committed to the developments at the universal council in Rome as well as the regional decisions of the Latin American bishops. But to be committed to a general course is not the same as to agree with what others thought the Council and Medellín could be said to mean. Romero was cautious as he followed the pastoral reflections on the situation in El Salvador in the 1970s.

His moderate approach may have had something to do with the fact that the following year Archbishop Chávez asked him to take charge of *Orientación,* the newspaper of the archdiocese. The previous editor had taken some controversial and unguarded positions, including praise for Camilo Torres, a priest who had left his duties to join the guerilla movement in Colombia.[15] Romero took a position that was later to be that of John Paul II toward social movements promising liberation through means that bordered on Marxism. First, he pointed out some of the specific intellectual problems in the literature generated by those movements. Then he contrasted them with what seemed to him a more authentic reading of the documents of Medellín and the Council. To be sure, Romero, like everyone else, had no easy solution for the long history of political and economic turmoil in El Salvador. But he seemed convinced that some of the remedies proposed might be worse than the disease.

Meanwhile, his years of work and the tense situation in El Salvador took their toll on his health and psychological well-being. He took a long, four-month break from work, going to Mexico for rest and reflection. Both before and after this interlude, he consulted several doctors and psychologists, less as a formal course of therapy than as a way of getting insight into his spiritual, emotional, and intellectual development. He identified elements of perfectionism in himself and of using work as an excuse not to deal with other matters. Emotional troubles, however, would dog him for the rest of his life. But his rest period refitted him to return to the increasing responsibilities he faced at home.

Those responsibilities grew immediately upon his return. Because of complaints that the Jesuits who ran the diocesan seminary were introducing new methods that most of the bishops disliked, Romero was made head of the seminary — a perfunctory solution to a deep problem. It was not clear what sort of seminary training could replace the old Jesuit system. Some bishops decided that, given the chaos, they would send their students elsewhere. Romero had to divide his time among his duties at the seminary, the diocesan paper, and the bishops conference. Without a strong and full-time hand to guide the seminary through a major reorganization, it is not surprising that within a few months it had to be closed.

Romero had to accept some of the blame, though the situation clearly involved a great deal more than his personal failure. Neither his fellow bishops nor Rome seem to have held it against him, however, because in 1974 he was named bishop of the diocese of Santiago de María, a relatively new diocese where his home town, Ciudad Barrios, was located. Contrary to the view that Romero was an apologist for the status quo during these years, he showed that, in line with Catholic social teaching, he was willing to support the government as the only available protector of the common good, but also willing to criticize it when it failed. An attack on a farm in his diocese, which resulted in several deaths, moved him to protest vigorously to the government about the violation of basic human rights. In the diocesan newspaper that he founded in Santiago de María, he directly applied the Gospel to those who were exploiting the coffee pickers: "Behold, the day wage of the laborers that cut your fields, defrauded by you, is crying out, and the cries of the reapers have reached the ears of the Lord of hosts" (James 5:4). The bishop who had worked a coffee plantation as a young boy even allowed the migrant workers to sleep in the cathedral, rectory, and clergy meeting hall, and encouraged others to provide food and other necessities. Characteristic of Romero, at the very moment he was doing these works of mercy, he was highly critical in reports to Rome, as a member of the Pontifical Commission for Latin America, about what he regarded as the mistaken radical ideals of some of his fellow Salvadoran priests. Though he would become more ardent as archbishop, it is clear that he never allowed his justified outrage at injustice to lead him into ideological blindness.

In the 1970s, concern for the poor and marginalized crystallized around the movement known as liberation theology. Liberation theology is a complex movement with various branches. But in its heyday it was an attempt, among other things, to use social analysis, often of Marxist tendencies, along with Christian principles to address the obvious situations of injustice throughout Latin America and other parts of the developing world. Whether the two worldviews could be combined as the liberation theologians thought without leading to tyrannies of its own was and is questionable. Cuban dictator Fidel Castro embraced it, and that welcome may indicate some of the problems that might have resulted had liberation theology, in its most typical form, achieved success in other Latin American countries.

John Paul II, who in the 1980s had to sift out what was good and bad in liberation theology, issued two "Instructions" on the movement that some have read as a repudiation of the kinds of positions Romero took in his last days. The technical theological arguments do not enter into the present story, though it is clear that, the holding open of the door to Marxism aside, Romero actually shared John Paul's basic position: solidarity with the poor, prophetic truth telling about clear evils, yet the independence of the Church from complete identification with any merely political group. The pope's view of Romero as a person is clear from the words he spoke after praying at Romero's tomb during a trip to El Salvador in 1983. John Paul II characterized him as a "zealous shepherd, inspired by the love of God and service to his brethren to offer up his very life, suffering a violent death while celebrating the sacrifice of forgiveness and reconciliation."[16]

In any case, Romero's view was not an uncritical adoption of liberation theology, though he drew closer to some of its practitioners during his later years. As archbishop, his third and fourth pastoral letters addressed some of the liberationists' themes. Written in the crucible of daily deaths, he weighed his words carefully, and it is therefore worth looking at them for what they say about his considered judgment. Besides Marxism, liberation theology raised the question of armed revolution. In itself, revolution is a legitimate response in Catholic social teaching under certain conditions. Thomas Aquinas had allowed for it.[17] But the harder question was whether civil war in El Salvador met the conditions for a just revolution and whether the regime that was likely to result would be worth the price. One sign of Romero's careful approach to these issues is that, when a highly popular revolution overthrew Anastasio Somoza in nearby Nicaragua, he expressed hope that freedom and justice could also be achieved in Salvador, but added, "May we not need to endure a bloodbath to obtain them."[18]

More immediately, however, he had to deal with organizations that were seeking change and to provide guidance for how religious people working with them should conduct themselves. Several such organizations, including the Christian Democratic Party, had roots in the teachings of the Church. In his third pastoral letter, Romero called such groups "signs of God's presence and purposes," as Vatican II had suggested they be. But he introduced several qualifications. First, the Church has a primarily religious mission. To interpret this in too strictly spiritual sense, however, would be to say that it had nothing to say about the day-to-day situation of most people in troubled countries like El Salvador. Vatican II had announced that, "out of this religious mission itself comes a function, a light and an energy which can serve to structure and consolidate the human community according to the divine law."[19] Paul VI and the Latin American bishops meeting in Medellín had spoken of the way the Church enlightens the conscience of those engaged in social struggles and the bishops stated it should be a pastoral policy "to encourage and favor the efforts of the people to create and develop their own grassroots organizations for the redress and consolidation of their rights and the search for true justice."[20]

So the Church could never simply identify itself with any movement or offer a political program: that is not its function. But it can make large-scale determinations in theory about whether groups are moving closer or further away from God's purposes for the people. In practice, however, such judgments are never easy:

> This is where the problem arises; faith and politics ought to be united in a Christian who has a political vocation, but they are not to be identified. The church wants both dimensions to be present in the total life of a Christian and has emphasized that faith lived out in isolation from life is not true faith. However, one also has to be aware that the task of the faith and a particular political task cannot be identified [with each other]. . . . Faith ought to inspire political action, but not be mistaken for it.[21]

Priests and other clergy, in particular, have to be careful that their zeal for the poor does not lead to idolatry of some political formation. For, as always happens in politics, partisan factions are not always faithful either to the Gospel or even to their own ideals. Romero repeatedly criticized popular organizations as well as the government for confusing the two missions and seeing their political identifications as the substance of their faith. One of his close advisers has particularly pointed to his criticism of the popular organizations as showing Romero's deepest principles: when popular organizations make their own goals more important than the good of the people, Romero criticizes them because they have become "anti-popular."[22]

One of the ways all sides violated this golden rule was through violence. Faithful to his idea that the Church must look into its own immediate reality, Romero gives a taxonomy of the various kinds of violence then common in El Salvador:

- *institutional violence,* wherein existing political and economic structures harm large segments of the people;

- *repression,* which stamps out all expression of popular aspirations to justice;

- *sedition or terrorism,* which some call revolutionary, but Romero prefers to call by these names, because, believing force is the only way to justice, it "produces and provokes" bloodshed;

- *spontaneous violence,* a desperate outbreak in reaction to attacks, which "cannot be an effective way of securing rights or bringing just solutions to conflicts";

- *legitimate self-defense,* which should be used more to protect rather than to destroy;

- *nonviolence,* for completeness included here, since "far from being passivity and cowardice, [it] is evidence of great moral strength and can leave an aggressor morally defeated and humiliated."[23]

Romero concludes with reflections on traditional just-war conditions for insurrection, cites Vatican statements discouraging violence, and then adds, "We cannot place all our trust in violent methods if we are true Christians or even simply honorable persons."[24] The government, then, must recognize that peace is the fruit of justice; and the rebels must use violence only as a last resort and always seek peace first. Jesus himself had friends who displayed "aggressive temperaments and deeds" such as Moses, Elias, Peter, James, and John. But the Lord "channeled the aggression of their temperaments toward a rich work of construction, of building up justice and peace in the world."[25] And he closes urging by name the various sectors in Salvadoran society — Catholics, the economically powerful, the middle class, professionals, intellectuals, political parties, popular organizations, and public authorities — *Listen to him!.... Obey him!*

This was a highly nuanced position. Unfortunately, even some of Romero's admirers have not been sufficiently faithful to all the nuances of his thought. For example, *Romero,* a film of the archbishop's life, succeeds in capturing the moral heroism and spiritual sensitivity of the man, but fails seriously in many other ways. To begin with, it falsely portrays Romero, prior to his election as archbishop, as a bumbling bookworm. As the brief account of Romero's life above indicated, from his return to El Salvador in 1943 until 1977, he was not only quite active for almost thirty-five years in ministering to people all over El Salvador. He had grown up in many ways as a *campesino* and did not suddenly discover the people, as many of his admirers mistakenly believe, when he became archbishop. Nor was he uninvolved in political struggles before becoming archbishop, as his work with *Orientación* makes clear. Romero can be thought of as inactive earlier only if it is assumed that only a certain kind of progressive activism is real activism. In addition, far from being timid and tongue-tied, he was much admired as a speaker, both in person and on the radio in the years before he became archbishop (By the end of his life, his diocesan radio broadcasts were being regularly followed by 73 percent of the rural and 47 percent of the urban population, even though the homilies often lasted an hour and a half; opponents noticed and twice bombed the station to put it out of commission.)[26] *Romero,* however, mixes many incidents together, which never occurred the way they are portrayed, for the sake of drama.

For example, Romero did not march into the desecrated church at Aguilares, as the film shows. Instead, he came a month later to install a new pastor and say a Mass for the dead in that conflict. His homily was, by all accounts, one of his most moving, remembered by people for years later. He quietly, but powerfully, presented the true Christian response to the outrages: "For God no one is lost. For God there is only the mystery of pain, which, if accepted with a sense of sanctification and redemption, will be like that of Christ our Lord, a redemptive pain." Such redemption was a liberation, both from the physical evils suffered and the moral hazards of hatred and revenge that might creep into the hearts of those who had experienced loss and sorrow. He called for the liberation of the new being in Christ "who does not speak with animosity in his heart, who never furthers violence, hatred, or rancor." Even those who desecrated the tabernacle, he said, deserve prayers for their conversion.[27] Five thousand people were present for this event, which in every account has the otherworldly freshness of a scene out of the New Testament. The true account would have been even more dramatic than the Hollywood version.

Just a month later, Archbishop Romero faced a delicate question: the inauguration of the new president, Carlos Humberto Romero (no relation) was to take place on July 1. The archbishop had stated after the deaths of the priests Rutilio Grande and Alfonso Navarro that, until the murders were investigated properly, the Church would suspend its usual presence at government events. Sadly for him, the bishops themselves were divided on whether it was a better idea to respect the legitimate authority that at least partly remained in the national government, and might therefore be recognized as "coming from God," or take a more uncompromising stand. Two bishops attended the inauguration, as did the papal nuncio, and the Vatican tried to influence Romero to take a more open position that could lead to dialogue. He was quite willing to dialogue but observed that dialogue must be based on truth if the Church were not to become an accomplice to crimes: "Dialogue, if it is to be engaged in with a truly constructive spirit, must open up thoroughly."[28] He was right, and bishops and bishops conferences around the world supported Romero. But a public division in the Salvadoran Church had become very visible.

If Romero took a firm line toward the government, he was not unaware that some of his priests had become politically partisan in identifying themselves with the armed opposition. As usual, though, he denied government charges that such people were simply Marxists or revolutionaries. He tried to persuade his clergy to take a more churchly view of their role as priests; they, in turn, accused him of too much caution about the popular organizations. It was a situation in which there was no perfect middle point, a classic conflict of the late twentieth century. The Church could make clear judgments about moral questions, especially justice. But it was not in a position to provide a political and social blueprint for a situation that, by its nature, admitted of no short-term solution. Though many priests and laity supported his position and his homilies broadcast on the Church's radio station YSAX were wildly popular and outright loved, he still had to endure criticism from all sides.

Typical of the kinds of situations he was forced to deal with was a government raid on what was, to all appearances, merely a gathering for Christian initiation at El Despertar. Early on the morning of January 20, 1979, while the clergy and young people attending the meeting were still sleeping, security forces broke into the building. They opened fire, killing Father Octavio Ortiz, a priest of poor background from a village close to Romero's own birthplace, and four young people. Once again the archbishop found himself saying a public Mass in the cathedral plaza and calling for a reform of the Salvadoran security forces. Those forces had manufactured, after the fact, stories that the meeting was in fact a terrorist training center, the usual charge against anyone in the Church they disliked. During his homily, Romero pointed out the increase in vocations in El Salvador, despite the growing danger to clergy. And he particularly warned those present and listening over the radio to beware of similar distortions that the military and the press might attempt to circulate.

It must be said that sometimes, however, Church people were improperly involved in armed uprising. Prior to the incident at El Despertar, another priest, Ernesto (Neto) Barrera died during a shootout with security forces at a house that appears to have been used by the FPL, the Popular Liberation Forces. Though Neto's membership in the FPL at first seemed just another trumped-up charge, further investigation indicated that, in violation of Romero's own strictures about formal participation in popular groups and prohibition of priest involvement in armed conflict, Barrera, a union adviser, had indeed belonged to the FPL. The FPL itself proudly proclaimed the fact. Whether Barrera had personally taken up arms remained unclear. Romero decided to preside at his funeral in the absence of any proof of such activity and commented later: "I sincerely feel that Father Neto did not always convey a message that was altogether priestly and that he yielded considerably to the political and revolutionary ideas of these organizations. Nevertheless, they always noted in him, they told me, an effort to guide them in a priestly way. What the fundamental ideology of this priest was remains unknown."[29] It was a rather weak defense of what Romero knew gave ammunition to his enemies inside and outside the Church.

Between situations like the El Despertar atrocities and the Barrera case, Romero went to Puebla, Mexico, for the 1980 meeting of the Latin American Bishops Conference. In his absence, the violence and counterviolence went on. The ERP, the People's Revolutionary Army, killed twenty people and wounded others with a bomb at the central police barracks in retaliation for El Despertar. Even in Mexico, Romero received death threats. But Romero was something of a celebrity at Puebla, even though he did not play a major role in the deliberations. His influence was exerted outside the formal meetings in discussions with delegates and in conversations with the press. He stated there that his so-called conversion was in fact a deepening, rather than a reversal, of his past attitudes, but that his new responsibilities had also brought him a new sense of the need for the Church to speak for those without a voice: "If we do not, we are not giving all the response that God wants to give to those who suffer."[30] Salvadoran Bishop Aparicio, however, told the press that Romero had been deluded by the Marxists, a remark that was widely reported in El Salvador. Aparicio even openly criticized Romero for "vanity" in claiming to defend human rights, saying that Romero wanted to be "the Latin American Jimmy Carter."[31]

After returning to El Salvador, Romero explained the Puebla documents. The "preferential option for the poor," he said, was not meant to exclude the rich, but to include them as Christians in thinking about how to deal with social and religious problems. As he would argue, "The best way to overcome Marxism is to take seriously the preferential option for the poor."[32] In one of his typically generous gestures, he allowed that he himself might be criticized:

> I say this with all sincerity. Whoever accuses must be ready to be accused. From the beginning I have said that I gladly accept criticism when it is constructive and means to improve whatever bit of good there may be in me. I truly ask pardon of all those to whom I have not succeeded in conveying the message as I should have. But let them understand that there is no pride or ill will or distortion of what the gospel bids me preach to this archdiocese entrusted to me.[33]

But he also expressed great hope in the riches of the Christian tradition in Latin America, both as a spiritual guide and a help on the way to greater justice and freedom.

Soon he was off to Rome again, nominally for a beatification, but really to speak with the Vatican officials and John Paul II himself about the Salvadoran situation. In his diary, he wrote that he again visited the tombs of the popes and prayed "very much for the faithfulness to my Christian faith and for the courage, if need be, to die as did all these martyrs, or else to live consecrating my life as these modern successors of Peter consecrated theirs."[34] The pope, who had had much experience with the wiles of Nazi and Communist governments, was sympathetic, and only suggested that Romero be both courageous and balanced. He advised more general statements rather than specific accusations, since the Church could not put its moral authority behind judgments of fact that might prove erroneous. Romero agreed in principle, but argued that specific murders, such as those of Father Octavio Ortiz and the four young people, called for specific replies. John Paul had had similar experiences in Poland and agreed, but also spoke of the importance of solidarity among the bishops. An Argentine bishop sent to report on the archdiocese of San Salvador had recommended that the pope appoint an apostolic administrator, in effect someone who would run the archdiocese while Romero remained its nominal head.

They discussed the situation and Romero was satisfied that the pope had listened to his point of view. But his position remained precarious. In later correspondence with Rome, it became clear that Vatican authorities hoped to appoint someone to handle his government relations who was less at loggerheads with national leaders. Romero would still have direction of spiritual activities. But he argued that this division of power would bring no solution, because in El Salvador religious and social justice questions could not be so neatly disentangled. Practically speaking, in a small country like El Salvador, unity in the leadership of the archdiocese, especially given its influence over the rest of the country, was essential.

While he was in Rome, the killing in Salvador went on. In one incident in front of the cathedral, police opened fire on a demonstration, killing twenty-five. Violence erupted in various parts of the country, people were summarily arrested and "disappeared," provoking the usual counter-attacks by militant organizations. Churches were occupied by protesters as were foreign embassies. Guerrillas were taking hostages. The minister of education had been ambushed and killed along with his driver. In his first homily after returning, Romero described how distressing it was for him in Rome to see El Salvador as Europeans and others see it in the newspapers and on television, as a place where violence was as natural an everyday occurrence as breathing. Yet he was back, he said, among his family and took comfort in sharing their fate. The government was continuing its tactic of saying it would investigate atrocities and doing nothing. Romero reminded the militant organizations of the basic ethical principle: one cannot do evil so that good may come out of it. In the month of his return alone, 115 people died and many more were wounded or disappeared. The next month, June, more peasants, workers, and even thirty teachers died in the violence. And Father Rafael

Palacios was assassinated in revenge, it was rumored, for the death of an army officer. Romero had returned to an unbelievable maelstrom of mayhem.

After one particularly bloody incident at the occupied Venezuelan embassy, he issued a statement: "As archbishop of San Salvador, I call on the consciences and hearts of those responsible not to continue their unyielding and intransigent position, but to yield and seek a way to break as soon as possible this endless chain of bloody deeds. What matters now is not to show the nation and the world who is the stronger or the winner but who is the more responsible and humane, capable of stopping this growing spiral of violence."[35] It was an eloquent and pointed plea, but had little effect.

More troubling, however, most of his fellows bishops formally went on record at this point against the archbishop. In a letter to Rome, Bishops Aparicio, Alvarez, Barrera, and Revelo — a bloc within the Salvadoran Bishops Conference (CEDES) — accused him indirectly of failing to see the Marxist positions he had come to adopt. They described various church groups, along with the archdiocesan radio and newspaper and the Jesuits, as virtual fronts for dissidents and centers for revolutionary indoctrination. Priests had criticized the papal nuncio as well as native bishops who did not take Romero's politicized pastoral line. He had allegedly set the so-called "popular church" above the Church proper. The priests who had been killed in El Salvador had been notorious subversives. More broadly, the critical bishops argued that world opinion had come to believe that the Church in El Salvador was being persecuted when in fact the government was only trying to maintain social order. They went so far as to say that the government was actually responding weakly to social disorder out of fear of international opinion. Romero's denunciations of the Salvadoran president as a liar and the justice system as venal during homilies they thought false or exaggerated. They even speculated that he was secretly meeting with the Christian Democrats, the business groups, and the Salvadoran president, hardly something that seems objectionable from their point of view. Their final charge, however, was the worst: "People ask how it is possible that a shepherd of the church should support cold-blooded criminals who openly declare themselves Marxist-Leninist."[36]

Had Romero taken a wrong turn? For the most part, his fellow bishops' charges were mistaken or presented in a one-sided fashion. Romero was not "sympathetic" to Marxism, despite his occasional jabs at Salvador's poor distribution of private property and U.S. "imperialism." Yet it also has to be said that Romero probably underestimated the extent to which El Salvador at that point in the Cold War was being used by Communist elements. Cuba was involved in widespread adventures around the world and was helping Salvadoran insurgents. Had they prevailed, might Salvador have gone through even more decades of tyranny, this time under Marxist oppressors?

Romero was certainly right to avoid giving security forces any excuse for further repression by not emphasizing this fact. But he was also limited in his view. The U.S. president at the time, Jimmy Carter, was notably interested in human rights, but even his administration backed the government against insurgents. In strict terms, Romero was right that the Marxist threat was invoked indiscriminately; but in Salvador in 1979, strict terms were impossible to maintain as passions boiled over. He probably would have helped his position enormously if, in addition to the correct criteria he laid down in his third pastoral letter about Church involvement with popular organizations, he had been more vigorous in enforcing them by appropriate disciplinary action against priests and religious who violated his norms.

Romero read the letter criticizing him and discussed it thoroughly with Bishop Rivera, who supported him. He knew he had failed in many ways but was confident that he was not guilty of the charges they presented. He consoled himself with the thought that "God will have the last word." But in the meantime he sent human words to the accusing bishops. After repeating his belief that the plain fact was that the people were being subjected to injustice, he raised the question of whether the bishops' silence on murders of clergy and the divisions within the CEDES had not made things worse. And he asked: "What have we done to prevent the murder of more than twenty teachers and the recent death of our fellow priest Father Rafael Palacios?" reminding them of God's ominous questions to Cain after he killed Abel.

His question was prophetic. Within a month, another priest, Father Alirio Napoleón Macías was gunned down in his church after sending out information about murders, arrests, and *desaparecidos* in his parish. This time the bishops issued a unanimous protest and called for a government investigation. The death occurred in Bishop Pedro Arnoldo Aparicio's diocese. Even this strong opponent of Romero admitted that the act was an outrage and condemned it publicly, excommunicating the perpetrators. He and the other bishops recalled their delegates from the National Forum. But Aparicio also made a public statement that all the priests who had been killed were members of popular organizations and were killed by leftists for trying to leave them. What the evidence for this was, he did not say. The Organization of American States had earlier asked the Inter-American Human Rights Commission to investigate El Salvador. Its view was that the government was persecuting the Church and that forces of the government or paramilitary death squads were responsible for the outrages. But supported or not, claims like these were a virtual death-warrant for priests suspected of sympathies with popular organizations. Everyone in Salvador knew it. Romero replied indirectly by asking CEDES to order clergy to refrain from public attacks on one another and to confront one another more discreetly through private ecclesial channels in order to avoid more bloodshed.

But more bloodshed seemed inevitable given the way that Salvador was going. In one of his most heartfelt statements of all, Romero proclaimed that the repression could not succeed if his people remained faithful to their Christian vocation: "If they ever take our radio, suspend our newspaper, silence us, put to death all of us priests, bishops included, and you are left alone—a people without priests—then each of you will have to be God's microphone. Each of you will have to be a messenger, a prophet. The church will always exist as long as even one baptized person is left alive!"[37] The vision he presented may have seemed extreme, even for El Salvador. Certainly, there was no organized attempt to suppress the whole Church as had been the case in Mexico, Spain, the Soviet Union, and other nations during the twentieth century. But beyond its apparent exaggeration, it pointed to a force among the people that would guarantee that truth and the desire for justice could not be stamped out.

Ironically, it was under a reform junta to which Romero gave some legitimacy that he was to die. In September of 1979, leaders planning a coup against President Romero came to the archbishop. They were part of the Juventud Militar, a group of young officers tired of the corruption, inefficiency, and violence of the existing regime. They discussed their intentions with Romero. He promised prayers and moral support insofar as the new junta fulfilled its promises. When the coup occurred, Romero remarked upon the leaders' "good will, clarity of ideas, and clear consciousness of their responsibility.... We lay down only one condition: that we both, government and church, be conscious that our reason for being is to serve the people, each in our proper capacity."[38]

The new junta did indeed promise a change. It included Román May-orga, president of the Central American University, Guillermo Ungo, a leader of an umbrella coalition, and a businessman from the Chamber of Commerce, along with other decent and prominent people. Nonetheless, some sectors of the people were restless. An uprising occurred and dozens of people died or were wounded during the fighting. Romero publicly declared such acts irresponsible. He called on the government to deal with such situations less brutally. But he also pointed out to insurgents that alternatives to the use of force existed with the new governing junta and, until there was evidence to the contrary, conscientious Catholics should try to take advantage of them.

Unfortunately, the new junta was no more capable than the old of controlling the armed forces. Other incidents soon followed. At the earliest stages, however, Romero thought some of the popular organizations were showing the kind of "fanaticism" he had deplored, fearing that if the government succeeded their organizations would lose their following. A group of his own more activist clerics and grassroots organizers issued a public statement disagreeing with his support of the new government. Shortly after, Romero was informed by the papal nuncio in Costa Rica that he had heard of a left-wing plot to assassinate him, this time for his support of the government and right-wing forces. The leftist charges were obviously untrue and contradicted everything we know about Romero's life. But El Salvador was so divided by then that a conscientious pastor like Romero could be threatened with death from every side.

Characteristic of Romero is the way he handled such threats. In a homily, he stated: "The shepherd does not want security while security is not given to his flock."[39] These were not mere words. When the Salvadoran president's brother was murdered by leftists trying to provoke the army on September 7, 1979, both the president and the minister of defense were concerned that Romero might be in danger, too. The government was either not willing or able to control the armed forces nor able to prosecute those in the various military and paramilitary groups who acted outside the law. But they offered Romero anything he wanted by way of protection, "even a bulletproof car." He respectfully declined the offer, regarding it as an "antipastoral witness were I to ride in such safety while my people are so insecure."[40]

Meanwhile, the new government continued to show some promising, if modest, signs of improvement. In December, Romero noted that a committee was investigating human rights violations and sketching future remedies. Under the junta, not only the Church but other organizations were free for the first time in a long while to speak out about problems and abuses. A genuine civic dialogue and political life might have flowered. Unfortunately, by the middle of the month, a shift occurred in the junta itself. More hardline military men were appointed to replace some of the reformers. The day after Christmas 1979, the civilian members were the target of attempted intimidation by the military figures. Within days, they resigned along with many judges and other government officials. Romero called on one of the military men to resign, without success. Finally, a compromise government of the military and the Christian Democrats formed. But this proved no better than its predecessors. Romero repeated: "To the government junta, I must say with my people that it is urgent to show, by ending the repression, that you are able to control the security forces, which at present seem to be a parallel government that is doing great harm to the junta. Each day that passes, marked by the security forces' repression, is a further weakening of the government and a new frustration for the people."[41] But by then it was too late; all roads to real reform seemed closed off.

Romero was offered an honorary degree in January 1980 by the University of Louvain in Belgium. He made a point of going to Rome afterward to consult again with the pope. During their discussion, John Paul expressed his appreciation for the difficulty of the situation and counseled Romero to continue defending human rights while being careful not to give comfort to ideologies that, in the long run, will ignore them. They were in total agreement about this strategy, as Romero's pastorals made clear, but he felt obliged to tell the pope: "In my country it is very dangerous to speak of anticommunism, because anticommunism is what the right proclaims, not out of love for Christian sentiments, but out of a selfish concern to preserve its own interests." The pope replied that the Church is not "anti" anything. Romero took up this line: "That is why I don't present it that way but, rather, positively, praising the spiritual, Christian values of my people and saying that we must always defend and preserve them." Romero told the pope that he preached what the pope preached at Puebla. They embraced, the pope promised his prayers, and Romero summed up this meeting in his diary: "I felt here God's confirmation and his force for my poor ministry."[42]

But that ministry was drawing to its earthly close. Romero wrote president Carter asking him not to send military aid to Salvador's repressive forces. The U.S. ambassador, Robert White, met with him and said the United States was as concerned as anyone to maintain order with the minimum of violence. When Romero mentioned some of this in his weekly homily over the radio, the station was bombed by a right-wing group. Secundo Azcue, Romero's confessor and spiritual director, states that Romero knew his days might be numbered and felt the agony in the garden, even though he willingly accepted the cup he was asked to drink. The willingness did not even specify what would be in the cup. He prayed during a retreat:

> I do not want to express my intention to him, such as that my death be for my country's peace or our church's flourishing. Christ's heart will know how to direct it to the purpose he wishes. For me to be happy and confident, it is sufficient to know with assurance that in him is my life and my death, that in spite of my sins I have placed my trust in him and I will not be confounded, and others will continue with greater wisdom and holiness the works of the church and the nation.[43]

In his next-to-last homily, he stated one last time his profound hope for reconciliation:

> The denunciations of the left against the right and the hatred of the right for the left appear irreconcilable, and those in the middle say, wherever the violence comes from be tough on them both. And thus we live in groups, polarized, and perhaps even those of the same group don't love each other, because there can be no love at all where people take sides to the point of hating others. We need to burst these dikes, we need to feel that there is a Father who loves us all and awaits us all. We need to learn to pray to Our Father and tell him: Forgive us as we forgive.[44]

The next week, his last, he was back in the basilica. Saying that he did not intend to meddle in politics, he put into simpler words what he had stated about the Christian guidance of politics in his pastoral letters:

> God's law must prevail that says: Thou shalt not kill! No soldier is obliged to obey an order against the law of God. No one has to fulfill an immoral law. It is time to take back your consciences rather than obey the orders of sin. The church, defender of the rights of God, of the law of God, of human dignity, of the person, cannot remain silent before such abomination. We want the government to understand seriously that reforms are worth nothing if they are stained with so much blood. In the name of God, and in the name of this suffering people, whose laments rise to heaven each day more

tumultuous, I beg you, I beseech you, I order you in the name of God: Stop the repression.

The following Monday seemed a normal day. Romero worked in his office. Around noon he went out to a study session; the archbishop that some accused of being a Marxist attended an event sponsored by Opus Dei, one of the more orthodox religious movements in Latin America, during his final hours. After, he stopped at the doctor's for advice about an ear infection. A friend drove him to Father Azcue for confession. "I want to feel clean in the Lord's presence," he said.[45] That evening this shepherd, beloved and hated by so many, criticized by his fellow bishops, the government, and, at times, his friends in the popular organizations and militant groups, was shot to death by paramilitary forces during Mass.

Perhaps the highest tribute paid Romero has come from the pen of one of his closest advisers, Jon Sobrino. Sobrino is a well-known liberation theologian who was himself embroiled in the political struggles of Central America in the 1970s and 1980s. He drafted several pastorals and other documents for Romero, and at times criticized Vatican efforts to purify liberation theology. But his ultimate praise of Romero concerns neither his liberationist nor political positions, his courage or dynamic leadership. Romero, he says, "is more than an analytical concept or a venerable myth. He was someone very real, someone whom 'we have seen, heard, and touched,' as the first Christians said of Jesus."[46] Perhaps that resemblance was the secret to Romero's appeal to the people. It is certain that, in any event, above all the other praise and honor he received during his life, the archbishop would have most treasured this comparison.

As remarkable a witness as Romero was to the truth and despite the inspiration he gave to millions of Salvadorans, his death was only the beginning of a brutal decade. Perhaps no atrocity in El Salvador captured more attention in the larger world than the murder of four American churchwomen — Dorothy Kazel, Jean Donovan, Ita Ford, and Maura Clarke — in December 1981. Unlike many of the other Salvadoran dead, these women were North Americans. For a press weary of Latin American turmoil, Latins killing other Latins seemed an everyday affair. But the murder, and brutal rape, of four female missioners from the United States struck a new chord.

Dorothy Kazel came from Lithuanian-American background and grew up in a middle-class home in Cleveland, Ohio, where she entered the Ursuline convent in the 1960s and taught at the Sacred Heart Academy for seven years.[47] Athletic, energetic, vivacious, she pursued her vocation in various ways, including periods in inner-city schools counseling students who had emotional and drug problems. In 1963, Pope John XXIII asked American dioceses to send 10 percent of their religious workers to mission territories. Bishops all over the United States responded. Dorothy Kazel was not chosen immediately, but in 1974 she was accepted into one of Cleveland's missions in Nuestra Señora de Guadalupe parish in Chirilagua, El Salvador.

Joining her shortly after was Jean Donovan, the daughter of Raymond Donovan, who would later become secretary of labor in the Reagan administration. Jean grew up in much better-off circumstances; her father was a very successful businessman before entering politics, and her mother devoted herself to helping the poor. Like many successful Catholic families, the Donovans encouraged the children to achieve, but also conveyed to them the need to develop strong "moral judgment."[48] Though Jean Donovan would never choose a formal religious vocation — indeed, she was planning on marrying after her work in El Salvador was over — her sense of responsibility for the poor, something she clearly inherited from her mother's efforts at home, led her to volunteer to work in El Salvador.

Ita Ford's family was familiar with death in the Catholic missions. Her uncle, Maryknoll Bishop Francis X. Ford, died in China in Communist prisons before she was a teenager. The family was middle-class from a modest Brooklyn, New York neighborhood. She sensed that a religious vocation was the only way she could realize her true self. After some health problems that delayed her acceptance, she joined the Maryknoll order.[49] The most literary of the four, Ford was moved by the deep piety she found among oppressed believers during a trip to Russia and Poland. She was also often disturbed by the images of repression she encountered in more than one Latin American country and depressed by the incomprehension she found during visits back home to the United States. By chance, she was assigned to Chile just before a coup led by General Augusto Pinochet overthrew the socialist government of

Salvador Allende. Ford witnessed first-hand the arbitrary arrests and tortures of many — including religious, despite protests by the Chilean Church — who were believed to oppose the new regime. One friend described her as a "seething volcano" after her return from Chile.[50] But through prayer and spiritual direction, she regained her calm and made a reasoned choice to go to a country then perhaps most troubled of all the Latin countries, El Salvador. As she wrote a friend about her work: "I believe in the Lord of the impossible."[51]

The fourth woman, Maura Clarke, also grew up in New York, the child of Irish-born parents. She seemed to have a Saint Francis-like generosity from her earliest years that would lead her, even toward the end of her life, to give away everything she had, including salary "advances" from Maryknoll, to anyone who needed it. After the disastrous 1972 earthquake in Nicaragua, she became outspoken in defending those who were being arrested by the brutal and corrupt Somoza regime and may even have saved several people from torture or death by timely interventions. She was transferred to El Salvador in August of 1980 and advocated remaining in the country to be with the people rather than escaping to safety, as prudence seemed to dictate.

All four women were primarily engaged in medical and relief work, often distributing help from the USAID and the Catholic agency Caritas. In regions with very few priests, they organized liturgies of the Word and administered the sacraments in appropriate ways. They also tried to empower people by educating them, organizing peasant groups, and teaching them to reflect on justice. In a heavily populated country like El Salvador, where land was held in a relatively few hands, suggesting that the poor had a right to land of their own threatened many established interests. But nothing in their backgrounds and little in their day-to-day practice indicates they were revolutionaries or primarily even activists of a political kind. More accurately, they were horrified at the random murders and mutilations they met with daily and had a typically American attitude that such things simply should not be. Democracy and respect for human rights were about all they advocated on the political side. But in El Salvador, where death squads (*escuadrones de muerte*) and military sweeps through whole villages were everyday occurrences, even their modest and generally nonideological efforts to help the people were viewed with the deepest suspicion. Ironically, the four women openly informed the military authorities in Chalatenango about the nature of their work to avoid any misunderstandings. They made it clear that their white Toyota minibus was a means of help to all, of whatever faction, who simply needed food or assistance, especially refugees. But their openness did little to mollify the armed forces. Colonel Ricardo Peña Abaiza, their local contact, mentioned to Ita Ford that he believed the Catholic Church was "indirectly subversive because it's on the side of the weak."[52]

Given such attitudes, an explosion was inevitable. The churchwomen went to Nicaragua for a regional assembly of Maryknoll sisters; they were already under surveillance. When they returned on December 2, 1981, they picked up the minibus and began driving from the airport to their base. A short distance from the airport they were stopped by a National Guard roadblock. In a brutal and senseless act, they were all raped and murdered. Days later, when the bodies were discovered in a shallow grave after a tip from local *campesinos*, Jean Donovan was unrecognizable: she had been beaten severely, as had Ita Ford, and shot in the face. All seem to have been found with their underwear and pants off, which the peasants had replaced out of respect.[53]

For almost a decade after Romero's and the four churchwomen's deaths, similarly bloody dynamics continued in Salvadoran society. On November 16, 1989, a terrible atrocity occurred even as the civil war in El Salvador was winding down. About thirty uniformed gunmen broke into a dormitory at the University of Central America (UCA). They took three of the Jesuits they found there out into the courtyard, tortured them, and then machine-gunned them all. Three other Jesuits were killed while they were sleeping in their beds. To add insult to injury, the Jesuits' cook, Julia Elba, and her daughter, Celina, were also executed in the process. In total, eight people died in one of the most heinous acts of the entire conflict.

Like Romero's death, these murders were by deliberate design. Father Ignacio Ellacuría, the best known of the group, had been a forceful witness against the ongoing violations of human rights. A Salvadoran woman who had seen him recently on television told a priest: "Not since they murdered Archbishop Romero has anyone spoken out so plainly in this country."[54]

But the others, in quieter ways, had continued Romero's work as well. Father Segundo Montes, a sociologist, had directed the UCA Institute of Human Rights; Nacho Martín-Baró, a psychologist and academic vice-rector, proposed religion as a force for liberation; Juan Ramón Moreno, Jesuit novice master, served as vice-rector of the Archbishop Romero Center, which was attacked and its library partly destroyed in the same incident; Father Armando López, rector of the San Salvador seminary, did energetic pastoral work in addition to his academic duties; and Father Joaquín López y López labored for twenty years in Fe y Alegría, a movement that taught the poor in both the countryside and the cities.[55] Their murders effectively eliminated some of the nation's most vigorous Catholic activities, particularly among the common people most in need.

Except for López y López, all the Jesuits had been born in Spain and might easily have had regular academic lives and less demanding circumstances at home. Instead, they committed themselves to living and working among a people suffering poverty and social turmoil even to the point of giving up their lives. They knew the risks quite well. For a decade and a half, they had received anonymous phone threats and public criticism. Bombs exploded fifteen times at the university, and residences were machine-gunned on several occasions. Ellacuría had agreed only once to leave the country, in November 1980, the same year that Romero and the four American churchwomen were killed, because his name was reported to be at the top of an assassination list. The Jesuits viewed their work as an extension of their Ignatian charism: "contemplatives in action for justice."[56]

In the overheated social conflict that gripped El Salvador in the 1980s, defense of the poor and helpless, as in Romero's case, was often identified as commitment to the guerrillas or Marxist analysis. The Jesuits often came under the same criticism. But their position was more nuanced than it was given credit for being at the time. They denounced violence and always preferred negotiations and dialogue. But dialogue itself was, for some in El Salvador, tantamount to capitulation. That was far from the Jesuits' minds. When guerrilla forces, the FMLN, murdered or when they were involved in terrorism, they, too, were criticized. Indeed, the Jesuits' stance resembles in some respects what Eastern Europeans facing Communism came to describe as "living in truth." Wherever regimes threaten those who tell the truth, a kind of slavery springs up. People begin to go along quietly with much they know to be false or wrong, simply because the price of truth is too high. To live for truth is not to claim that one has simple answers for terrible and complex social circumstances. But it does entail an honest decision not to ignore hard facts, about whatever faction, as a way to ultimate reconciliation. If Christ, among other things, is the Truth, then telling the truth is a way of witnessing to him. Romero had taken that approach, and the six Jesuits also tried with no little courage to practice this form of truth telling in circumstances in which the truth was guaranteed to inflame murderous passions on one side or the other.

Those passions were not long in manifesting themselves. Archbishop
Rivera y Damas, Romero's successor, when asked who killed the Jesuits,
replied: "It was those who murdered Archbishop Romero and who are
not satisfied with seventy thousand dead."[57] We know that the perpetrators wore uniforms, and we may speculate that almost certainly they
were Salvadoran military forces or a covert force directed by the upper
echelons of the army and the government.

The killing of the four churchwomen and the six Jesuits however, was
part of a pattern common in many Latin American countries in the second half of the twentieth century. El Salvador was only the most flagrant
example. But from Argentina and Chile, two countries with democratic traditions, to Paraguay, a long-standing dictatorship, to Chiapas in
southern Mexico, religious were subjected to intimidation, violence, and
"disappearances." Alleged political involvement was not always the reason why religious died. In Honduras, for example, Franciscan Casimir
Cypher, a decidedly apolitical man, was executed in July of 1975. Jesuit
James Carney, a professed revolutionary priest, died in the hands of security forces in 1982. Three Catholic missionaries died in Guatemala:
Maryknoller William Woods in a suspicious plane crash, Father Stanley
Rother in his own rectory, and Christian Brother James Miller, machine-
gunned while repairing a wall at the Casa Indígena. Clergy from other
denominations perished in the turmoil as well.

   Guatemala, in particular, has had a long history of widespread and
flagrant abuse of human rights that has resulted in the death of religious.
During the thirty years when civil war raged in Guatemala, until the December 29, 1996, signing of a peace accord between the Guatemalan
government and the National Revolutionary Unity (URNG), at least
150,000 people died, and countless others were "disappeared." In addition, a million people were displaced and hundreds of thousands fled to
other countries, primarily Mexico. The accord halted the bulk of the conflict, but passions and problems smolder and occasionally break out in
ways that indicate that human rights problems continue in Guatemala,
sometimes in old ways, sometimes in new ones, that involve religious
issues.

   The most graphic confirmation of this occurred on April 26, 1998.
Just two days after issuing "Guatemala: Never Again!" a fourteen-
hundred-page report that blamed the Guatemalan army or government

paramilitaries for over 80 percent of the dead and for 401 out of 422 documented massacres, Juan José Gerardi, a seventy-five-year-old Catholic bishop, was brutally murdered. Gerardi, founder of the Guatemala City archdiocesan human rights office, had his head crushed by repeated blows of a cement block in the rectory where he lived. The official government investigation tried to place the blame on a priest who lived in the same house, alleging that the violence was the result of a homosexual relationship gone bad. But there is no evidence that confirms this charge. Such evidence as there is, phone records and vehicles reported to have been outside the residence that night, points to more likely culprits — some of the figures named in the human rights report.

Guatemala has created the Truth Commission to try to sort out responsibility for human rights violations committed in the past. The Guatemalan Catholic bishops have founded the Project to Recover Historic Memory and assembled a forensic team to exhume and examine bodies of massacre victims. As these investigations continue, other members of religious groups involved in pursuing justice and reconciliation are likely to be the targets of death threats and intimidation and perhaps will suffer further outrages.

Many of the victims of human rights abuses during the civil conflict were indigenous peoples of the various Mayan groups in the country who constitute about half the population. As elsewhere in Latin America where Spanish settlers intermingled with large indigenous groups, religion in indigenous areas was and remains a syncretism of Catholic and traditional Mayan beliefs. Rural indigenous people were economically marginalized to a great extent during Guatemala's history by the concentration of land ownership within a small percentage of the population. When liberation theology began to emerge in the 1970s throughout Latin America, some of the Guatemalan proponents of that movement organized indigenous communities to challenge perceived injustices.

Massive human rights abuses were visited upon individuals and groups who saw in their religious commitments obligations to reform governmental practice and promote social justice. Government forces, death squads, and "civilian patrols" violently repressed anyone seen as an "enemy of the people" during the civil war. Guerrilla forces, too, if in lesser numbers, attacked indigenous communities they perceived as loyal to the government. Many indigenous people died, others were displaced to different areas within Guatemala, still others crossed the border into southern Mexico. The peace accord has led to a sharp reduction in the kinds of politically driven attacks on religious groups characteristic of the past. But until Guatemala achieves profound social reform, human rights violations against religious reformers are very likely to continue.

Since the 1959 revolution, the Communist government of Cuba under Fidel Castro has engaged in the most systematic repression of religion in the history of the Americas. Pre-Columbian empires imposed religious uniformity to bolster political power, as did the Spaniards in many places after their arrival. Modern Mexico tried to control the Church after its revolution earlier in the century. But no American regime before revolutionary Cuba's has so thoroughly opposed religion per se. Recent concessions by the regime, under duress, have not basically altered that pattern.

Though the Cuban constitution, like the constitutions of the old Soviet bloc, formally allows freedom of religion and purports to treat all religions equally, its clauses mask widespread official and unofficial discrimination against believers and limitations on religious exercise. For many years, active believers were both openly and subtly threatened about the consequences of continued practice. Some were simply arrested and given long prison sentences as counterrevolutionaries, often dying in obscurity. Others were dismissed from government posts and forced to take menial jobs. Still others were — and still are — denied access to the more prestigious educational institutions that are the gateway to employment in the entirely state-owned economy. The few exceptions prove the rule.

The regime claims that religion was never very strong on the island and that it largely functioned as a prop for exploitative elites. Though figures are difficult to come by and are uncertain, nominal Catholics probably still constitute about 40 percent of the population, with only 2 percent actively attending Mass. Protestantism is growing and by some estimates may now have reached 10 percent of the Cuban population. Official government studies of religion like to point to Santería, a combination of African, indigenous, and Catholic practices that poses few challenges to the regime, as the most widespread form of spirituality on the island. After decades of repression, it is difficult to say what the religious makeup of a free Cuba might have been.

In any case, Fidel Castro's own history tells a somewhat different story than the official version of Cuban religiosity. The son of a poor Spanish immigrant who later became a wealthy landowner, Castro was educated by the Marists and the Jesuits. He and his brother Raúl were saved from execution by the intervention of Bishop Enrique Pérez Serrantes, a family friend, when they had been captured and tried by the Batista regime after their infamous failed 1953 attack on the Moncada Barracks. From before the triumph of the revolution on January 1, 1959, to early in the 1960s (when the move into Communism became apparent), many in the churches supported the as yet ideologically uncommitted revolutionary government. Many priests, with the blessing of their bishops, served as chaplains to the revolutionaries.[58] But Catholic concern for social justice did not extend to the embrace of Marxism, whose basic atheism conflicted with the Church. In the early days of the revolution, most Christians regarded Castro as an idealist; Raúl Castro and Che Guevara were the Marxists. A great divide opened in December 1960 when Fidel declared, "To be anti-Communist is tantamount to being anti-revolutionary." Just a few months earlier, he had put out feelers trying to find a leader for a national Church, independent from Rome and dependent upon Havana, on the Communist Chinese model.

After the failed U.S.-backed Bay of Pigs invasion in April 1961, the regime immediately arrested many Catholic laymen, priests, and all the bishops. The next month, all private religious schools, Catholic and Protestant, were "nationalized." That fall, over a hundred priests were expelled, public religious observances were banned, and discrimination against believers began in earnest. For decades, the churches in Cuba were subjected to a slow strangulation. The Castro regime adopted a shrewd tactic. Knowing that the open killing of believers would have negative international repercussions, Castro told his followers: "We will not fall into the historical error of planting our way with Christian martyrs, for we know well that it was precisely martyrdom that strengthened the Church. We will create apostates, thousands of apostates."[59]

The apostates, however, were not many, at least not publicly. And there were quite a few martyrs, though their stories remain little known. For instance, Armando Valladares, an Evangelical Christian, was imprisoned for twenty-two years in Castro's prisons, where he witnessed many who died after being apprehended for their faith. In his memoir *Beyond All Hope*, he documents the fates of some of these witnesses. His own case is indicative: he was a post office worker who lost his position because, as a Christian, he would not agree to display a sign saying: *Si Fidel es communista que me pongan en la lista, yo estoy de acuerdo con él* ("If Fidel is Communist, then put me on the list, I agree with him").[60]

A quiet and apolitical man, this was enough, however, to earn him a long sentence that, unlike many others, he was fortunate to survive.

Louis Boitel, a Catholic, was not so fortunate. In the 1950s, Boitel had been a prominent Catholic student leader who opposed Batista and welcomed the Castro revolution. But since, as a Catholic, he would not join the Cuban Communist Party, he was arrested in 1960 and sentenced to ten years. When he completed his sentence, however, he was not released. In 1972 he died after being tortured and having his back broken at the Castillo del Príncipe Prison. The torture was only the end of a long period of mistreatment. At his death, he weighed less than eighty pounds; his family and the International Red Cross had petitioned Castro on his behalf without success. Family members were not allowed to attend his funeral.[61]

Cases like these cropped up over decades. The 1976 constitution officially declared Cuba an atheist state. In addition to attacks on believers who were not compliant, building permits for churches were withheld, repairs were unauthorized, and activities in public and private strictly regulated. Even so, the churches remained the only partly independent sector: politics, the press, labor, education, and almost the entire economy were in party hands. After the fall of the Soviet Union, there was some slight opening to real freedom of practice. The "special period within Socialism," which is to say the current crisis in which Cuba no longer receives Soviet subsidies and remains under U.S. embargo, has made some accommodation with the churches a necessity.

In 1992, the Cuban People's National Assembly slightly modified the constitution. Christians were allowed to become members of the Cuban Communist Party, with the social and economic benefits that might bring them. The clause in the constitution declaring Cuba to be an atheist state was modified so that Cuba is now officially secularist. But even the revised constitution warned Cubans that none of their rights may be used "contrary to the Cuban people's decision to build Socialism and Communism." Christmas was permitted as a legal holiday in 1997 in anticipation of John Paul II's visit in January 1998. (In December of 1998 the regime announced it would make that arrangement permanent.) Havana's Cardinal Ortega was allowed to broadcast a message about the Holy Father's pilgrimage to the island over Cuban television and radio. Some church figures now have limited access to the media. Open-air masses have been allowed and a procession took place in downtown Havana at Eastertime 1998.

These tentative steps of accommodation toward religion, however, must largely be viewed as a tactical necessity in a time of desperation. Caritas, a Catholic relief organization, has been allowed to import medicines and other materials, but the regime has demanded a large percentage of those imports for its own hospitals and services as the price for the private relief efforts. Tellingly, after the 1998 papal visit, Cuba expelled Father Patrick Sullivan, an American missionary who had been actively promoting human rights in the city of Santa Clara, probably as a warning to native and other foreign priests that strict limits on the Church's social role still exist.

Even the papal pilgrimage to Cuba seems to have been viewed by the regime as an opportunity to gain international sympathy. Immediately upon the pope's arrival in Havana, Castro delivered a welcome in which he tried to make it appear as if Cuban Communism and Roman Catholicism shared a common vision of social justice. John Paul II — knowing full well the record of brutal repression and continuing curtailment of religious freedom — was careful to distance himself from this clumsy embrace, preferring to point to other elements in Cuban history, culture, and religion that should lead to a more authentic care for the weak and freedom for all. Though he and the Cuban bishops have long condemned the U.S. embargo, they continue to press for an end to denials of basic human rights.

Large crowds turned out for the papal events, spurred both by quiet activity within the parishes and by the desire of the regime to present a favorable international face. The papal homilies contained several carefully worded calls for the opening up of Cuban society. The archbishop of Santiago de Cuba, the oldest see in the nation, felt emboldened to denounce people who claimed a monopoly on Cuban history and social space. These references were not lost on the people.

The papal visit also galvanized public ecumenical alliances. Prior to the visit, Catholics and Protestants in Cuba, like their counterparts elsewhere in Latin America, felt themselves in a kind of competition. Except for Protestant groups that have collaborated with the regime through an ecumenical council, Protestant congregations, stifled by the same discrimination as Catholics and lacking the Catholic Church's more substantial presence, have had to make do at the margins of Cuban society. Faced with a chance to present a united public witness of all of those "who confessed Christ as Lord," as one Baptist pastor put it during the papal visit, Protestants joined with Catholics in the public celebrations. The ground for this reconciliation had long been prepared. In the 1960s, many young Catholics and Protestants found themselves imprisoned together in the Military Units to Aid Production (UMAP), in reality concentration camps. Today, now older, they form the religious leadership of the island, among them Jaime Ortega, cardinal archbishop of Havana.

Though modest, even the small social opening has had explosive effects. In recent years there have been tens of thousands of baptisms, many of them among adults. Religious weddings, Confirmations, and First Communions have increased sharply. The Catholic and Protestant churches alike are growing in numbers. Though to date these indications of popular religiosity have led to little change in the way the government treats religion, they may suggest a far different future for Cuba after Castro's demise. But in the meantime, Cuba remains a sad and continuing reminder of a century of religious suffering throughout Latin America.

# -FOURTEEN-

# GENERAL INTRODUCTION TO THE ASIAN MARTYRS

POPE JOHN PAUL II visited New Delhi in November 1999 to promulgate a special document, *Ecclesia in Asia* ("The Church in Asia"), which lays out a vision of that continent and the Church's future there for the new millennium. It is a sign of the difficult situation that Catholics face almost uniformly throughout the vast Asian continent that Hindu and other Eastern religious protested and demonstrated during his visit. In all the largest Asian nations — China, India, Indonesia, and Pakistan — Catholics and other Christians, who are a minority in every Asian country but the Philippines, have been subjected to human rights violations, persecutions, and martyrdom. Even in the Philippines, Catholics died for their social witness under the Marcos dictatorship and, more recently, Muslim terrorists have killed many Catholics in outlying islands. The Muslim threat is so pervasive that, when John Paul II visited the nation in 1995, Cardinal Sin of Manila warned that the terrorists might pose a threat to his life.

Just a few months before the pope's visit, a hate campaign by Hindu fundamentalists led to riots that caused the murder of a Catholic, Father Arul Das, and a Muslim shopkeeper, Sheikh Rahman, on August 25, in the state of Orissa. Similar deaths and mob destruction of churches and mosques are, unfortunately, not uncommon in India. Even Mother Teresa of Calcutta is a controversial figure in this environment. Fundamentalist Hindu leaders associated with the Bharatiya Janata Party (BJP) and the Reshtriya Swayamsevak Sangh (RSS), a Hindu paramilitary organization, have attacked Christians they believe are thwarting their aims. In February 1995, for example, Sister Rani Maria was stabbed more than forty times in broad daylight and her body was mutilated by the BJP because she had helped Indians who disagreed with the party.[1] The previous year, three priests were savagely murdered and their church bombed in the south Chotanagpur region.[2] One priest was strangled and another disappeared around the same time. Early in 1995 five Franciscan nuns died near the border between Delhi and Ghaziabad.[3]

The month after the pope's visit, a group of Christian leaders met with Indian Prime Minister Atal Behari Vajpayee to seek the government's support for the rights of Christians and protection from the attacks of regional governments and unchecked crowds. Sister Dolores Rego, the general secretary of a Christian religious women's group that numbers seventy thousand members, told the prime minister that they were all committed to the people of India, but feared increasingly for their basic security. She had good reason. All Christians — and Muslims — in India might say the same. In Madhavan Madras, forty-four nuns at the Saint Anne's Convent have earned brown belts in karate to defend themselves against the burgeoning violence.[4]

In some ways, the Hindu reaction is understandable. Though India counts almost a billion people within its borders, it has at least twenty-five million Christians; and most Indians think of Christianity as a holdover from the British *Raj*. In fact, Christianity may have arrived in India earlier than it did in Britain. Legends suggest that India may have first been evangelized by the Apostle Thomas; Christianity did not come to England until centuries later. The special opposition to Christians, however, may stem from more than religious motives. Indian unity is not easy to maintain. When the British were withdrawing in the 1940s, Winston Churchill, a shrewd observer, remarked that India was not a nation but a geographical description. Language and culture vary a great deal from one region to another. Amid this ethnic diversity, Hinduism is one of the most important unifying elements. Though Hinduism and its offshoot Buddhism are often thought of as peaceful faiths, in fact they can inspire quite militant movements. Mahatma Gandhi himself was assassinated by a Hindu who thought the Indian leader was deviating from Hindu orthodoxy. The Hindu caste system discriminates sharply against certain social groups. The lower castes have been particularly responsive to the Christian teaching that all people are the children of God and equal before God.

But it is not only Hindus in India who react violently when some of their people are converted. In the mostly animist region of Assam, converts are often ostracized and forbidden to use village wells or graze their cattle on common grounds. Their own relatives may disown them. It is no surprise that matters sometimes go further. In the 1990s, three new Catholics were martyred in that region alone. Laria Simon Sutilal Bosumatary and his family were tried by their village and beaten for accepting a "foreign religion." When they would not recant, their house was invaded and all Christian objects destroyed. Other beatings followed. Finally, to put an end to the situation, some village leaders took Bosumatary out of town and cut his throat. Another convert, Muaya Binod Bernard Wary, had his head cut off. In the village of Kuntaibari, Maloti Mary Bosumatary was beaten to death and her body thrown into the Longa River.[5]

Many such conflicts are inevitable all across Asia in the years to come. Christianity is an evangelizing faith and, in India, the pope laid out a bold program for the Church in the new millennium: "Just as in the first millennium the Cross was planted on the soil of Europe, and in the second on that of the Americas and Africa, we can pray that in the Third Christian Millennium *a great harvest of faith* will be reaped in this vast and vital continent."[6] In his view, Asia stretches from the Middle East to the Pacific and this means that: "It was in fact in Asia that God revealed and fulfilled his saving purpose." The pope acknowledged that many Asians look on Christianity as a foreign Western import, but argued that like Judaism, Islam, and other world religions, Christianity took its rise within Asia itself. He called it "a mystery why the Savior of the world, born in Asia, has until now remained largely unknown to the people of the continent."[7] Yet for all his care in outlining the need for respectful dialogue with Asian philosophies, theologies, and cultures, and in pointing out that Jesus was close to the poor, the forgotten, and the lonely, it is clear that most Asian countries regard Christianity as a danger to be curtailed, sometimes for religious reasons, sometimes for political reasons.

Noting that believers in many Asian countries were bearing a heavy cross to the point of martyrdom, John Paul went so far as to recommend new institutional arrangements to ease their plight:

> I encourage the various national Episcopal Conferences in Asia to establish an office to help these Churches; and I pledge the Holy See's continued closeness to and concern for all those who are suffering persecution for their faith in Christ. I appeal to the governments and the leaders of nations to adopt and implement policies that guarantee religious freedom for all their citizens.[8]

After outlining various strategies for respectful evangelization, however, he notes, "in the end *it is martyrdom which reveals to the world the very essence of the Christian message.*"[9] John Paul himself seemed to recognize that the international instruments, however desirable in themselves, were not going to be of much avail against cultural and religious inertia and backlash for the foreseeable future, or even as important as the many, often unknown witnesses to the faith in Asian nations, whose numbers grow daily.

Persecution and martyrdom in Asia constitute a vast subject and, in a book such as the present, one that cannot be treated fully here. The following chapters examine three of the worst cases in the Asian continent: China, Korea, and Vietnam. In other deeply troubled countries such as Kampuchea, where genocide eliminated one million out of a population of seven million in 1975, Christian communities were among the hardest hit. Ninety percent of the Protestants and about a third of the Catholics died during the turmoil. Since Vietnam installed a puppet government there in 1978, the general situation has not improved for believers. But there are many smaller persecutions worth noting in Asia, some an indication of past problems, others ominous signs for the future.

In Pakistan, for example, the relatively small Christian community of two million, about 3 percent of the population, of which about two-thirds is Catholic, has been subjected to systematic repression and death. Pakistan became an independent nation in the 1940s when India, which had previously included the region now known as Pakistan, ended its long existence as a British colony under the leadership of Mohandas Gandhi. An overwhelmingly Islamic country, Pakistan clashed and continues to clash with largely Hindu India. Though created to secure religious security for its own population, the Pakistani government has not extended religious rights to non-Muslims. In fact, in 1986 Pakistan adopted a religious blasphemy law. Section 295.C of the new Penal Code declares: "Whoever by words, either spoken, or written, or by visual representation, or by any imputation, innuendo, or insinuation, directly, or indirectly, defiles the sacred name of the Holy prophet Muhammed (peace be upon him) shall be punished with death." Given the ease with which such a sweeping law can be abused, it made it all but inevitable that Christians would be condemned to death.

Trials, when they occur, are far from impartial or peaceful. In 1993, Salamat Masih, a twelve-year-old, and two other Christians were accused of having written a blasphemous slogan on a village mosque, even though all three were only semiliterate and were unlikely to have been able to write anything at all. During the course of their trial, they were attacked by an armed band. Salamat and one of his codefendants were wounded, and Manzoor Masih was killed. International pressure forced the Lahore High Court to overturn the conviction of the surviving youths. The judge who made the decision, Arif Iqbal Bhatti, was assassinated shortly after. The two young Christians went into exile, but they are marked men. Islamic fundamentalists have offered a $30,000 bounty for their deaths.[10]

This incident was only one of many such unfounded charges against members of Pakistan's Christian community. In February 1997, thirty thousand Muslims in the Punjab province burned and looted thirteen Catholic churches and a Salvation Army center. Christian schools, businesses, and homes were sacked. The village of Shantigar, with a mostly Catholic population of fifteen thousand, was destroyed. Police were slow to respond to reports of such illegal attacks by one group of citizens on another. Several Catholics were killed in the mob violence and John Paul II took the unusual step of sending a personal protest to the government. A public demonstration in the Pakistani capital, Islamabad, against the Shantigar violence only led to further arrests and beatings. Violent incidents occur almost daily. In May 1998, Ayub Masih was arrested merely for mentioning the controversial Islamic novelist Salman Rushdie — a charge he denied. But the blasphemy law makes it easy for anyone with a grudge against a Christian to bring unsubstantiated complaints that may lead to a mandatory death sentence. The prime minister of Pakistan has tried to deflect criticism of the nation's religious policies by claiming that the anti-Christian action is merely the application of *Shari'a,* or Islamic law.[11]

Perhaps the most blatant instance of Christian martyrdom in Pakistan occurred in May of 1997. John Joseph, bishop of Faisalabad and the first native Pakistani to run that diocese, died under suspect circumstances in front of a court building. Pakistani officials claimed later that the bishop had committed suicide out of protest against anti-Catholic repression. Suicide by a courageous Catholic bishop, who had advocated nonviolence, would, of course, have been an unorthodox way to protest. The bishop had already distinguished himself for his public defense of those condemned under the blasphemy laws. For that work, he had received multiple death threats. A night watchman at the court reported to police that he had seen a car pull up to the gate and two men throw out a body. Though he called the police, they did not arrive for two hours. The bishop's death evoked international outrage, but the Pakistani government has not carried out any credible investigation into the matter.

At Bishop John Joseph's funeral, Muslim mobs burned and looted Christian homes, and the police fired on the ten thousand people gathered to mourn his passing.[12]

The case of Pakistan is an important one because it reflects an emerging pattern in the Muslim world. Under the guise of religious law, Pakistan is making it all but impossible for Christians and other non-Muslims to find work. According to a Pakistani bishop, 90 percent of them are unemployed, and those who find jobs usually have to work at the most menial tasks such as street cleaning. They are discriminated against when they look for housing. The blasphemy law is merely the strongest weapon in the government's battles against non-Muslims. This type of forced Islamization is by no means accepted by all scholars of the Koran in the Muslim world. But some Muslim countries, under fundamentalist pressure, have even petitioned the United Nations to block the very use of terms such as "Islamization" to describe growing fundamentalist campaigns of religious purity that involve persecution and death.

Saudi Arabia, the homeland of Islam, is far more restrictive than Pakistan. Public Christianity is absolutely forbidden and, at least in theory, it is a punishable offense to say Christian prayers in your own home. When the Coalition Forces were stationed in Saudi Arabia during the 1991 Gulf War, for example, they were told they were not allowed to offer Christian prayers before battle. As elsewhere in the Islamic world, a Muslim who converts to Christianity is subject to the death penalty. Saudi Arabia has a large contingent of guest workers, almost a quarter of the population, many of whom are Catholics from the Philippines. Those caught trying to organize Christian services have been arrested and beaten; almost a thousand cases have been documented since 1990 alone.[13] But penalties can be far worse: flogging, amputation, and beheading. Oswaldo Magdanal and Renato Poesdio, two Filipinos, were scheduled for beheading on Christmas day 1992 until an international protest led to their deportation. Just before Christmas day 1999, another Filipino was arrested for having an English-language Bible in a locked cabinet at his workplace. Information on similar cases is difficult to come by in Saudi Arabia's carefully controlled society. But roughly equivalent abuses of rights occur throughout the Muslim Middle East in Kuwait, Qatar, Oman, and the United Arab Emirates. Even Turkey, the most secular and Westernized of the Islamic countries, still restricts open Christian practice, and converts from Islam may face death there. Turkey and Iran have also been trying to extend their influence into the mostly Islamic Central Asian Republics that have become independent since the breakup of the Soviet Union.

The world was horrified in 1999 by the slaughter of thousands of East Timorese as that small former Portuguese colony became independent from Indonesia, the world's largest Islamic nation. All sides were careful to avoid attributing any religious motive to the conflict, but that religion played a role in the massacres seems indisputable. The Indonesian government took no serious action to stop the murders of mostly Catholic East Timorese. Nor has it done much within its own traditional territories to protect minority Christians from an increasingly militant Muslim majority. Hundreds of Christians died in Indonesia in 1999 outside the East Timorese conflict. More than 170 Christian homes, churches, and other buildings have been burned. In a particularly bloody outburst of violence just days before Christmas 1999, at least forty-three Christians died in eastern Indonesia.[14] In the Spice Islands, several hundred Christians died in clashes with Muslims.

In many smaller and little studied Asian nations — from the Asian part of Turkey on the Bosphorous to the island archipelagoes in the South Pacific — the struggle between missionaries and local interests is constant. In the Far East, little noticed by the world at large, waves of missionaries have come out from the West with the intrepidity and bravery in facing dangers that distinguished the great missionary efforts in the sixteenth and seventeenth centuries. Many of these new initiatives are aimed at some of the poorest and most forgotten regions of the smaller Asian states. Far from being directed by crafty Western imperialists, the missions are often manned by young, idealistic men attracted to the work by a sometimes romantic notion of spreading the Good News, but also by a sincere love and enthusiasm. They often spend decades in remote rural areas largely unknown even to the rulers in the national capitals.

When Bangladesh proclaimed itself a new independent nation in 1971, for instance, the person chosen, even by Hindus and Muslims, to raise the flag in the Jonrail district for the first time was Father Angelo Rusconi, a priest of the Pontifical Institute for Foreign Missions (PIME).[15] The choice paid tribute not only to Father Rusconi's contributions to the people of Bangladesh, but to the many members of his order who had labored among a people virtually unknown to the world until several disasters, natural and man-made, brought them to international attention. Several had lived and died among the more than hundred million people of Bangladesh. Father Angelo Maggioni, for instance, the son of a desperately poor farming family in Italy, chose to become a missioner and work there. He was killed in 1972 by brigands after twenty-three years working in the area that became Bangladesh. Despite the religious rivalry that exists in the subcontinent, a Muslim high school teacher said at his death: "This priest of yours embodies what we Muslims have of sanctity. We are strong in faith, but rarely do we also achieve humility; he was able to blend those two qualities."[16] Such mutual admiration between Christians and Muslims in Asia may be more common at a personal level than the large-scale political forces and fundamentalist religious movements allow to appear.

But personal respect will have a hard time against entrenched social conditions throughout Asia in the new century. In Israel, historic Christian communities are slowly dying out, forced into exile by the conflict between Jewish Israelis and Muslim Palestinians. Across the Asian continent, fundamentalisms in several religions combine with national interests to produce a virulent mixture of anti-Westernism and anti-Christianity that will not dissipate any time soon. The Church has dealt with similar difficulties in the past and not only triumphed, but flourished because of the challenges. For the time being, however, John Paul's vision of the third millennium as the age of peaceful dialogue and evangelization of Asia remains a visionary hope indeed.

# -FIFTEEN-

# CHINESE CARNAGE

CHINA IS A MASSIVE COUNTRY, in terms of both land and population, with a long and rich cultural and political history and influence. Chinese art, food, poetry, and culture are much admired and studied around the world. For much of its history, however, China sought to keep outside influences at bay, regarding itself as cultivated and the outside world as barbarous, fit only to pay tribute to the Son of Heaven, the Chinese emperor. Its culture has been primarily shaped over the past twenty-five hundred years by Confucian philosophy and the religious movement known as Taoism. Buddhism gradually insinuated itself into some sectors of the vast Chinese social fabric and produced distinctive forms, as it did in Japanese Zen Buddhism. But China is also a place where Christianity has found fertile soil. An old legend claims that Saint Thomas the Apostle traveled to China and preached there. Though there is no solid historical evidence for this claim, the legend may be a popular recognition that Christianity discovered an opening in Chinese culture from the moment missionaries first found their way into the "Middle Kingdom."

The first documented appearance of Christianity in China dates back quite far, to the seventh century when a Nestorian monk from Syria took up residence in the Shensi province. Nestorius was the heretical patriarch of Constantinople who was deposed because he objected to the naming of the Virgin Mary as the Mother of God. For him, Jesus was God by descent from the Father and man by birth from Mary. The Councils of Ephesus and Chalcedon authoritatively proclaimed the constant orthodox understanding that Christ had two natures, human and divine, inseparably linked in one person. Nestorianism effectively disappeared from Europe in the fifth century. But China received several dozen Nestorian missionaries who founded monasteries and translated Christian texts into Chinese. Though both Christian and Buddhist monasteries were largely suppressed in the ninth century, they later recovered. Marco Polo discovered Nestorians in several parts of China at the end of the thirteenth century. Beginning around Polo's time, Europe began a serious second missionary effort. Maffeo and Nicolò Polo brought the pope a letter from Kublai Khan requesting that a hundred Catholic missionaries come to China. The Franciscans had some success, but with the advent of the Ming Dynasty (1368), Christianity was again suppressed, probably creating several martyrs, though we have no good information about this.

During the great period of Western missions, the Jesuit Saint Francis Xavier tried to enter China but died before he could do so. Other Jesuits, along with Dominicans, Franciscans, and Augustinians, also tried and failed to penetrate Ming China's xenophobia. But in the late sixteenth century, two remarkable Italians, Michele Ruggieri and Matteo Ricci, by careful study of the Chinese language and by respectful approaches through well-established cultural channels, impressed the cultivated Chinese with their own cultivation and learning. Ricci also amazed the Chinese scholars and rulers with prodigious feats of memory, which he was able to accomplish by a system of memorization he had invented.[1] The Chinese asked the Europeans for help in reforming their calendar, and experts arrived who presented the emperor with the requested information, raising the status of the Westerners still further. It took eighteen years before Ricci was allowed to go to the Chinese capital, Beijing. But by the time he died, this genius and tireless missionary had drawn twenty-five hundred to the Church. There were eighteen Jesuits active in his community — half of them native Chinese.

Other orders began to arrive, including a new one founded for just such purposes: the Paris Foreign Mission Society, which would contribute missionaries and martyrs to several countries in Asia and around the world. The natural affinities between the learned missionaries and the educated classes of China led to hundreds of conversions among the Chinese nobility and their households. It was unfortunate for both sides in this process, then, that the arrival of the Manchus in Beijing upset a growing interrelationship. At first, the Jesuit missionaries were highly valued for their learning; then, in a wave of suppression, they were arrested or exiled. In a turnaround, the Manchu emperor K'ang Hsi ordered toleration, and three hundred thousand Chinese had become Catholics by 1700. Then he changed his mind and a series of emperors persecuted the Church, going so far as to threaten death for preachers or converts. For the rest of the eighteenth century, China was a land of martyrs. The reasons for this were complex. In part, the religious were viewed, as they would be periodically in modern times, as representatives of Western imperialism, even though that had not been their primary role throughout centuries of Christian presence in China.

But the growing global power of Europe and the United States was confused with the Christian preaching for some Chinese leaders. Europe and America took the lead in convincing China to permit religious liberty in the second half of the nineteenth century. This came at a price. As periodic fits of anti-Westernism arose in modern China, not only the Europeans but all Christians, native-born Chinese as well as foreign missionaries, felt the reaction. China was painfully seeking for ways to reconcile its long past with the needs of the modern world. Such a vast and rich country naturally tried to find ways of playing a prominent role in the contemporary international order. Out of this political and social struggle, which provides the backdrop for much of what follows in these pages, many Catholic and Protestant martyrs were to come.

The heart of China's problem was the question of whether to adopt some Western ways as a means of competing with the Western powers or to expel Westerners and Western influence and pursue a purely Chinese path toward the future. Opinions varied among Chinese leaders. Ch'ing emperor Kwang Hsŭ took a moderate path of accepting some Western forms but of rejecting others. It was too late for a moderate path, however. In 1899, the *I Ho Ch'ŭan* (Chinese: "righteous fists"), or Boxers, a secret society opposed to foreign influence, began open rebellion. Despite their name, the Boxers often operated less as idealistic nationalists than as leaders of a kind of organized crime. Bosses claimed to be acting on behalf of China, but in fact frequently sought only to enrich themselves. As late as the 1920s, long after the period usually thought of as the Boxer Rebellion, the Boxers controlled several rackets. But in 1900, numbering around 140,000, the militants moved swiftly against Western enterprises in various regions, including the railroads, a symbol of foreign presence. They identified three main categories of enemies: foreigners in China; Christians, even if native-born; and Chinese merchants who dealt with foreigner merchants. An estimated thirty thousand Christians died, among them five bishops and several dozen priests.[2]

Typical of this group of martyrs was the PIME (Pontifical Institute for Foreign Missions) priest, Father Alberic Crescitelli from the Italian region of Campania, south of Rome. Like many European missionaries who went to work in the poorer regions of China, Crescitelli came from a relatively humble background himself. He worked his father's fields in Italy from about age fifteen until he decided to enter the seminary. In addition, Crescitelli's father and sister had died, buried by an earthquake in 1883, just after his ordination. Then cholera broke out and the young priest postponed his departure for the Chinese missions for four months to work with the sick in his home region. When he felt he had done all he could, he set out for China, where he spent nine months enduring "the intellectual torture of studying the Chinese language."[3] He was sent to the Sijiyang district on the Han River, where there were about a thousand Catholics distributed among seven villages. Then he was transferred to the mountainous area of Ningqiang.

Despite the Boxer uprising, he wrote home that he was safe, "unless something absolutely unforeseen should happen."[4] At that moment, the Boxers were training militants, attacking railroad and telegraph, and placing the blame for all problems in China on "the foreign devils." But Crescitelli was not involved in these events. His only complaint amid many hardships is that "the Chinese remain indifferent, if not directly hostile." The plight of many Chinese in the countryside — their goods exploited and lives disrupted by various political factions — attracted his attention. When famine ensued, the public granaries had already been looted by the militias. Help arrived from other provinces, but Chinese Christians were barred from receiving any aid. Crescitelli convinced the local mandarin that this discrimination was wrong.

Shortly thereafter, one of the factions in Beijing succeeded in obtaining an imperial decree that all Chinese Christians who will not denounce the faith should be killed and all foreign missionaries expelled. To his credit, the imperial viceroy in Shaanxi did not publicize this hateful message out of regard for fair treatment. But it became known through unofficial channels. The local mandarin whom Crescitelli had confronted began to plot how to eliminate him. Though the imperial decree ordered expulsion — not execution — for foreigners, the mandarin seems to have regarded the distinction as a legal technicality. Crescitelli's catechumens found out about the plot and counseled him to flee. A government customs official took him in at night, claiming that his home was the only safe place for the priest. In fact, the man was part of the plot. Crescitelli was driven outside, beaten, and then carried hanging from a pole by his hands and feet like an animal killed in a hunt. The next morning, soldiers dragged him to the river by rope and decapitated him. His dismembered body was thrown into the river. He has since been beatified.[5]

Father Crescitelli's fate was repeated many times in the two months that the Boxer's went on their rampage. Tens of thousands died, mostly in rural areas where the bulk of missionary activities were located. The

Franciscans paid a heavy price: Cesidio Giacomantonio, Bishop Antonio Fantosati, and Giuseppe Gambaro, vicar apostolic of Southern Hunan, were martyred. In Shansi, the Boxers eliminated a French and Italian community of women Franciscan Missionaries of Mary: Marie Hermine de Jésus, Maria della Pace, Maria Chiara, Marie de Sainte Nathalie, Marie de Saint Just, Anne François Moreau, and Marie Amandine. In line with their opposition to unrepentant native Chinese Christians, the Boxers also did away with the seminarians John Chang, Patrick Tung, John Wang, and Philip Chiang, together with a group of Chinese lay people who worked with them. All were beatified in 1946. Five thousand more Catholics died in similar circumstances in the Hopeh province, of whom fifty-six — four French Jesuits and fifty-two Chinese — were also beatified in 1951.[6] Twenty-five thousand more fell in various locations.

Though the Boxer persecution was heavy, it soon ended. Remarkably, the missionary activity and indigenous Chinese Church rebounded vigorously. At the beginning of the twentieth century, 886 missionaries were working in China. By the time of the Communist Revolution in 1949, despite other waves of persecution, they had increased to 4,415. Similarly, the communities of missionary nuns during the same period grew from ten to fifty-eight, and sixty-three native Chinese congregations of women, numbering 6,927 members, sprang up. The Catholic population of China grew from about three-quarters of a million to nearly four million.[7]

These figures are even more remarkable in light of the fact that severe persecution of the Church by several factions continued over that half century. Anti-Catholic violence swelled again during the Sino-Japanese war (1937–45). The Japanese had invaded Korea in 1910 and tried to stir up trouble for the Chinese in Mongolia and Manchuria. But they also created a dangerous atmosphere for Catholic missionaries, as Japanese invaders, nationalist Chinese, Chinese Communists, and bands of brigands operating within widespread disorder, each sought to advance their interests. Those interests were quite different from one another, but almost all the competing forces had reason, at times, to eliminate a Catholic presence. The Chinese Communists were the only ones to do so on ideological principles, but the other groups found multiple occasions to kill foreign and native Catholics.

Contrary to the claims of these groups and of charges outside China

about the role of the Church in Western "imperialism," most of the missionaries in China and their Chinese converts operated in remote rural
areas where they used great ingenuity to improve the basic day-to-day
existence of poor Chinese peasants. Perhaps no other area of the world
demanded so much from people who had been trained primarily as evan-
gelists, not as engineers, road builders, agriculturalists, or flood control
experts. PIME Father Cesare Mencattini provides a moving image of the
scene soon after he arrived in Shanghai:

> Immense populations live here in desolation and misery in re-
> gions which extend for hundreds of kilometers. We missionaries
> could not reach everyone, even if we had wings. We're limited to
> doing very little in comparison with the immense work there is
> to accomplish. The inhabitants of these areas are reduced to the
> most extreme poverty, the result of brigands' passing, war, and
> the flooding of the Yellow River. Along the roads you see groups
> of vagabonds, who don't even have a hole in which to spend the
> night nor sufficient clothes to guard against the cold, which is so
> intense here in Henan.[8]

And if the natural challenges were not enough, the political turmoil
added still others. In 1939, Father Mencattini described a rather typical
situation:

> The Chinese, so lacking in arms and unable to resist the Japanese,
> who advance with cannons and automobiles, have adopted this
> defensive tactic: they destroy all the roads.... Thousands of people
> have been commandeered for this immense work; night and day
> for two months, they have dug deep pits in the streets. The painful
> effort, which the people must put forth with no compensation, is
> more than you can imagine. There is the added danger of being
> surprised by the Japanese.[9]

These primitive measures were not very successful at stopping Japanese troop movements. Even when the Chinese forces succeeded, the
effects on the rural populations were disastrous: "The places once occupied by the Japanese and often abandoned because of their poor
condition, fall into the hands of the communists or other soldiers, or
brigands. The city of Huaxian has suffered this fate five times in one
year: occupied by regular [Chinese] troops, the Japanese, brigands, the
communists, and now once again the Japanese, who are quickly working
to rebuild it." But what the Japanese built, the Chinese felt obliged to

tear down: "After a voluntary retreat of the Japanese, when the Chinese take over the city again, everything is destroyed. Railway stations, city walls, everything must be reduced to heaps of rubble."[10]

For four years, this was the day-to-day situation of most Catholic missionaries in China. Father Mencattini several times found himself caught in the crossfire of the various parties, or sometimes deliberately targeted, only narrowly escaping. Two of his lay Chinese catechists had worse luck: they were abducted and decapitated. Still, he writes to his friends back home: "The opportunities for doing good are so great here! Many of the poor have no one else to help them. . . . We have no fear of death here. We would really be leaving nothing behind in this poor world. All of our strength, energy, and health must be dedicated to the Chinese, until we can do no more."[11] It is unfortunate that those, then and now, who see in the Christian missions nothing but Western imperialism are largely unaware of men like Father Mencattini.

As often happened in the chaos, this good priest met his end almost by chance. A band of Chinese regular army troops took charge of the town of Qimen, where Father Mencattini and Fathers Angelo Bagnoli and Leo Cavallini happened to be celebrating Mass and working with the people. Another military faction under the command of a local mandarin named Rencun arrived shortly after. For no known reason, the latter group concealed themselves near the town market and then opened fire on the priests. Father Mencattini was seriously wounded, but died only after being bayoneted. Then the soldiers stole everything from the body and buried it. Strangely, the other two priests, also wounded, were not killed. One told the troops that they were Christian missionaries and received the reply: "We know." Perhaps to make an example of them, the soldiers put the two wounded men in an open pagoda where they would be visible, but forbade anyone from going near them on pain of death. Their lives were saved because a Christian with local influence happened to hear about the incident and was able to get the two priests released to a hospital.[12]

Though the large Communist persecutions would reach their peak only after the Red Army took control of the country in the late 1940s, they began much earlier. Father Antonio Barosi, who would later become bishop of Kaifeng, the capital of the Henan province, felt the anti-Catholic wrath of the Communists in July of 1927. That summer, seventy thousand disorderly Communist soldiers invaded Henan shouting "death to the foreigners" and introducing Communist propagandists to indoctrinate the people. Their stated aim was to "save the homeland," but Barosi observed that "it is all too clear that they are really out to enrich themselves and win some fame." A severe famine struck the following year, and the Communists did little to help. The mission Barosi was overseeing had to find food and shelter for over a hundred people. Over the next fourteen years, he did remarkable work in building up the moral and physical infrastructure as various occupiers came and went, leaving the usual destruction in their wake.

Virtually without outside support, Father Barosi built schools, provided relief to the poor, and even started to erect a cathedral. At one point, his dispensaries were treating three hundred refugees, sick, and wounded a day. As his talents became known, in a region "about half the size of Lombardy," he directed various construction projects made necessary by the general poverty, periodic flooding, and the ravages of war: "As you can imagine, I have to be an engineer, an architect, and a laborer too. Here you become well versed in all fields. . . . The day begins at 4:00 in the morning and ends at 10:00 at night. And I'm not even mentioning the excursions and trips that have to be done."[13] It was his remarkable success in these demanding tasks that led to his appointment as successor to Henan bishop Giuseppe Tacconi, a forty-five year veteran of the missions, in 1940.

In November of 1941, Bishop Barosi and three other priests — Fathers Mario Zanardi, Bruno Zanelli, and Girolamo Lazzaroni — journeyed to the city of Dingcunji to perform Confirmation. The ceremony went on normally, and the clerics, the confirmed people, and their relatives went their separate ways afterward to lunch. Without warning, a local official appeared with a small platoon of soldiers. After imposing a kind of curfew on the town, the soldiers confronted the priests and accused them of being "spies of the enemy and agents of capitalism." Nothing in the previous lives of the four could be even remotely described in such terms. But Bishop Barosi and Father Zanelli were tied up and their mouths stuffed with paper. Then the atrocities began.

Father Zanelli was forced to drink boiling oil and water poured out from large containers. He may have died then, or afterward when his body was thrown into a well. No witnesses saw what happened to the other three. The soldiers departed at evening by boat as a cold rain began to fall. The townspeople at first believed that the priests had been taken hostage. But when they looked around, they noticed a well that had been closed with debris. Using bamboo poles, they retrieved, one by one, the bodies of Barosi, Zanelli, and Zanardi. It was not until the next morning that they also found Lazzaroni's body in the well. By all indications, he had been buried alive. They all had spent several years in the Chinese missions, Barosi, the senior among them, sixteen of his forty years of life.[14]

The early Communist persecutions were aimed at whole communities as well as individuals. In July 1947, for example, the Cistercian monastery at Yang Kia Ping with eighteen monks experienced the growing boldness of the Communist forces after the retreat of the Japanese. The monastery was invaded and a judicial process begun against all the inhabitants. Special attention was devoted to two native Chinese Cistercians, Fathers Seraphim and Chrysostom, who represented the future of the community. The monastery was sacked by mobs who destroyed all the vestments and the library. The church was converted into a courtroom and a formal process began.

From the outset, it was clear what the outcome of the "trial" would be. All the monks who had glasses had them removed. Each was ordered to plead guilty to various charges and, when they refused, were beaten without mercy. Father Seraphim was charged with being a Japanese spy. Maria Chang, a catechist called as a witness to confirm the charges in public, instead pleaded that all the monks were innocent. She was beaten so severely for making this truthful statement that she was left for dead, but survived. Not wishing to give an opportunity for any more "witnesses" to disrupt the proceedings, the court had the monks stripped of their belts and scapulars and bound. During the night, they were given loads to carry and marched for twenty-four hours through the mountains. Two aged Cistercians, Brothers Bruno and Clement, died from the ordeal.

After a brief respite, the survivors were driven through bad weather another hundred miles over the mountains to Ta Lung Men, near the Great Wall, and then up a steep incline toward a village. Father William Camborieu, who had earlier been imprisoned by the Japanese, fell when the person who was helping him walk slipped. The priest bled to death from his wounds. Father Stephen Maury, being carried in a litter by the other monks, followed him. A Canadian, Father Alphonsus, perished after being separated from his brethren owing to illness. But his end was not entirely terrible. The guard who found him told the monks that "he died peacefully. He looks like the man on the figure-ten frame [i.e., the cross] in your church." The other brothers found his body in a Christ-like pose.

At the village of Teng Chia Yu, the interrogations, beatings, and brainwashing started again. Brothers Aloysius, Bartholomew, Conrad,

Jerome, and Mark died from the mistreatment. Buried in shallow graves, their bodies were dug up and eaten by wild dogs and wolves. In the meantime, the guards taunted those still living with the news that their monastery had been burned to the ground.

But even this humiliation was not enough for their captors. Father Seraphim was bound in an awkward way with wire. Father Chrysostom was confined in a pig sty. Mistreatment produced two more martyrs: Father Anthony Fan, the prior, and the French priest Augustine Faure. Death came quickly after that. The Dutch priest Aelred Drost died. Then the guards speeded the process. Fathers Seraphim and Chrysostom first had their heads crushed with large stones, then cut off. Brother Alexis Liu, Damian Hang, Eligius Sui, and John Miu were shot on February 5, 1948. Thirty-three people from the monastery disappeared, a number of them whose fates are unknown.[15]

Similar events occurred all over China during the 1940s. It is impossible, given the closed nature of the Communist regime since its creation, to reconstruct all of them at present. Which of the actors — Japanese, Communists, irregular nationalists, or simple brigands — did the most damage would also be difficult to determine. All of them, by design or inattention, were responsible for many unjust deaths among the common people, Chinese Christians, and Catholic and Protestant missionaries.

One example of the odd combinations of circumstances that led to martyrdom in China is the case of Swiss Father Maurice Tornay, whose cause for beatification had been underway since 1953 and whom John Paul II declared "Martyr of the Faith" on July 11, 1992. Tornay, a member of the Congregation of Saints Nicholas and Bernard of Mont-Joux, died in an ambush among the high mountains near "the roof of the world" on the border between China and Tibet in 1949 at the age of thirty-nine. Tibetan armed Lamas, who had kept Tornay under close surveillance, attacked the caravan in which he was traveling, deliberately seeking to eliminate the priest. He had spent the thirteen previous years as a missionary in the Chinese area of Yunnan, just south of Tibet.

Tibet was an independent nation from 1912 until the Communist Chinese victory. As a center of Buddhist monasticism and seat of the Dalai Lama, it claimed the right to self-governance. By the end of the twentieth century, it was one of the most prominent international instances of religious repression. The Dalai Lama himself has become a highly visible exponent of religious tolerance since his experiences of Communist oppression and the harsh treatment of his people. But in the 1940s, threatened by the Red Chinese, the Tibetan Lamas feared Father Tornay's influence. Ironically, the region in which he died was filled with signs meant to remind travelers of the omnipresence of the Compassionate Buddha. *Chorten* — towers in which a cube, a sphere, and a cone were piled up symbolizing the Buddha — dotted the landscape. So, too, did *mani*, stones usually engraved with the Sanskrit prayer *O mani padme oum,* "O may I achieve perfection and be absorbed by the Buddha. Amen."[16]

Tornay walked through these monuments reciting prayers of his own, saying Mass, the rosary, and the breviary in between the necessary work of the caravan. As the group picked its way across a high mountain pasture, officials from the Karmda lamasery, apparently alerted by an informant, were combing the area with an arrest warrant for the priest "to finish once and for all, with this intruder, the missionary and man of God."[17] Tornay had come by an odd route to face such hatred.

Born the seventh of eight children in the Swiss village of La Rosiere, among peaks that almost rivaled those of Tibet, Tornay had early learned the various crafts of poor mountain life: milking cows, making cheese, butter, and wine, taking care of the crops and, his favorites, the animals. Tornay did not hesitate at spending nights alone to help with the work of his poor family during bad weather in mountain huts at altitudes over six thousand feet. Though he was by all accounts bright, energetic, imaginative, playful, headstrong (bordering on pugnacious) but still somehow kind, he was also the most pious boy his teachers had ever seen.[18] All these qualities were to serve him well in his future vocation. Informed that being a priest and a martyr were among the highest callings, he determined to become both.

Delayed from beginning higher education by his work on behalf of his family, Tornay did not enter the College of the Abbey of Saint Maurice until he was fifteen. But he was like a force of nature there for the next six years. Any difficulties he encountered in his seminary work paled in comparison with the work he had done in his family. He was first in every subject and at various times impressed the superiors as capable of becoming almost anything, including a doctor or lawyer. The local doctor thought his determination so great that Tornay could complete the medical course in a year. But the Novice Master reports that Tornay's constant question was "What must I do to become holy?" and that Tornay was ready to obey orders on that urgent quest.[19]

A chance for a heroic life arose when Pius XI, an enthusiastic mountain climber before his election as pope, caught fire about the idea of a Tibetan mission in conversations with missionaries. He encouraged communication between the Paris Foreign Mission Society and Tornay's abbey. It was a natural step for Tornay to volunteer. Though he had not yet finished his studies for the priesthood, no one thought of this as an obstacle. In fact, one of his superiors wrote to the Tibetan mission: "As for his formation, do not be anxious. He is a chosen subject and could work on his own. You can count completely on his tenacity."[20] This opinion proved accurate: Tornay successfully continued his studies while learning Tibetan and Chinese as well as carrying out astonishing pastoral activity. He was later ordained in Hanoi.

It was almost a foregone conclusion that such an energetic priest would run afoul of the local authorities. While the Tibetan capital, Lhasa, had often protected the religious freedom of the missionaries, the local Lamas were feudal lords and virtually slave masters over the local populations. They resented any threat to their monopoly of power. Though the Lamas were religious leaders as well as political figures, they also usually practiced magic, witchcraft, and other forms of superstition, along with extortion. Tornay and the missions upset this profitable existence in several ways: they bought land and did not allow themselves to be dictated to; they educated children and adults to draw them away from superstition; and, even given large material interests among the local population to remain Tibetan Buddhists, they drew people away from Buddhist belief. There were quite a few Tibetans and local Chinese who were attracted by what the mission had to offer.

In addition, the area was in turmoil, as were other parts of China, from the various military forces already mentioned. In the disorder left by the retreating Japanese, wolves came into the missions and carried off pigs. Brigands arrived, looted, and left. In 1940, the Lamas killed ten missionaries in an effort to get control of the areas in which they worked. Gun-Akio, the Lama in power near Tornay's mission, took a more and more belligerent stance toward him. He ordered the priest to vacate his land. Father Tornay replied that he would leave only if carried away tied up like an animal. Gun-Akio had to be cautious since the Swiss and French governments had delegations in Lhasa, and the Tibetan government wished to have good relations with the Europeans.

Tornay finally decided that the only way to end the harassment was to go to Lhasa to plead his case, a difficult journey for physical reasons, but also because it entailed passing through land controlled by the Lamas.

It was a brave step, but under the circumstances, his chances of success were slim. Gun-Akio could not risk Tornay's turning the Dalai Lama against him or curtailing his powers. Instead, he bribed various traveling companions of Tornay's to keep him informed about the priest's whereabouts. It would only take patience to wait for the right moment to strike. On a very steep slope near a town called Thotong, Gun-Akio's men jumped up and opened fire. Father Tornay had repeatedly said: "If the stem bears the flower for too long, the fruit cannot ripen before the cold and death approach." He had made an early sacrifice.

The subsequent history of Tibet is well known. The Lamas were helpless against the advance of massive Chinese forces. The Dalai Lama was driven into exile in India, and Tibetan independence was destroyed. The remaining Christian missionaries were transferred first to Hong Kong and ultimately to Taiwan. In the 1980s, during a period of relaxation, the Communists allowed some of the missionaries back to examine their former post. The heroic efforts of Father Tornay and many others resulted in a small concession. The Communist Office of Religious Affairs gave official recognition to the small Christian communities on the Tibetan border, not out of any love for the work but hoping to get international credit for religious liberty.[21]

But these small concessions have to be viewed in light of the widespread persecutions unleashed by the Communist Revolution under Mao Tse-tung in China.[22] The severity of the Chinese Communist persecutions may be gauged from the testimony of an interesting witness. Father Robert Juigner, of the venerable Paris Foreign Mission Society, was still a young man (only thirty-four), when he was arrested in China and sentenced to deportation in 1952. Juigner had spent a year and a half in a Nazi concentration camp during World War II and had the misfortune of passing another three months in a Chinese Communist prison after becoming a missionary in China. The young priest was subjected to vigorous attempts at brainwashing intended to convince him of the truth of Communism and the falsehood of his previous beliefs. Every day he endured four hours of "instruction" in Marxism-Leninism; in the evenings, for two hours, he and his fellow prisoners were forced to make "confessions" and "self-accusations" of past "errors." Needless to say, these sessions had little effect on a man who had already braved the terrors of Hitler. When his captors threatened not to release him until he "converted," Father Juigner simply stated: "Keep me here twenty or thirty years, if you like. But you might just as well execute me straight away, because I shall never become a Communist."[23]

Juigner's protests that he had never done anything illegal, even under Chinese Communist law, were of no avail. To up the ante, the jailers put a leper into the cell with him and the other prisoners. Instead of recoiling in horror, as the others did, Juigner treated the man with kindness and tried to comfort him. Guards and prisoners alike were astonished by this. When it became clear that Juigner would never submit to forced conversion, the authorities decided to pretend they had succeeded: "You have followed a course of indoctrination, so that now you know that you are a wicked sinner, who has spoken and worked against the Chinese Communists. Now we are going to punish you more severely by banishing you from China. Begone!" This political excommunication did not faze Juigner: "I was a prisoner in the hands of the Germans for eighteen months. But they never treated me like this, and above all they did not try to make me believe in Nazism. You, on the other hand, want to convert us all to Communism by force."[24] Juigner was "punished" by being sent to Hong Kong.

What might be called the "missionary" nature of Chinese Communism is one of the strangest elements in its makeup. The Chinese Communists attempted, as perhaps no other totalitarian system in the twentieth century, not only to control, but to convert those who resisted it. The Communist Chinese emphasis on anti-imperialism and ideological purity, however, was singular not only for its vehemence but for its fundamental self-contradiction. It is entirely understandable that a people, or some portion of it, would decide to reject outside influences as foreign or imperialistic. The Chinese Communists viewed Christians in particular and Westerners more generally in those terms. The self-contradiction arose, however, when they turned to Marxism — itself a Western ideology drawing heavily on German idealistic philosophy and Marx's interpretation of Europe's experience of industrialization — as an antidote to alleged European imperialism. Marxism was as foreign to Chinese culture as Christianity and, given the Church's long history in China and its indigenous adherents, even more so. In addition, Marxism in the twentieth century led to no small imperialism and hegemony of its own, even as it professed anti-imperialism. The Chinese Communists had put themselves into a badly confused and self-defeating position.

But incoherence notwithstanding, they pursued their mission with a vengeance. If it was convenient for them to expel a figure like Father

Juigner on occasion, more often they imposed far more diabolical penalties. The Soviet Union had made psychiatry an instrument of repression and had occasionally used psychological measures to try to break recalcitrant religious believers. The Chinese Communists, in both the Chinese mainland and in conquered North Korea, used psychological measures in a far more systematic way. They seem to have felt a need to convince themselves that resistance to Communist truth could be overcome by the right combination of physical and mental tortures, thus proving that the vaunted virtues of believers were illusory. At a later stage, they might content themselves with driving believers into the Patriotic Church controlled by Beijing. But in the beginning they wanted, more typically, to turn them into Communists, or drive them to madness or suicide.

That intention may have reflected their worry about the moral influence the Church already had, even though Catholics remained a small percentage of the Chinese population. In 1948, the number of native Chinese priests was beginning to approach that of the foreign missionaries: 2,676 Chinese compared to 3,015 foreigners. In training were 924 Chinese in the major seminaries and 2,705 in minor seminaries.[25] Absent persecution during the twentieth century, Chinese Catholicism would have quickly become a basically indigenous movement. Native Christians were most numerous where the Church missions had been present longest: Mongolia (the Scheut Fathers), Beijing (Lazarists), Hopeh and Kiansu (Jesuits), Shantung, Shansi, and Shensi (Franciscans), and Manchuria and the Southeast (Paris Foreign Mission Society).[26] Several of the most prestigious educational institutions were headed by Chinese Catholics and Chinese bishops were common. In the rural districts, Christianity was penetrating slowly and, as a result, was still largely dependent on foreign missionaries.

The Communists struck hard at both foreign and native Christians, however exemplary their contributions to the Chinese people. One of the most distinguished figures among the early martyrs was Kaying Bishop Francis Xavier Ford. Father Ford had been the first student at Maryknoll and the first Maryknoller to be sent abroad. From 1918 until 1950, he worked in China. Among his other firsts, he was one of the first bishops to be rounded up by the Communists. Ford was subjected to torture and brainwashing for eleven months, which left him so dazed he was uncertain about his own identity. According to reports, he had to pinch himself and repeated to himself, "My name is Francis Xavier Ford, My name is Francis Xavier Ford."[27] Several people caught glimpses of him tied up or being dragged to and from interrogations. He died in unknown circumstances in February 1952; news of his death leaked out only about six months later.

The German Franciscan Cyrill Jarre spent over forty-five years as a missionary in China, ending his life as archbishop of Tsinan. Seventy-four when he was arrested in 1952, he died without the sacraments after several illnesses that his jailers did not treat. In reply to their nagging questions, he said: "My answer will come to you from the tomb." His words were prophetic. An enormous crowd attended his funeral. The archbishop's body was dressed in red, the color, the police were informed, of martyrs. They ordered the body to be disinterred and the clothing changed to white. During the reburial, the people jostled each other in search of relics.[28] Jarre shared the early martyr's crown with two other foreign bishops, Scheut Father Leon de Smedt and Paris Foreign Mission Society Alexandre Carlo.

The Communists were somewhat less murderous toward native Chinese bishops, apparently because they wanted to use them to set up a Patriotic Church independent of the Vatican. Archbishop of Nanchang Joseph Chow Chi-Shih, a gifted and cultured man, was offered the chance to become "pope of China" by the Communists. He replied that if they thought him worthy of such a position that he preferred "to be pope of the whole world." His flippancy did not endear him to the authorities. He was arrested and subjected to two months of indoctrination aimed at brainwashing him into thinking that an independent church would not be in schism with Rome. Under pressure to break off political relations with the Vatican, the archbishop adamantly denied that such political relations existed.[29] He was imprisoned and died in January 1977.

The most eminent figure among the Chinese hierarchy, however, was a man who belongs among the honored names of other well-known prelates such as Cardinals Mindszenty, Wyszyński, Stepinac, and Slipyi, who heroically resisted persecution in the twentieth century: Ignatius Kung, bishop of Shanghai. Kung was born in that city in 1901. His family could trace Catholic roots back five generations, and its adherence to the faith may go back even further. His obvious talents led to his appointment as headmaster of several distinguished Catholic schools while he was still a young man. When he was made bishop of Soochow in 1949, students and teachers lamented his departure. It was only to be expected that such a man would be appointed bishop of Shanghai, an important center for Catholicism in China, which occurred the next year.

The early 1950s witnessed the most savage attack by the Communists on the Church. It is clear that they regarded bishop Kung as one of their principal religious opponents. In addition to being Bishop of Shanghai, Kung was apostolic administrator of Soochow and Nanking, and he put considerable energy and ingenuity into building up Catholic resistance in all three cities. In China, the Legion of Mary had been a major force for religious formation and expression. Kung made it even more so. The government responded by outlawing the Legion under the pretext that it was a spy network. Members either had to declare themselves as such and register with the Public Security Bureau or face government action. Kung counseled them not to register and hundreds were given long sentences at hard labor.

Hundreds more were arrested with Bishop Kung in 1955 after his further defense of the rights of Catholics against the impositions of the regime. Kung would pay a great price for his courage. For the next thirty years he would be held incommunicado. It was only during a visit to China by Philippine Cardinal Jaime Sin that the by then aged bishop's courage appeared again to the outside world. He was allowed to attend a banquet given by the state in Sin's honor. But the two were seated at opposite sides of the room and not allowed to talk. In fact, the banquet was mostly quiet, even for those who were free to speak, and Sin, a brave man himself, proposed that he and Kung each sing a song to liven things up. In one of the most notorious acts of fidelity and boldness in a century of horrors, Kung rose and sang out the hymn, *Tu es Petrus et super hanc petram aedificabo Ecclesiam meam,* the Latin words of Christ's giving of the Keys of the Kingdom to the first pope, "You are Peter and upon this rock I will build my Church." One of the bishops from the Patriotic Church informed the Chinese officials about what was happening, but it was too late. Cardinal Sin was able to report to the outside world that Kung had not only survived three decades in Chinese prisons, but had done so with his faith still fully intact.

Kung was allowed to leave China in 1987. In Rome, he met with John Paul II, who told the elderly Chinese bishop that he had made him a secret cardinal, *in pectore* as the Latin form puts it, in 1979. Four years later, the pope announced the fact to the world. In exile in the United States, Cardinal Kung set up a foundation that, throughout the 1990s and into the new millennium, was dedicated to publishing the truth about Chinese persecution and helping to support those still faithful to their beliefs who remained in the People's Republic.

From the time he became bishop until the end of the century, the plight of believers in China has been a story of almost unrelieved misery. Kung had witnessed himself, and presided over the funeral Mass for Jesuit Father Bede Tsang in 1951. Tsang was one of the most cultivated men of the Church in his native Shanghai, having studied in Paris and taken a doctorate in literature at the Sorbonne. He had been appointed dean of the Faculty of Literature at the prestigious Catholic institute of higher learning, the Aurora University in Shanghai, and was one of the most prominent Catholics in the city.[30] When the Communists took over, one of their first aims was to get the Church leaders to submit to Party control. This took the form of pushing for the so-called "Three-Self," or Triple Autonomy, Movement. Believers in China, Catholic and Protestant, were expected to detach themselves from all foreign influence by recognizing no authority abroad (especially the pope), accepting only native-born priests and catechists, and relying solely on local contributions. The Communists propagandized that only these three measures would guarantee true "freedom of religion," since they would allegedly free the Chinese from imperialism.

Father Tsang opposed these steps in the public meeting held to ratify them. He argued that neither authentic Church teaching nor his own personal views would in any way detract from patriotism toward China. After that he was a marked man. The police arrested him on August 9, 1951. At first, they tried to bribe him with the usual offer: he could become the head of the "Reformed" Church in Shanghai. When he refused, they resorted to more brutal means of persuasion. Within a month, he was lying in a coma in a prison hospital. But it was too late for medicine to save him. The authorities claimed he had died from natural causes. But his brother, a doctor, examined the body, which was merely thrown on the floor in a room and so disfigured that he could only confirm its identity from dental records. During Bishop Kung's funeral Mass for Tsang, the choir sang verses from the Sermon on the Mount (Matt. 5:11) in Latin, "Blessed are you when they insult you and persecute you and utter every kind of falsehood against you because of me." Similar ends came to Father Matthew Su, Peter Sun (provincial of the Lazarists in North China), Father Joseph Seng, Father Michael Chang, Father Vincent Shih (a Trappist who was hung for six days straight by his wrists), among many other native and foreign born clerics.

Harsh punishments also touched Bishop Kung's own family. Maria Kung Chu, Cardinal Kung's niece, was arrested in September of 1958 and spent twenty-one years in Communist prisons for refusing to join the so-called Patriotic Church.[31] She was not arrested in the initial strike against the Shanghai Church in September of 1955, but she, like the other Catholics in Shanghai, was subjected to brainwashing aimed at making her denounce the Church as antirevolutionary. Those who did not do so were denied access to the university or lost jobs with little hope of finding others in the party-dominated economy. Prison was usually added to the penalties. We know of her story because she was able to escape to the United States in 1979. Her story, however, may be taken to represent similar treatment of perhaps tens of thousands of Chinese martyrs and confessors, who have disappeared without a trace since the 1940s.

Given the deep commitment of the Kung family and many others to God, which they viewed as entailing loyalty to the head of Christ's Church in Rome as well, Maria Kung's fate was virtually decided in advance. Hoping for a university degree and a chance to make a significant contribution to Chinese society, she had her application denied because of her religious background. The priests who still remained at large and many lay people crumbled under terrible pressures, leaving the faithful remnant virtually without support. Confessions were heard by the few priests at large walking in parks, Masses were held furtively, and sermons were distributed secretly. Maria participated often in the few remaining bits of authentic Catholicism.

But state surveillance was everywhere. A spy who had infiltrated clandestine Catholic circles reported on various individuals in the movement, who were not engaged in anything remotely political. But on May 28, 1958, Maria Kung's house was broken into by members of the Patriotic Church, and she was dragged off to a propaganda meeting. She prayed the rosary while others shouted at her and abused her for three days. In those early hours, she decided that to renounce the pope would be to renounce Christ, and she steeled herself for the prison camps that she knew would be her punishment for her beliefs. She was arrested three months later at age twenty-two.

Her first cell was a filthy, smelly hole with about sixteen people crammed into a small, dark space. For discussing the faith with other Catholics she found there, Maria was assigned to a cage. She was sentenced a few months later to eight years imprisonment for "counter-revolutionary activities." Work in the camps was numbing — eighteen hours a day, seven days a week. Two Catholic friends died after a brief period; others were beaten and hung from the ceiling. Indoctrination was constant. Maria was a special target for the brainwashers because of her uncle and her adamant refusal to admit to having committed any crime. Her sentence was scheduled to end just around the time that Chairman Mao began his "Cultural Revolution," which would destroy many remnants of traditional Chinese culture and prevent people from practicing others.

She was not released at the end of her sentence, but transferred to a less rigorous labor camp. Nonetheless, life became harder for her in the atmosphere of the Cultural Revolution. When she refused again to admit to any crime during an interrogation session, half her hair was cut off and her arms tied behind her in a way that produced excruciating pain at the slightest movement. After the session, she was handcuffed, day and night, for the next hundred days. Fellow prisoners who even made a sign toward her paid for it. "Everyone was encouraged to insult me," she recalled. Her tormentors blasphemed and used foul language about God and the Church. Too upset even to cry, she hoped added burdens would put an end to her misery and prayed for death. She was too distressed to sleep. Her condition was so unbearable that this heroic woman, who had decided to die rather than renounce God, candidly confesses she began to feel impatience that God allowed her trials to go on so long. Her only place of refuge was a latrine so foul that when she was there no one would bother her.

Transferred to a third camp, she was made to pick tea and vegetables and sometimes to carry burdens of firewood weighing as much as one hundred pounds. She found she liked these tasks, despite their burdensome nature, because at least she was free of abuse outside the camp and in the open air. The future promised nothing besides more of the same. But grace of a sort found her in these seemingly hopeless circumstances. She ran into Joseph Chu, a Catholic she had known many years earlier and who had been imprisoned for the same reason she had. His family, too, were staunch Catholics; all seven of his brothers had, at varying times, been imprisoned for the faith as well. The two decided to marry secretly. Francis Chu, one of Joseph's brothers, who as a Jesuit priest had been imprisoned in another camp, performed the ceremony (Francis later died in the camps). Before long, Maria received word from her brother, then living in the United States, that U.S. authorities had approved her request to emigrate. But she and Joseph would both need passports, and it was extremely unlikely that two would be issued together.

A letter writing campaign from the United States on their behalf initially failed. In 1978, relations between Communist China and the United States were normalized, and, the following year, after over three years of trying, the couple were granted passports. On September 5,

1979, they walked into Hong Kong and shortly thereafter flew to New York City. Since then, they have worked at exposing the lack of press coverage, concern by Western governments, and outrage by many Catholics themselves, over the ongoing persecution of the Church in China. The Communist Chinese government, they have argued, has little fear that anything they do against the Church will lead to unfavorable economic or political consequences on the part of the free world. As a result, the regime continues to deal however it wishes with any religious resistance.

By the 1990s, Human Rights Watch Asia had assembled a carefully researched list of over a thousand religious people imprisoned in China and Tibet. Hundreds more are listed, though little is known of their whereabouts.[32] Many, no doubt, are suffering under the system of *laojiao,* forced labor aimed at "reeducation." In some regions, owing to the views of local officials, religious activities are tolerated if they keep a low profile. But the standard government policy is to regulate publications and even seminary studies — reminding all religious institutions that they exist only at government sufferance. Catholicism is officially banned because of its connection with the "foreign" authorities in the Vatican. Only the Patriotic Catholic Church, subservient to the government, is officially recognized.

The Vatican, however, takes a less absolute approach to the situation. While maintaining that only churches in full communion with Rome should be the norm, and supporting the underground Church, the Holy See recognizes some of the clerics in the Patriotic Church. But the Chinese treatment of unrepentant Roman Catholics remains harsh. Following the 1989 pro-democracy demonstrations in Tiananmen Square, the government cracked down hard against all resistance. The success of Polish Solidarity and John Paul II against Communism in Eastern Europe scared the Chinese leaders. One of the most prominent Catholic leaders still alive in China, Bishop Fan Xueyan, died on April 13, 1992, while in police custody, one day before his prison sentence was to expire. Bishop Su Zhimin was released in 1993 after fifteen years of prison and torture. Some voices in the West have spoken of a relaxation of control in light of international dialogue with the Chinese about religious liberty. But the reality of such an opening is doubtful. In 1996, Bishop Su himself was arrested again. And since 1996 the regime has cracked down hard on "house churches," destroyed churches and temples, and repressed any activity not officially recognized. As usual, the Communists claim that such arrests are for political, not religious, reasons. Liu Bainan, a member of the Standing Committee of the Catholic Patriotic Association, has gone so far as to claim that, since the Cultural Revolution, no one has ever been arrested in China for religious reasons.[33] China's stringent "one-child policy" has also struck hard at Catholics who do not believe in the morality of birth-control and abortion. Catholic women have been taken from their homes and forced to have abortions. Coerced sterilization is a common practice.

Yet in spite of all pressures, religion — not least Christianity — flourishes among the Chinese. In 1999, members of a new cult, the Falun Gong, claimed ten million members and were brutally suppressed by the government. Accurate figures for all denominations are difficult to come by, but the government estimates that there are twenty-five million Christians — a large percentage of them Protestants suffering persecution similar to the Catholic persecution — in the country. Independent estimates hazard the guess that there may be as many as a hundred million, several million of them Communist party members who quietly worship on the side. Paul Marshall, one of the most reliable scholars of religious persecution at the end of the twentieth century, believes that "there are more Christians attending regular church worship services in China than there are in all of Western Europe combined."[34] If true, this means that the martyrs and confessors in China may ultimately prevail in the struggle with Communist repression. China has the largest population of any nation, and what happens there will largely determine how many martyrs will be produced in the early part of the new millennium. Though some signs are promising, the odds are that, for the foreseeable future, China will continue to be the preeminent land of Christian martyrs in the world.

# -SIXTEEN-

# KOREA'S DEATH MARCH

**K**OREA IS A HIGHLY MOUNTAINOUS PENINSULA situated among the political and cultural influences of China, Japan, and Eastern Siberia. To its own people, it is known as *Chosŏn*, "The Land of the Morning Calm," perhaps because of the serenity associated with its many mountain valleys and ocean inlets. The outside world gave it the name "The Hermit Kingdom" owing to a Korean tendency to close itself to foreign influences except for the traditional culture of China. Indeed, so strong has the Chinese presence been that, for most of its history, Korea has had little in the way of national identity. Such identity as it has acquired has been strongly marked by Western Christian currents of thought, especially early Catholic growth, combined with modern political developments.

Korea has long been a land of martyrs. The twentieth century produced a large harvest of witnesses to the faith in Korea, beginning with fifty who died in 1901 in an anti-Christian uprising.[1] Japanese colonial rule (1910–45) martyred others. But thousands of Catholics were killed particularly during the Korean War (1950–53) between Communist-occupied North Korea and Western-backed South Korea. Soviet armies occupied North Korea after the defeat of Japan and immediately set up a government linked with Moscow under Red Army major Kim Il Sung. A group of countries tried to negotiate a reunification of Korea through the United Nations, but had to content themselves with establishing a Republic of Korea in the South. U.S. forces withdrew in June of 1949. A year later, the North Korean Army crossed the thirty-eighth parallel dividing the two political entities and the Korean War began.

The U.N. Security Council condemned the invasion, and U.S. president Harry Truman sent American troops under General Douglas MacArthur along with contingents from sixteen other nations to hold off the Communist advance. Red China sent troops into the fray on the Northern side, which quickly led to a stalemate. By June 1951 both sides were negotiating a cease-fire and an armistice. Negotiations dragged on until the 1953 death of Joseph Stalin and the election of a new American president, Dwight Eisenhower, mostly because of disagreements about returning prisoners. But in 1953, an agreement was reached and, despite continuing disagreements over what to do with prisoners who did not wish to return to the Communist North, the fighting and holding of cap-tives came to an end. In those three years, however, many people lost their lives, for both political and religious reasons.

Like the troops battling for the South, the martyrs of Korea were a veritable United Nations of faithful heroes. Many, of course, came from Korea itself. But others had arrived in Korea as missionaries from various parts of the globe, some dating back to the end of the nineteenth century. Because of growth of the missions, in 1933 the Holy See had asked the Missionary Society of Saint Columban to send some of its members to then Japanese-controlled Korea. In October of that year, ten missionar-ies set out on a journey that would bring many of them to martyrdom. But missionary/martyrs also arrived from many orders and countries: Benedictine abbot and bishop Bonifatius Sauer from Oberufhanusen, Germany; Maryknoll bishop and apostolic delegate Patrick Byrne from Washington, D.C.; Columban father Francis Canavan, from Galway, Ireland; Columban James Maginn, from Butte, Montana; Paris Foreign Mission father Joseph Bulteau from the French Vendée; and Carmelite sister Thérèse Irene Bastin of Belgium, just to name a few.

The fact that persecution and martyrdom fell on both native-born Catholics and foreign-born missionaries reflects a hatred of Christianity in itself by the Korean Communist regime, irrespective of any nationalist resentment of foreigners. This point is further confirmed by the half-dozen Anglican martyrs in Korea. A mixture of native- and foreign-born Anglican priests — Timothy Cho Yong-ho, Charles Hunt, Michael Lee Won-chang, Albert W. Lee, and Mose Yun Tal-yong — as well as Anglican sister Mary Clare, perished under Korean Communist control. Clearly, the widespread persecution of all Christians makes it evident that the repression of the Catholic Church had nothing to do with ties to Rome. Korean Communist ideology could not bear Christianity, whether indigenous or not, and sought to wipe it out.

Despite its long history as a primarily Buddhist and Confucian society, with indigenous Ch'ŏndogyo believers, Korea had a growing Christian presence for hundreds of years. In the seventeenth century, Western thought began to spread in Korea, mostly through a small group of scholars called the Silhak School, who had been converted to Catholicism through contacts with European missionaries while conducting official missions in Beijing.[2] Their ideas, however, also found a willing reception among the common people, because Christianity taught the equality of all. Even so, persecution began shortly after. Various elements in Korean society who did not stand to benefit from these new ideas took strong steps. A Chinese Catholic priest who came to Korea at the end of the eighteenth century found a Catholic community of four thousand, even though there were no priests in the country. Some members of the community had already been martyred and the priest himself soon joined them. But Korean culture clearly resonated to the Gospel even in the most unlikely circumstances.

Early in the nineteenth century, Catholic thought and Catholics themselves were virtually crushed, with around three hundred converts being put to death. This had unfortunate consequences for agriculture, as the peasants rebelled against the religious and social oppression.[3] Though the government prohibited Christian proselytizing and the ruler Tae Wongun martyred about seven thousand of the twenty-three thousand Catholics in Korea in the 1860s, along with a dozen French missionary priests,[4] their Western views continued to undergird progressive thought in Korea in future decades.[5] Pope John Paul II canonized 103 martyrs from Korea's history prior to the twentieth century in 1979, the bicentennial of the formal birth of Korean Catholicism.[6]

Toward the end of the nineteenth century, Protestant missionaries from the United States and England also began to arrive and achieve some success. All the Christian denominations, with their Western views about human dignity and equality, were seen as part of the Western Silhak School, while the age-old Confucian and Eastern advocates formed the Tonghak faction. When the Japanese took control of Korea in 1910, however, Christian missionaries spoke up for Korean national interests. Sensitive to Western opinion, the Japanese conquerors did not dare move openly against the missionaries. So by a strange political development, the Christianity, both Catholic and Protestant, that had earlier seemed to one political wing a foreign element took on at least some aspects of a specifically Korean nationalism.

To counterbalance that influence, the Japanese colonial government subsidized the Confucians and Buddhists.[7] Japanese repression could also take far more brutal forms: anti-Japanese guerillas could be crucified and shot mercilessly.[8] Though not all guerrillas were Christian by any means, the Japanese maintained the constant belief that Christian and Japanese interests were fundamentally opposed to one another in Korea. In the 1930s, Bibles were banned by the Japanese in at least one region. After World War II erupted, Japan tried to introduce Shintoism into Korea by ordering all homes to erect a Shinto shrine. Two thousand Christians who resisted were arrested and fifty shot.[9]

In 1939, Buddhists were by far the largest religious body in Korea, but Christianity had made marked progress in a culture that, like China's, appears to have a certain openness toward the New Testament. Eminent intellectuals of the past had labored to find a way to reconcile Confucianism and Catholic theology.[10] Figures are not very reliable, but there were probably around 287,000 Presbyterians and 114,000 Catholics together with another 60,000 Christians of other denominations.[11] By 1988, there were 6.5 million Protestants and 1.9 million Catholics alongside 8 million Buddhists in non-Communist South Korea, making Christianity the largest religious denomination there. Christians, particularly Cardinal Stephen Kim of Seoul, played a central role in calling for opening the South toward democracy — long one of the Christian contributions to Korean political developments. This stance brought the churches into some conflict with South Korea's authoritarian regime as well.

These democratic growing pains were nothing, however, compared with the Communist persecutions which have virtually obliterated all religious practice in North Korea.[12] According to South Korea's Catholic bishops, Communist repression fell only slightly more harshly on the Church than on other segments of the Korean population. But the numbers are still shocking. Between 1950 and 1953, at the height of the Korean War between North and South, half of all churches had been destroyed or suffered major damage. Fifty percent of the hierarchy, one-third of the clergy, and at least fifteen thousand lay persons perished.[13] Korea's martyrology is atypical of other Communist persecutions in that it includes so many nonclerics. The Catholic Bishops Conference of Korea has officially identified 215 "witnesses to the faith" from the period.[14]

But the martyrdoms began before the Korean War broke out. As the Japanese war effort was failing, Soviet forces invaded Manchuria and North Korea. It did not take the Russians long to begin the same kind of summary elimination of the Church in Korea that they had carried out in the previous three decades in their own lands. Father Servatius Ludwig and a Brother Engelmar Zellner of the Yenki Diocese were shot by the Soviet invaders. In addition, the Russians arrested Theodor Breher, Bishop of Yenki, along with almost forty German priests and nuns, and an Italian missionary sister. One of the prisoners, Bonifatius Köstler, died as the result of mistreatment. In another region, Father Witmar Farrenkopf was the victim of twofold hatred. The retreating Japanese burned his church and the convent in Hoe-ryŏng; the advancing Soviets summarily executed him. But this was only the start of Soviet-inspired religious persecution, which the native North Korean forces would carry still further.[15]

In May 1949, The Soviets took possession of the Tŏk-won Abbey and arrested the abbot, prior, subprior, and a theology professor, all of whom were German missionaries. Four Korean priests — Kim Ch'i-ho, Kim Chong-su, Kim I-sik, and Ch'oe Pyŏng-kwon — were also taken into custody. The entire Benedictine community of Wonsan disappeared. Large numbers of native priests, including Bishop Francis Hong Yong-ho, were apprehended in the P'yong-yang vicariate. All of them were subjected to a common pattern after their arrest. They were tortured, interrogated, and charged with espionage. Only a small percentage survived the ordeal and imprisonment.[16] A Protestant Pastor Han has given an account of how the religious "special prisoners" were often taken to air-raid bunkers where their executions could not be observed. The corpses were left to rot. Han survived to tell the tale because his would-be executioner got confused among the bodies, which were piled four deep, and put a bullet in the head of a corpse lying next to him.[17] Some of the wounded lay in agony two days in the death piles. Han was rescued by a fellow survivor, Kwon Hyŏk-ki, who had been arrested because he was a Catholic supposedly engaged in "reactionary activities."[18] Both felt their survival a miracle. But Fathers Maurus Kim Pong-sik and Lee Kwang-jae did not receive that grace and died in the incident. When the bunker was recaptured by anti-Communist forces, 298 bodies were found inside.

The brutality of the invaders touched off a mass wave of refugees to the South. Those who managed to get away safely gathered at the Cathedral of the Immaculate Conception in Seoul to plan ways to train new priests and support them and their fellows.[19] But when the North Korean forces launched their invasion of the South by crossing the thirty-eighth parallel on June 25, 1950, the Feast of Saint John the Baptist, all the priests and religious remaining in North Korea were arrested. Authorities killed or imprisoned any priests and religious they came upon along their advance.[20] Among the first clerics to fall was Father Anthony

Collier, an Irish Columban missionary. The Columbans not only were the largest missionary order in Korea when the war broke out; they were exposed to particular danger because their northern mission was in Chunchon, which straddled the thirty-eighth parallel — the line of demarcation between North and South. In June 1950, Father Collier and Gabriel Kim, his houseboy, were apprehended by Communist North Korean troops as they were walking to the Chunchon post office. After interrogating them, the soldiers tied the two together with a rope and told them to march toward the river. En route, without warning, a machine gun burst killed Collier. But the priest had thrown himself over Kim's body at the first sound. Kim was wounded through the throat and lay in a heap, still tied to Collier's corpse. Thinking they both were dead, the soldiers left them there. Thirty-six hours later, Gabriel Kim was able to get free from the ropes and find help. The story of Father Collier's death is known only because Kim survived.[21]

The fate of other early martyrs in the conflict is not so clear. A month after Father Collier's death, three other missionaries — the prefect apostolic of Kwangju Patrick Brennan and Columban fathers Thomas Cusack and John O'Brien — disappeared. They had been warned by the American embassy that their mission in Mopko was in peril. All adamantly refused to abandon their people. The Church in the region was flourishing and growing. All over Korea, there were record numbers of converts at the time, about a thousand a year in Kwangju alone. The Church also had to care for masses of refugees. Just a year before, Father Brennan had requested fifteen more priests to help in the crush of work. The three were engaged in continuing that demanding ministry when the conflict engulfed them and their entire body of believers.

On July 24, 1950, a truckload of North Korean soldiers entered the town. Monsignor Brennan, it was later reported, knelt down and began saying the rosary when he heard the news. Soldiers came up to his front door, but when they learned that it was a church, they made a public statement that they would not interfere in religious liberty. The next day, however, they returned and took Brennan and Cusack and marched around the town with them. It quickly became obvious that their initial restraint had been a ploy to find out who the Catholics were in Mopko. Shortly thereafter, all three priests were transferred to a prison in Kwangju, and then forwarded to a prisoner-of-war camp near Seoul. Their hands were bound with ropes and they were forced to cover part of the journey on foot, even though they were without shoes and the road was rocky. They all arrived at the Franciscan monastery in Tae-jon, which was being used as a prison, but were then removed from their cell when it appeared that United Nations forces were advancing toward the town. The Communists massacred a large number of prisoners at that point. No word was ever heard about the priests again. By the time church people were able to examine the thousand or so corpses in the monastery courtyard, they had decomposed to the point of being unrecognizable. It can only be presumed that the three priests were part of the massacre.

Many more priests fell victim to the "Death March" that they and other captives were forced to make through North Korea to the Yalu River. Among the hundreds on the march were Monsignor Thomas Quinlan, prefect apostolic of Chunchon (Chunchon and Kwangju being the two large mission areas in Korea, the Communists had effectively destroyed the leadership by killing Father Brennan and imprisoning Father Quinlan). He was joined by Columban fathers Francis Canavan and Philip Crosbie. After being transferred among several prisons, they and several hundred others, including journalists, civil servants, and captured soldiers, were lined up to avoid the approaching U.S. Army. The Death March began on October 31, 1950, the vigil of All Saints' Day. The snow was deep and the temperatures were low at that time of year. Sick and aged people along with those severely weakened by malnutrition were driven through the elements.

In pursuit of some humanitarian concessions, the Salvation Army's Commissioner Herbert Lord pleaded with the officer in charge of the march, known as "the Tiger" to the prisoners: "These people will die if they have to march!" The Tiger replied: "Then let them march until they die. This is a military order."[22] Within the ten days the march lasted, ninety-two prisoners died from the rigors of the trek — or by bullets if they refused to walk any further. Father Canavan succumbed. But Philip Crosbie lived to write a harrowing memoir, *March till They Die*. We also have a confirmation of Crosbie's story in the diary of another survivor, an anonymous French Carmelite nun who was kidnapped after she and her co-nationals refused to board a plane for safety because it would have meant leaving their Korean sisters behind.[23]

Crosbie had been caught early after the first Northern incursion into the South in 1945. After a day carrying out pastoral duties, he tried to return to Chunchon to take care of some business matters. As he neared the city, he had to thread his way through a mass of people moving south, away from the fighting:

> It was not a pleasant spectacle, this sudden flight of most of the townspeople from their homes. Young and old, rich and poor, weak and strong: all alike were here. The majority carried some of their belongings with them, the women gracefully upright with huge bundles balanced on their heads and some with babies tied to their backs, the men bowed down under great loads carried on their shoulders. Some few trundled their possessions along in handcarts. A very few walked beside heavily laden carts drawn by meek-eyed, plodding oxen.[24]

Children had already become separated from their parents and were crying in the crowd. Everyone was uncertain about what the next few dozen hours would bring.

When he finally made his way back to his parish in Hongchon, which was further South, things looked bad even there. Peasants were streaming south in front of the advancing Northern army. Some stopped to see their *Sin-bu,* Father Crosbie, and make what might turn out to be a last confession. Local Catholics, as well as some catechumens still under instruction, were determined to stay with the priest. Others came thinking the church would be a place of sanctuary. Crosbie warned them that it would more likely be the first place the Communists would take control over. The Red Army arrived and Father Crosbie's journey began: "We had just passed, in a matter of seconds, from one world to another — by merely standing still."[25] The Communists requisitioned the church, but promised the priest that he would not be harmed so long as he stayed on church grounds.

Father Crosbie did so, but the bargain fell apart. A few days later he was taken in for interrogation. Despite some reasonable discussion, his questioners concluded that, since all religion is nonsense, the priest's real reason for being in Korea was that he was a political agent for his country. Crosbie was an Australian; it is difficult to say what Australian interest he was advancing in Korea. Though these soldiers were not very sophisticated, they had been thoroughly indoctrinated in Marxist ideology. One spontaneously informed the priest that "the most potent weapon the West held against its enemies was not the atom bomb, but religion."[26]

That this attitude had been so deeply implanted in simple soldiers is no small evidence of the special animus against faith in North Korea.

The Carmelite nun who has written her own separate memoir recalls that after one interrogation, the North Korean officer lost his temper and proclaimed: "There is nothing for it but to destroy Rome and the Vatican!" In his view, the nuns were nothing but hags who had corrupted women. And he took pleasure in speaking to a colleague — just loud enough for the prisoners to overhear: "We are going to kill all the priests and nuns tonight."[27]

The indoctrination ran against Korean traditions as well as Christian ones. In one conversation with a particularly ideological guard, Crosbie asked the man if his mother was alive:

"No, she is dead."

"Do you really believe that your mother died as animals do, that now she exists no more and you will never see her again?"

"Yes, that is what I believe."

Father Crosbie comments: "That answer, from a man belonging to a people who are devout ancestor-worshipers, staggered me."[28]

He was taken to a prison where Quinlan and Canavan were already being held in a cell. Quinlan, a big-hearted fifty-four-year-old Irishman from Tipperary, was familiar with prison life, having been detained during the earlier occupation by the Japanese. Canavan, thirty-five, was a quiet, intense man from Galway. Food — mostly rice and water — appeared sporadically and only in small quantities. Interrogations, however, were regular and extensive. Though the questioners were representatives of a sort of creed, they could not believe that missionaries had come to Korea without some tangible interest and assumed colonialism drove the foreigners. The Korean prisoners, mostly simple peasants, were constantly badgered to sign "confessions" of wrongdoing and were brutally brainwashed into accepting Communist teaching.

Crosbie was transferred to various places of detention, some better, others near-starvation camps. In one he came upon Bishop Byrne and another Maryknoll priest, William Booth, along with members of the Paris Foreign Mission Society (Antoine and Julien Gombert and Celestine Coyos — the only one to survive). A group of French and Belgian Carmelite nuns was also there — Prioress Thérèse Bastin, Mother Henriette de Lobit, Mother Mechtilde Devriese, and Sisters Marie-Madeleine and Bernardette Descayaux. Laywomen arrested included a German, Charlotte Gliese, a Turk, Maisara Daulatsch, and a Polish-Korean named Helena.[29] Three more French religious from the Congregation of Saint Paul de Chartres soon joined the group: Paul Villemot, Béatrix Edouard, and Eugénie Demeusy. All lived at death's door, a condition occasionally lightened by Korean Father John Yu who risked retribution by bringing food and other amenities for the foreign prisoners.

Crosbie and the two Irish priests were trucked to Pyong-yang, the Northern capital, and taken to a courtroom where pictures of Stalin and Kim Il Sung, the North Korean premier, hung on the walls. After perfunctory reports were written, they were interned in a prison that contained several Anglican, Methodist, and Salvation Army missionaries from various nations, as well as diplomats from foreign legations. During one of their periodic displacements, they joined a large line of American POWs. All were huddled onto a ramshackle train and sent further North. Travel by train was dangerous at that point in the Korean War. American planes strafed trains, unknowingly putting their wounded and captured comrades, some of whom were placed on flat-bed cars, and the religious and foreigners who had been sequestered, in mortal danger. After this occurred, the train moved only at night. Eventually it arrived in Manpo.

There an elderly French priest, Father Joseph Cadars, joined the group. By that time, many foreigners — Russians, Austrians, Germans, and others — cast up in Korea by the First and Second World Wars or by dissatisfaction with their lives and labors in North or South America and thinking Korea a place to make, perhaps, a modest recovery were also in custody. Camp life was not hard that far north, but it was no picnic. Food was ample, but the situation always precarious. The prisoners were a remarkably resilient lot, given the rigors they faced. But they were about to encounter far worse challenges. One of the worst deprivations for the Catholics was that priests were not allowed to say Mass in the camps, a restriction even the Japanese had not imposed on clerical prisoners. But the stage was set for the main event: the Death March.

Though many of the prisoners were old or sick — some were mothers with babies in their arms, and one of the Carmelites was blind — the North Koreans announced they were expected to walk through the November cold to a new destination, far distant. All implements that might be used as weapons, including walking sticks, were confiscated. The stronger internees propped up the weak ones. And the guards, apparently in order to fulfill some order unknown to the prisoners, drove them along. The sheer exertion of the forced marching was responsible for the majority of those who died. Food was meager; POWs sometimes got none at all. "The Tiger," who commanded the marching line, allowed no one to fall out. When some GIs who were sick did so, he furiously executed the American officer in charge of their group. Terror of a maniacal officer was added to the terror of the conditions.

Bishop Byrne passed the word down the line that he would give General Absolution to all the Catholics — many of whom now feared immediate death — once the march started again. After a day of exhausting movement, the prisoners slept in a cold, open field. The next morning, about a dozen of the POWs were dead, from overexertion or the cold. The same fate awaited anyone left behind the column. Those who continued encountered maddening moments. At one point hundreds were crowded into a building and the doors were locked. The crowding was so bad that panic ensued, people trying to crawl over each other to get out all night. Some died standing up and were found that way the next morning. Ironically, the Tiger lectured the survivors that the North Korean government was doing everything for their welfare and they should be grateful that they were being moved out of the reach of U.N. belligerents to People's Hospitals.

The guards deliberately separated the women, many of whom were in bad shape, from the men, promising they would be provided with transportation. When the men left, the guards ordered the women to start walking. Mother Béatrix, born Anne Marie Edouard, soon succumbed. At the point she could no longer walk, she was left behind in the cold. The guards allowed no one to stay behind to help. The elderly nun tranquilly told Mother Eugénie, "Go, my Sister, go." She was never seen again. Father Villemot looked to be next. This sturdy eighty-two-year-old marched sixty miles before he could go no further. He had started his missionary work in Korea in 1892 — almost fifty years before his death. His companions dragged him along as far as they were able. Then they managed to get him on a supply cart for a few miles. This was reason for hope, though guards had begun shooting anyone who stopped by the roadside to rest. Despite the talk of the People's Hospitals ahead, there was no mercy here.

Dozens began dying per day. Blood-red patches appeared in the snow alongside the road, the telltale signs of executions carried out ahead. Brutality increased. Bishop Byrne tried to tie a shoelace and was shoved into the snow. Helped to his feet, he moved on. Then, in a burst of leniency, transportation was suddenly found for the women and children, the old and weak, including some of the POWs. Like much else in prison life, the leniency was as inexplicable as the brutality. Father Villemot ultimately succumbed to one of the typical accidents of such circumstances.

Toothless and unable to eat the whole corn the prisoners were given, he died after five days of virtual starvation. Anglican Sister Mary Clare died at the same time of exhaustion.

Over a hundred people had died along the way. But fatalities owing to the march did not end when the column reached its destination; an equal number perished soon after. The Tiger cruelly told the sick that their condition was the result of neglect of their own health. Consequently, fresh air and exercise were prescribed for everyone, including those on the brink of pneumonia. Father Villemot died peacefully as a result, Fathers Julien and Antoine Gombert thereafter. Within a few days, Carmelite Mother Mechtilde succumbed. Bishop Byrne, Fathers Coyos and Canavan, and Bill Evans — all gravely ill — were moved to a cottage to isolate them from the other prisoners since Byrne was showing symptoms of meningitis. The bishop declined steadily, became delirious, and finally expired. Father Canavan, who was only thirty-five, and Father Coyos approached death, but made a miraculous recovery. Then Canavan had a relapse and went to his eternal reward. Father Cadars died a week before Christmas, and Father Bulteau on the Epiphany, after being forced to turn a grindstone wheel.[30] The regular rhythm of death took its toll on the survivors as well.

Beri-beri struck several internees because of poor nutrition. A few soy beans could have remedied this problem, but they were provided only sporadically. The weather was still bitter cold. They suffered a little less from it, however, because the living inherited the clothes of the dead. The prisoners were subjected to indoctrination. At one point, the Tiger informed the group that all capitalists were filthy and that the United States was the filthiest country in the world. Why? "Because most Americans had toilets *inside* their houses."[31] After repeated failures in this comic instruction, the officers gave up on the civilians. They were too reactionary. The POWs, however, continued with their lessons. In these they learned that, in the West, women were oppressed, college was only for a privileged elite, and elections were not free. No experience to the contrary counted for anything with the indoctrinators. "Examinations" on the lessons were held periodically. Salvation Army Commissioner Lord, serving as translator, would make up answers to the examination to satisfy the guards while POWs talked about other matters with him.

A new camp commandant, "Gooseneck," replaced the Tiger. In one of his first conversations with Commissioner Lord, he asked, "Do you believe in God?" "I do." "Then from now on I'll be your god and you can thank me for the benefits you receive." It is a testimony to the spirit of these worn-down internees, however, that when Saint Patrick's Day came, they managed to find some green cloth and the many Irish among the prisoners were allowed a little wearing of the green. Their condition slowly improved. The surviving nuns, such as Mother Eugénie and Sister Marie-Madeleine, the latter blind, were allowed to resume their ministry to the suffering again. Another figure, Mother Henriette, was too frail to help out but showed a tranquillity born of her Carmelite contemplation that strengthened her companions. By spring, when food became available on the land again, and summer, with its abundance, some continued to die, but the life of the remaining band was relatively easy.

Despite regular reports of U.N. troops about to land, a year came and went. The prisoners, more accustomed to camp life, found ways to cope and even the guards relaxed somewhat during a second year. It was during that time that the guards showed up one day wearing black armbands. Stalin had died. Foreigners began to be shipped away. Some were repatriated to their home countries. Crosbie himself went by a circuitous route. A Soviet representative took charge of him. They crossed China together; then he was sent without guards from Siberia to Moscow, where the Australian embassy took him in. Afterward, he prayed for the ultimate redemption of all captors, those who had been freed, and the many who remained in North Korea awaiting the Resurrection.

Meanwhile, outside the camps, those who had not been interned lived a hard existence. Around the same time that the Death March began, various forms of martyrdom took place in the rest of the country, mostly among native priests who had not been immediately apprehended, as the foreigners had been. Father Lee Chae-ch'ŏl was one of the few priests to remain in the North after the general round-up and internment following the start of hostilities between North and South. Father Lee, therefore, had to fill up the empty space left by the arrest of many others. He was constantly watched and was soon arrested, but, owing to negotiations with the military command, he was set free. Forced into hiding, he took refuge in some mountain caves near Ch'ŏng-jin. Life in the mountains was hard and it was made even harder by the several hundred refugees who had taken shelter there. The Communists raided the caves and caught about eighty religious leaders. Apparently, they were imprisoned in a lighthouse, and all of them were executed. Their bodies were thrown into the sea; Lee's body was never found.[32]

Father Andrew Chon Tok-pyo died in December of 1950 in his church at Sariwon. But his body was not recovered until U.N. forces retook the town. They found him bound with an electric cord and bearing signs of electric shock torture. Cotton had been stuffed in his mouth and both mouth and eyes appeared to have been sewn shut during his final hours.[33] Native priests Timothy Lee Kwang-je and Francisco So Ki-chang were disposed of after similar treatment. Father Francis Yu Chae-ok was buried alive on the seashore east of Haeju.[34] Father Benedict Kim Chi-ho was beaten to death with a stick.[35] Sisters of Saint Paul de Chartres Angela Kim Jeong-ja and Marianna Kim Jeong-suk were hacheted to death.[36] And many more, lay and clerical, died by similar or more ordinary executions, massacres, and harsh treatment, their bodies unidentified or disappeared, merely because they were open Catholics or refused to abjure the faith under torture.

Communist oppression of Catholics did not end with the end of the war. Many remained in prison camps. In 1965, Father Pius Yang Se-hwan refused to accept Communist orders to break with the Holy See and was sent to his death in a work camp. As late as 1972, Father Joseph Kim Son-yong was imprisoned in Manchuria for refusing to join the so-called "Patriotic Church" and died while breaking rocks in a labor camp.[37] Needless to say, almost no religious activity of any kind has been allowed since 1953 in North Korea, which remains one of the world's foremost totalitarian regimes and religious persecutors.

One unexpected consequence of the war has been that, after the conflict, the Christian churches, Catholic and Protestant, expanded quickly in the South. Many Koreans, their traditional ways of life disrupted, were looking for some way to make sense of their experience and turned to Christianity. From 1964 to 1994, the Catholic Church went from 628,000 members to over three million, mostly through adult baptisms, to become about 7 percent of the population.[38] The number of native priests grew from 338 to 1,820, enabling the Korean Church to become a source of missionaries to other countries. In line with its traditional role as a transmission belt for Western ideas, the Church has been an advocate of democracy and has had ties going back before the Korean conflict to the period of Japanese colonization (1910–45) with student and worker groups.[39]

In 1960, protests resulted in a short-lived democratic regime in the

South that ended the following year in a coup by Chung-hee Park. Park made some attempts at democratization, but settled into an authoritarian pattern. When Park announced a state of emergency that gave him wide-ranging powers, Cardinal Kim of Seoul remarked on Christmas 1972: "Your action will help widen the already existing gap between the people and the government, and will eventually lead to a government without people and a people without a leader."[40] Though the South and North still remained in uneasy tension, the cardinal pressed for economic reform and greater justice throughout the 1970s.

In recent years, Catholic confessors have suffered even in South Korea. Though much less harsh than its Northern counterpart, which has brought all religious practice to a virtual standstill, the Southern government has taken vigorous steps to curtail opposition. Particularly after Saigon fell in 1975, the South Koreans felt justified in using strong-arm tactics to prevent "Communism." The prominent Catholic presidential candidate Kim Dae-jung was abducted in 1973 and arrested during a 1975 pro-democracy demonstration at the Myongdong Cathedral in Seoul. Cardinal Kim led a protest for him and twenty-six others imprisoned. Protestant and Catholic leadership alike have supported the government against a potential Communist incursion. But the Catholic Church has been unusual in that it combined that hard stance with advocacy of reform.

Maryknoll priest Father James Sinnott was expelled for criticizing the government, and Church-sponsored protesters have been arrested. South Korean intelligence agencies threatened publication of damaging information about some Korean priests — a threat Cardinal Kim bravely resisted by challenging them to publish and substantiate their claims. A North Korean bishop who had escaped into the South, Bishop Daniel Tji, was arrested for supposedly stirring up destabilizing protest and a Catholic poet and friend, Kim Chi-ha, joined him in prison. The charges against Tji were absurd on the face; he had been tortured in North Korea and had no sympathy either with Communism or with attempts to weaken the South vis-à-vis the North. At a Holy Year celebration in 1974, according to Korean scholar Eric O. Hanson, "Five bishops, one hundred priests, three hundred nuns, and three thousand lay persons marched to demand Bishop Tji's release, restoration of democracy and human rights, relief for the poor, and recovery of freedom of the press."[41] The U.S. State Department also protested.[42] Given its need for continued Church and international (especially American) support, however, the government was careful not to create any outright martyrs. It used only tear gas and pepper spray to disperse the crowd. Kim Chi-ha was tortured in prison, however, which might easily have ended in disaster.

President Park was assassinated in 1979, which sent the country into turmoil. Military forces set up martial law. Further protests followed. In Kwangju, one of the centers of North Korean persecution during the war, students demonstrated and hundreds were brutally slaughtered despite the interventions of Kwangju's Archbishop Youn. Catholics who got information about this massacre to the outside world received long prison sentences.[43] But the Church's courage and outspokenness has made it a much esteemed institution in South Korea and one that has become a largely indigenous force.

The Church is valued for its presence in conflicts such as the one in Kwangju, but also for its work with young people, women (who were traditionally subordinate in Korean society), and in education, journalism, book publishing, and movements for social development. The Korean Church, only forty-five years after its cruel Calvary, has created a network of colleges and high schools, hospitals, retirement homes, leper colonies, and a host of other institutions. It took great bravery on the part of the Catholics between 1950 and 1953 to keep faith alive and the vigorous intervention of U.N. and other forces to keep the South from being overrrun. Korea still wrestles with many problems, but it owes a large debt of gratitude to the many thousand who labored and still labor for its ultimate salvation.

# -SEVENTEEN-

# THE SPIRIT IN VIETNAM

A S WORLD WAR II was coming to an end, Vietnam began to suffer the same types of persecution and martyrdoms that Communism was bringing to China and Korea. But at that very moment a spiritual story was unfolding that enriches our understanding of how grace operates even in the most terrible circumstances. Marie-Michel Marcel Van, a young man who had been born in 1928 in the small village of Ngam Giao, between Hanoi and Haiphong in the Northern Tonkin Delta, had had visions for much of his life in which he conversed with the French saint Thérèse of Lisieux. Like Thérèse, he only wrote down an account of them in obedience to a religious superior. Most of those visions had to do with learning to train the will for love and obedience, and, though cast in a heavily pious language similar to Thérèse's, reveal a real spiritual awakening in the soul of a remarkable Vietnamese boy. Those spiritual experiences would carry him to his death in the Vietnamese Gulag, but also opened a future path for reconciliation in Vietnam that still remains to be explored.

Van needed a great deal of spiritual help during his precarious early life. His family were simple rice farmers, subject to periodic famine when the dikes of the rice paddies burst or the crops failed. Van's father was a basically decent man, but had a weakness for gambling. His mother was very devout, but overwhelmed by work and the care of the children. Van remembered beautiful poetic days in the small village with them both. They instilled a pure, childlike faith in him from his earliest years which, though tried, was never shaken. His religious interests clearly marked him out for some sort of vocation, but his family sent him away to work in a parish, less for the sake of his vocation than to get this stubborn, oversensitive, and somewhat eccentric boy out of the house.

In the Vietnam of the 1930s, this exposed Van to several dangers. He unfortunately came into contact with harsh and sadistic catechists and priests. He had never reacted well to imposed tasks, only those he was encouraged to do out of love and affection. But at his minor seminary he was frequently beaten with a rattan cane by a particularly vicious young catechist. The same teacher tried to sexually abuse the seven-year-old Van and the other boys, who all resisted violently. They were all threatened, "If you talk I will bury you alive!"[1] This catechist was eventually dismissed, but the others were only a little better, mocking Van's piety and trying to put temptation in his way. In various parishes to which he later went to study, the pastors were often corrupt, using the boys as free servants and taking their pleasures with alcohol and women on the side. Remarkably, the young Van never let these gross vices change his view of the Church's goodness.

Van was driven to petty thievery to buy matches to light the altar candles; after a beating, he stole a few pennies so that he would have paper for his school work. The scruples these forced thefts caused a sensitive boy are understandable. But he showed great spiritual and moral maturity from the first. He writes of this period: "The more I discover the superficiality of love in this world, the more I feel drawn into the depth of the heart of God."[2] Transfer to another parish and even a visit home were all to no avail. Everyone believed he was just making trouble. Rather than submit to further temptations and injustice, Van escaped at around age twelve to become a street urchin, living any way he could to earn a few pennies. At one point, he was almost sold into slavery by a woman who had pretended to befriend him.

During this period, he also came into contact with Vietnamese revolutionaries trying to drive out the French colonial power. Though a firm Catholic and grateful to the French for bringing Catholicism to Vietnam, Van — probably like many boys his age — hated the French forces and hoped for their withdrawal. He had seen the Japanese invading forces during the Second World War and hated them too. The time seemed right to him for Vietnam to have its own independence, as it had in the past. But he also thought about the need for a revolution to reform the Church: "I wanted to be a revolutionary too: the struggle would be to create a better future for the Church in Vietnam, to reform the parishes, encourage and support vocations in the priesthood, etc."[3]

Sleeping under the stars, contemplating on hillsides, living by handouts, even eating wax that had dripped from altar candles in church, he found himself experiencing great humility and littleness before everything. Even before he had read Saint Thérèse of Lisieux, his experiences moved him in directions similar to those she took. A sweet tenderness remained with him in the midst of his lonely and challenging circumstances. When he was finally admitted into another parish for religious training, he encountered the same corruptions he had met with else-where. But by now he had a new attitude: he would become a leader of spiritual resistance, helping form the other boys to lead better lives and make little sacrifices for the poor.

Transferred to the minor seminary of Saint Thérèse of Lisieux at Lang-Son, he almost by chance came upon the saint's spiritual autobiography, *Diary of a Soul*. Immediately, he recognized in the saint's "little way" something he had been looking for all his life. From age fourteen on, he always had a copy of the book with him. But then an odd thing hap-pened. In prayer, he found himself in conversation with Saint Thérèse, his little sister, as he called her. She began giving him good advice about how to conduct his life. He was taught how to overcome fear and a lack of trust. Thérèse told him that, like everyone else, he was distant from God because he had a wrong conception of the Almighty. God, she said to him, loves us: "Never be afraid of God. All He can do is love."[4] And she explained: "To love means to give everything and to give oneself," not to become embroiled in attempts to do things that are beyond weak human nature. It was a lesson that the young boy, who had recoiled from harsh masters but flourished under loving ones, could take to heart. Just as a good father bends down to kiss a child, and does not make the child try to jump higher than he can to kiss his own face, so does God deal with us in coming down to our level, if we let him, Thérèse explained.

These conversations went on for years. At times, quite surprising lessons emerged. Thérèse made a point of asking Van to pray for the French. He replied heatedly to her:

> I have no difficulty praying for Vietnam, but I can never pray for those wretched French Colonialists. Sister, I'm sorry if that offends you.... I'll make an exception for the Missionary priests and nuns because I regard them as the Fathers and Mothers of the Faith for the Vietnamese. But as far as the French Colonialists are concerned, they can go to Hell until they realize who we are.... I've seen too much of the cruelty and contempt they have for my race.[5]

He told the French saint that, if he had a gun, it would give him great pleasure even to kill just one Frenchman.

Exchanges like these may convince even a skeptic that Van was not merely imagining these conversations. Something outside his normal consciousness was beginning to break through. Thérèse sympathized with Vietnam's suffering and deplored the bad behavior of the French, but she advised him, instead of taking up arms, to use the "tactic of prayer." Only the profound Christian response of praying for enemies, and for a change of heart that will reveal to them the evil they are doing, was the right response, she counseled. France and Vietnam had to cease to be enemies because diabolic forces were at work, not only Communism but apathy and infidelity in France itself: "There is an urgent need for someone to offer himself quietly in prayer and sacrifice. This will reconcile the two countries and the power of evil will be brought to an end."[6]

All his life, Van had wanted to be a priest. He was told another hard truth in these sessions: he would not be a priest but a lay member of the Redemptorists in Hanoi to serve God as God wanted to be served. Van was also warned that he would face hard trials, but should remember that just as Jesus was present in the boat when it was in danger of capsizing on the Sea of Galilee and stilled the storms. Van would have divine help in the trials that awaited him. Conversations with Christ himself and mystical experiences followed. At one point, he says, "My soul seemed to be outside itself; I felt that I was plunged into the depths of Love and disappearing into the Heart of God."[7] Though the language used here is not a modern idiom, it strongly resembles the mystical experience in all ages.

A friendship with God began that reminds the reader of Teresa of Avila and other great mystics. At one point, Christ even asked Van to tell him some funny stories.[8] During a Mass, Van had a vision of the millions upon millions who assault Christ through their sins while he can only take it and love. The crowd had surprising members: adults, men and women, certainly, but "the most painful part of it was seeing innocent children throwing stones at Jesus." Later he was told that he had a special mission to children, who were being led away from God by the world.

Van received dark prophecies about coming trials in which the Apostles would seem weak and overcome by evil. But they would triumph on the way to restoring love in the world: "Be sure you tell everyone that my reign will be established on the solid foundation of prayer."[9] God gave Van a special mission to pray for the conversion of France, since the Devil wanted to make it a place of great conflict. Communism was a threat there, as in Vietnam, but after that problem was conquered, Freemasonry, a long-standing challenge to the Church in Europe, would come to the fore. Whatever is to be thought of these last instructions, it is remarkable that a young Vietnamese boy of no particular education would have received and written down these warnings.

On September 2, 1945, Vietnamese Communist leader Ho Chi Minh proclaimed the country's independence, and war again ensued between the French and the Vietnamese. Van flew to Saigon in the South, away from the greatest Communist influence, to work there during the war. He took final vows with the Redemptorists in 1952 and busied himself at various simple tasks, but he was unsatisfied with his life. He wrote to his sister: "The more I go on...the more I realize that holiness is about turning sadness into joy!"[10] In 1954, when the country was cut in two after the fall of Dien Bien Phu, masses of people, Catholic and not, fled to the South. But, according to Van, "Jesus had insisted"[11] that he was needed where the trouble was greatest. Van immediately flew to the North on September 14, the Feast of the Cross. He did not like the North, but he accepted his mission: "I am going so that in the midst of the Communists, there will be someone who loves Our Dear Lord."

Van joined the reduced staff at Our Lady of Perpetual Help and was quietly conducting his duties when one day he was sent out to do the shopping. Hearing some *agents provocateurs* spreading rumors in the markets about atrocities and imperialism in the South, he blurted out, "I have just come from the South and the government has never done anything like that!"[12] It was a small detail, but, as Saint Thérèse had taught Van, God cares for every detail. His remark unmasked the seeming friendliness of the authorities in the North to the presence of religious. He was taken to Sureté headquarters, where an all-too-familiar pattern began. Interrogations went on for several days from seven in the morning until midnight seeking Van's confession — of what is not clear. Then the questioners tried to "convert" him to the North Vietnamese cause or at least to convince him to join the "Catholic Patriots and Friends of Peace," a group subservient to the regime. When that too failed, they accused him of having a relationship with a woman in the police headquarters and advised him it was best to marry her despite his religious vows.

All Van's life had hardened him to resist such pressures. He spent five months in solitary confinement during sweltering summer heat. Then he was transferred to the main Hanoi prison and locked up with other alleged "reactionaries." Notes he wrote were smuggled out by another prisoner who was released. One to his religious superior read: "It would be easy for me to stay alive: all I would have to do is make an accusation against you. Don't be afraid, I would never do it....I will resist to the death."[13] The prison officials used brainwashing techniques to break him and prevent his dying a "heroic" death. Near the end, he got out a message, "Today, I am a corpse who can still breathe. . . . I am the victim of Love. Love is my joy, an indestructible joy."

A show trial, during which he displayed great calm and dignity, ensued, and he was sentenced to fifteen years for spreading propaganda. His first prison was Camp 1 in Mo Chen, where he was subjected to reeducation. Other prisoners flocked to him because of the strength he displayed: "They all come to me thinking I am inexhaustible. They can see that I am feeble like themselves, but where else can they go for consolation! I have to be there for them." Perhaps because of this good effect on the others, he was transferred to a new prison: Camp 2 at Yeh Binh. There he endured the worst treatment of all: he was beaten and put in a dark cell for two years and, at the beginning of 1958, chained up for three months with no outside contacts. When he was finally set loose from the special confinement, he had tuberculosis and beri-beri. His body was emaciated. On June 10, 1959, he groaned and quietly passed away, leaving some future Vietnam to take the measure of his life.

Vietnam stretches along the coast of Asia south of China and its geography has played a large role in the shaping of its culture and religious history. The early Vietnamese moved slowly down the curve of land alongside the South China Sea. Chinese invaders came after them, establishing Chinese cultural and political dominance in the region for over a thousand years and at intervals thereafter. The Chinese instilled Confucianism in the ruling class. Traders coming to the Red River Delta and Vietnam's good harbors from India added Buddhism to the religious mixture. In the seventeenth century, European explorers brought Christianity. It is only an illusion of perspective, then, that has made it appear to some opponents of Vietnamese Christianity that missionaries constituted a unique colonial element. In fact, they were merely continuing a history, several thousand years old, of the interchange of culture at the crossroads of Vietnam.

The most remarkable figure among the early missionaries was the French Jesuit Alexandre de Rhodes, who arrived in Hanoi in 1627. An energetic man, he learned Vietnamese quickly and was well received by the royal court. By 1630, when he was expelled — probably because of his growing influence — he had baptized over six thousand people. In addition, Father de Rhodes wrote a Vietnamese catechism and organized a Vietnamese-Latin-Portuguese dictionary. Though he never personally returned to Vietnam, de Rhodes left a large influence on the country's subsequent history.

For Christianity persisted in Vietnam despite persecutions. As in other parts of the world, changing political alignments might favor or harm religious interests. Vietnamese rulers martyred both Buddhists and Christians at different times. In the nineteenth century, growing French colonialism in Vietnam promoted Catholicism and evoked a backlash. Vietnam became a French Protectorate in 1883, partly owing to sheer force of arms but also because the ruling dynasty had become badly out of touch with the people. Some Vietnamese, non-Christians among them, welcomed the French as perhaps a force that might modernize a still largely feudal system. But in the fifty years prior to the French takeover, somewhere between 100,000 and 300,000 Christians were slaughtered or persecuted. The Vatican later beatified 117 of these nineteenth-century martyrs.

Within a few years, there were over 700,000 Catholics in Vietnam. But the situation of the French — especially after their defeat by the Nazis and need to rebuild their own nation after the war — became more and more precarious. In 1954, owing to the Geneva Armistice Agreements, the country was partitioned at the seventeenth parallel into a Communist North and democratic South. As the French began to withdraw and American troops began to replace them in the South, the Communist movement in the North, led by Ho Chi Minh, was establishing itself. By that time, there were close to 1,600,000 Catholics in the country, all but 480,000 in the Communist-dominated regions. Persecution of believers began immediately and 670,000 Catholics plus another 210,000 non-Catholics left their native lands and fled to the South. The rest were forced to stay in the North; bishops, priests, other religious, and laity frequently wound up in prison.[14] Ironically, as in other parts of Asia that turned Communist, North Vietnam used a European ideology, allegedly with the aim of throwing off European influence. Ho Chi Minh had studied Marxism in Paris.

The Geneva Agreements had stipulated that the Vietnamese people would be given three hundred days in which to decide where they wanted to live. Even before the agreement, Communist forces had intimidated and arrested those wishing to leave, blockading roads, rivers, and other ways of escape. Boats were commandeered. They demanded that anyone wishing to emigrate possess a "travel permit," which they made difficult to obtain. Many of the Catholics of Tonkin, one of the traditional centers of Vietnamese Catholicism, made the journey south anyway by moving down canals and rice paddies. Some died in overloaded *sampans* or in the shipwreck of makeshift rafts. Others were intercepted by armed patrols. Once the Vietnamese Communists took full possession of Hanoi, they used vast armed forces to control any movement. The Communists denied that there was a spontaneous exodus. Instead, they proclaimed that fear of the atom bomb, or the bad influence of the Catholic clergy, or American propaganda were responsible. However, when the International Control Commission, at the request of the North, interviewed refugees in the South, not one of them expressed a desire to return to the North.[15] A similar exodus would occur when the North Vietnamese moved into the South after the 1975 U.S. withdrawal: around 1.5 million South Vietnamese sought refuge in various countries, especially the United States.[16]

The North Vietnamese government professed to allow freedom of religion. Ho Chi Minh included messages to Catholics in many of his early speeches. But the actions of the government spoke louder than his words. Priests and prominent believers were harassed and arrested. The people themselves had a good idea of what the new government would mean for religious belief. In the early stages, the persecution was carefully concealed. Once the Vietnam War broke out into the open, however, the government engaged in open persecutions. Concentration camps and Communist "reeducation centers" sprouted around the country. Catholic schools were closed and Catholic philanthropic enterprises curtailed. A "patriotic" Catholic association was formed to try introducing a split between the people and official Catholic institutions. Like all such "patriotic churches" in Communist lands, it was subservient to the government.

Several incidents recounted by eyewitnesses give a sense of the terror:

- In the village of Haiduong, Viet Minh (Communist) forces entered the school and accused students and teachers of "conspiring" because they had been discussing religion. The punishments were made to fit the several crimes. Two school children had chopsticks shoved into their ears so that they would never hear such things — or anything — again. The teacher had his tongue held out by pliers and cut off with a bayonet so that he would never speak of religion again. Fortunately, none of the victims died and they were able to escape to the South shortly thereafter.[17]

- A priest who had been left at liberty in the North suffered a similar incident. He was allowed to say Mass only between six and seven in the morning when the peasants were already starting work. One evening the local Communist soldiers decided he needed reeducation. They hung him by his feet and beat him with bamboo to drive the evil out of him. The altar boys found him hanging in the chapel. The local townspeople smuggled him across the border, where he survived.[18]

- Since priests were not good at being reeducated, they often encountered even worse. One was sentenced for "treason" and given a crown of thorns. Eight nails were hammered into his head. He staggered to a nearby hut. The people pulled out the nails and sought medical help from the South. He managed to recover. When he did, he refused to remain in the South, but crossed back over into the North to resume his parish duties.[19]

And these were the lucky ones who managed to survive.

The treatment of Catholics in the South could not have been more different. The South Vietnamese Premier Ngo Dinh Diem was himself a professed Catholic. Indeed, his government tended to favor Catholics in various ways, which led to no little resentment among the non-Catholic population. Though the Diem regime was reputedly very corrupt, its religious injustices may have weakened popular support for the government even more than the corruption did among the majority of South Vietnamese, who were non-Catholics. Diem offered a welcome to Catholic refugees, and they helped support his regime. Until his assassination in 1963, probably in part owing to the influence of another Catholic president, John F. Kennedy of the United States, Diem combined religion and politics to create an anti-Communist coalition that had both good and bad elements.

Tracing individual martyrs during the tumultuous war in Vietnam is still not easy because, given the continued Communist control over the country, there has been no way to make a comprehensive assessment. It will likely be decades before even part of the story will be known. But we have some representative cases. In June of 1953, two Belgian priests, the Abbés Künsch and Bruneau, together with a catechist, were forcibly removed from the seminary at Bui-Chu in North Vietnam by the Viet Minh. When the priests refused to take off their cassocks, the clothes were torn off. The priests were tied together and marched away. The road they traveled was so muddy that their sandals came off en route.

In October, four months later, they were still bound together in a prison camp. Künsch died from severe dysentery, which had gone untreated, and was buried in an unmarked grave. Bruneau survived until June of 1954, a year after he was first apprehended. Camp conditions killed him as well.[20]

In South Vietnam, the escalating war made things difficult, but the Church was at least spared persecution. As soon as Saigon fell in 1975 after the Paris Peace Talks, however, the usual persecutions began in the South as well. Perhaps the most eloquent and deeply spiritual witness to the situation in the Communist-occupied South is François-Xavier Nguyen Van Thuan. He had just been appointed titular archbishop of Vadesi and coadjutor archbishop of Saigon before the Communists arrived. The Vatican had made the appointment because the existing archbishop, Paul Nguyen Van Binh, was quite ill and worn out from his onerous duties during the war years. The Communists chose to view things differently, calling the appointment "a conspiracy between the Vatican and the imperialists," which was obviously meant to bolster resistance.[21]

In some ways, their worries were understandable. The new archbishop had been born in Huê, the ancient imperial capital, in 1928 to an old Catholic family that traced its faith back three centuries. Family members had suffered and died along with many other Vietnamese Christians under Emperor Tu Duc in the nineteenth century. The family was also prominent in both Vietnamese politics and the Church: Ngo Dinh Diem, the future president of South Vietnam, was one of the archbishop's uncles as was Pierre-Martin Ngo Dinh Thuc, archbishop of Huê.[22] In addition, Archbishop François-Xavier had studied abroad, taking degrees in canon law in Rome, and had frequently traveled outside the country seeking material and moral support. An active bishop who had trained almost eight hundred seminarians in the eight years prior to the Communist takeover, he had also been instrumental in setting up Radio Veritas, an Asia-wide Catholic network. Given the archbishop's background and accomplishments, it is no surprise that the regime brought the charges it did, though they were entirely untrue.

Archbishop François-Xavier was, therefore, never even allowed to take up his new post. As he was en route to Saigon, having already installed his successor in his old diocese of Nha Trang, he was stopped and forced to turn back. On the Feast of the Assumption, August 15, 1975 — a date to which he attached great importance — he was confined to house arrest. Most of the South's bishops were also taken into custody along with a large number of priests, army chaplains, and human rights advocates.[23] They all wound up in reeducation camps. The archbishop followed the same route, eventually spending a dozen years in prison, nine years among them in isolation cells. In November 1988, he was released but forbidden to conduct religious services. Three years later, he was expelled from Vietnam. Since the mid-1990s, he has been vice president of the Pontifical Council for Justice and Peace in Rome.

In many respects, the archbishop's story is all but identical to many others in Vietnam, and even in China and North Korea in recent decades. But his reaction in these sadly familiar situations in the twentieth century was, like Marcel Van's, perhaps a sign of something more hopeful in the future of Vietnam. During his incarceration, he produced a series of spiritual meditations that were smuggled out and copied and became a kind of consolation to Catholics suffering in Vietnam, even those who put their lives in peril as "Boat People." The meditations do not go much into the details of the bishop's trials or those of his fellow prisoners. In fact, he makes a point of not describing the wrongs they suffered very much, precisely, it seems, out of a pastor's desire to find a way past the usual human desire for revenge and dwelling on the hurts inflicted by others: "Many times I suffer deeply because the mass media want to make me tell sensationalistic stories, to accuse, to denounce, to incite opposition, to seek revenge.... This is not my goal. My greatest desire is to transmit my message of love, in serenity and truth, in forgiveness and reconciliation."[24] In another place, he advises people to "take your problems to Jesus in the Sacrament and to Mary. Then when the suffering has passed, resist any impulse to recrimination and vengeance. Forget about it, never speak about it again except to say 'Alleluia!' "[25]

The archbishop does, however, tell how he turned his many years in prison into a kind of spiritual practice. He recalls Bishop John Walsh, who spent a dozen years in a Chinese Communist prison, as having remarked upon his release, "I spent half my life waiting." The archbishop, too, felt time heavy on his hands at first and was tormented by thoughts of all the pastoral projects he had to leave undone. The fact that his people were going through many trials without pastoral guidance kept him awake until, one night, he received a powerful inspiration: "Francis, it is very simple. Do what Saint Paul did when he was in prison: write letters to the different communities."[26] From that moment, he decided to make his time in prison fruitful in whatever way God was allowing him to live. Mother Teresa of Calcutta had written him: "What is important is not how many actions we perform, but the intensity of love that we put into each action." In his limited circumstances, he meditated:

> How does one achieve this intensity of love in the present moment? I simply think that I must live each day, each minute as the last of my life. To leave aside everything accidental, to concentrate only on the essential. Each word, each gesture, each telephone call, each decision is the most beautiful of my life. I keep my love for everyone, my smile; I am afraid of wasting even one second by living it without meaning.[27]

This was the principle that kept him vibrant during the long years of imprisonment. Among the worst moments were periods in the hold of a ship with fifteen hundred desperate people being transported North. In the Phú-Khánh prison, he had no windows in his cell and spent the first hundred days with his nose up against a tiny hole for fresh air. During rains, even that relief was taken away; spiders, earthworms, and millipedes rushed in, and he was too weak to drive them away. Worst of all was the simple length of time he spent in solitary confinement. The archbishop confesses that there were whole days when he was so exhausted or ill that not a single conscious prayer passed through his mind.

But over and above these trials, a pure and simple dedication emerged in him. The effect on those he came into contact with was nothing short of miraculous. One Communist guard, impressed by his spirit, promised to pray for him at the partly destroyed sanctuary of the Madonna of Lavong. The archbishop did not know what to make of this promise, but received a note from the guard shortly after, confirming that he was going weekly and making this touching petition: "I pray for you like this: Madonna, I am not a Christian; I do not know how to pray; I ask you to give Mr. Francis what he desires."[28]

The prayer must have been heard. One thing the archbishop was able to do frequently was to say Mass with a little wine, shrewdly labeled "stomach medicine," that he had sent to him, along with some concealed hosts. Camp officials noticed that the guards assigned to watch him soon became "contaminated," so they stopped rotating the detail to prevent the contamination from spreading further. He told guards stories of trips abroad, taught them a little French and English. Some of them even began studying Latin; one of them asked the archbishop to teach him a Latin hymn and chose the "Veni Creator." He went around the camp singing the ancient words and music happily.[29] One guard even let the archbishop make a cross and chain out of a piece of wood and some wire. Later, in freedom, it became the archbishop's pectoral cross: "I wear this cross and chain every day, not because they are reminders of prison, but because they indicate my profound conviction, a constant reference point for me: only Christian love can change hearts, not weapons, threats, or the media."[30]

By his own report, he made a point of discussing Christ's command to forgive our enemies with his captors, which led to this exchange:

> "Do you really love us?"
> "Yes. I sincerely love you."
> "Even when we treat you so badly? When you suffer because you have been in prison for so many years without a trial!"
> "Think about the years we have lived together. I really love you!"
> "When you are free, you won't send your people to take revenge on us and our families?"
> "No, I will continue to love you, even if you want to kill me."
> "But why?"
> "Because Jesus has taught me how to love you. If I do not, I am no longer worthy to be called a Christian."[31]

Or as the archbishop sums up his conclusions from his prison experiences: "Charity has no boundaries; if it has boundaries it is no longer charity."[32]

Vietnam is still not free and it may be some time before the slow introduction of real charity by figures such as Marcel Van and Cardinal François-Xavier Nguyen Van Thuan bears fruit. Churches already seem to be growing quickly. But the experience of countries like Poland and Czechoslovakia suggests that a real resolution will require both charity and a public spirit of truth. In the late 1990s, the Vietnamese government launched another crackdown on both Protestant and Catholic leaders, sending a new wave of mostly unknown believers into detention. Vietnam's Catholic bishops have issued a public statement protesting the move. A dozen members of the Congregation of Mother Coredemptrix have been in prison since 1987. And harsh restrictions seem to be increasing.[33]

Asian societies have a history of long imperial dynasties, and it may take the millennial perspective that John Paul II announced in *Ecclesia in Asia* before we see a social evolution and powerful evangelization that reforms the tyrannies that have sprung up in the absence of traditional orders. But there is no question that history now seems on the side of the Vans and Thuans and not the ruling cliques that seem so potent in their ideological rigor and intimidation of dissidents. It is the old story of the charity that overcame persecution and tyranny in the ancient world of the West. The new millennium may witness a reproduction of that evangelical revolution in the East.

# -EIGHTEEN-

# OUT OF AFRICA

O N CHRISTMAS EVE 1993, in the remote Atlas Mountains of Algeria, several men carrying machine guns appeared in the courtyard of the Trappist monastery at Tibhirine. Besides the unexpected presence, recent events made their appearance ominous. On December 1 of the same year, a one-month grace period had expired in which the Armed Islamic Group (GIA), rebels fighting the government, had warned all foreigners to leave the country. Two weeks later, twelve Croatians working at a hydraulic plant nine miles away from the monastery had had their throats cut, partly in retaliation for what the rebels regarded as ongoing mistreatment of Muslims in Bosnia at the time, partly because the Croatians were foreign Christians. The same man who had ordered the slaughter of the Croatians, Sayat-Attya, led the armed group that entered the Trappist monastery and demanded to see the Trappist father superior.

Father Christian de Chergé, a Frenchmen like all the other monks, appeared, but was not intimidated: "This is a house of peace. No one has ever come in here carrying weapons. If you want to talk with us, come in, but leave your arms outside. If you cannot do that, we will talk outside."[1] It was a bold gesture, but Dom Christian had learned something living among the Algerian Muslims for almost twenty-five years: in their own way, even the armed bands respected religious commitment to peace. Nonetheless, the intruders made three demands. First, the monastery was rich and had to support the rebels; second, the Trappists had to send their doctor to take care of the GIA wounded; finally, as religious, the monks should donate medicine to the revolutionary cause.

Dom Christian deftly parried each of these requests. The community might seem rich, but was in fact poor, earning its own daily bread by working. The doctor was too old to travel into the Atlas mountains. But most importantly, as religious, the monks would care for whoever appeared in need before them, without taking sides in political or military conflicts. Besides, it was Christmas Eve and they were at the moment preparing to celebrate the feast commemorating Christ's birth; it was outrageous for soldiers to interrupt them in their sacred duties. With what appears to an outsider as an odd mixture of chivalry and brutality, Emir Sayat-Attya apologized: "In that case, please excuse us. We did not know."[2] But he promised to return. Dom Christian had turned aside the threat — for the moment.

A little over two-and-a-half years later, Dom Christian and six of his companions would have their throats cut in cold blood. Their case is one of the most widely reported martyrdoms in Africa in the twentieth century, besides those connected with the genocide in Rwanda. Some may say that the event was widely reported because it involved Europeans rather than native Africans, and there is some truth in this claim. But the manner of their deaths and the extensive documentation that exists about it have made it easy, unlike the cases of thousands of native black African martyrs, to reconstruct how one group of Christians was willing to expose itself to danger as a religious witness, knowing in advance that the gesture would probably bear little immediate fruit.

We have already seen in the chapter about Charles Foucauld that Algeria, as a French colony, presented many difficulties to missionaries at the beginning of the twentieth century. At the century's end, if anything, the difficulties were even worse. In the first half of this century, large numbers of mostly Christian French and mostly Muslim Algerians managed to find a rough *modus vivendi* with each other. But the French departed in the 1960s, under serious indigenous pressures. Their withdrawal amid much turmoil led to various atrocities. Even as decent a moral commentator as Albert Camus, a native French Algerian, did not know what to recommend any longer near the end. Algeria entered a tumultuous period in which various indigenous factions vied for power, some involving predominantly Islamic elements, others of a basically secular cast.

But in the 1980s and 1990s, Algeria, like many other countries with large Muslim populations, began to feel the pressure of fundamentalist Islamic groups that were springing up around the world. Algeria had already damaged its relations with France. But with the new fundamentalist groups, some of which practiced terrorism against Westerners and even against their own government, a new type of intolerance arrived. Many devout Muslims around the world have denounced the terrorism as not in harmony with the principles of Islam, which proclaims that Allah is the All-Merciful. But for the extremists, fundamentalist Islam presented a potent combination of political power and religious enthusiasm that could be used to assert national identity in the world over against the influential, wealthy nations.

Dom Bernardo Olivera, the abbot general of the Trappists, has written a moving account of the lives of the seven Algerian martyrs,[3] which includes many of their last letters and, therefore, enables us to know very clearly both what happened and what the monks believed they were doing. Like all the monks and nuns in the Benedictine/Cistercian tradition, they took a vow of "stability," which is meant to link them to the community in which they live until death. During the same period, because of threats to monastic establishments in many parts of the world, Trappist monasteries in Angola, Uganda, Bosnia, and Zaire also had to decide whether it was more prudent to stay or leave. In most cases (the monastery in Mokoto, Zaire, being the only exception), they have decided to stay. The decision is voted on by the whole community after thorough discussion among the members.[4]

In the Algerian case, the monks knew quite well what they were facing. The monastery at Tibhirine, Our Lady of Atlas, had been founded in 1934 as an offshoot of the Yugoslavian Abbey of Our Lady of Liberation. Though Atlas went through ups and downs, like any monastery, it had committed itself to a continuous witness among the people of Atlas for over half a century of Algerian history, including the most troubled periods. Indeed, one of the most touching statements about their feelings toward the area emerged immediately after the Christmas Eve 1993 visit when the guerilla fighters wanted the monastery to give them medical, financial, and logistical support in exchange for security. On the government side, the *Wali*, or prefect, of the nearby town of Medea offered the monks military protection or at least a more secure place to live within the city. The Trappists turned down both offers, however, because they preferred being a sign of peace to all sides even at the risk to their own safety. But they also pointed out that even temporary transfer to the prefect's protection might make it impossible to return and "our neighbors would not understand."[5]

So they remained in the monastery with basically no change in their way of life. The only modifications in policy that they voted for were to offer medical aid to all comers at the monastery itself, to reduce for the moment the number of monks, to halt taking on new novices for the time being, and, in case of emergency, to move to Morocco instead of France, so that they could return as soon as conditions allowed. Their commitment to being open witnesses to God's love was so firm that they even turned down an offer by the apostolic nuncio to move the monastery within the nunciature. The following year they voted again to confirm their commitment to be living witnesses of God's love in

Algeria — through prayer, a simple life, manual labor, and openness and sharing with everyone, especially the poorest.

The calmness and lucidity of these decisions were a marked contrast to the fact that armed conflict was increasing all around the Trappists. The violence struck at Christians in particular. First, a Little Sister of the Assumption, Paule Hélène Saint Raymond, and a Marist brother, Henri Vergès, were killed by Islamic militants on May 8, 1994. Vergès's death called forth from Dom Christian this reflection:

> His death seems so natural, so fitting to a long life entirely given, intentionally, from the first. He seems to me to belong to the category of those whom I call "martyrs of hope," who are never spoken of because it is in the patience of daily life that they spill all their blood. I understand "monastic martyrdom" in the same way. And it is this instinct that currently leads us not to change anything, unless toward a permanent effort of conversion (but even in this there is no change!).[6]

Two women religious, the Augustinians Caridad María Alvarez and Esther Alonso, were assassinated in October of 1994 as they left a church in Algiers. In a letter to the abbot general, Dom Christian described the funeral for the two women in terms of the effects it had on the small remnant of what had once been a large church in Algiers: "The celebration had a beautiful climate of serenity and self-offering. It brought together a tiny church whose still living members all realize that the logic of their presence must now include the possibility of violent death. For many, it is an occasion for a new and radical immersion in the very charism of their congregation . . . as well as a return to the very fount of their first calling. Furthermore, it is clear that all desire that none of these Algerians, to whom our consecration links us in the name of the love that God has for them, should wound that love by killing any of us, any of our Brothers."[7]

Christians continued to be killed, however. Dom Christian noted that like the Jesuits, Little Brothers of Jesus, the White Fathers, and others, his Trappists had all decided to stay in their African posts despite the risks, as a gesture of faith in the future. The risks were growing rapidly. First two more nuns, Odile Prévost and a Sister Chantal, both members of Foucauld's Little Sisters of the Sacred Heart, perished. Then Jean Chevillar, Christian Cheissel, Alain Dieulangard, and Charles Deckers — four White Fathers, a community with longstanding ties to Africa, were killed in Tizi Ouzou.

The Trappist community received another "visit," this time from the "brothers of the mountain," a different armed group. They claimed only to want to use the monastery telephone and gave the monks guarantees that they would not be harmed, even after they had not been allowed to enter. But Dom Christian and his colleagues knew that a veiled threat remained.[8] When some sisters of Our Lady of the Apostles also fell to armed bands, a visiting papal delegate told the Trappists at the funeral that he admired and agreed with their decision, but encouraged them not to ignore basic prudence and discretion despite their commitments. The monks had long ago made up their minds to give a certain kind of witness: "We see that we are at a juncture between two groups [i.e., government and Fundamentalist rebels] who are in conflict here and, to some extent, everywhere in the West and the Near East."[9]

Father Christopher Lebreton, another of the Trappists, wrote of how the slow process with all its threats affected them all. He had been one of the student revolutionaries in France in 1968, a generation supposedly afraid of commitment. But events since then had carried him to a far different place:

> There is something unique in our way of being Church: how we react to events, how we wait for them and live them out in practice. It has to do with a certain awareness, that we are responsible not for doing something, but for being something here, in response to Truth and to Love. Are we facing eternity? There is a sense of that. "Our Lady of Atlas, a sign on the mountains," *signum in montibus,* as our coat of arms declares.[10]

And he observes: "The martyr no longer desires anything for himself, not even the glory of martyrdom."[11] In all of this, it is difficult not to feel that we have a window into something of the same spirit with which Christ himself remained firm in his decision to go up to Jerusalem near his end, even though he knew what the result would be.

The Trappists, of course, had Christ's example constantly in mind. But they were also mindful that to claim for themselves some kind of special virtue in the circumstances would be to betray the humble love that they felt for the Algerians. For one thing, they feared that the outside world, knowing little of the good Muslim people (who later condemned the killing of the monks), would take their death as a triumphalistic mark of Christian superiority. Dom Christian in particular, with his long experience of Algiers and of life, reflects in a document that has become known as his *Testament:*

I have lived long enough to know that I am an accomplice in the evil which seems, alas, to prevail in the world, even in the evil which might blindly strike me down. I would like, when the time comes, to have a moment of spiritual clarity which would allow me to beg forgiveness of God and of my fellow human beings, and at the same time forgive with all my heart the one who will strike me down. I could not desire such a death. It seems to me important to state this. I do not see, in fact, how I could rejoice if the people I love were indiscriminately accused of my murder. It would be too high a price to pay for what will perhaps be called the "grace of martyrdom."[12]

Dom Christian had long been one of the guiding spirits of the Ribat es Salam ("Bond of Peace"), a group engaged in Islamic-Christian dialogue. If anything were likely to overcome centuries of conflict and mistrust between Muslims and Christians, it would have to be the kind of initiative, backed up by willingness to give everything, that he and his brothers engaged in. His final words in the *Testament* are addressed to the person who may, someday, cause his death: "In God's face I see yours. May we meet again as happy thieves in Paradise, if it please God, the Father of us both. *Amen! In H'Allah!*"

That heartfelt prayer was soon tested. As we have seen is often the case with martyrdom, the finale was mixed up with politics and human passions in a way that, for some observers, might obscure the offering of self that was present among the monks for years before the end. During the night of March 27, 1996, seven of the monks were abducted in a two-month ordeal that would stretch out almost until Pentecost. A month after the abduction, a GIA communiqué offered several reasons why the monks were seized and several conditions for their safe release. Among the reasons given for why the action was licit, the GIA emir, Abou Abdel Rahmân Amîn (popularly called Djamel Zitouni), argued that the previous protection (*aman*) was improper because the monks "have not ceased to invite the Muslims to be evangelized. They have continued to display their Christian slogans and symbols and to commemorate their feasts with solemnity."[13] Gone was the mutual religious respect manifested by the dark visitors on Christmas Eve two years earlier.

Citing selectively from Muslim law, the emir also stated: "It is therefore licit to apply to these monks what applies to unbelievers who are prisoners of war, namely: death, slavery or exchange for Muslim prisoners." Despite the religious forms, it was the last point — political advantages — that seems to have really motivated the GIA. They demanded the release of GIA members held by Algeria and France with this threat: "The choice is yours. If you liberate, we shall liberate. If you do not free your prisoners, we will cut the throats of ours. Glory to God."[14]

Governments that are given ultimatums by terrorists cannot give in without inviting more terrorism. That reasoning guided the French and Algerian authorities, though they sought ways to negotiate a solution. Pope John Paul II asked the abductors during his Palm Sunday Angelus that March, "Let them go back to their monastery safe and sound, and let them take up their place again among their Algerian friends." But all outside pleas were to no avail. On May 23, the GIA announced that they had cut the throats of all seven monks — Dom Christian de Chergé, Brother Luke Dochier, Father Christopher Lebreton, Brother Michael Fleury, Father Bruno Lemarchand, Father Celestine Ringeard, and Brother Paul Favre Miville — two days before.

Their heads were found, but not their bodies, reminding some present of the story of John the Baptist. The funeral Mass took place in the Algiers Basilica of Our Lady of Africa. Cardinal Arinze, an African himself, presided along with various French, Algerian, and other dignitaries. The remains were then quietly taken, with military security, back to the monastery for burial together in the cemetery there. Several Algerians, including the neighbors of the monastery, offered their sincere condolences for the loss of seven men who were both monks and friends to Muslims. The neighbors told the departing Christians, "Don't leave us, you must return."[15] Cardinal Lustiger of Paris celebrated Mass the next day and commended "the faith of this small local church which gives life and support to the decadent faith of old Europe."[16] But all was not over. Pierre Lucien Caverie, bishop of the Algerian city of Oran, was killed by terrorists while driving. A year later, John Paul II, hospitalized at the Gemelli Clinic in Rome, sent a message to the Trappists reminding them of a duty toward the seven, the bishop, and all the other victims of the conflict: "You are the custodians of this martyrdom, the persons on watch in prayer...so that the memory of this event remains fruitful in the future for Trappists and for the whole Church."[17]

John Paul's words might be applied to the many little-known martyrs of the rest of Africa as well, because their memories should bear fruit in the places where they made their sacrifices. Africa is a vast continent that, for the most part, is still in the early stages of development. Though there have been large numbers of martyrs in Africa during the twentieth century, there are few materials in print that tell their stories. Often the best information arises when a non-African missionary is killed in some corner of the Dark Continent. Material on indigenous African martyrs is less common in the media and even in scholarly studies. Such material as exists often derives from oral anecdotes written down, if at all, years after the events. Other material can only record the death of large masses of people, many of whom are known only by name, and many more not even by that. The story of the vast majority of African martyrs then has to be pieced together from less than ideal sources; but the sources still paint a portrait of vibrant Catholic communities in several countries that were willing to make the ultimate sacrifice for the faith. We will give only a few examples here in order to suggest the flavor of what life — and death — were like for many African Christians in the twentieth century.

As elsewhere in the world, martyrdom in Africa usually occurs in the context of political, religious, or social turmoil and, often, brutal tyranny. But Africa's vast tropical lands provide many opportunities for oppression far from internal or external monitors. So there is a certain similarity among the cases, whether they come from Sudan or Angola, Rwanda or the Congo. More than in most regions of the world, however, it is difficult to keep track of martyrdoms. Yet mere justice and Christian concern for every one of God's children singly makes it a moral imperative to study as closely and as comprehensively as possible the many who gave their lives in hard conditions, usually because they refused to abandon their pastoral or spiritual responsibilities as clear threats emerged all around them. As Cardinal Gantin, an African himself, has observed "Some of them have followed their master even further [than laying down their lives for their friends], by giving their life for their enemies."[18]

For instance, in the former Portuguese colony of Angola during the protracted wars that began in 1975, the year of Angola's independence, and continued for about a decade, almost one hundred priests and religious, Angolan and foreign, were abducted or murdered.[19] Carrying out the simplest pastoral and humanitarian duties exposed them to sudden death from one of the several factions fighting in the country. Some were deliberately sought out for execution, as was Father Leonardo Sikufinde, who was shot to death on August 30, 1985, along with several co-workers as he was taking a woman in labor to the Chiulu missionary hospital.

Opposing forces knew Sikufinde's mission car quite well and must have viewed these humanitarian gestures as comforting an enemy, when in fact they were merely part of the charitable mission. But the real reason for his murder seems to have been Sikufinde's work with young people. After studying Marxist philosophy in Rome, he returned to Africa as a professor and head of the Newman Academy for university students. His informed criticism of Marxism and influence over young people made him a natural target for the Marxist government of Angola, which was trying to keep an ideological stranglehold over education. Yet it is significant that he was gunned down on a mission of mercy rather than in an academic setting. It was easy in Angola to kill the priest anonymously in circumstances that few people would have even braved during such a conflict. The local bishop described the death of Sikufinde and others thus: "It was their dedication to the service of mankind that pushed the heroic missionaries to venture out on that practically deserted road in search of salvation and survival."[20] John Paul II sent his condolences from Rome for this all too common occurrence.

The sheer bravery of missionaries in Angola was a necessary factor to the ongoing survival and operation of the Church. If a priest or other Catholic leader avoided such dangerous circumstances out of fear, it gave the persecutors a hold over the situation. Once a priest was prevented from following his usual round or responding to an emergency situation, the people themselves would naturally refuse to leave their homes. Regular meeting places were always dangerous and, without an assurance that a priest would appear, attending religious events hardly seemed worth the exposure. Priests and leaders had to be careful not to concentrate themselves too much in one place or use one vehicle too often because these routines offered opportunities to wipe out entire pastoral teams. Two priests, Dutch Father Ligthart and Angolan priest Adriano Kasala, earned a reputation for exceptional bravery in carrying out scheduled rounds. This meant that catechists could prepare people for the sacraments and promise regular pastoral services to the faithful. On February 24, 1987, they were traveling in separate vehicles to try helping in Katchiungo, a town where armed forces had looted a Red Cross depot. Both were shot within seconds of one another during an ambush. Father Ligthart had written a Dutch proverb on his dashboard: "A ship that remains in harbor is safe, but is a ship made to remain in the harbor?" Evidently, this Dutchman and his Angolan comrade, who had formed an effective pastoral team, thought not, and joined many others who left harbor for work from which they would not return alive.

In Mozambique, another former Portuguese colony that gained independence in 1975, an outright civil war arose that did not end until 1992, and led to "one of the worst holocausts since the second world war."[21] About a million people fled the country, three million were internally displaced, and almost a million killed in one way or another. Naturally, the massive turmoil touched Catholics carrying out pastoral work. Two Jesuits, João de Deus Gonçalves Kamtezda and Silvio Alves Moreira, were killed near their residence in Chapotera on an unknown date in October 1985; their bodies were found only after they failed to appear for a scheduled meeting.

They had been warned several times by military forces to leave the area. This, of course, presents the classic missionary's dilemma. If they leave when times are hard, people think they are not really with them; if they remain, they face trouble and perhaps death. The two Jesuits took the latter course and paid the price for their decision to remain with their otherwise peaceful people. They brought the people the sacraments during the time that they were most terrified, wracked with hunger, sleeping out in the bush, away from the villages, to avoid military units.

Among others who found a similar but even less clear fate in Mozambique: Father Frederico Samuel Guimboa, who spoke up for justice and died from multiple gunshots wounds by unknown assassins, on November 23, 1984. Father Estêvão Mirassi worked in a bank after religious houses were nationalized; but he continued to criticize the Marxist government, local authorities, and human rights abuses. He could have escaped but preferred to be sent to a "reeducation" camp in 1978. At several points, the local governor promised his release, but he was never heard from again and is presumed dead. Even party identification was not sure protection in the tumultuous Mozambican situation. Another priest, Mateus Guengere, supported Frelimo, the Marxist party in Mozambique, but sought reforms within it. After several stays abroad to avoid arrest or worse, he was rounded up with a group of others. Though his fate is not known, he, along with the group, was probably executed.

Small-scale murders like these have occurred by the hundreds and thousands all over Africa. But the really large numbers — approaching millions — stemmed from much greater social upheavals. One of the first hot spots, Burundi, erupted soon after that nation achieved independence on July 1, 1962. Burundi went through five governments in its first three and a half years. In addition, one of the most unfortunate features of life in some parts of Africa also contributed to the slaughter: tribal warfare. In October 1965, when a coup failed, the Tutsi tribe came to power. Several thousand Hutus, the rival tribe, died. Michel Micombero, a Tutsi military leader who formed yet another government, made a habit of blaming all problems in the country on the rival Hutus. Though Burundi is over 80 percent Hutu, very few members of the tribe were admitted to the highest level of government. Instead, they experienced repeated waves of elimination and the whole tribe underwent relentless repression. Eyewitnesses reported a dozen truckloads of bodies per day being dumped openly in mass graves.

Sadly, at the time, few people among the victims or their families spoke up about what was clearly an attempt at genocide. The Burundian bishops wrote a 1973 pastoral letter calling for peace: otherwise the people seemed all but resigned to their fate. Priests who might have raised their voices because of contacts in Europe and elsewhere were rounded up and eliminated. One such figure, Father Melchior Bivanda, had earned a degree in theology *summa cum laude* at the Urbiana University in Rome. Around the time of the bishops' pastoral, he was summoned to a military office along with two other priests, Joseph Nikoyaggize and Donatien Nzeyimana. None of them was heard from again. Though the government tried to make it appear that they had all been released and fled the country, word leaked out that they had been beaten to death with sticks and hammers. An old woman gave church officials a tip about where to look for their bodies; the corpses showed obvious signs of torture.

Such summary treatment was common. Though many priests were arrested in Burundi and given long prison sentences of up to twenty-five years for "subversive activity," they hardly ever served their sentences, disappearing without a trace along the way. "Subversion" was broadly defined. If there was even a suspicion of unwanted activity, the harshest penalties could be imposed. A Father Théophile Karenzo, who came to the authorities' attention, was found transporting spare parts for his refrigerator to the parish house at Mekebuko. Since questions about where he got the money to buy the refrigerator did not produce incriminating answers, the military raised doubts about whether the parts were really for a refrigerator or for a machine gun. He was taken to a prison in Gitega, where he was kept for eight days without food or water. Later, 463 prisoners were machine-gunned *en masse*: Karenzo's body was found among them.[22]

Some priests at Mugera risked their lives to give Communion and the last rites to the thousands of prisoners. The inability of the Church to do much amid this carnage in Burundi drove more than one priest to criticize pastoral practice, though it is difficult to say what might have eliminated or even softened what were centuries-old ethnic and tribal hatreds. For instance, Father Michel Kayoya achieved a certain visibility in Africa with two books of poems, *Father's Footprints* and *Entre deux mondes*. Kayoya's verses do not rise to any great literary height, but they express what many felt at the time:

> After one colonization, were we undergoing
> Another more terrible colonization?
> A colonization by the meanness which
> every heart conceals, laziness
> and pride,
> Burdens that weigh on the heart of man
> and prevent him from growing.
> The struggle for liberation becomes
> a struggle between brothers tearing each
> other apart.[23]

Kayoya also objected to the government's curbs on development that would have helped the people; a kind of home-grown feudalism, which profited many high officials, dominated Burundi after independence. But Kayoya was not content merely to complain about what others were doing wrong. He tried to do something right that would show African initiative. Kayoya established a kind of lay order for native girls who would work with the very poor. Nuns came to Burundi from Europe, of course, but Kayoya thought it important for there to be native women in religious orders so that Burundians could care for other Burundians. The idea worked beautifully. The young girls cared for orphans, cultivated crops to be distributed to those who needed food, and worked humbly among all sectors of Burundian society dressed in simple clothing. It was Kayoya's way of suggesting how the Church might draw closer to the people in ways that had never been tried.[24]

Unfortunately, Father Kayoya did not have time to develop these initiatives further. First, he was arrested by the government for unknown reasons. It would not be mere speculation to think that perhaps his attempt to make peace between Burundians may have angered those who profited from war. By all accounts, Kayoya was constantly calm and cheerful in prison, leading others in prayers and song. At one point, he gave his stole to a guard, asking that the sacred object be returned to his bishop. But Kayoya's gentle life came to a terrible and swift end. Under the Mugera Hill, where he was held, the soldiers had dug mass graves. Father Kayoya was taken to the Ruvubu Bridge, which extended above them. Before they shot him, he forgave the soldiers and sang the Magnificat. Forgiveness and joy are common elements in the last moments of true martyrs, but Father Kayoya may have added a special and indigenous African element in that he was forswearing traditional tribal belief in vengeance. Another priest, right before dying, had "cursed his killers to the fifth generation," a more typical reaction in that culture.[25] According to one witness, the soldiers themselves were in tears at Kayoya's death.[26] With his passing and that of many other pastoral workers, a pathway to a different future for Burundi also died.

As late as 1993, during a new wave of violence, the Burundian bishops were officially remarking that "there will never be a church, but a caricature of a church, up until such time as the Hutu and Tutsi are able to find together and, with sincerity, the means for peaceful coexistence; up until such time as the Hutu and Tutsi priests, Brothers and Sisters are able to doubt themselves, in fraternal charity."[27] And they added: "Thousands of dead, thousands of homeless, thousands without a country and a future. In most cases, those who planned and committed these massacres are Christians."[28] This, of course, raises a question that has often appeared in the present volume: are these martyrs properly speaking, or incidental casualties in secular conflicts? The Church has its own criteria by which it officially declares people to have been martyred. But it would not be stretching the point too far to say that Christians may, indeed, martyr other Christians, whether it is Protestants killing Catholics, as in the case of the English martyrs, or Christians with one view of the nation murdering a figure like Archbishop Oscar Romero in El Salvador. In most African cases, it might be said that a culture of tribal violence martyred many for carrying on pastoral ministries or trying to preach a Gospel of reconciliation among age-old enemies, even in those cases where both sides were Catholic.

During the upheaval of the mid-1990s in Burundi, not only individual priests and catechists, but churches and chapels were attacked. At times, whole congregations of parishioners were caught in the violence and religious leaders were subjected to prolonged tortures, such as having their bodies mutilated with machetes, before being killed. In 1993 alone, though exact figures are difficult to come by, something like a hundred thousand people died and a million became refugees. Quite a few of the religious leaders had been intimidated many times and warned to leave before they met their ends. Yet they continued trying to bridge a gap that seemed unbridgeable. One of them, Father Michel Sinankwa, for instance, in the Ngagara area stated just before he died: "It's true I am a Hutu, while the parish priest is a Tutsi, but I don't see why I have to go. We could work together for peace." He fell victim to a radical Tutsi group with the ominous nickname *Sans échecs* ("Never defeated").[29]

Around the same time, the world became aware of similar large-scale atrocities going on in nearby Rwanda. But the momentary attention brought little in the way of positive action. Though the international community deplored the violence, there was very little outside nations could do to stop the deaths of over a million people (100,000 to 300,000 from 1990 to 1993 and somewhere between 500,000 and 800,000 at the height of the genocide in 1994) and the flight of another 2.5 million within a little over a year.[30] Two out of three Rwandans died, went to jail, or were displaced overall. Sadly, the greatest violence followed upon a peace agreement signed in 1993 that seemed to have put an end to the Rwandan civil war. But when Juvenal Habyarimana, the Rwandan president, and Cyprien Ntaryamira, the Burundian president, both died on April 6, 1994, in an unexplained plane crash, tribal animosity between Rwandan Hutus and Tutsis exploded once more.

If anything, the Rwandan atrocities were worse than those in Burundi. They displayed similar patterns to those described above, but marauding bands now attacked not only churches but hospitals and even diplomatic residences. Some of the bishops who survived the killing spree described them as following "a logic of mutual extermination" perpetrated by "a caste without a human horizon."[31] Faced with evidence of these events, U.N. Secretary General Boutros Boutros Ghali admitted that he, the United Nations, and the whole international community had failed. The diplomats could only continue talking about what to do while thousands were being slaughtered.

The Church itself could do little but suffer along with the rest of Rwanda. In earlier periods of unrest in Rwanda, churches had been used as sanctuaries. Now they became places where mass executions could more easily be carried out. Cardinal Roger Etchegaray, head of the Pontifical Commission for Justice and Peace, visited Rwanda in June of 1994 and lamented that the church buildings themselves had been turned into "slaughterhouses of innocents."[32] Just a few years earlier, in preparation for a visit by Pope John Paul II, the Church in Rwanda had been described as "young, beautiful, but fragile." By the end of the massacres, the condition of believers was horrible beyond words. In some areas, over half of the priests and other church leaders died. By one estimate, the death toll included: 3 bishops, 96 priests, 64 sisters, 45 brothers, and 28 consecrated lay people, in addition to the thousands of other murders.[33]

As terrible as these figures are, it is clear that they represent something even more sinister than mere carnage. It appears to have been the deliberate policy of the Rwandan government to break popular confidence in the Church's ability to protect them, to desecrate religious centers that protested human rights violations and that offered alternative visions of human existence, and particularly to cut off links between Rwandan priests and their contacts abroad. As in all such confused situations, clergy, including bishops, were accused of links with past or present regimes. Often this merely meant they tried to act as mediators with "the enemy." Bishop of Kabgayi Thaddée Nsengiyumva was charged with engaging in such efforts at reconciliation and noted that "the civilization of love is still far from getting possession of our hearts." The bishop had organized "Contacts Committees" that tried to bring together people of different backgrounds.

Church leaders protested atrocities of all kinds, but their voices were muted for a variety of reasons. In retrospect, it seems that perhaps they might have somehow done more. But in a vexed situation like Rwanda's, they faced armed opponents who turned a deaf ear to moral exhortations. Before a massacre at Gakurazo, for example, three bishops — Joseph Ruzindana, Vincent Nsengiyumva, and Thadée Nsengiyumva — tried to stop rampaging military forces, telling them that they needed written orders to carry out the operation they intended. The military leaders ordered the bishops to get out of the way or they would set the city of Kabgayi on fire. All three, along with priests and nuns, were taken for interrogation and held in a detention room. Without warning, soldiers burst in and machine-gunned all of them. Officials tried to attribute the deaths of these high-ranking church leaders to an "undisciplined soldier." But the homilist at the funeral for the three spoke frankly of the moral disaster that was growing alongside the physical one: "Nowadays in Rwanda, to do well or to do evil seems to be the same."[34]

Military forces made other attempts at large groups of clerics. The Christus Center, a place where various pastoral activities, retreats, and other harmless religious events took place, was brutally attacked in 1994 leaving seventeen dead. During the annual meeting of diocesan priests at Nyundo that same year, the militia attacked: two priests and thirty other people died. Many fled to the house of Bishop W. Kalibushi, who, in turn, was driven away in a car by security forces and spared only when an officer came by at the moment he was about to be executed. His residence, however, was completely destroyed. The militia attacked with grenades and machine guns and entered the sacristy, which was full of the wounded from previous days. All were killed. In the residence proper, eight priests and other people died. By chance, some people hiding in the cathedral survived because the soldier's thought they had gotten all the available "game."[35] Indeed, in this one attack alone, three hundred people fell.

In many places, for a priest to harbor and feed refugees was enough in itself to draw the ire of the military. Father Joseph Boneza, the pastor of a church at Mibilizi, for example, refused to turn over people who had fled to him and were on a military list. When the soldiers threatened to kill everyone, women and children included, if the designated people were not handed over, some of those who were not being sought heroically offered themselves in their places and were taken away, no doubt to death. Unfortunately, the names of these Christians who gave up their lives for others remain unknown. The local bishop suggested that Father Boneza come to his house for protection, but the people said to him: "If you abandon us, we are done for." A short while later, as he was driving toward a regional center, soldiers pulled him from his car, tore the cross off his neck, and crushed his skull with a club, killing him.[36]

Given all this mayhem, it is surprising that many who died, from both sides in the ethnic conflict, continued to work for reconciliation right up until the end. Some, like Fathers Alfred Kayibanda and Ananie Rugasira were Hutus who hid and protected Tutsis. Others, like Hutu Father Fidèle Mulinda, made a commitment to the rule: "Every man is my brother." The stories often show some detail that recalls Christ's passion and death. Tutsi Father Joseph Niyomugabo was stripped, beaten, and then killed. The murderers of Tutsi Father Sylvère Mutiganda of the Nyundo diocese were at first bribed to leave him alone, but eventually decided he had to be silenced, saying, "We will answer for his blood!"[37] Like the Good Shepherd who refused to abandon his sheep, Tutsi Father Félicien Muvara remarked before he died: "I cannot abandon these people. What shall I say to them when we meet in heaven?"[38]

And there is the remarkable story of two choirboys in the parish of Mwague who got lost in an area controlled by the Rwanda armed forces. They were captured and a soldier told one of them that he was going to kill the other to make him confess to some misdeed. The boy who heard this volunteered himself in place of his friend: "No, kill me instead!" Fortunately, another officer was passing by at that moment, recognized the two boys, and set them free. When the local priest, a Polish missionary, asked the boy what ever made him offer himself in the place of his friend, the boy answered: "Didn't you tell me once about a priest in Poland who gave his life for another...?" In the midst of a terrible genocide in Africa, a Rwandan boy had been inspired by the story of Maximilian Kolbe.[39]

Martyrdoms have taken place in various African countries for complex religious and political reasons as well as tribal hatreds. The notorious leader of Uganda, Idi Amin Dada, carried out a ruthless program of repression against anyone who stood in his way. Of Sudanese origin, Amin had plans to turn Uganda into a Muslim state, receiving money from Saudi Arabia and Libya to carry out a Jihad. And, like the Sudanese in the 1990s, he had a particular animosity toward Catholicism. Catholics, both lay persons and clerics, did not endear themselves to Amin by their frequent opposition to human rights violations.

For instance, Benedicto Kiwanuka, president of the Ugandan Supreme Court, used to go early every morning to the cathedral in Rubaga to pray for Uganda. He told his wife: "All of us must pray insistently for our country." And a priest reported him saying: "We cannot abandon our country because we are menaced. If we have to die, better to die as martyrs."[40] Kiwanuka seems to have gotten strength from his spirituality to stand up to one of Africa's most consistently ruthless dictators. He opposed Amin in the Supreme Court when the Ugandan leader would try to abrogate the rights of Ugandans or resident aliens. Kiwanuka repeatedly tried to make the army and other security forces obey rules of arrest and interrogation. He himself was illegally arrested and taken to a military prison in Makindye in September 1972. Within days he was killed with a hammer blow to the head and his body was taken away never to be found.

Amin's savagery also struck out at Father Clement Kiggundu, a Catholic priest and journalist who edited a church paper called *Munno*. Father Kiggundu pulled no punches in detailing the atrocities of Amin's Uganda. Amin replied in kind: when Kiggundu's body was found near his burnt-out car in early 1973, an autopsy revealed that he had been strangled, shot, and burned. Even that treatment was mild compared with the death of Father Gabriel Banduga. Apprehended on the pretext that he was traveling toward a rebel area (a mere coincidence) Banduga was beaten from 9:30 in the morning until 5:00 in the evening. The soldiers tied a rope around his waist and dragged him around the area; finally, tiring of the game, they cut off his ears and ordered him to eat them.[41]

After Idi Amin fled into exile, priests in Uganda still fell foul of indigenous forces. At least one, Father William Nyadru, a brilliant philosopher, ethnologist, and journalist who studied for several years in England, seems to have been ritually sacrificed in 1991 because a sorcerer in the area said a human victim was needed to assure the success of a raid.[42] Ironically, Father Nyadru had studied the cultures and languages of East Africa at the University of London precisely so that he would be able to return to Uganda with greater understanding and greater effectiveness in evangelizing. Even knowing all the dangers and challenges in Uganda, Nyadru believed the Church's future was great.

At the end of the twentieth century, however, the most vicious persecution of religious believers in the world was occurring in the Sudan. A fundamentalist Islamic government in Khartoum seeking to impose Islam on the whole country unleashed a *Jihad,* a holy war, that killed two million of its own people and displaced another four million. Radio, television, the press, and education have all been enlisted in proclaiming the Jihad. This assault fell heavily on Christians in the Nuba mountains and Southern Sudan, communities that proudly trace back their religious beliefs to the Nubian official from Candace who in the New Testament is described as having been converted by the deacon Philip. Both Egypt and Sudan became Christian in the early centuries until Islam arrived in the seventh century. Nonetheless, pockets of Christian believers survived and were strengthened by European missionaries in the nineteenth century. The Comboni missionaries in particular were founded to stimulate evangelization of Africans by other Africans.

The Khartoum government has targeted the Christian regions to the South for forced Islamization. In those regions, Christians and animists form the large majority of believers, but Muslims of a less fundamentalist bent live harmoniously with their neighbors. Nonfundamentalist Islam is persecuted by the Sudanese government as well. In a notorious case, Mahmoud Mohamed Taha, a scholar who argued that the Koran did not authorize brutality toward non-Muslims, was himself sentenced to death in 1985. Given the degree of religious purity that Sudan's leaders are determined to impose on fellow Muslims, it is no wonder that they have drawn the line at nothing against non-Muslims.

Priests imprisoned in Khartoum have been threatened with crucifixion, and there have been reports of actual crucifixions in the South.[43] But the Sudanese have brought back practices that Charles de Foucauld hoped France would help to stop and the world had thought were over forever. Slavery of black Christians from the South has become a common occurrence. Young children are often taken from parents and sold on national and, it is believed, international slave markets. The Dinka people, in particular, have been taken in large numbers. Some groups, Christian Solidarity prominently among them, have redeemed slaves with monetary payments. The practice is controversial, as it was in Foucauld's day: some applaud it; others believe it only encourages slavers. But there is no question that slavery of the most heinous kind has reemerged. As one Sudanese has described the situation:

> At the end of the twentieth century and at the dawn of a new millennium, our people are still being branded like cattle so that their masters will recognize them; their Achilles tendons are cut so that they are no longer able to walk, their hands only being freed for slave labor; our women are forcibly infibulated, that is, genitally mutilated, to gratify the sexual tastes of their masters.[44]

Sudan also attacks non-Muslims on a large scale. Villages and churches are bombed. Catholic schools set up in refugee camps have been repeatedly bulldozed. Military units are unleashed without restraints against any community that resists the forced Islamization. As difficult as it is to believe, the Sudanese government has gone so far as to starve, intentionally, regions that remain Christian. Wells have been poisoned to induce further attrition. In 1988, in the town of Bahr al-Ghazal, military forces drove Dinkas and Christians into cattle cars and then burned them alive. Sudanese Anglican Bishop Daniel Deng told his fellow bishops in London at the 1998 Lambeth Conference that "genocide is taking place now."[45]

Some individual stories may help to put a human face on the mayhem. Catechists are regularly tortured and shot (as happened to Younan Kuwa Paolo Adlan). Another catechist, Agostino El Nur, was tortured for four months: nails were driven into his head, his beard was pulled out, he was cut with a knife and his genitals were mutilated with pliers, and he was crucified for twenty-four hours tied to poles while lighted cigarettes were put in his ears. An Anglican priest, Kamal Tutue, would not convert to Islam and was burned so badly that, though he did not die, he lost all four limbs. In 1988, in Omdruman, Muslims incited by an imam attacked one of the convents of Mother Teresa's Missionaries of Charity, with serious injuries.[46]

The rampage against non-Muslims in Sudan shows no sign of slowing. Indeed, many of those captured have been warned, "Convert, or die like Jesus Christ!"[47]

# -CONCLUSION-

# MEMORY, COMMUNION, HOPE

"**C**ONVERT, OR DIE LIKE CHRIST." Those words from the most flagrant religious oppression in the world at the dawn of a new millennium might serve as an epitaph for all the hundreds of thousands who suffered persecution and death in the twentieth century — or, for that matter, since the very beginnings of Christianity. Christ made a point of telling his followers: "They have persecuted me and they will persecute you." And the Gospel of John, after noting that Jesus knew what was in human hearts, records that the master said, "The light has come into the world, and people loved darkness rather than light because their deeds were evil." It has never much mattered whether the rejection of the light came from moral, religious, or political evils. All evils share a common root, and the results have everywhere been very much the same wherever the forces of light and the forces of darkness clash.

The survey of the twentieth century's martyrs in the preceding pages has necessarily been long. But this book could easily be several times its current length even with the partial information we possess at this point in history. Recovering every name of every person who suffered persecution and death in the twentieth century and honoring his or her memory is a matter of simple justice. But if the foregoing pages show anything, they indicate that justice is not the only reason we ought to recover the memories of these brave and holy men and women. Death through injustice, whether individually or in groups, is an unfortunate feature of all human history, religious and secular. The twentieth century, alongside its great advances, was perhaps the bloodiest on record. Leaving religious passions aside, scholars have calculated that something like 170 million people died violently during this century, without even counting soldiers who died in wars. The passions that led to those deaths did not die with the coming of the new millennium.

We should not, therefore, believe that with the new millennium, the demise of totalitarian systems, or the spread of human rights' agreements, that injustice, much less martyrdom, will come to an end. The rule of law and democratic procedures, desirable as they are, will not abolish sin, but merely make it more difficult for malefactors to gain control of power and wield it unchecked. The age-old struggle over the things that are Caesar's and the things that are God's will continue forever. The very revelation of that truth has been one of Christianity's greatest contributions to a world in which various powers — political, religious, cultural — are always seeking to exert total control over human life. The martyrs stake their lives on a truth beyond all human powers.

There is no other group of victims throughout history who so consistently faced terrifying ends with calm hope and sincerely forgave their persecutors. Martyrs rarely even assume a posture of moral superiority toward their executioners — people that most of us would regard as inhuman monsters. The martyrs are aware of the evil in themselves and the redemption that has come to them from outside the usual human darkness. By the specific dynamics of martyrdom, the desire for vengeance or sense of superiority are ruled out at the beginning.

Remembering martyrs then is different than the kind of process whereby, say, the truth commissions set up after various conflicts try to bring perpetrators of crimes to justice and to uncover the facts about people's deaths. As important as these activities are in human terms, they are worlds away from the ambience of the martyrs. The whole point in remembering those who died as witnesses for truth and goodness is that they literally participate in the Passion of Christ. The remembrance of his Passion and death throughout history has not brought all evildoers to justice or established a paradise on earth. His death revealed, for Christians, an unexpected structure inherent in the very world we inhabit. That world is always enslaved to passion, greed, hunger for power, envy, and a host of other vices. The only way out of the endless cycle of wrong and punishment is the free willingness to suffer wrong and forgive without revenge. The Christian story changed several cultures on those principles. It is still available to change our own.

For a Christian, martyrs are not merely models to be imitated, but, like all saints, spirits with whom we are in communion, waiting with a common hope. Martyrdom is in a deep sense the paradigm for the Christian life. Any person who starts to follow the Master seriously cannot help but find himself or herself attacked by the same forces that attacked him. Happy is the age that does not produce a large crop of martyrs. But even happier is the age whose people are willing to remain with Christ whether it means martyrdom or not, for from that willingness to die springs everything that makes it worthwhile to live.

And so we should end this account of a remarkable and little known group of witnesses with profound thanks and a simple prayer:

*Requiem eternam dona eis, Domine,*
*et lux perpetua luceat eis.*

# NOTES

## Introduction

1. Raymond Etteldorf, *The Catholic Church in the Middle East* (New York: Macmillan, 1959), 153.

2. These facts were made public in November 1999 when the Italian Parliamentary commission dedicated to the continuing investigation of the assassination attempt confirmed to the Roman newspaper *La Repubblica* that secret files from the former Czechoslovakia, released in 1990 by dissident turned president Václav Havel, suggested quick KGB action.

3. John Henry Newman, *Parochial and Plain Sermons* (San Francisco: Ignatius Press, 1997), 131–32.

4. Václav Benda, "Life as a Dissident," in Janice Broun, *Conscience and Captivity in Eastern Europe* (Washington, D.C.: Ethics & Public Policy Center, 1988), 309.

5. Quoted in Ray Kerrison, *Bishop Walsh of Maryknoll: Prisoner of Red China* (New York: Putnam, 1962), 13.

6. Tacitus, *Annales,* Book xv, chapter 44.

7. On these spectacles, see Henri Daniel-Rops, *The Church of Apostles and Martyrs* (New York: Image Books, 1962), 1:201–4.

8. Quoted from Tertullian's *Apology,* Book V, in Daniel-Rops, ibid., 209.

9. Jack Sparks, ed., *The Apostolic Fathers* (New York: Thomas Nelson, 1978), 73.

10. Daniel-Rops, *The Church,* 221.

11. See the account of their deaths in Anne Freemantle, *A Treasury of Early Christianity* (New York: Mentor, 1953), 183–85.

12. Quoted in Daniel-Rops, *The Church,* 236.

13. Quoted from Justin Martyr, *Apology* ii. 12, in ibid., 249.

14. Freemantle, *Treasury,* 169.

15. Though all such figures are less than reliable, these are the best estimates available. See Stéphane Courtois, Nicolas Werth, Jean-Louis Panné, Andrzej Paczkowski, Karel Bartosek, and Jean-Louis Margolin, *The Black Book of Communism: Crimes, Terror, Repression,* trans. Jonathan Murphy and Mark Kramer (Cambridge, Mass.: Harvard University Press, 1999).

16. *Lumen Gentium,* 42.

## Chapter 1: Miguel Pro and the Mexican Tragedy

1. Michael Kenney, S.J., *No God Next Door: Red Rule in Mexico and Our Responsibility* (New York: William J. Hirten, 1935), 9.

2. Graham Greene, *The Lawless Roads* (New York: Penguin, 1982), 100. The first edition of this volume was dated 1939, and Greene was an eyewitness to this destruction.

3. Quoted in Francis Clement Kelley, *Blood Drenched Altars: A Catholic Commentary on the History of Mexico* (Milwaukee: Bruce, 1935), 342–43. The American bishop is presumably Kelley himself, who, in addition to being a historian of Mexico, was the bishop of Oklahoma City and Tulsa.

4. Gerald F. Muller, C.S.C., *With Life and Laughter: The Life of Father Pro* (Boston: Pauline Books, 1996), 15. Muller's work was reviewed before publication by Pro's last surviving sister, Ana María, who regarded it as the most factual account of her brother to appear.

5. Ramiro Valdés Sánchez and Guillermo Ma. Havers, *Tuyo es el Reino: Mártires mexicanos del siglo XX* (Guadalajara: Libros Católicos, 1992), 43–46.

6. See the reproduction in Antonio Dragon, *Pour le Christ-Roi: Miguel-Augustin Pro de la Compagnie de Jésus* (Montreal: Imprimerie du Messager, 1928), 127.

7. Muller, *With Life and Laughter,* 32.

8. Fanchón Royer, *Padre Pro* (New York: P. J. Kenedy & Sons, 1954), 87.

9. Ibid., 102–5.

10. Muller, *With Life and Laughter,* 34.

11. Valdés Sánchez and Havers, *Tuyo es el Reino,* 19–23.

12. Quoted from Humboldt's *Political Essay on New Spain* in Kelley, *Blood Drenched Altars,* 372, n. 4.

13. Enrique Krauze, *Mexico: A Biography of Power, A History of Modern Mexico, 1810–1996,* trans. Hank Heifetz (New York: HarperCollins, 1997), 436.

14. Royer, *Padre Pro,* 132.

15. Muller, *With Life and Laughter,* 58. The American was Joseph F. Howard, S.J.

16. Adriano Xavier's study *Entre Obreros,* 3d ed. (Mexico City: Buena Prensa, 1952), recounts these matters.

17. Muller, *With Life and Laughter,* 98.

18. Quoted in ibid., 106–7.

19. Ibid., 112.

20. Royer, *Padre Pro,* 155–56.

21. See the account of this incident in Valdés Sánchez and Havers, *Tuyo es el Reino,* 24–38.

22. Ibid., 25.

23. Walsh, *Men of Mexico,* 543–44.

24. See Wilfrid Parson, *Mexican Martyrdom* (New York: Macmillan, 1936), 29. The journalist, who interviewed Calles in January of 1928, was John Gregory Mason of the London *Daily Telegraph.*

25. Parson, *Mexican Martyrdom,* 30–31.

26. Muller, *With Life and Laughter,* 138.

27. Quoted in Royer, *Padre Pro,* 223.

28. George W. Grayson, *The Church in Contemporary Mexico* (Washington, D.C.: Center for Strategic and International Studies, 1992), 15.

29. Quoted in Greene, *The Lawless Roads,* 39.

30. Donald J. Mabry, "Mexican Anticlerics, Bishops, Cristeros, and the Devout during the 1920s: A Scholarly Debate," *Journal of Church and State* 20, no. 1 (1978): 81.

31. Ann Ball, *Blessed Miguel Pro: Twentieth Century Martyr* (Rockford, Ill.: Tan Books, 1996), xi.

32. FBIS, *Daily Report (Latin America),* November 13, 1991, p. 27.

## Chapter 2: In Soviet Russia and Its Territories

1. Quoted in Antoine Wenger, *Catholiques en Russie d'après les Archives du KGB, 1920–1960* (Paris: Desclée de Brouwer, 1998), 155.

2. V. I. Lenin, *Collected Works* (New York: International Publishers, 1927 ), 14:70.

3. This letter is translated in *The Unknown Lenin: From the Secret Archive,* ed. Richard Pipes (New Haven: Yale University Press, 1996), 152–55.

4. Ibid., 11, n. 17.

5. Father Leopold Braun, *Worldmission,* December 1950.

6. Gary MacEoin, *The Communist War on Religion* (New York: Devin-Adair, 1951), 19.

7. Stéphane Courtois, Nicolas Werth, Jean-Louis Panné, Andrzej Paczkowski, Karol Bartosek, and Jean-Louis Margolin, *The Black Book of Communism: Crimes, Terror, Repression,* trans. Jonathan Murphy and Mark Kramer (Cambridge, Mass.: Harvard University Press, 1999). See in particular chapter 10, "The Great Terror 1936–1938." The only reference to the religious terror is at the bottom of page 200.

8. A full account of this pre-Soviet period may be found in James J. Zatko, *Descent into Darkness: The Destruction of the Roman Catholic Church in Russia, 1917–1923* (South Bend, Ind.: University of Notre Dame Press, 1965).

9. Ibid., 62.

10. Ibid., 70–71.

11. Ibid., 76–77.

12. Ibid., 79–80.

13. Ibid., 121.

14. Ibid., 83.

15. Quoted in Irina Osipova, *Se il mondo vi odia . . . Martiri per la fede nel regime sovietico* (Rome: La Casa di Matriona, 1997), 33.

16. Zatko, *Descent into Darkness,* 119.

17. Ibid., 114.

18. Cited from *Izvestia* in ibid., 144.

19. Zatko, *Descent into Darkness,* 171.

20. Ibid., 180.

21. Ibid., 178.

22. Osipova, *Se il mondo vi odia,* 28.

23. In addition to the Osipova book mentioned above, which is based on some KGB materials, we have Antoine Wenger, *Catholiques en Russie d'après les Archives du KGB, 1920–1960,* which quotes extensively from recently available files.

24. Osipova, *Se il mondo vi odia,* 141–42.

25. Ibid., 145.

26. Ibid., 147.

27. Ibid., 149.

28. Quoted in Wenger, *Catholiques en Russie,* 94, from a January 16, 1934, document of the secretariat of the central committee of the Ukrainian Communist Party.

29. Osipova, *Se il mondo vi odia,* 58.

30. Ibid., 46.

31. Quoted in ibid., 65.

32. Ibid., 77.

33. Ibid. 60 and 217.

34. Ibid., 237.

35. Ibid., 195.

36. Entry for January 30, 1929, quoted in ibid., 103.

37. Quoted from the interrogation file in ibid., 87.

38. Ibid., 93.

39. Quoted in Wenger, *Catholiques en Russie*, 96.

40. Quoted from the 1997, "New Europe" by ibid., 100.

41. Ibid., 74.

42. Antoine Wenger, *Rome et Moscou, 1900–1950* (Paris: Desclée de Brouwer, 1987), 336–37.

43. Ibid., 83.

44. Wenger, *Rome et Moscou*, 552.

45. Quoted in Kent Hill, *The Puzzle of the Soviet Church: An Inside Look at Christianity and Glasnost* (Portland, Ore.: Multnomah, 1989), 127.

## Chapter 3: The Terror in Ukraine

1. See in particular the account published by Monsignor Giuseppe Moioli of the Roman Congregation for the Eastern Churches. That account is excerpted and amplified in Athanasius B. Pekar, O.S.B.M., *History of the Church in Carpathian Rus'*, trans. Marta Skorupsky (New York: Eastern European Monographs of the Columbia University Press, 1992), 151–52.

2. Pekar, *History*, 150.

3. Ibid., 147–48.

4. Pavel Sudoplatov, *Special Tasks: The Memoirs of an Unwanted Witness — A Soviet Spymaster* (New York: Little, Brown, 1994), 253.

5. Pekar, *History*, 150.

6. See Serge Keleher, *Passion and Resurrection: The Greek Catholic Church in Soviet Ukraine* (Lviv: Stauropegion, 1993), 11–17.

7. For a brief history of Ukrainian Christianity before, during, and after Brest, with a bibliography that lays out the case for the various claims, see Bohdan Rostyslav Bociurkiw, *The Ukrainian Greek Catholic Church and the Soviet State (1939–1950)* (Toronto: Canadian Institute of Ukrainian Studies Press, 1996).

8. Ibid., 10, also cites this figure.

9. John Paul II, "Letter to European Bishops on the Recent Changes in Central and Eastern Europe," Vatican, May 31, 1991, section 1.

10. Didier Rance, *Catholiques d'Ukraine, des catacombes...à la lumière* (Paris: Bibliothèque AED, 1992), 13.

11. Keleher, *Passion and Resurrection*, 19.

12. Bociurkiw, *The Ukrainian Greek Catholic Church*, 25.

13. Ibid., 23.

14. Kurt I. Lewin, *A Journey through Illusions* (Santa Barbara: Fithian Press, 1994), 254.

15. Ibid., 265.

16. Rance, *Catholiques d'Ukraine*, 36.

17. Ibid., 36.

18. Ibid., 37.

19. Ibid., 37–38.

20. Quoted from the October 9, 1939, issue of *Komunist* in Bociurkiw, *The Ukrainian Greek Catholic Church*, 34.

21. See Robert Conquest, *Harvest of Sorrow: Soviet Collectivization and the Terror-Famine* (New York: Oxford University Press, 1986).

22. Gregory Luznycky, *Persecution and Destruction of the Ukrainian Church by the Russian Bolscheviks* (New York: Ukrainian Congress Committee of America, 1966), 47.

23. Bociurkiw, *The Ukrainian Greek Catholic Church*, 37.

24. Ibid., 52.

25. Ibid.

26. Ibid., 235.

27. Ibid., 56.

28. Quoted in Bociurkiw, ibid., 57.

29. Keleher, *Passion and Resurrection*, 35.

30. Kurt I. Lewin, "Archbishop Andreas Sheptytskyi and the Jewish Community in Galicia during the Second World War," *Unitas* (Summer 1960): 137–38.

31. Keleher, *Passion and Resurrection*, 38.

32. Bociurkiw, *The Ukrainian Greek Catholic Church*, 63.

33. Ibid., 71.

34. Ibid., 104.

35. Quoted in Jaroslav Pelikan, *Confessor between East and West: A Portrait of Ukrainian Cardinal Josyf Slipyi* (Grand Rapids: William B. Eerdmans, 1990), 151.

36. All quotations from Halan are cited by Bohdan R. Bociurkiw in *Ukrainian Churches under Soviet Rule: Two Case Studies* (Cambridge: Ukrainian Studies Fund of the Harvard University Press, 1984), 99.

37. Bociurkiw, *Ukrainian Churches*, 106.

38. Bohdan R. Bociurkiw, "The Ukrainian Catholic Church in the USSR under Gorbachev," in *Problems of Communism* 39 (November–December 1990): 2.

39. Bociurkiw, *Ukrainian Churches*, 107.

40. Ibid., 206.

41. Ibid., 201.

42. Luznycky, *Persecution and Destruction,*, 54, and Keleher, *Passion and Resurrection*, 43–44.

43. Personal letter (September 16, 1999) to the author from Greek Catholic Exarch Michael Hrynchyshyn.

44. Keleher, *Passion and Resurrection*, 42.

45. Jaroslav Pelikan, *Confessor between East and West*, 149.

46. Quoted in ibid., 150.

47. Ibid., 156.

48. Bociurkiw, *Ukrainian Churches*, 91.

49. Pelikan, *Confessor between East and West*, 157.

50. Ibid., 164.

51. Quoted in ibid., 165.

52. See ibid., 170.

53. Quoted in ibid., 167.

54. For a balanced assessment of these problems see Bociurkiw, *The Ukrainian Greek Catholic Church*, 245.

55. Ibid., 236.

56. Ibid., 244.

57. Keleher, *Passion and Resurrection*, 61.

58. Bociurkiw, *The Ukrainian Greek Catholic Church*, 203.

59. Quoted in Bociurkiw, "The Ukrainian Church in the USSR under Gorbachev," 4.

60. Myroslaw Tataryn, "The Ukrainian (Greek) Catholic Church in the USSR," in *Religious Policy in the Soviet Union,* ed. Sabrina Petra Ramet (New York: Cambridge University Press, 1993), 294.

61. Bociurkiw, "The Ukrainian Catholic Church in the USSR under Gorbachev, 5.

62. Vasili Mitrokhin, who smuggled out notes in 1992 from the KGB archives, which he made while still working as a KGB agent, recorded that Yuvenalyi had the KGB code name ADAMANT, a point also confirmed by the *Washington Post.* Yuvenalyi inherited the name from his uncle, Metropolitan Nikodim, after the latter's death. See Christopher Andrew and Vasili Mitrokhin, *The Sword and the Shield: The Mitrokhin Archive and the Secret History of the KGB* (New York: Basic Books, 1999), 660, note 18. Their chapter entitled "The Penetration and Persecution of the Soviet Churches," though not accurate in every detail, is also worth reading for what it reveals about the often conflicted motives of Orthodox collaborators with the Soviet regime.

63. Bociurkiw, "The Ukrainian Church in the USSR under Gorbachev," 8.

64. Tataryn, "The Ukrainian (Greek) Catholic Church in the USSR," 295.

65. Ibid., 296.

66. Ibid., 297.

67. Quoted in Bociurkiw, "The Ukrainian Church in the USSR under Gorbachev," 9.

68. Tataryn, "The Ukrainian (Greek) Catholic Church in the USSR," 294.

69. Quoted in Bociurkiw, "The Ukrainian Church in the USSR under Gorbachev," 15.

70. Tataryn, "The Ukrainian (Greek) Catholic Church in the USSR," 309.

## Chapter 4: A French Prodigal Son

1. Charles de Foucauld, *Meditations of a Hermit,* trans. by Charlotte Balfour (London: Burns & Oates, 1930), 156.

2. For the most recent review of the details of Foucauld's death, see Jean-Jacques Antier, *Charles de Foucauld (Charles of Jesus),* trans. Julia Shirek Smith (San Francisco: Ignatius Press, 1999). The original French edition appeared in 1997.

3. Thomas Merton, *Entering the Silence* (San Francisco: HarperSanFrancisco, 1996), 417.

4. Ibid., 200.

5. Thomas Merton, *Witness to Freedom* (New York: Farrar, Strauss & Giroux, 1994), 204.

6. *Meditations,* II:5.

7. Quoted in Robert Ellsberg, "Little Brother of Jesus," in *Martyrs: Contemporary Writers on Modern Lives of Faith,* ed. Susan Bergman (Maryknoll, N.Y.: Orbis Books, 1996), 295.

8. Anne Freemantle, *Desert Calling* (New York: Henry Holt, 1949), 8–9.

9. Ibid., 48.

10. Ibid., 44.

11. Ibid., 53.

12. Ibid., 74.

13. Ibid., 86.

14. Ibid., 99.

15. Ibid., 124.

16. Ibid., 107.

17. Ibid., 151.

18. Ibid., 185.

19. Ibid., 209.

20. Ibid., 215–16.

21. Ibid., 227.

22. See chapter 18 of the present volume for the ongoing slave trade in Sudan.

23. Freemantle, *Desert Calling,* 232.

24. Ibid., 13.

25. Ibid., 266.

26. Ibid., 271.

27. Foucauld, *Meditations of a Hermit,* 178.

28. Ibid., 171.

29. Charles de Foucauld, *Lettres et carnets* (Paris: Éditions du Seuil, 1966), 162 (December 1902).

30. Foucauld, *Meditations of a Hermit,* 180.

31. Ibid., 186.

32. Ibid., 179.

33. Ibid., 181.

34. Ibid., 183.

35. Ibid., 180.

36. Foucauld, *Lettres et carnets,* 170.

37. Ibid., 179.

38. Freemantle, *Desert Calling,* 277.

39. Ibid., 283.

40. Ibid., 302.

41. Ibid., 322.

42. Ibid., 301.

43. Antier, *Charles de Foucauld,* 316–17.

44. Marion Mill Preminger, *The Sands of Tamanrasset: The Story of Charles de Foucauld* (New York: Hawthorn Books, 1961), 267.

## Chapter 5: Spanish Holocaust

1. Sister Martina López, *And They Gave Their Lives...* (Fremont, Ohio: Lesher Printers, 1997), 139.

2. All the figures draw on the careful review of the various estimates in José M. Sánchez, *The Spanish Civil War as a Religious Tragedy* (Notre Dame: University of Notre Dame Press, 1985), 9–10. The quotation is from pp. 10–11.

3. Miguel Mauta, *Así cayó Alfonso XIII* (Barcelona, 1966), 251.

4. George Orwell, *Homage to Catalonia* (Boston: Beacon Press, 1953).

5. George Orwell, "Looking Back on the Spanish Civil War," in *A Collection of Essays by George Orwell* (New York: Doubleday Anchor, 1954), 197. The essay dates from 1945.

6. Ibid., 202.

7. Ernest Hemingway, *For Whom the Bell Tolls* (New York: Charles Scribner's Sons, 1940), 244.

8. Ibid., 135.

9. Opus Dei, "Remembrances of Our Founder during the Spanish Civil War," unpublished typescript, 25.

10. Paul Johnson, *Modern Times: The World from the Twenties to the Eighties* (New York: Harper & Row, 1983), 330–31.

11. Warren H. Carroll, *The Last Crusade* (Front Royal, Va.: Christendom Press, 1996), 86.

12. Quoted in ibid., 75, from Antonio Montero Moreno, *Historia de la persecución religiosa en España, 1936–1939* (Madrid, 1961).

13. Carroll, *The Last Crusade,* 84.

14. Montero Moreno, *Historia de la persecución,* 521–23.

15. Sánchez, *The Spanish Civil War as a Religious Tragedy,* 12–13.

16. Hugh Thomas, *The Spanish Civil War* (New York: Simon & Schuster, 1986), 271.

17. On this lack of hard evidence, see Sánchez, *The Spanish Civil War as a Religious Tragedy,* 45, and Montero Moreno, *Historia de la persecución,* 63.

18. Montero Moreno, *Historia de la persecución,* 610–12, for these various stories and the quotation.

19. Ibid., 613–14.

20. Ibid., 615.

21. Thomas, *The Spanish Civil War,* 274–75.

22. Ibid., 276–77.

23. Quoted in Carroll, *The Last Crusade,* 194–95, from H. Edward Knoblaugh, *Correspondent in Spain* (New York: Sheed & Ward, 1937), 167–68.

24. Orwell, *Homage to Catalonia,* 4–5.

25. Sánchez, *The Spanish Civil War as a Religious Tragedy,* 21, n. 5.

26. Gregorio Gallego, *Madrid, corazón que se desangra* (Madrid: G. del Toro, 1976), 46–47, quoted in Sánchez, *The Spanish Civil War as a Religious Tragedy,* 27.

27. Quoted in Sánchez, *The Spanish Civil War as a Religious Tragedy,* 27.

28. Thomas, *The Spanish Civil War,* 269.

29. Montero Moreno, *Historia de la persecución religiosa,* 365–67.

30. Ibid., 376–77.

31. Thomas, *The Spanish Civil War,* 272.

32. Montero Moreno, *Historia de la persecución religiosa,* 619–23.

33. Thomas, *The Spanish Civil War,* 269–70.

34. Ibid., 271–72.

35. Ibid., 276. See H. L. Kirk, *Pablo Casals* (New York, 1971), 401.

36. Montero Moreno, *Historia de la persecución religiosa,* 623.

37. See ibid., 623–24.

38. Thomas, *The Spanish Civil War,* 513.

39. Ibid., 277.

40. Ibid., 271.

## Chapter 6: The Nazi Juggernaut

1. Josef Levit, S.M., *Blessed Jakob Gapp, Marianist* (Dayton: North American Center for Marianist Studies, 1998), 96–109.

2. A transcript of these minutes is in Appendix 1 of Levit, *Blessed Jakob Gapp.*

3. Levit, *Blessed Jakob Gapp,* 41.

4. Figures cited from the German census in Donald J. Dietrich, *Catholic Citizens in the Third Reich* (New Brunswick, N.J.: Transaction Books, 1986), 39.

5. This is the figure arrived at for the West German Catholic Bishops Commission for the Study of Contemporary History in 1984. See Vincent A. Lapomarda, *The Jesuits and the Third Reich* (Lewiston, N.Y.: Edwin Mellen Press, 1989), 66, n. 92.

6. Helmut Moll (on behalf of the German Bishops Conference), *Die Katholischen Deutschen Martyrer des 20. Jahrhunderts: Ein Verzeichnis* (Paderborn: Ferdinand Schöningh, 1999).

7. Hermann Rauschnig, *Conversations with Hitler* (Zurich: Europa-Verlag, 1988), 50.

8. Ibid., 53.

9. See the statistics and individual accounts of prisoners in Bedřich Hoffmann, *And Who Will Kill You: The Chronicle of the Life and Sufferings of Priests in the Concentration Camps* (Preroc, Poland: Pallottinum, 1994), 287–88 for the raw statistics and 288–581 for individuals.

10. Ibid., 176.

11. John M. Lenz, *Christ in Dachau or Christ Victorious,* trans. Countess Barbara Waldstein (Mödling bei Wien, Austria: Missionsdruckerei Saint Gabriel, 1960), 102.

12. Ibid., 103.

13. Ibid., 123.

14. Ibid., 129.

15. Quoted from Dr. Felix Hurdes's book *Our Father,* in Lenz, *Christ in Dachau,* 164.

16. Lenz, *Christ in Dachau,* 163. See also Jan Mikrut, *Blutzeugen des Glaubens: Martyrologium des 20. Jahrhunderts* (Vienna: Dom Verlag, 1999), 119–33.

17. Jan Mikrut, "Sr. Angela Autsch Ott: Der Engel von Auschwitz," in Mikrut, *Blutzeugen des Glaubens,* 29.

18. Ibid., 38.

19. Hoffmann, *And Who Will Kill You,* 11.

20. Lenz, *Christ in Dachau,* 20.

21. Ibid., 31.

22. Ibid., 35.

23. Ibid., 40.

24. Ibid.

25. Ibid., 48.

26. Ibid., 50.

27. Ibid., 62.

28. Ibid., 67.

29. Ibid., 73.

30. Ibid., 152.

31. Ibid., vi.

32. Ibid., 114.

33. Francis J. Murphy, *Père Jacques: Resplendent in Victory* (Washington, D.C.: ICS Press, 1998), 89.

34. Ibid., 72.

35. Ibid., 78.

36. Ibid., 86.

37. Ibid., 136.

38. Ibid., 96.

39. Ibid., 98–99.

40. Ibid., 102.

41. Ibid., 103.

42. Ibid., 108.

43. Lenz, *Christ in Dachau,* 74.

44. Murphy, *Père Jacques,* 109.

45. For a brief summary of this history see William L. Shirer, *The Rise and Fall of the Third Reich* (New York: Simon and Schuster, 1960), 234–40.

46. Quoted from the *Frankfurter Zeitung,* August 28, 1934, in Nathaniel Micklem, *National Socialism and the Roman Catholic Church* (New York: Oxford University Press, 1939), 2.

47. Quoted from Alfred Rosenberg's *Protestantische Rompilger* in Micklem, *National Socialism,* 23.

48. See Micklem, *National Socialism,* 16.

49. Ibid., 17.

50. Quoted from the September 1937 *Nationalsozialistische Monatshefte* in ibid., 57.

51. See *National Socialism,* 60–61.

52. Ibid., 32–33.

53. Quoted in ibid., 70.

54. Quoted in ibid., 75.

55. Annedore Leber, ed., *The Conscience in Revolt: Portraits of the German Resistance 1933–1945,* trans. Thomas S. McClymont (Speyer: Hase & Koehler, 1994), 317.

56. Ibid., 318.

57. Quoted in Micklem, *National Socialism,* 82.

58. Quoted in ibid., 78.

59. Leber, *Conscience in Revolt,* 333.

60. Giorgio Acquaviva, *Rupert Mayer: Un Gesuita contro il nazismo* (Rome: La Civiltà Cattolica, 1987), 77.

61. Ibid., 81.

62. See P. Walbert Weber, O.P., *P Titus Horten, O.P.: Ein Lebensbild* (Vechta: Dominikanerkloster, 1986).

63. Shirer, *Rise and Fall,* 1060.

64. Ibid., 1048.

65. Quoted from Hitler's *Table Talk* in Hugh Gallagher, *By Trust Betrayed: Patients, Physicians and the License to Kill in the Third Reich* (New York: Henry Holt, 1990), 245.

66. Gallagher, *By Trust Betrayed,* 239.

67. Quoted in Levit, *Blessed Jakob Gapp,* 57.

68. Quoted in ibid., 81.

69. Günther van Norden, "Opposition by Churches and Christians," in Wolfgang Benz and Walter H. Pehle, eds., *Encyclopedia of German Resistance to the Nazi Movement,* trans. Lance W. Garmer (New York: Continuum, 1997), 51.

70. Quoted in Leber, *Conscience in Revolt,* 159.

71. Cf. van Norden, "Opposition by Churches and Christians," 54–56.

72. Van Norden's summary, ibid., 52.

73. Leber, *Conscience in Revolt,* 336.

74. Ibid., 337.

75. Ibid., 146.

76. Shirer, *Rise and Fall,* 223.

77. Benz and Pehle, *Encyclopedia,* 72 and 288.

78. Ibid., 251.

79. Quoted in Leber, *Conscience in Revolt,* 356.

80. See Gordon C. Zahn, *In Solitary Witness: The Life and Death of Franz Jägerstätter* (New York: Holt, Rinehart and Winston, 1964), 5.

81. Ibid., 71.

82. See ibid., 30–31.

83. Quoted in ibid., 33.

84. Quoted in ibid., 34.

85. Ibid., 104, n. 2.

86. Ibid., 42.

87. Ibid., 48–49.

88. Ibid., 34.

89. Ibid., 53.

90. Ibid., 58.

91. Quoted in Micklem, *National Socialism,* 218.

92. Ibid., 219.

93. Zahn, *In Solitary Witness,* 59.

94. Ibid., 66.

95. Ibid., 63.

96. Ibid., 61.

97. Ibid., 86.

98. Ibid., 97.

99. Ibid., 99.

100. Ibid., 101.

101. Ibid., 107.

## Chapter 7: Martyr for Truth

1. Waltraud Herbstrith, *Edith Stein: A Biography,* trans. Bernard Bonowitz, O.C.S.C. (New York: Harper & Row, 1985), 2.

2. Josephine Koeppel, O.C.D., translator's afterword to Edith Stein, *Life in a Jewish Family* (Washington, D.C.: Institute of Carmelite Studies, 1985), 442.

3. *Life in a Jewish Family,* 445.

4. Ibid.

5. Ibid., 437.

6. Quoted in Hilda Graef, *The Scholar and the Cross: The Life and Work of Edith Stein* (London: Longman, Green, 1955), 10.

7. Quoted in Henry Bordeaux, *Edith Stein: Thoughts on Her Life and Times,* trans. Donald and Idela Gallagher (Milwaukee: Bruce, 1959), 20.

8. Herbstrith, *Edith Stein,* 6.

9. Ibid., 8.

10. Ibid., 14.

11. Graef, *The Scholar and the Cross,* 12.

12. Herbstrith, *Edith Stein,* 20.

13. Ibid., 25.

14. Edith Stein, *Self Portrait in Letters, 1916–1942,* trans. Josephine Koeppel, O.C.D. (Washington, D.C.: Institute for Carmelite Studies, 1993), 6.

15. Ibid.

16. Ibid., 7–8, 9.

17. Herbstrith, *Edith Stein*, 27.
18. Ibid., 28.
19. Graef, *The Scholar and the Cross*, 61.
20. Ibid., 67.
21. Quoted in ibid., 54.
22. Quoted from a 1932 speech given in Essen in Herbstrith, *Edith Stein*, 53. For Stein's views on women, see Edith Stein (Sister Teresa Benedicta of the Cross), *Essays on Woman*, trans. Frieda Mary Oben (Washington, D.C.: Institute of Carmelite Studies, 1996).
23. See Hilda Graef's introduction to *The Writings of Edith Stein* (London: Peter Owen Ltd., 1956), 9.
24. Quoted in Graef, *The Scholar and the Cross*, 88.
25. Herbstrith, *Edith Stein*, 66.
26. Ibid., 53.
27. Bordeaux, *Edith Stein*, 50.
28. Graef, *The Scholar and the Cross*, 112.
29. Stein,"The Prayer of the Church," in *Writings*, 40.
30. Graef, *The Scholar and the Cross*, 141–42.
31. Ibid., 130.
32. Ibid., 143.
33. Ibid., 128–30.
34. Ibid., 145.
35. Ibid., 151.
36. Bourdeaux, *Edith Stein*, 11.
37. Herbstrith, *Edith Stein*, 92.
38. Graef, *The Scholar and the Cross*, 184.
39. Herbstrith, *Edith Stein*, 95.
40. Graef, *The Scholar and the Cross*, 188.
41. Bordeaux, *Edith Stein*, 15.
42. Graef, *The Scholar and the Cross*, 225.
43. *L'Osservatore Romano*, October 14, 1998, p. 1.
44. Herbstrith, *Edith Stein*, 102.
45. Graef, *The Scholar and the Cross*, 31.
46. Herbstrith, *Edith Stein*, 105–7.

### Chapter 8: Saint Maximilian Kolbe and Some Polish Victims of Nazism

1. Patricia Treece, *A Man for Others: Maximilian Kolbe, Saint of Auschwitz, in the Words of Those Who Knew Him* (New York: Harper & Row, 1982), 134–35.
2. Ibid., 132.
3. Sergius C. Lorit, *The Last Days of Maximilian* Kolbe (New York: New City Press, 1988), 16–17.
4. Ibid., 20.
5. Quoted in ibid., 23.
6. Ibid., 24–25.
7. Ibid., 136.
8. Ibid., 138–39.
9. Ibid., 134.
10. Ibid., 139.

11. Ibid., 140–41.

12. Ibid., 42.

13. Ibid., 99.

14. Treece, *A Man for Others,* 131.

15. Ibid., 1–2.

16. Ibid., 17.

17. Antonio Ricciardi, O.F.M. Conv., *Saint Maximilian Kolbe, Apostle of Our Difficult Age,* trans. and adapted by the Daughters of Saint Paul (Boston: Saint Paul Editions, 1982), 45–46.

18. Ibid., 74.

19. Ibid., 88.

20. Ricciardi, *Saint Maximilian Kolbe,* 71.

21. Treece, *A Man for Others,* 44–45.

22. See the selections from these in Ricciardi, *Saint Maximilian Kolbe,* 149–50.

23. Lorit, *The Last Days,* 124.

24. Ibid., 128.

25. Ibid.

26. Ibid., 128–30.

27. See André Frossard, *"N'Oubliez pas l'amour: La Passion de Maximilien Kolbe* (Paris: Éditions Robert Laffont, 1987), 203.

28. Ibid., 131.

29. Ricciardi, *Saint Maximilian Kolbe,* 256.

30. Treece, *A Man for Others,* 133.

31. Quoted in ibid., 138.

32. For the background to this debate and a more temperate reading of the whole question, see Ronald Modras, "Explorations and Responses: John Paul II, St. Maximilian Kolbe, and Anti-Semitism, Some Current Problems and Perceptions Affecting Catholic-Jewish Relations, *Journal of Ecumenical Studies* 20, no. 4 (Fall 1983): 630–39.

33. E.g., *Commonweal,* February 11, 1983.

34. Modras, "Explorations and Responses, 632–33.

35. Ibid.

36. Ibid.

37. Diana Dewar, *Saint of Auschwitz: The Story of Maximilian Kolbe* (New York: Harper & Row, 1982), 92.

38. Ibid.

39. Treece, *A Man for Others,* 122.

40. Ibid., 123.

41. Ibid., 126.

42. Ibid., 139.

43. Ibid., 142.

44. Ibid., 147.

45. Ibid., 154.

46. Ibid., 149.

47. Ibid., 166.

48. Ibid., 176.

49. Vladislavien, et al., *Beatificationis seu Declarationis Martyrii Servorum et Servarum Dei Antonii Juliani Nowowiejski (Archiepiscopi), Henrici Kaczorowski et Aniceti Kopliński (Sacerdotum), Mariae Annae Biernacka (Laicae) atque Cen-*

*tum Trium Sociorum in Odium Fidei, Uti Fertur, Annis 1939–1945 Interfectorum: Introduzione Generale della Causa* (Vatican City State, 1999), 3.

50. Ibid., 24.

51. Ibid., 25.

52. Ibid., 28.

53. Ibid., 29.

54. Ibid., 17.

55. Ibid., 17–18.

56. Ibid., 39–40.

57. Maria Starzyíka, *Eleven Prie-Dieux,* trans. M. Roselita Bradley, C.S.F.N., and M. Frances Sikorski, C.S.F.N. (Rome: Tipografia Poliglotta della Pontificia Università Gregoriana, 1992), 11.

58. Adam Mickiewicz, *Poems,* edited by George Rapall Noyes (New York: Polish Institute of Arts and Sciences in America, 1944), 237–38.

59. Starzyíka, *Eleven Prie-Dieux,* 18.

## Chapter 9: A Brief Introduction to the Martyrs of Eastern and Central Europe

1. Grażina Sikorska, "Poland," in Janice Broun, *Conscience and Captivity: Religion in Eastern Europe* (Washington, D.C.: Ethics and Public Policy Center, 1988), 193.

2. Sikorska, "Poland," 193–94.

3. Janice Broun, "Poland's Progress Towards Democracy," *The First Freedom,* Puebla Institute, Washington, D.C., July–August 1991, p. 3.

4. Quoted from a December 1982 homily in Bruno Chenu, Claude Prud'homme, Frances Quéré, and Jean-Claude Thomas, *The Book of Christian Martyrs* (London: SCM Press, 1990), 211.

5. See chapters 6 and 7 of the present volume.

6. Sikorska, "Poland," 166.

7. Ibid.

8. Albert Galter, *The Red Book of the Persecuted Church* (Westminster, Md.: Newman Press, 1957), 259.

9. Ibid., 261.

10. Sikorska, "Poland," 178.

11. Cf. Andrzej Micewski, *Cardinal Wyszyński: A Biography* (San Diego: Harcourt Brace Jovanovich, 1984), 93.

12. Sikorska, "Poland," 180.

13. George Weigel, *The Final Revolution: The Resistance Church and the Collapse of Communism* (New York: Oxford University Press, 1992), 111.

14. Quoted in ibid., 128.

15. Chenu et al., *The Book of Christian Martyrs,* 207.

16. Leslie László, "Religion and Nationalism in Hungary," in *Religion and Nationalism in Soviet and East European Politics,* ed. Pedro Ramet (Durham, N.C.: Duke University Press, 1989), 291.

17. Broun, *Conscience and Captivity,* 140.

18. "Marton Hartai," in ibid., 329.

19. See V. Chalupa, *Situation of the Catholic Church in Czechoslovakia* (Chicago: Czechoslovak Foreign Institute in Exile, 1959), 5–6.

20. Ibid., 9.

21. Ibid., 11.

22. Ibid., 15–16.

23. Ibid., 20.

24. Ludvík Němec, *Episcopal and Vatican Reaction to the Persecution of the Catholic Church in Czechoslovakia* (Washington D.C.: Catholic University of America Press, 1953), 40.

25. Broun, "Czechoslovakia," in *Conscience and Captivity,* 69.

26. Ibid., 72.

27. Ibid.

28. Ibid., 76.

29. Ibid., 79.

30. Ibid., 85.

31. Ibid., 88.

32. Ibid., 89.

33. Ibid., 93.

34. Ibid., 94–95.

35. Ibid., 98.

36. Václav Havel, "Politics and Conscience," in *Living in Truth* (New York: Faber and Faber, 1986), 156–57.

37. ZENIT News Agency report, September 14, 1999.

## Chapter 10: The First Atheist State: Albania

1. Cf. Romans, 15:19: "My own work has been to complete the preaching of Christ's Gospel, in a wide sweep from Jerusalem as far as Illyricum" (Knox translation). The ancient Roman province of Illyricum included much of northern Albania and the regions of Albanian-speaking peoples who lie outside current national borders. Paul may have also passed through Dalmatia, which contained southern Albania, on his way north.

2. On this history see Gjon Sinishta, *The Fulfilled Promise: A Documentary Account of Religious Persecution in Albania* (Santa Clara, Calif., 1976).

3. Ibid., 14.

4. Michael Marku, "The Martyrdom of Father Anton Harapi, O.F.M.," in ibid., 102.

5. Didier Rance, *Albanie: Ils ont voulu tuer Dieu* (Paris: Bibliothèque AED), 27.

6. Enver Hoxha, *Selected Works* (Tirana: "8 Nentori" Publishing House, 1974), 1:438–39, quoted in Sinishta, *The Fulfilled Promise,* 20.

7. Sinishta, *The Fulfilled Promise,* 26.

8. Rance, *Albanie,* 100–101.

9. Quoted in ibid., 125.

10. Ibid., 89.

11. As recorded in the documentary service Fides (March 1953), no. 291, 6, quoted in Sinishta, *The Fulfilled Promise,* 53.

12. Ernest Koliqi, "The Tragic End of One of the Most Brilliant Stylists of Albanian Literature," in ibid., 115.

13. Arshi Pipa, "In Memory of Archbishop Vincent Prendushi," in ibid., 79–87.

14. Vala Jeh, "Bishop Frano Gjini — Dignified Defender of His Flock," in ibid., 91–94.

15. Illir Bali, " ... The Suffering, My Son, Makes the Victory More Noble," in ibid., 118–21.

16. Anton Gaspri, "Mother Do Not Weep for What You See Now, Weep for What Is to Come," in ibid., 95.

17. Rance, *Albanie*, 90.

18. Sinishta, *The Fulfilled Promise*, 159.

19. Rance, *Albanie*, 83.

20. Sinishta, *The Fulfilled Promise*, 167.

21. Ibid., 56.

22. Jak Gardin, S.J., diary excerpt of November 1950, in ibid., 146.

23. Sinishta, *The Fulfilled Promise*, 60.

24. Rance, *Albanie*, 100.

25. Sinishta, *The Fulfilled Promise*, 62.

26. Broadcast of Radio Tirana, April 28, 1972, recorded in *Albania Report* vol. 3, no. 5 (April–May 1973).

27. Rance, *Albanie*, 108.

28. Ibid., 204.

29. Quoted in ibid., 5.

## Chapter 11: A Steady Light in Lithuania

1. Nijole Sadunaite, *A Radiance in the Gulag: The Catholic Witness of Nijole Sadunaite,* trans. Rev. Casmir Pugevicius and Marian Skabeikis (Manassas, Va.: Trinity Communications, 1987), 30–33.

2. Ibid., 46.

3. Ibid., 48–49.

4. Ibid., 56.

5. Ibid., 58.

6. Ibid., 60.

7. See Czeslaw Milosz, *Native Realm: A Search for Self-Definition* (Berkeley: University of California Press, 1981).

8. The figures are drawn from the book assembled by the "Christians of the East," *Catholiques de Lituanie* (Paris: Bibliothèque AED, 1987), 11 ff.

9. V. Stanley Vardys, *The Catholic Church, Dissent and Nationality in Soviet Lithuania* (New York: Columbia University Press, 1978), 46.

10. Ibid., 48.

11. *Catholiques de Lituanie*, 53.

12. Quoted from *Lietuvių archyvas,* in Vardys, *The Catholic Church*, 58.

13. Vardys, *The Catholic Church*, 75.

14. Reprinted in Lino Gussoni and Aristede Brunello, *The Silent Church: Facts and Documents concerning Religious Persecution behind the Iron Curtain* (New York: Veritas Publishers, 1954), 52.

15. Lists taken from the archives of the *Chronicle of the Catholic Church in Lithuania,* no. 28 (n.d.), 44–45.

16. Sadunaite, *A Radiance in the Gulag,* 74.

17. Ibid., 113.

18. *Catholiques de Lituanie*, 155.

19. Ibid., 152. The story first appeared in *Chronicle of the Catholic Church in Lithuania,* no. 50 (December 8, 1981): 8–11.

20. *Catholiques de Lituanie*, 156–57.

21. From "Freedom Appeals," January–February 1982, cited in ibid., 157–58.

## Chapter 12: The Calvary of Romania

1. Didier Rance, *Roumanie: Courage et Fidélité, L'église gréco-catholique unie* (Paris: Bibliothèque AED, 1994), 22.

2. Abbé Pierre Gherman, *L'âme roumaine écartelée: Faits et documents* (Paris: Les Editions du Cèdre, 1955), 135.

3. R. G. Roberson, "The Church in Romania," *New Catholic Encyclopedia,* supplemental vol. 14, 335.

4. Gherman, *L'âme roumaine écartelée,* 135–36.

5. Alexander Ratiu and William Virtue, *Stolen Church: Martyrdom in Communist Romania* (Huntington, Ind.: Our Sunday Visitor Press, 1979), 27.

6. Gherman, *L'âme roumaine écartelée,* 136.

7. Alexander F. C. Webster, *The Price of Prophecy: Orthodox Churches on Peace, Freedom, and Security* (Washington, D.C.: Ethics and Public Policy Center, 1993), 119.

8. Ion Ploscaru lists these subsequent recanters in *Lanturi si teroare* (Timişoara: Signata, 1993).

9. Rance, *Roumanie,* 39.

10. Gherman, *L'âme roumaine écartelée,* 136.

11. Ibid., 142.

12. Webster, *The Price of Prophecy,* 119.

13. Ratiu and Virtue, *Stolen Church,* 17.

14. Ibid., 119.

15. S. A. Prunduş, O.S.B.M., and C. Plăianu, *Cardinalul Iuliu Hossu* (Cluj: Unitas, 1995), 131–32.

16. Ratiu and Virtue, *Stolen Church,* 17.

17. Quoted from his October 12, 1948, letter to Cardinal Tisserant in Gherman, *L'âme roumaine écartelée,* 148.

18. Richard Wurmbrand, *Tortured for Christ: Today's Martyr Church* (London: Hodder & Staughton, 1967).

19. Gherman, *L'âme roumaine écartelée,* 147.

20. Ibid., 153.

21. Webster, *The Price of Prophecy,* 91.

22. Janice Broun, "The Latin-Rite Roman Catholic Church in Romania," *Religion in Communist Lands* 12, no. 2 (Summer 1984): 168.

23. Ratiu and Virtue, *Stolen Church,* 126.

24. Gherman, *L'âme roumaine écartelée,* 162.

25. Ibid., 163.

26. Ibid., 172.

27. Broun, "The Latin-Rite Roman Catholic Church in Romania," 170.

28. Ibid., 169.

29. Rance, *Roumanie,* 167.

30. Ibid., 167–68.

31. Ibid., 170.

32. Ibid., 172.

33. Ibid., 166.

34. Ibid.

35. Ratiu and Virtue, *Stolen Church,* 158.

36. Stéphane Courtois, Nicolas Werth, Jean-Louis Panné, Andrzej Paczkowski, Karel Bartosek, and Jean-Louis Margolin, *The Black Book of Communism: Crimes,*

*Terror, Repression,* trans. Jonathan Murphy and Mark Kramer (Cambridge, Mass.: Harvard University Press, 1999), 400.

37. Ibid., 419.

38. Ibid., 420.

39. Ibid., 421.

40. Ibid. This account is drawn from Virgil Ierunca, *Piteşti, laboratoire concentrationnaire (1949–1952)* (Paris: Michalon, 1996), 59–61.

41. Ratiu and Virtue, *Stolen Church,* 111.

42. Quoted from D. Bacu's account, *The Anti-Humans,* in Ratiu and Virtue, *Stolen Church,* 92.

43. Ratiu and Virtue, *Stolen Church,* 100–101.

44. From Bacu, quoted in ibid., 108.

45. Ibid., 110.

46. Ibid., 98.

47. Rance, *Roumanie,* 186.

48. Ibid., 187.

49. On Ghika, see Hélène Danubia, *Prince et Martyr: Monseigneur Vladimir Ghika, l'apôtre du Danube* (Paris: Pierre Téqui, 1993).

50. Ratiu and Virtue, *Stolen Church,* 26.

51. Ibid., 73.

52. Broun, "The Latin-Rite Roman Catholic Church in Romania," 175.

53. Quoted in Ratiu and Virtue, *Stolen Church,* 170.

54. Broun, "The Latin-Rite Roman Catholic Church in Romania," 173.

55. Quoted in Rance, *Roumanie,* 12.

56. Quoted in Ratiu and Virtue, *Stolen Church,* 175.

## Chapter 13: Murder in the Cathedral

1. Jon Sobrino, *Archbishop Romero: Memories and Reflections,* trans. Robert R. Barr (Maryknoll, N.Y.: Orbis Books, 1990), 43.

2. James R. Brockman, S.J., *Romero: A Life* (Maryknoll, N.Y.: Orbis Books, 1990), 3. Brockman's life is the best researched and most authoritative source that has so far appeared and is followed with some differences here.

3. Ibid., 4.

4. Ibid.

5. Quoted, in a slightly different translation, in ibid., 7.

6. Ibid., 10.

7. Quoted in ibid., 20.

8. Ibid., 23.

9. Ibid., 30.

10. See, for example, Aquinas's points in *Summa Theologiae* IIa IIae, q. 66.

11. Brockman *Romero,* 30.

12. Ibid., 31–32.

13. Brockman, for example, disputes the alleged "conversion" in ibid., 128. Sobrino says that Romero himself disliked this idea; see Sobrino, *Archbishop Romero,* 7.

14. Brockman, *Romero,* 35.

15. Ibid., 47.

16. Sobrino, *Archbishop Romero,* 49.

17. *Summa Theologiae* IIa IIae, q. 42.

18. Brockman, *Romero*, 186.

19. Oscar Romero, *Voice of the Voiceless: The Four Pastoral Letters and Other Statements* (Maryknoll, N.Y.: Orbis Books, 1985), 95. The citation is from *Gaudium et Spes*, 42.

20. *Voice of the Voiceless*, 97. The citation is from the Medellín document "Peace," 27.

21. *Voice of the Voiceless*, 100.

22. Sobrino, *Archbishop Romero*, 36.

23. *Voice of the Voiceless*, 107–8.

24. Ibid., 109.

25. Ibid., 110.

26. Figures quoted by Thomas E. Quigley in his foreword to Oscar Romero, *A Shepherd's Diary*, trans. Irene B. Hodgson (Cincinnati: St. Anthony Messenger Press, 1993), 2.

27. Brockman, *Romero*, 63.

28. Ibid., 70.

29. Ibid., 153.

30. Ibid., 161.

31. Sobrino, *Archbishop Romero*, 21.

32. Brockman, *Romero*, 192.

33. Ibid., 164.

34. Ibid., 166.

35. Ibid., 174.

36. Ibid., 179.

37. Sobrino, *Archbishop Romero*, 34.

38. Brockman, *Romero*, 201.

39. Ibid., 195.

40. Romero, *A Shepherd's Diary*, 322.

41. Brockman, *Romero*, 223.

42. Ibid., 224.

43. Ibid., 235.

44. Ibid., 238.

45. Ibid., 243.

46. Sobrino, *Archbishop Romero*, viii.

47. Donna Whitson Brett and Edward T. Brett, *Murdered in Central America: The Stories of Eleven U.S. Missionaries* (Maryknoll, N.Y.: Orbis Books, 1988), 197–99.

48. Ibid., 216.

49. Ibid., 257.

50. Ibid., 267.

51. Ibid., 273.

52. Quoted in ibid., 297.

53. Ana Carrigan, *Salvador Witness: The Life and Calling of Jean Donovan* (New York: Simon and Schuster, 1984), 250–51.

54. Jon Sobrino, S.J., *Company of Jesus: The Murder and Martyrdom of the Salvadorean Jesuits* (London: Catholic Fund for Overseas Development, 1990), 3.

55. Ibid., 9–10.

56. Ibid., 18.

57. Quoted in ibid., 30.

58. Juan Clark, *Religious Repression in Cuba* (Miami: Cuban Living Conditions Project, 1998), 1.
59. Ibid., 32.
60. Armando Valladares, *Contra Toda Esperanza: 22 años en el "Gulag de Las Américas"* (Panama: Kosmos-Editorial, 1985), 8.
61. Sergiu Grossu, ed., *The Church in Today's Catacombs* (New Rochelle, N.Y.: Arlington House, 1975), 196.

### Chapter 14: General Introduction to the Asian Martyrs

1. Paul Marshall, *Their Blood Cries Out: The Worldwide Tragedy of Modern Christians Who Are Dying for Their Faith* (Dallas: Word Publishing, 1997), 97–98.
2. Ibid., 102.
3. Ibid., 103.
4. Ibid.
5. All accounts of the Assam martyrs are from personal correspondence with Father Edward D'Souza, S.D.B., director of the Catholic Church in Dotma, Kokrjhar.
6. *Ecclesia in Asia,* Section 1.
7. Ibid., section 2.
8. Ibid., section 28.
9. Ibid., section 49, emphasis in the original.
10. Nina Shea, "A Still Darker Era for Pakistan's Christians," *National Catholic Register,* March 9–15, 1997.
11. Ibid.
12. "Pakistani Catholic Cleric Buried; Muslims Burn Christian Homes," *New York Times,* May 11, 1998.
13. Nina Shea, *In the Lion's Den* (Nashville: Broadman & Holman Publishers, 1997), 41.
14. *New York Times,* December 24, 1999, A6.
15. Mariagrazia Zambon, *Crimson Seeds: Eighteen PIME Martyrs,* trans. Steve Baumbusch (Detroit: PIME World Press, 1997), 164.
16. Ibid., 170.

### Chapter 15: Chinese Carnage

1. For a colorful account of Ricci's life, see Jonathan D. Spence, *The Memory Palace of Matteo Ricci* (New York: Viking, 1984).
2. Mariagrazia Zambon, *Crimson Seeds: Eighteen PIME Martyrs,* trans. Steve Baumbusch (Detroit: PIME World Press, 1997), 37.
3. Ibid., 41.
4. Ibid., 42.
5. On February 18, 1951, by Pius XII.
6. J. Krahl, "Martyrs of China," in *The New Catholic Encyclopedia* (1967), 3:602–3.
7. Ibid., 598.
8. Quoted in Zambon, *Crimson Seeds,* 54–55.
9. Quoted in ibid., 57.
10. Ibid., 58.
11. Ibid., 60–61.
12. Ibid., 61–62.
13. Ibid., 68–69.

14. Ibid., 95.

15. The data on the martyrs of the Yang Kia Ping monastery was collected from various sources by Father M. Basil Pennington, O.C.S.O. Though some of the details may be inaccurate, given the difficulty of establishing the truth after the fact, the basic lines of the story seem to be confirmed by several witnesses.

16. Claire Marquis-Oggier and Jacques Darbellay, *Maurice Tornay: A Man Seized by God,* trans. Sister Edmond Veronica, R.A. (London: Saint Paul, 1993), 92.

17. Ibid., 94.

18. Ibid., 17.

19. Ibid., 35.

20. Ibid., 46.

21. Ibid., 104.

22. For a comprehensive list of Catholics martyred by various forces diocese by diocese, see Giancarlo Politi, *Martiri in Cina: I martiri cattolici dell Cina imperiale e repubblicana e della Repubblica popolare cinese* (Bologna: Editrice Missionaria Italiana, 1998).

23. Jean Monsterleet, S.J., *Martyrs in China,* trans. Antonia Pakenham (Chicago: Henry Regnery, 1956), 74.

24. Ibid., 75.

25. Ibid., 31.

26. Ibid., 32.

27. Ibid., 40.

28. Ibid., 43–44.

29. Ibid., 45–48.

30. Ibid., 59.

31. Taped presentation to the Cardinal Mindszenty Foundation, Saint Louis, Missouri, April 1990.

32. See Paul Marshall, *Their Blood Cries Out* (Nashville: Word, 1994), 75.

33. Ibid., 81.

34. Ibid., 83.

## Chapter 16: Korea's Death March

1. See Catholic Bishops Conference of Korea, *Korean Witnesses to the Faith throughout the XX Century* (Seoul, 1999), 141–43.

2. Stewart Lone and Gavan McCormack, *Korea since 1850* (New York: St. Martin's Press, 1993), 7.

3. Andrea Matles Savada, ed., *North Korea: A Country Study* (Washington, D.C.: Library of Congress, 1994), 22.

4. Robert T. Oliver, *A History of the Korean People in Modern Times: 1800 to the Present* (Newark: University of Delaware Press, 1993), 43.

5. Savada, ed., *North Korea,* 81.

6. On these earlier martyrs, see Father Kim Chang-seok Thaddeus, *Lives of 103 Martyr Saints of Korea* (Seoul: Catholic Publishing House, 1984).

7. Lone and McCormack, *Korea since 1850,* 54.

8. See photo in ibid., 57.

9. Oliver, *A History,* 119.

10. Ibid., 30.

11. Lone and McCormack, *Korea Since 1850,* 55.

12. Ibid., 133.

13. Korean Bishops Conference document, "Korea's Holocaust" (Seoul: n.d.), 23.

14. See Catholic Bishops Conference of Korea, *Korean Witnesses to the Faith*.

15. Father Joseph Chang-mun Kim and catechist John Jae-sun Chung, editors and compilers, *Catholic Korea: Yesterday and Today* (Seoul: Catholic Korea Publishing, 1964), 341.

16. For a breakdown of the fates of the missionary and native religious, see the tables in ibid., 354–55, and 360–63.

17. Ibid., 357.

18. Ibid., 358.

19. Ibid., 342.

20. Ibid., 343.

21. Ibid., 26.

22. Edward Fischer, *Light in the Far East: Archbishop Harold Henry's Forty-Two Years in Korea* (New York: Seabury Press, 1976), 112.

23. See "The Death March (From the Diary of a Kidnapped Carmelite Nun)" in *Catholic Korea,* Appendix III, 473–536.

24. Philip Crosbie, *March till They Die* (Westminster, Md.: Newman Press, 1956), 13.

25. Ibid., 24.

26. Ibid., 32.

27. *Catholic Korea,* 477.

28. Ibid., 43.

29. Ibid., 54.

30. Catholic Bishops Conference of Korea, *Korean Witnesses to the Faith,* 23.

31. Ibid., 180.

32. Ibid., 359.

33. Ibid., 9.

34. Ibid., 15.

35. Ibid., 36.

36. Ibid., 69–70.

37. Ibid., 11.

38. *New Catholic Encyclopedia,* Supplement 1989–95 (Washington, D.C.: Catholic University of America Press, 1996), 19:230.

39. Eric O. Hanson, *Catholic Politics in China and Korea* (Maryknoll, N.Y.: Orbis Books, 1980), 101.

40. Quoted in ibid.

41. Ibid., 104.

42. Ibid., 106.

43. *New Catholic Encyclopedia,* 19: 232.

### Chapter 17: The Spirit in Vietnam

1. Marie-Michel, *Love Cannot Die: A Life of Marcel Van* (Montpellier: Librairie Arthème Fayard, 1990), 84.

2. Ibid., 106.

3. Ibid., 116.

4. Ibid., 161.

5. Ibid., 172.

6. Ibid., 175.

7. Ibid., 201.

8. Ibid., 202.

9. Ibid., 217.

10. Ibid., 225.

11. Ibid., 230.

12. Ibid., 231.

13. Ibid., 234.

14. A. Gélinas, "Vietnam," *The New Catholic Encyclopedia* (1967), 14:661–63.

15. See Albert Galter, *The Red Book of the Persecuted Church* (Westminster, Md.: Newman Press, 1957).

16. Peter Pham, "The Catholic Church in Vietnam," *The New Catholic Encyclopedia,* supplemental vol. 19 (Washington, D.C.: Catholic University of America Press, 1998), 395.

17. Thomas A. Dooley, *Deliver Us from Evil: The Story of Viet Nam's Flight to Freedom* (New York: Farrar, Straus and Cudahy, 1956), 174–75.

18. Ibid., 178–80.

19. Ibid., 182–83.

20. Tran-Minh-Tiet, *Histoire des Persécutions au Viêt-nam* (Paris, 1955), 246.

21. John Peter Pham, "Introduction" to F. X. Nguyen Van Thuan, *Thoughts of Light from a Prison Cell* (London: New City, 1997), 13.

22. Ibid., 11–12.

23. Ibid., 14.

24. François-Xavier Nguyen Van Thuan, "Five Loaves and Two Fish," unpublished typescript to be released by Morley Books, Washington, D.C., in 2000, p. 4.

25. Nguyen Van Thuan, *Thoughts of Light from a Prison Cell,* 148.

26. Ibid., 9.

27. Ibid., 10.

28. Ibid., 28.

29. Ibid., 44.

30. Ibid., 45.

31. Ibid., 45–46.

32. Ibid., 47.

33. Nina Shea, *The Lion's Den* (Nashville: Broadman & Holman, 1997), 77.

## Chapter 18: Out of Africa

1. Bernardo Olivera, *How Far to Follow? The Martyrs of Atlas* (Petersham, Mass.: St. Bede's Publications, 1997), 70.

2. Ibid., 72.

3. Bernardo Olivera, O.C.S.O., *Martiri in Algeria: La vicenda dei sette monaci trappisti* (Rome: Ancora, 1997).

4. Ibid., 20.

5. Olivera, *How Far to Follow?* 55.

6. Quoted from a letter (July 5, 1994), in Olivera, *Martiri in Algeria,* 23.

7. Quoted in Olivera, *Martiri in Algeria,* 22.

8. Ibid., 23.

9. Olivera, *How Far to Follow?* 55.

10. Ibid., 59.

11. Ibid., 117.

12. Ibid., 127–28.

13. Quoted in ibid., 21.

14. Quoted in ibid., 22.
15. Ibid., 94.
16. Quoted in ibid., 40.
17. Quoted in ibid., 105.
18. Bernardin Cardinal Gantin, "Introduction," to Fr. Neno Contran, M.C.C.J., *They Are a Target: 200 African Priests Killed* (Nairobi: Paulines Publications Africa, 1996), 6.
19. Contran, *They Are a Target,* 7.
20. Ibid., 9.
21. Ibid., 53.
22. Ibid., 20.
23. Quoted in ibid., 22, from *Entre deux mondes,* 83.
24. Contran, *They Are a Target,* 24.
25. Ibid., 27.
26. Ibid., 24.
27. Ibid., 29–30.
28. September 22, 1993, statement of the Burundian Bishops, quoted in ibid., 29.
29. Ibid., 36.
30. Didier Rance, "Impossible Réconciliation?" in *Rwanda: Le pardon ou le chaos,* dossiers, Aide à l'Eglise en détresse, no. 2 (October 1995): 5.
31. Contran, *They Are a Target,* 65.
32. From his message to the people of Rwanda, quoted in ibid., 66.
33. Ibid., 66.
34. Ibid., 68–69.
35. Ibid., 70.
36. Ibid., 72.
37. Ibid., 91.
38. Ibid., 93.
39. Joël Courtois, "Au dèla des apparences...," in *Rwanda: Le pardon ou le Chaos,* dossiers, Aide à l'Eglise en détresse, no. 2 (October 1995): 26.
40. Contran, *They Are a Target,* 163.
41. Ibid., 174.
42. Ibid., 182.
43. Karl Vick, "Priests in Sudan Could Face Crucifixion," *Washington Post,* December 3, 1998.
44. Quoted in William L. Saunders, "Genocide in Sudan," Washington, D.C.: Family Research Council, 1999, 4.
45. Ibid., 6.
46. Cases communicated to the author by William L. Saunders after consultation with Bishop Macram Max Gassis, Catholic Bishop from the South of Sudan.
47. William L. Saunders, "Christmas in Sudan," *First Things* (May 1999): 15.

# INDEX

Abrikosova, Anna, Dominican, Russia, 51, 55
*Act and Potency* (Stein), 180
ADAMANT, KGB Agent, 83
Adlan, Younan Kuwa Paolo, catechist, Sudan, 387
Adoratrice nuns, execution of, Spain, 124
Africa, 93, 375–76, 385
Aftenie, Vasile, Bishop, Romania, 256, 263
Agca, Mehmet Ali, 2, 216
Akulov, Epifany, Father, Russia, 56
Albani, Gian Francesco, 231
Albania
    Catholic Church, elimination of, 233–34, 236, 239
    cultural revolution in, 241
    families, campaign against, 241–42
    history of, 231–33
    property, religious, return of, 242
    religion, repression of, 234–35
Algeria, 369–75
Alonso, Esther, Sister, Augustinian, Algeria, 372
Aloysius, Brother, Cistercian, China, 325
Alphonsus, Father, Cistercian, China, 325
Alvarez, Bishop, El Salvador, 291
Alvarez, Caridad María, Sister, Augustinian, Algeria, 372
Alves Moreira, Silvio, Father, Jesuit, Mozambique, 378
Amandine, Marie, Franciscan, China, 321
Amîn, Abou Abdel Rahmân, Emir, GIA, 374
Amin, Idi. *See* Dada, Idi Amin
Angela, Sister, prisoner, Auschwitz, 136–37
Angola, 376–77
animists, Assam, India, ostracizing of converts, 310
Aparicio, Bishop, El Salvador, 291, 292
apostasy, 6, 121, 138, 248, 305
Aquinas, Thomas, 178, 277, 283
Arinze, Cardinal, Algeria, 375
Armed Islamic Group (GIA), Algeria, 369, 374–75
Armenian Catholics, killed by Turks, 1
Arrupe, Pedro, Jesuit, 275
Assumptionists, religious order
    Neveu, Eugène, 52–53, 60–61
*Au Revoir les Enfants* (film), 141, 143
Augustine, Saint, and Foucauld, 91, 94
Augustinians, religious order
    Alonso, Esther, 372
    Alvarez, Caridad María, 372
    Ciscar Puig, Felipe, 121
    Nieves, Elías, 33

Aurelius, Marcus, 88
Auschwitz prison camp, Germany, 192–94, 195
Autsch, Maria Cäcilia, prisoner, Germany, 135–36. *See also* Angela, Sister
Azaña y Díaz, Manuel, President, Spain, 111, 127
Azcue, Secundo, Father, El Salvador, 296, 297

Bachmeier, Franz (father of Jägerstätter), 160
Bagnoli, Angelo, Father, China, 323
Bainan, Liu, China, 338
Bal, Joseph, Father, Romania, 256
Bălan, Ion, Bishop, Romania, 256
Baltrymas, Benediktas Šveikauskas Stasys, Father, Lithuania, 250
Banduga, Gabriel, Father, Uganda, 385
Bangladesh, 315–16
Barosi, Antonio, Father, China, 323–25
Barrera, Bishop, El Salvador, 291
Barrera, Ernesto (Neto), Father, El Salvador, 288
Barrera, Josefa María, Sister, Visitandine, Spain, 108
Bárta, Jan, Father, Franciscan, Czechoslovakia, 227
Bartholomew, Brother, Cistercian, China, 325
Basilians, order of, Russia, 82
Bastin, Thérèse Irene, Prioress, Carmelite missionary, Korea, 340, 347
Batiz Sáinz, Luis, Father, Mexico, 31
Beionoravičius, Balys, Lithuania, 250
Benda, Václav, dissident, Czechoslovakia, 3
Beran, Josef, Archbishop, Czechoslovakia, 223–24
Beria, Lavrentii, Russia, 76, 82
Bertram, Adolph, Cardinal, Germany, 152, 157
*Beyond All Hope* (Valladares), 305–6
Bharatiya Janata Party (BJP), India, 309
Bhatti, Arif Iqbal, Judge, India, 313
Biernacka, Marianna, layperson, prisoner, Germany, 212
Binh, Paul Nguyen Van, Archbishop, Vietnam, 364
Bisoc, Anton, Franciscan, Romania, 260
Bivanda, Melchior, Father, Burundi, 379
BJP (Bharatiya Janata Party), India, 309
Black Madonna, painting of Virgin Mary, 220
Blandina, slave girl, 7

**Glen Cove Public Library**

Glen Cove, New York

Phone: OR 6-2130

GL